THE LAST TSAR

THE
LAST
TSAR

The Life and Death of
Nicholas II

EDVARD
RADZINSKY

Translated from the Russian by
MARIAN SCHWARTZ

ANCHOR BOOKS
DOUBLEDAY
New York London Toronto Sydney Auckland

AN ANCHOR BOOK

PUBLISHED BY DOUBLEDAY
a division of Bantam Doubleday Dell Publishing Group, Inc.
1540 Broadway, New York, New York 10036

ANCHOR BOOKS, DOUBLEDAY, and the portrayal of an anchor
are trademarks of Doubleday, a division of Bantam Doubleday Dell
Publishing Group, Inc.

The Last Tsar was originally published in hardcover by
Doubleday in 1992. The Anchor Books edition is
published by arrangement with Doubleday.

Book design by Marysarah Quinn
Map and Family Tree by Claire N. Vaccaro

Library of Congress Cataloging-in-Publication Data
Radzinskiĭ, Edvard.
[Zhizn' i smert' Nikolaia II. English]
The last Tsar : the life and death of Nicholas II / Edvard Radzinsky ; translated
from the Russian by Marian Schwartz. — 1st Anchor Books ed.
p.   cm.
Reprint. Originally published: New York : Doubleday, 1992.
Includes bibliographical references and index.
I. Title.
DK258.R2813   1993b
947.08'3'092—dc20
[B]   93-16757
                                                                   CIP

ISBN 0-385-46962-4

English language translation copyright © 1992
by Doubleday, a division of
Bantam Doubleday Dell Publishing Group, Inc.

Russian language version by Edvard Radzinsky
Translated from the Russian by Marian Schwartz

10 9 8 7 6 5 4 3 2

CONTENTS

ACKNOWLEDGMENTS

Grateful acknowledgment is made for use of photographs compiled by Tatiana Makarova and supplied by Novosti Publishers working in cooperation with and with permission from the Central State Archives of Cinematographic and Photo Documents, the October Revolution Central State Archives, the Central Revolution Museum Archives, and the Archives of Novosti Russian Information Agency.

The editor would like to acknowledge the assistance of the staff of the Slavic and Baltic Division, The New York Public Library in the preparation of this publication. The following staff members deserve particular mention: Edward Kasinec, Chief, for his review and commentary regarding both the original, and translated versions of the manuscript, and for his advice on the selection and description of the illustrations; Robert H. Davis, Librarian, for his annotations and editing of the plate captions; and Benjamin E. Goldsmith, Technical Assistant, for his work on the verification of bibliographic citations.

Grateful acknowledgment is made for use of photographs supplied by The Wernher Collection of The Luton Hoo Foundation.

Though thou exalt thyself as the eagle, and thou set thy nest among the stars, thence I will bring thee down, saith the Lord.

—OBADIAH 1:4

"Lord, save Russia and bring her peace."
—TSAR NICHOLAS II, *October 17, 1905*

THE DATES USED IN THIS BOOK FOLLOW
THE OLD-STYLE JULIAN CALENDAR IN
USE IN RUSSIA UNTIL FEBRUARY 1918.
IN THE NINETEENTH CENTURY THAT
CALENDAR LAGGED TWELVE DAYS BEHIND
THE GREGORIAN CALENDAR USED IN THE
WEST; IN THE TWENTIETH, IT LAGGED
THIRTEEN DAYS BEHIND. NICHOLAS AND
ALIX USED A DOUBLE-DATING SYSTEM IN
THEIR DIARIES AND LETTERS BEGINNING
IN FEBRUARY 1918, BUT NICHOLAS SOON
RETURNED TO THE OLD-STYLE DATING.

Tsaritsa Alexandra

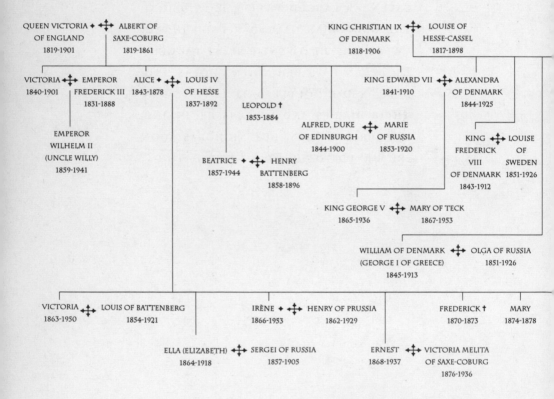

QUEEN VICTORIA ✦ ✦†✦ ALBERT OF
OF ENGLAND   SAXE-COBURG
1819-1901   1819-1861

KING CHRISTIAN IX ✦†✦ LOUISE OF
OF DENMARK   HESSE-CASSEL
1818-1906   1817-1898

VICTORIA ✦†✦ EMPEROR   ALICE ✦ ✦†✦ LOUIS IV
1840-1901   FREDERICK III   1843-1878   OF HESSE
    1831-1888   1837-1892

KING EDWARD VII ✦†✦ ALEXANDRA
1841-1910   OF DENMARK
   1844-1925

LEOPOLD †
1853-1884

EMPEROR
WILHELM II
(UNCLE WILLY)
1859-1941

ALFRED, DUKE ✦†✦ MARIE
OF EDINBURGH   OF RUSSIA
1844-1900   1853-1920

KING ✦†✦ LOUISE
FREDERICK   OF
VIII   SWEDEN
OF DENMARK 1851-1926
1843-1912

BEATRICE ✦ ✦†✦ HENRY
1857-1944   BATTENBERG
   1858-1896

KING GEORGE V ✦†✦ MARY OF TECK
1865-1936   1867-1953

WILLIAM OF DENMARK ✦†✦ OLGA OF RUSSIA
(GEORGE I OF GREECE)   1851-1926
1845-1913

VICTORIA ✦†✦ LOUIS OF BATTENBERG
1863-1950   1854-1921

IRÈNE ✦ ✦†✦ HENRY OF PRUSSIA
1866-1953   1862-1929

FREDERICK †   MARY
1870-1873   1874-1878

ELLA (ELIZABETH) ✦†✦ SERGEI OF RUSSIA
1864-1918   1857-1905

ERNEST ✦†✦ VICTORIA MELITA
1868-1937   OF SAXE-COBURG
   1876-1936

✦ FEMALE HEMOPHILIA CARRIER

† HEMOPHILIAC

Tsar Nicholas II

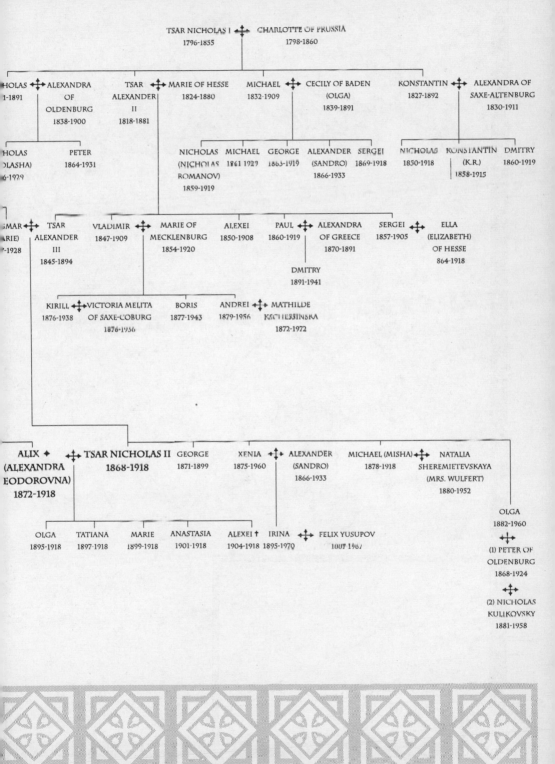

TSAR NICHOLAS I ✛ CHARLOTTE OF PRUSSIA
1796-1855   1798-1860

...HOLAS ✛ ALEXANDRA   TSAR ✛ MARIE OF HESSE   MICHAEL ✛ CECILY OF BADEN   KONSTANTIN ✛ ALEXANDRA OF
1-1891   OF   ALEXANDER   1824-1880   1832-1909   (OLGA)   1827-1892   SAXE-ALTENBURG
OLDENBURG   II   1839-1891   1830-1911
1838-1900   1818-1881

...HOLAS   PETER   NICHOLAS   MICHAEL   GEORGE   ALEXANDER   SERGEI   NICHOLAS   KONSTANTIN   DMITRY
OLASHA)   1864-1931   (NICHOLAS   1861-1929   1863-1919   (SANDRO)   1869-1918   1850-1918   (K.R.)   1860-1919
6-1929   ROMANOV)   1866-1933   1858-1915
     1859-1919

...GMAR ✛ TSAR   VLADIMIR ✛ MARIE OF   ALEXEI   PAUL ✛ ALEXANDRA   SERGEI ✛ ELLA
...ARIE)   ALEXANDER   1847-1909   MECKLENBURG   1850-1908   1860-1919   OF GREECE   1857-1905   (ELIZABETH)
...-1928   III   1854-1920   1870-1891   OF HESSE
   1845-1894   864-1918

                   DMITRY
                   1891-1941

KIRILL ✛ VICTORIA MELITA   BORIS   ANDREI ✛ MATHILDE
1876-1938   OF SAXE-COBURG   1877-1943   1879-1956   KSCHESSINSKA
     1876-1936   1872-1972

ALIX ✦ ✛ TSAR NICHOLAS II   GEORGE   XENIA ✛ ALEXANDER   MICHAEL (MISHA) ✛ NATALIA
(ALEXANDRA   1868-1918   1871-1899   1875-1960   (SANDRO)   1878-1918   SHEREMIETEVSKAYA
EODOROVNA)   1866-1933   (MRS. WULFERT)
1872-1918   1880-1952

                                        OLGA
                                        1882-1960

OLGA   TATIANA   MARIE   ANASTASIA   ALEXEI †   IRINA ✛ FELIX YUSUPOV   ✛
1895-1918   1897-1918   1899-1918   1901-1918   1904-1918   1895-1970   1887-1967   (1) PETER OF
                                              OLDENBURG
                                              1868-1924

                                              ✛

                                              (2) NICHOLAS
                                              KULIKOVSKY
                                              1881-1958

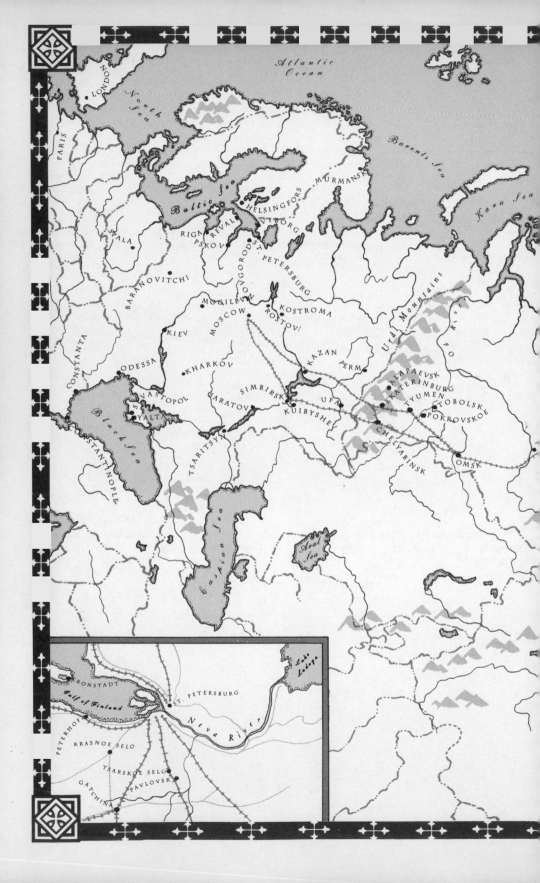

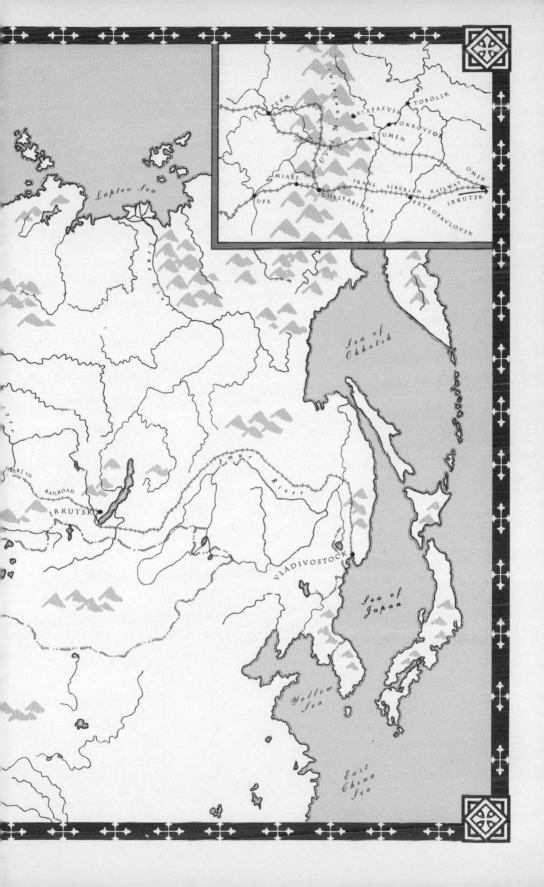

THE LAST TSAR

PROLOGUE

✦

As now, the century then was living out its last years. And as now, old people felt a sadness that what was coming, which promised mankind the flowering of science and serene well-being, had nothing to do with them. Young people, though, were living with a presentiment of what was to be.

The two happiest of young people, Nicky and Alix, in love, joined in marriage, and rulers of one-sixth of the world, were also living this happy future. The day of their coronation, set for 1896, promised to be the prologue to the even happier life that awaited them in the new century.

May 14, 1896. Moscow, the Kremlin. In ancient Assumption Cathedral, the sacred coronation rite was in progress. Candles burned . . . cherubic singing a cappella. . . . He took the large crown from the metropolitan's hands and placed it on his own head. She went down on her knees before him. . , . A small diamond crown already sparkled on her golden hair.

July 17, 1918. Ekaterinburg. "The bodies were put in the hole and the faces and all the bodies generally doused with sulfuric acid, both so they couldn't be recognized and to prevent any stink from them rotting [it was not a deep hole]. We scattered it with dirt and lime, put boards on top, and rode over it several times—no trace of the hole remained. The secret was kept" (from the Note of Yakov Yurovsky, who directed the execution of the last tsar and his family).

"Though thou exalt thyself as the eagle, and though thou set thy nest among the stars, thence will I bring thee down, saith the Lord."

The last tsaritsa from the house of Romanov read these words from the prophet Obadiah (1:4) to her daughter in the Ipatiev house. On the family's last day of life.

The progenitor of the Romanov clan was Andrei Ivanovich Kobyla, a distinguished émigré from the land of Prussia, where, in the four-teenth century, a long and fruitful line that included many of Rus-sia's most distinguished families began with Kobyla and his brother Feodor. Kobyla's great-great-granddaughter Anastasia became wife and tsaritsa to Tsar Ivan the Terrible. Thus Andrei Kobyla's descen-dants allied themselves with the ancient dynasty of Muscovite tsars.

The tsaritsa's brother, Nikita Romanovich, was particularly close to the cruel tsar. But Ivan the Terrible died, and in his will and testament he appointed Nikita Romanovich guardian and councilor to his son, the new tsar, Feodor.

The struggle for power commenced.

Slandered by the all-powerful Boris Godunov, Tsar Feodor's brother-in-law, the eldest of Nikita Romanovich's sons was forced to take monastic vows under the name Filaret.

With the death of Tsar Feodor in 1598 Rurik's ancient dynasty came to an end, whereupon ensued a period of unprecedented tur-bulence for old Russia—the Time of Troubles. Selected to be tsar was Boris Godunov, whom the people suspected of having murdered the infant Dmitry, heir to the throne. In the midst of unimaginable famine and death, Godunov died and the Poles invaded Russia, put-ting a tsar-pretender, the False Dmitry, on the Russian throne. Rus-sia suffered widespread impoverishment, cannibalism, brigandage.

It was then, during the Time of Troubles, that Filaret Romanov was returned from exile and made metropolitan of Rostov.

The Poles were driven from Moscow, and the false tsar perished. And at last, in 1613, the Assembly of the Land put an end to the terrible interregnum.

The son of Metropolitan Filaret, Michael Romanov, who was at that moment at Kostroma's Ipatiev monastery, was unanimously elected tsar by the Assembly of the Land on February 21, 1613. Thus began the three-hundred-year history of the house of Romanov.

The mysticism of history: the monastery whence the first Romanov was called upon to rule was the Ipatiev; the house where the last ruling Romanov, Nicholas II, parted with his life was the Ipatiev house, named after the building's owner, the engineer N. N. Ipatiev.

A Michael was the first tsar from the house of Romanov; a Michael was also the last, in whose favor Nicholas II tried unsuccessfully to abdicate the throne.

Part I

LEAFING THROUGH THE TSAR'S DIARIES

PRELUDE:
FROM THE
ARCHIVE OF
BLOOD

✛

*I*n the seventh decade of our century, in Moscow, lived a strange old woman: her wrinkled face was plastered with a grotesque layer of theatrical makeup; her bent figure tottered on high heels. She moved almost by feel, but nothing could induce her to don glasses. Oh, no, she had no intention of looking like an old woman!

According to the *Theatrical Encyclopedia* she was then in her tenth decade.

This was Vera Leonidovna Yureneva—a star of the stage from the turn of the century. Once, her student admirers harnessed themselves to her carriage in place of horses to take her home from her performances. Now, yesterday's femme fatale was living out her life in a communal apartment on a miserable pension. And she had rented one of her two rooms to me, a sorry student at the Historical Archival Institute.

Evenings, when I returned home, I often had long talks with her in the communal kitchen. The suites of Petersburg restaurants, the glamorous Yacht Club with its grand dukes, the palaces on translucent White Nights—this drowned world where she had once lived Vera Leonidovna ironically referred to as Atlantis. She scattered names: "Anya"—just Anya— turned out to be Anna Vyrubova, the empress's fateful friend; and "Sana"— to the rest of Russia the Em-

press Alexandra Feodorovna. Thus began our nightly conversations
in a Moscow kitchen, our journey to a drowned Atlantis. I recorded
her stories greedily. And now that I have read so many reminiscences by participants in those stormy events, her opinions retain a
distinct charm for me, precisely because she was not a participant.
Participants are, after all, biased. It reminds me of the expression
"He lies like someone who was there." Vera Leonidovna was merely a
contemporary, an interested but disinterested party.

Here is one of Vera Leonidovna's stories about Atlantis's demise:

"Only after the revolution did Mikhail K. become my husband.
[Mikhail Koltsov was a distinguished journalist in Bolshevik Russia.]
'Yet Another Bolshevik Victory'—that was what the émigré press
wrote about our union.

"At that time many prominent Bolsheviks lived in the Metropole
Hotel. For relaxation they often invited writers and journalists serving the new authorities. Koltsov, too, was often at the Metropole.
Once he met two people there. One had been the head of the Ekaterinburg Bolsheviks when the tsar's family was executed. The other
had been in charge of the execution itself. And they reminisced
about how it all had been. They sipped unsweetened tea through a
sugar lump, crunched the cube, and told stories about how *the bullets bounced off the girls and flew about the room.* Gripped with fear,
they had been utterly unable to get the boy. He kept crawling across
the floor, warding off their shots with his hand. Only later did they
learn that the grand duchesses had been wearing corsets sewn solidly with diamonds, which had protected them. Later Misha [Kol-
tsov] used to say that there must be a photograph of that horror
somewhere. 'After all, they were very proud—they had liquidated
Nicholas the Bloody. How could they have resisted taking their picture with the slain afterward, especially since the chief assassin had
once been a photographer.' He never did stop searching for that
photograph."

This picture: the tsar's murderers drinking tea in a room at the
Metropole . . . and the bullets bouncing off the girls and the boy
on the floor, and the terrible photograph. I could not put it out of my
mind.

Later at the Historical Archives Institute I heard about a secret
note written by that same former photographer who had led the
execution of the tsar's family. His name: Yakov Yurovsky. In the note
he purportedly told all.

Once I had completed my archival internship, I found myself in
the Central State Archive of the October Revolution in Moscow.
Immediately I made a naive inquiry about the Yurovsky "note."

"There is no Yurovsky note," my colleague replied brusquely, as if to point up the question's lack of tact.

I was shown the Romanov archive, however. To my surprise, at a time when everything was classified, these documents were not.

First I looked through albums of Romanov photographs. The same colleague with the bloodless (archival) face carried in huge scrapbooks—Moroccan leather, with the tsarist seal and without—and carried them out, one after the other. She refused to leave me alone with those photographs for a second. At first she was cold, indifferent, but then, forgetting herself, she waxed enthusiastic and explained each one to me, as if boasting of this amazing vanished life. The dim pictures in those tsarist photographs were a window out of her destitute, boring life.

"They took pictures of everything," she explained with a certain pride. "The whole family had cameras: they took photos of the girls, the tsar and the tsaritsa."

Photographs, photographs. A tall, slender beauty and a sweet young man—the period of their engagement.

Their first child—a little girl on spindly legs.

The four girls sitting on a leather sofa. Then the boy, the long-awaited heir to the throne. The boy and his dog, the boy on a bicycle with an enormous wheel, the amusing bicycle of that era. But most often he is in bed, the empress beside him. She has aged so. She looks into the camera, she looks at us. A bitter crease circles her mouth. The thin nose now hooked—a sad young woman. And here is Nicholas and the future king of England, George. They are looking at each other—astonishingly, ridiculously alike (their mothers were sisters).

A photograph of a hunt: a huge deer with giant antlers lying in the snow. And here is a vacation: Nicholas swimming—he has dived and is swimming underwater, naked—his bare strong body from the back.

Since then I have often recalled those photographs—the dead deer and the naked tsar—when thinking about him lying dead and naked on the warm July ground by the mine shaft into which they later tossed his body.

Then I was given his diary.

In July 1918, the Czechs and Cossacks were advancing on Ekaterinburg. The Bolsheviks would have to surrender the town. Yakov Yurovsky left Ekaterinburg on the last train out. The "secret courier" (as he was officially referred to in the documents) was carrying the tsar's leather cases—one of which contained the family archive of the very recently executed Romanovs.

So there he was riding the train, looking through the albums of photographs. The former photographer must have found this very interesting. But the main thing, naturally, was that he read the tsar's diary. The diary of the man with whom his name would be linked from then on and always. Imagine what he felt as he leafed through it on his long journey, trying to picture this life lived in full view of the entire world.

That is how the diary of Nicholas II, kept in the Romanov archive, came to be in the Central State Archive of the October Revolution. The Romanov archive. I call it the Archive of Blood.

Nicholas kept a diary for thirty-six years without interruption. He began it at the age of fourteen, in 1882, in the palace at Gatchina, and ended it as a fifty-year-old prisoner in Ekaterinburg.

Fifty notebooks filled from beginning to end with his neat hand-writing. But the final, fifty-first notebook is only half filled: his life was cut short, and yawning blank pages remain, conscientiously numbered by the author in advance.

This diary contains no reflections, and opinions are rare. He is terse—this taciturn, retiring man. The diary is a record of the principal events of the day, no more. But his voice lingers on its pages.

The mystical force of genuine speech.

The revolution punished him without trial, not allowing him a final say. The portrait of this puzzling man was created only after his death—by his opponents and his supporters. Now he himself can speak in the words he himself once wrote. I leaf through his diary. One experiences an eternal yet banal sensation in the archive: one feels *other* hands, the touch of hands across a century. He himself will lead us through his life. He is the Author.

Chapter 1

DIARY OF THE YOUNG MAN

✧

HE DIARY BEGINS

The author of the diary was born on May 6, 1868.

An old postcard: an angelic infant in long curls. Here Nicholas is all of a year.

Another photograph: a youth with his hair fashionably parted.

In 1882 Nicholas received a gift from his mother: a gilt-edged "book of souvenirs" bound in precious inlaid wood. This luxurious book became the first notebook of his diary. Nicholas was moved to begin keeping a diary conscientiously by a fateful date in Russian history: March 1, 1881.

On the dank night of February 28, 1881, in a Petersburg apartment, the light stayed on for a long time. All that day, from early morning, certain young people had been going in and out of the apartment. Since eight o'clock in the evening six had remained, four young men and two young women. One of them was Vera Figner, distinguished leader of People's Will, the revolutionary terrorist organization. Subsequently she would describe that day in her autobiography.

The other woman was Sofia Perovskaya, who in the morning was going to take a direct part in the *cause*. They had convinced her to get some sleep.

Vera Figner and the four men worked through the night. Only toward morning did they fill the kerosene cans with blasting jelly. They now had four homemade bombs.

The cause was the assassination of Tsar Alexander II, one of the greatest reformers in the history of Russia. That spring he had been preparing to give Russia its longed-for constitution, which would have brought his feudal despotism into the ranks of civilized European states.

But the young people were afraid that the constitution would create false contentment in society and distract Russia from the coming revolution. Also, the tsar's reforms seemed to them too gradual. The young people were in a hurry.

By that time People's Will terrorists had already made seven unsuccessful attempts on the tsar's life. The price had been twenty-one death sentences. And now, once again, they were going out onto a Petersburg street—to kill Alexander II.

That day in the Pavlovsky Regiment barracks, which had a view on the Moika Canal and the Field of Mars, the young soldier Alexander Volkov was standing guard. From the direction of the Ekaterininsky Canal came two powerful explosions. Volkov saw the smoke disperse slowly over the canal and the police chief's sleigh dash past.

Three Cossacks from the tsar's escort were propping up the dying tsar: two standing to the side on the runners and one in front whose Circassian coat was black with Alexander's blood. The savaged muscles of the tsar's legs were gushing blood.

The sleigh was heading toward the Winter Palace. "I want to die there," the tsar kept repeating. Alexander II had been mortally wounded by a bomb made in that same Petersburg apartment. The bomb that killed the Orthodox tsar had been disguised as an Easter cake, a fine-looking Easter gift—the young people had not overlooked the irony.

Then a coach under escort sped past Volkov. A huge, heavy, bald man and a thirteen-year-old boy were sitting in the coach—the new Tsar Alexander III and his thirteen-year-old son Nicholas, who that day became heir to the Russian throne.

The entire life of the soldier standing guard that day, Alexander Volkov, would be linked with this boy sitting in the coach. His life would rush by between two regicides.

Meanwhile Vera Figner and her friends had already learned of the mortal wounds to Alexander II. Their gruesome success evoked a strange exultation in the young woman: "In my agitation I could scarcely get the words out, that the tsar had been killed, and I wept: the terrible nightmare that had oppressed young Russia for so many decades had been broken off. All had been redeemed by this moment, this tsarist blood we had shed." And they embraced for joy— the young people who had killed the tsar-reformer.

"The revolutionary is a *doomed* man." This is a quotation from Mikhail Bakunin's famous *Revolutionary Catechism*, according to which the revolutionary must break with the civilized world's laws and conventions and renounce any personal life and blood ties in the name of the revolution. He must despise society and be ruthless toward it (and must himself expect no mercy from society and be prepared to die), intensifying the people's misfortunes by all possible means, spurring them on toward revolution. He must know that all means are justified by a single goal: revolution.

They had resolved to smear the stalled Russian cart of history with blood. And roll on, roll on—to 1917, the Ekaterinburg cellar, and the Great Red Terror.

Tsar Alexander II passed away in the palace in agony.

This picture: the murdered grandfather bleeding profusely. It would not quit Nicholas his whole life long.

In blood, he became heir to the throne.

"A tsar's blood shed" gave birth to his diary. Nicholas was the heir, and now his life belonged to history. Starting with the New Year he must record his life.

*H*IS FAMILY

As a result of countless dynastic marriages, by the twentieth century scarcely any Russian blood flowed in the veins of the Russian Romanov tsars.

But "Russian tsar" is a nationality in itself, and the German princess who ascended to the Russian throne and brought glory on herself in Russian history as Empress Catherine the Great felt truly

Russian. So Russian that when her own brother prepared to visit Russia she was indignant: "Why? There are more than enough Germans in Russia without him." Nicholas's father, Alexander III, was in his appearance and habits a typical Russian landowner who loved everything Russian. The proud formula "Autocracy, Orthodoxy, and Nationality" flowed in the non-Russian blood of Russia's tsars.

Nicholas's mother was the Danish Princess Dagmar; his grandmother, the Danish queen. He called his grandmother "the mother-in-law of all Europe": her numerous daughters, sons, and grandchildren had allied nearly all the royal houses, uniting the continent in this entertaining manner from England to Greece.

Princess Dagmar was first engaged to the elder son of Alexander II—Nicholas. But Nicholas died from consumption in Nice, and Alexander became heir to the throne. Along with his title, the new heir took his deceased brother's fiancée for his wife: on his deathbed Nicholas himself joined their hands. The Danish Princess Dagmar became Her Imperial Highness Marie Feodorovna.

The marriage was a happy one. They had many children. Nicholas's father proved to be a marvelous family man: his main precept was to preserve the foundations of the family and the state.

Constancy was the motto of Nicholas's father, the future Emperor Alexander III.

Reform—that is, change and quest—had been the motto of Nicholas's grandfather, Emperor Alexander II.

His grandfather's frequent enthusiasms for new ideas found a unique extension in his many romantic involvements. Alexander II's love affairs followed one after the other, until *she*—the beauty—appeared: Princess Catherine Dolgorukaya. To everyone's astonishment, Alexander II was faithful to his new mistress. Children were born. An official second imperial family appeared, and Alexander II spent nearly all his time with them. And when the revolutionaries began their tsar hunt, Nicholas's grandfather took an extravagant step: for their safety he settled both his families in the Winter Palace.

In 1880 Nicholas's grandmother, Marie Feodorovna, Alexander II's official wife, died, whereupon Nicholas's grandfather married his mistress. Although the intelligent and punctilious Princess Catherine was quick to renounce all rights to the throne for her eldest son, who knew? Today, perhaps tomorrow, the impossible. . . . Alexander II was sixty-two years old, but he was at the dawn of his powers and health. Nicholas's father took a marked step into the background. But now, just a few months after Alexander II's shameful marriage, a bomb exploding on the Ekaterininsky Canal carried

Nicholas's grandfather to his grave. Naturally, Nicholas heard what people around him were saying: divine retribution for the sinful tsar!

In the fall of 1882 Nicholas sang a song which so impressed him that when he got home he wrote it out on the inside cover of his very first diary ("The song we sang while one of us hid"). This folk song about the old hag death combing out the curls of the slain lad opens his diary. Yet another mysterious portent.

"Began writing my diary on the 1st of January 1882. In the morning drank hot chocolate, dressed in my Life Guard reserves uniform. . . . Took a walk in the garden with Papa. We chopped and sawed wood and made a great bonfire. Went to bed at about half past 9. . . . Papa, Mama, and I received two deputations. Presented me with a magnificent wooden platter inscribed 'The peasants of Voronezh to their Tsarevich.' With bread and salt and a Russian towel."

Games at Gatchina, visits with his cousins the grand dukes, who were his age. The large Romanov family.

"This morning the canaries were moved into a small wooden cage. . . . Sandro [Alexander] and Sergei . . . skated and played ball, and when Papa left we started a snowball fight."

Boys at play. A carefree life. Sergei and Sandro were the sons of Grand Duke Michael, his grandfather's brother.

Nicholas (or Nicky, as everyone called him) was especially friendly with Michael's sons. Sergei, Sandro, and George Mikhailovich were his diary's favorite characters, the comrades of his childhood games, his youth. The eldest was also a Nicholas, later the distinguished liberal historian Nicholas Romanov, who looked bemusedly on their play. He would always regard Emperor Nicky with gentle irony.

Later, outside at the Fortress of Peter and Paul, Nicholas Mikhailovich and George Mikhailovich would be executed, and Sergei Mikhailovich would lie at the bottom of a mine shaft with a bullet in his head.

"We worked in the garden. Cleared three trees that had fallen on top of one another. Then made a huge bonfire. Mama came to look at our bonfire it was so inviting."

Burning, burning, a huge bonfire in the dark of night. Many years later this gray-eyed adolescent would kindle another bonfire in which an empire would perish.

THE CIRCUMSTANCES OF HIS LIFE
All this went on at Gatchina, where Alexander III shut himself in
with his family after his father's assassination. The tsar appeared in
Petersburg from the New Year until Lent, during which time he gave
royal balls whose Asiatic splendor stunned the foreign emissaries.
But this was window dressing. The family's real life was at Gatchina,
where they lived in a magnificent palace whose formal rooms were
empty. Alexander and his family occupied the mezzanine, once the
servant's quarters. His numerous family lived in small rooms so narrow one could scarcely bring in a piano. The shade of his murdered
father haunted Alexander III. There was a chain of sentries along the
fence, guards around the palace, and guards inside the park. The life
of the young Nicholas began with a prison accent.

Meanwhile, the young soldier Alexander Volkov was beginning to
make a career for himself: he was brought into the inner Palace
Guard. After midnight he watched the emperor fish on the lake.

A moonlit night over the Gatchina park. Volkov stood all alone on
the bank, demonstrating the guard's small numbers. The real guard,
comprising thirty men, was hiding in the bushes around the lake.
Beyond the tsar's boat was another guard with a convoy.

In the tsar's boat the huntsman held up a lantern, the fish swam
toward the light, and the huge, heavy tsar speared the surfacing fish.

Fishing and hunting at times even pushed back affairs of state.
"Europe can wait while the Russian tsar fishes." This aphorism of
the powerful monarch, the master of one-sixth of the earth's surface,
circulated through the newspapers of the world.

Nicholas was taken hunting and fishing, but more often his father took Michael, the younger brother. The hardy rascal Michael
was his father's and mother's favorite.

The tsar is drinking tea with guests on the balcony, and below
Misha, as Michael is called, is playing. The father gets an idea for a
bullyish prank: he takes a watering can and douses the boy from
above with water. Misha is pleased. Misha laughs, the tsar laughs,
the guests laugh.

But suddenly, an unexpected cry: "And now, Papa, your turn."

The tsar obediently presents his bald spot—and Misha douses him with the watering can from head to foot.

But the father's iron will broke Michael's childish independence. Both brothers would grow up good, gentle, and timid, as often happens with children of strong fathers.

This was when Nicholas grasped what is for an adolescent the bitterest truth: They don't love me, they love my brother! His adolescent insight did not make him mean, sullen, or less obedient. He simply became reticent.

Alexander appointed the distinguished K. P. Pobedonostsev, chief procurator of the Holy Synod, Nicholas's tutor.

Alexander III ascended to the throne with an understandable logic: there were reforms under my father, and what was the result? His murder. So Pobedonostsev was called to power. The desiccated old man with protruding ears had the dry wheeze of a grand inquisitor wasted away from fasting.

Pobedonostsev would explain that Russia was a special country where reforms and a free press would inevitably result in decadence and disorder. "Like frost he inhibits any further decay, but nothing will grow under him," a Russian commentator pinpointed Pobedonostsev. But the frost-man was then already feeling the heat of the fiery luminescence advancing on the empire: revolution. Who was going to stand up to it? This kind boy whose nature was anything but that of a tsar? Pobedonostsev respected Nicholas as the future monarch, but he could not love him. Nicholas found no love in his tutor.

Instead of love he got—the army!

Alexander III had the nickname "Peacemaker." He avoided wars, but the army loomed over society as imposing as ever. The army, which had always made Russia strong. "Not by its laws, nor its civilization, but by its army," as Count Witte, the powerful minister and adviser to both Nicholas and his father, wrote. "Russia as a state is neither commercial nor agricultural but military, and its calling is to be the wrath of the world," said a Cadet Corps textbook. The army meant obedience and diligence above all else. Both these qualities, which the shy youth already possessed, the army would foster ruinously.

The heir to the throne did his service in the Guards. Ever since the eighteenth century Russia's wealthiest, most distinguished families had sent their children to Petersburg and the Guards. The richest grandees, having retired to live out their days away from Petersburg in hospitable Moscow's magnificent palaces, sent their children off to Petersburg and the Guards. Drinking, gypsies, duels—these were the Guards' gentlemanly occupations. The Guards had been responsible for all of Russia's palace revolutions. Guards had brought the Romanov empresses—Elizabeth and Catherine—to the throne and killed Emperors Peter III and Paul I. But the Guards had done more than plot against the imperial court. In all of Russia's great battles, the Guards had been in the van.

Nicholas began his service in a mixed regiment of a Guards battalion. The first half company was commanded by the heir, and the second by Alexander Volkov, who was a noncommissioned officer by then. At Alexandria, the tsar's dacha, Volkov taught the heir the art of marching.

Nicholas adored physical exercise, and he was indefatigable. During his trials with Volkov in the art of square-bashing, his middle brother George would watch from the bushes. George, chronically ill and painfully ashamed of his persistent weakness, followed his brother's every move ecstatically.

"6 May 1888. Am twenty and becoming quite the old man. . . .

"7 May. Liked this costume ball very much. All the ladies wore white dresses, and the men wore red. . . . Danced the mazurka and cotillion."

Balls, the regiment, a life without care.

Then on October 17, 1888, for the first time, miraculously, Nicholas eluded death when the tsar's train had a terrible wreck at Borki, not far from Kharkov (and for the first time in his life the number 17 appeared in conjunction with calamity).

"A fateful day for us all. We might all have been killed, but by the Lord's will we were not. During breakfast our train jumped the rails. The dining car and coach were demolished, but we emerged from it all unscathed. However, 20 people were killed and 16 injured."

So the holiday resumed: 1889.

"Returned from the ball at half past 1. Slept through my first lesson. . . .

"A gay old time getting an eyeful of that gypsy. Returned home at 2. . . .

"Surprised at awakening in Gatchina. The sight of my room lit by sunshine. After tea fenced at Mama's.

"Couldn't help myself and began to smoke, assuring myself this is all right. . . .

"At midnight went with Papa after grouse. Sat in the cabin, the mating place was remarkable. Slept until 10. . . .

"6 May. . . . Was made a member of Council of State and Committee of Ministers."

The pleasure with which gentle, retiring Nicholas threw himself into the unruly world of the Guards was striking. Nicholas's regimental superior was his father's brother Grand Duke Sergei Alexandrovich. A powerful giant, the peremptory and strict commander was the unhappiest of men. Profoundly religious, he suffered endlessly from what he felt were unnatural inclinations: Sergei Alexandrovich was a homosexual.

The Guards, a closed male fraternity, encouraged pederasty and heavy drinking.

The tradition of the hard-drinking Russian Guards! The poetry of that famous hero and hard drinker the hussar Denis Davydov was set to music and his ballads sung all through the Guards' barracks:

> Old men! I remember you,
> Draining dippers round the fire,
> Your noses red and blue.

"Yesterday [during training at Krasnoe Selo] we drank 125 bottles of champ[agne]. Was sen[try] for the division. At 1 took my squadron out on the battlefield. At 5 an inspection of military institutes under a pouring rain."

But by that night he was draining the dipper again.

"Woke up and felt as if a squadron had spent the night in my mouth." It was all as Davydov had devised: they drank "elbows" (filling a glass the length of a forearm and draining it at one draft), "the staircase" (setting glasses all the way up the stairs and emptying them one step at a time, ascending, but often falling down dead drunk before reaching the top), or "till the wolves" (stripping naked and jumping out in the savage frost, where an obliging barman carried out a tub of champagne for the gentlemen guardsmen, who sipped from the tub, howling all the while like wolves). People said this strange entertainment had been dreamed up personally by Grand Duke Sergei Alexandrovich, who was famous for his remarkable, truly guardsmanly drinking.

"16 March 1892. . . . Have never seen such a profusion of gypsies. There were four choruses. We supped, like that time, with the ladies. Sojourned in vinous fumes until 6 in the morning."

Amid these rather awful, noisy amusements Nicholas had the good sense to remain gentle, chaste, and lonely. There was the anticipation of love, ideal love.

"19 January 1890. . . . Don't know how to explain it but a mood has come over me: neither sad nor happy. Almost over now, drank tea and read."

Only *she* could break this loneliness.

A rather short young officer strides briskly with the crowd down Nevsky Avenue.

Meanwhile, the coach of Petersburg's governor rolls down Nevsky as the governor searches the faces on the street.

Finally he spots the young officer, the carriage slows, and respectfully but firmly the governor transmits the father's order to return to the palace.

Vera Leonidovna Yureneva:

"He adored walking. . . . There was a rumor that he had met a beautiful Jewess on a walk. . . . And a romance had sprung up. There was a lot of gossip about that in Petersburg. But his father acted as decisively as ever: the Jewess was sent away along with her entire household. Nicholas was in her home while all this was going on. 'Only over my dead body,' he declared to the governor. Matters did not go as far as dead bodies, however. He was an obedient son, and eventually he was broken and taken away to his father at Anichkov Palace, and the Jewess was never seen in the capital again."

"ALIX H."

That was how he referred to her then in his diary: Alix H.

I'm sitting in the archive. Before me is a stack of papers. All that remains from the life of Alix H.

They too have made a journey, and they bear the dust of the terrible Ipatiev house.

Endless letters from Nicholas, hundreds of letters. Her diaries—or, rather, what remains of them. Evidently she burned her diaries early in March of 1917, when the empire perished.

What survives are brief notes for the years 1917 and 1918, the last two years of her life.

Notebooks with excerpts from the works of theologians and philosophers, lines from favorite poems she had copied out: Maikov, Fet, Lermontov, Pushkin, Grand Duke Konstantin Romanov (a well-known poet from the first part of the century who wrote under the pseudonym K.R.), a certain Bronitskaya, and again Pushkin, and again Fet, and again K.R.—*her* poets.

But here is one other particular notebook. It is also a collection of utterances, true from a somewhat unlikely philosopher who ruled over the mind and soul of the brilliantly educated Alix H.: the half-literate Russian peasant Grigory Rasputin.

The English Alix, the daughter of the Grand Duke of Hesse-Darmstadt, Louis IV, was born in Darmstadt in May 1872.

Hills grown up in forest descended into the misty valley of the Rhine, places beloved of Goethe. Here lay Darmstadt, the tiny capital of a tiny German state, the grand duchy of Hesse. At the season of Alix's birth the town would have been drowning in flowers, and in the palace museum hung a tender Madonna of Hans Holbein.

Alix's father, Louis IV, sovereign of Hesse, was married to Alice, daughter of the English Queen Victoria. The Exalted English Alice was renowned for her fanatical (albeit wholly platonic) passion for the famous German philosopher and theologian David Strauss. Her worship of Strauss was a deification reminiscent of her daughter's future deification of Rasputin. Both the nerves and the dreadful headaches—everything that led Alice to an early grave—remind us very much of the portrait of her daughter Alix. The mother passed down more than just her name.

To this familial exaltation was added the dark memory of the ages. In the blood of Alix H. flowed the blood of Queen Mary Stuart.

Alix's mother died at age thirty-five, leaving a large family, of whom Alix was the youngest. Her oldest sister, Victoria, married Prince Louis of Battenberg, who would become commander-in-chief of the British Navy; her second sister, Ella, would marry Grand Duke Sergei Alexandrovich. Finally Irène, the third sister, became the wife of Prince Henry, her first cousin and the brother of German Emperor Wilhelm II. Thus, by forging familial bonds, these Hesse princesses would unite the Russian, English, and German royal houses.

After her mother's death, Alix's grandmother took the child under her wing. Her grandmother, the English Queen Victoria, observed the constitution scrupulously. Power belonged to Parliament, sage counsel to the queen.

Alix H. was one of the liberal queen's favorite granddaughters.

A pale blond little beauty. For her radiant nature her mother called her "Sunny." For her mischief and recalcitrance, the German court had called her *spitzbube* ("scamp," "troublemaker"). Was the orphan, taken away from her sisters, brother, and father, really so very lighthearted and gay? Or is that how her grandmother Victoria chose to see her? And did Alix, with the cunning of a child, make a point of playing up to her grandmother's expectations?

She was a troublemaker, however.

Queen Victoria did not favor the German princes, especially Emperor Wilhelm. And Alix, who spoke and thought in English, must have smiled at the old queen's caustic jokes. But she must have missed them as well—her father, her brother Ernie, and the blooming Hesse landscape. And her family. That large family that fell apart when she was six years old.

When she married she would attempt to re-create the same kind of large family.

The lonely girl made the circuit of the royal courts of her numerous relatives.

In 1884 twelve-year-old Alix was brought to Russia.

Her sister Ella was marrying Grand Duke Sergei Alexandrovich. Her cousin, the future German Emperor Wilhelm II ("Uncle Willy") followed beautiful blond Alix's debut at the Russian court closely. The wedding of Sergei Alexandrovich—the brother of the Russian tsar to a German princess—could have a reprise. The heir to the Russian throne was already sixteen, and the Hesse line occupied a special place in the history of the Romanov family. Emperor Paul's first wife, who died in childbirth, had come from that line. And Empress Maria Alexandrovna, Nicholas's grandmother, was also a princess of Hesse-Darmstadt.

This was how they came to meet for the first time: Alix and Nicky. It was an idyll: he fell in love with her at first sight. And there was a day when they found themselves in Peterhof, at Alexandria, the small imperial dacha.

Much later, a year after their marriage, Nicholas and Alix would come back to Alexandria, and Nicholas would write in his diary, "Rained the entire day, after coffee we went upstairs . . . we saw the window we had both cut our names into in 1884." (She liked to draw on glass with the precious stone on her ring. One can see her signature on the grand windows of the Winter Palace.)

Subsequently they would come to love old Alexandria, which preserved a precious memory.

A window and a couple. They were looking out at that day in 1884. Standing at a window at the inception of their destiny.

It was after this that Nicholas spoke with his sister Xenia, the only one with whom the not very sociable English-Hessian princess had become friendly. And Xenia gave him her advice.

He asked his mother for a diamond brooch, which he gave to Alix. She accepted it. Nicholas was happy, but he did not know Alix H. Her consciousness had been formed in the puritanical English court. Uncompromising, militantly stern, and proud—these were the necessary attributes of an English princess. Alix decided she had acted improperly. The next day, while dancing with him at a children's ball in Anichkov Palace, she stabbed the brooch into his hand. Silently, without a word.

Also without a word, Nicholas gave the brooch to his sister Xenia.

Only to take it back ten years later.

This brooch would know a terrible fate.

It would be five years before Alix H., now seventeen, would appear at the Russian court again. Ostensibly she had come to see her sister Ella. In fact, she was being inspected as a prospective bride. All those years he had clung to his memory of the young beauty, and now he had got his way.

"Devoid of charm, wooden, cold eyes, holds herself as if she'd swallowed a yardstick"—this was the court's obliging sentence. It was made known that the empress-mother did not like the princess. The voice of the empress-mother always rang out when the emperor-father did not want his own heard.

It was all a simple matter of politics. Alexander's policy was alliance between Russia and France. The princess from the house of Orléans, the daughter of the Comte de Paris—that was the desired party right now. Moreover, Alix's English upbringing (England, the eternal symbol of liberalism) might revive the hopes of the liberal party, which Alexander and Pobedonostsev had smothered.

No one in the country or the family dared cross the powerful emperor. Especially the soft-spoken Nicky, who hated conflict. Father and son had a serious talk at Peterhof, and Nicky meekly agreed not to insist on marrying Alix, but. . . . But he adamantly rejected the Orléans princess. He chose a third path: to wait, silently, without complaint or hope. To wait until the Lord joined him to Alix. That was the only possible way: very quiet and meek—but rebellious.

His diary of 1889 opens with a photograph of the young Alix, which he pasted in after she was gone. He had begun to wait.

Her sister Ella (after her conversion to Orthodoxy, Grand Duchess Elizaveta Feodorovna) helped him out of his unpleasant situation with the rejected Alix. It was announced that there could be no question of any prospective marriage: Alix had no intention of converting.

Alix returned to England. But what was most surprising was that she did so with a strange relief. She told herself: My sister is right, I cannot convert so simply. Faith occupied too great a place in her life.

On the blond princess's next visit, a year later, the unhappy Nicholas was not permitted to see her.

Alix H. stayed with her sister Ella at Ilinskoe, Ella's estate outside Moscow.

"20 August 1890. Lord! Am dying to go to Ilinskoe. . . . Otherwise, if not now, then I might have to wait an entire year to see her, and that is hard!!!"

Ilinskoe exists to this day, outside Moscow. Alix stayed at the estate a few weeks and watched with astonishment. The ties between Darmstadt, London, and Petersburg were too close not to know the details about each other: Ella's marriage was fictitious because of her husband's inclinations, and she was never to have a child. At the same time Sergei Alexandrovich tormented her with his drinking bouts and groundless jealousy. Alix was astonished to see that her sister nonetheless was happy; her eyes shone. Ella loved her husband because the Lord so ordained. Her love for her unlucky husband was the fulfillment of the Lord's commandments. The transitory joys of life and the eternal joy of serving God.

The church still stands at Ilinskoe. Then candles burned there, singers' voices rang out, and the two sisters stood in the sanctuary.

Nicholas continued his meek rebellion. He carried out Papa's order, but. . . . He could be forbidden to see her but not to wait for her.

"21 December 1890. This evening with Mama we discussed the family life of today's young society people. Unintentionally this conversation brushed a most vital chord in my soul, the dream and hope that carries me from one day to the next. Already a year and a half has gone by since discussed this with Papa at Peterhof, and nothing has changed in either the bad or the good sense. My dream is one day to marry Alix H. Have loved her for a long time, but even more deeply and strongly since 1889, when she spent 6 weeks of the winter in Petersburg. Have fought my feeling for a long time, trying to deceive myself with the impossibility of my cherished dream coming true. . . . The only obstacle or gap between her and me is the matter of religion. Other than that barrier there is no other, am nearly convinced that our feelings are mutual. All is up to God's will, and am putting my trust in his mercy, calmly and meekly, looking to the future."

He was sent away to travel and forget the whole business.

"The Mediterranean Sea, the Adriatic, Venice. . . . Life truly is a holiday! A ball! A ball!"

When Nicholas returned to Petersburg his father realized that nothing had changed—and it was time to act.

Soon in Nicholas's diary yet another important character would appear: "Little K."

"*I*'VE FALLEN MADLY IN LOVE . . . WITH LITTLE K." All the brilliant Guards officers, the imperial suite, and the imperial family belonged to the famous Yacht Club. It was in March 1890 that the name of Little K. was heard there for the first time.

All the club members were balletomanes. For a century the Rossi Street colonnade, where the Petersburg ballet school was located, had been a favorite spot for the dandies of the capital to take the air. It was an old tradition of the Petersburg elite to have a ballerina for a mistress.

Like the Guards, the ballet was closely linked with the court.

Grand Duke X. (various names could be substituted here) fell in love with a ballerina, lived with her openly, bought her a house, and fathered her children. The list of these scandalous tales was long. The director of the imperial theaters had to be a diplomat and strategist, always current on the complicated disposition of relationships between his wards and the members of the imperial family. Arriving at the ballet, the public first turned to notice the "imperial presence": which member of the imperial family was sitting in the imperial box. This often determined a ballerina's status.

Vera Leonidovna Yureneva:

"She wasn't beautiful, her legs were too short. But her eyes! Two pools. She was enticing, a little temptress. She had studied with the Italians and was magnificent technically. She once danced thirty-two *fouettés* and, after a storm of applause, sweetly danced thirty-two more. Someone said about her: 'She loved ballet in general and life in particular.' On the contrary: she loved ballet in particular and life in general. All her life she aspired to become a great ballerina, but she never was considered great. . . . In society at that time it was fashionable to show one's displeasure: she was doomed to the audience's disfavor the moment the future tsar fell in love with her. My ballerina girlfriend tried to have her hissed off the stage. . . . This was duly noted. . . . And at her own performance my girlfriend received a huge bouquet of flowers and a note: 'Mathilde Kschessinska thanks you very much.' She could be splendid. Because of her eyes she was called the 'fairy of the Parc des Cerfs': the French King Louis XV had kept his harem at the Parc des Cerfs."

It was a ballet family. Her father was the Pole Felix Kschessinski, who had taught all of Petersburg high society to dance the mazurka. He produced ballets and himself had danced with all the famous ballerinas of his day. By the end of the century, his children were already dancing on the imperial stage, Iosif and Yulia (or Kschessinska the First, as they would call her when her younger sister's star skyrocketed).

Nicholas's diary:

"23 March 1890. Took a carriage to Elagin Island to see a stable of young horses. Came back in a new troika. Had a bite to eat at 8. Went to a performance at the theatrical institute. There were some short plays and a ballet.

"We had a fine supper with the pupils."

Behind this awkward sentence lies the beginning of the romance.

Mathilde Kschessinska was born in 1872. She would die in Paris in 1971, just shy of one hundred years. In Paris she would write her memoirs, the touching story of the love of a young ballerina for the heir to the throne. She would write about that evening of March 23, 1890, as well, about an evening in vanished Atlantis.

After the graduation performance and ball, which the emperor and the heir attended, the tables were set. *Unexpectedly* they stayed for supper. They were seated at a separate table and *suddenly* the tsar said: "And where is Kschessinska the Second?"

The young ballerina was brought to the tsar's table; the sovereign paid her several compliments and added that he knew her father. The emperor-father *himself* seated the young ballerina next to the heir and added jokingly: "Only please don't flirt too much." To the young ballerina's amazement, Nicholas sat by her the entire evening without saying a word. His tender blue eyes watched her helplessly.

Let us switch from Kschessinska's romantic tale to prosaic narrative. So the tsar himself sat the girl next to his son and even offered some advice: "Just don't flirt." He could scarcely have made himself any clearer.

Vera Yureneva: "This was common. When young boys from wealthy families were coming of age, a beautiful and, even more important, pure servant would be brought into the house. This was a dangerous era."

Indeed, syphilis carried away young men by the thousands. Heavy drinking, homosexuality, and brothels were a part of life in the Guards. But the heir's health affected the destiny of the entire country. The affair with the Jewess had been an ominous warning, and the father of the family and the country had decided to take action. Kschessinska was a brilliant candidate: a romance with a future ballet star could only enhance the young man's biography. But still, the main thing was to make him forget the Hesse princess. The visit to the institute had been devised for just that purpose.

Did the young ballerina understand the rules of the game? Or for her was it all, in fact, cast in a romantic light: the heir, the tsarevich! But then the game was being orchestrated by adults. Whatever the scenario, this was a *game*.

Only in the summer did the little girl with the big eyes manage to resume the romance. In June 1890 Mathilde Kschessinska was accepted into the troupe of the Mariinsky Imperial Theater. Guards training, in which Nicholas was taking part, went on at Krasnoe Selo, where the imperial ballet danced the summer season.

She knew it would happen during the intermission: the grand dukes liked to come backstage, and he would probably come with them, because she knew he wanted to come.

And he did. So they met backstage. He was talking incoherently, and she was still waiting. The next day he was backstage again, and again—nothing. Once during an intermission she was detained, and when she ran out onto the stage, flushed, eyes blazing, so afraid was she of missing her timid admirer, he had already left. When he did see her he burst out with a jealous, helpless "I'm certain you were only flirting!" And, flustered, ran out. Thus he declared himself.

The tsar's family had the first box on the left, which was practically on the stage. Dancing nearby, the new ballerina Kschessinska the Second devoured the heir, who was sitting in the box alongside his father, with her huge eyes. What was most surprising was that she evoked no displeasure from the terrible emperor. From that moment the director of the imperial theaters took pains to ensure that any available parts went to this ballerina. In a very short time she would win the place of prima donna in the imperial ballet.

"17 June. Detachment maneuvers. Like Kschessinska the Second quite well."

"30 June. Krasnoe Selo. The growing affair has heated up powerfully. . . . Was at the theater, talked with little K. at the window [of the box]."

In Paris she recalled how he stood at the box window and she onstage down front. And again the conversation ended in a delightful nothing. Later he came to say goodbye: he was leaving for a trip around the world.

"Went for the last time to the dear Krasnoe Selo theater to say goodbye to K. Dined with Mama until 1."

She did not understand him. But it was all so simple: he was saving himself for Alix H.

Little K. read the newspapers daily—she was following his travels. News came that left Petersburg dumbfounded: a Japanese policeman had attacked the heir on the street of a small Japanese town and tried to behead him with a sword. By a miracle, Nicholas had survived.

The capital was full of rumors. Fantastic stories about inadmissible courting by a most adventuresome Nicholas. (Well aware of her timid admirer's character, Little K. did not believe it possible.) Finally the attacker was declared an insane fanatic.

"27 April 1891. Arrived in Kyoto. My eyes didn't know where to look first, such were the wonders. Watched archery and horseracing in ancient costumes. . . . At 9 set out with Georgie [the Greek

Prince George, who had accompanied him on his travels] for a teahouse. Georgie danced, provoking gales of laughter from the geishas."

"Even in my dreams the waters of the Gion [the teahouse quarter in Kyoto] flow under my pillow. . . . Hundreds of geishas filled Gion's narrow streets. The teahouses' residents are brocade dolls in kimonos woven with gold thread. Japanese erotica is more refined and subtle than the crude proffers of love on European streets. . . . The tea ceremony ends. . . . All that follows remains a secret."

"29 April. Woke up to a marvelous day whose end I would not have seen had I not been saved by the Lord God's great mercy.

"We set out from Kyoto in a jinrikisha for the small town of Otsu, where we went to the house of the little round governor. In his house, which was utterly European, he had set up a bazaar where each of us ruined ourselves on some knickknack. This was where Georgie bought his bamboo cane, which was to do me such a great service an hour later. After lunch we prepared to make the return trip, and Georgie and I were glad we would be able to take a rest in Kyoto before evening. We rode out in our jinrikishas and turned left down a narrow street crowded to either side. At that point received a strong blow to the right side of my head, above my ear. Turned and saw the loathsome scowl of a policeman, who was waving his saber over me in both hands a second time. Could only cry out: 'What, what do you want?' He jumped out over the jinrikisha onto the pavement. Seeing that the monster was headed toward me and that no one was attempting to restrain him, I ran off down the street, stopping the blood spurting from the wound with my hand. Wanted to hide in the crowd but couldn't, because the Japanese themselves were terrified and had scattered in all directions. . . . Turning around once more as I ran, noticed Georgie chasing the policeman pursuing me. . . . Finally, having run an entire 60 paces, I ducked around the corner of a side street and looked back. By then, thank God, it was all over. Georgie, my savior, had felled the loathsome creature with one blow of his cane, and as I approached our jinrikishas, several policemen were dragging him off by the legs. One of them was holding a saber to his neck. What I couldn't understand was how Georgie, that fanatic, and I had ended up alone, in the middle of the street, why no one from the crowd rushed to my aid. . . . No one from our suite could have helped, evidently, since they were riding in a long file. Even Prince Ari Sugava, who was third in line, didn't see anything. Had to reassure everyone and stay on my feet as long as possible. Rambakh [the doctor] did the first bandage and, most important, stanched the blood. The people on the street were touching: most of them got down on their knees and raised their arms in a sign of regret. More than anything I was upset at the thought of alarming dear Papa and Mama and about how to write them of this incident."

Nicholas's outcry in this deadly moment as he himself recorded it is striking: *"What, what . . . ?"*

Twenty-seven years later he would repeat this same cry, also at a deadly moment, as he stood in that cellar in Ekaterinburg—to be recorded by his assassin, Yurovsky.

So in 1891, for the second time in his life, he eluded death, and Nicholas began to feel that he was under His protection; He would not let Nicholas die. Did this mean he had another purpose?

"1 May. Tokyo. Am not so very angry at the good Japanese for the repulsive act of one fanatic. As before, their model order and cleanliness is a pleasure, and I must confess I keep on watching . . . whom I see on the street from afar. Received the Mikado at 11 o'clock."

His father ordered him to return to Petersburg, and again all was joyous; life was a never-ending ball. In Vladivostok he helped lay the first stone at the eastern terminus of the great railway that was to cross all of Siberia. And there was a pleasant journey down the rivers of Siberia, with plenty of card playing and drinking—to celebrate death twice cheated.

On the return trip he visited Tobolsk.

"10 July 1891. At 7 arrived in Tobolsk in a dim, gray light. On the wharf, as always was met by the mayor with bread and salt, the citizens of the town of Tyumen, with platters by the craft guild, and an honor guard. . . . Took a carriage and rode up the hill to the cathedral—through the original wooden streets of the town. From the cathedral we went to view the vestry, where they keep most of the objects relating to the subdual of Siberia. Went to the museum; here I found most interesting the bell sent away from Uglich because it had been sounded as an alarm on the day Tsarevich Dmitry died."

Subsequently he himself, like this bell, would be exiled to Tobolsk. As a prisoner he would climb an icy slope to look over a fence at the very edge of the streets and town he had admired in his happy youth.

He returned. Not stopping in Petersburg, he continued on to Kras-noe Selo to see his parents.

"7 August 1891. Strange not to have to go anywhere or have any more night lodgings with late arrivals and early departures."

He resumed his old familiar life.

"15 December. This morning received an entire shipment of papers from the Council of State and Committee of Ministers. Simply cannot understand how anyone can read so many papers in one week. Always limit myself to one or two matters, the most interesting, and the rest go straight into the fire. . . .

"31 December. Cannot say I have regretted 1891 coming to a close. It was definitely fateful for the entire family: the death of Aunt Olga [the mother of his friends Sergei and Sandro Mikhailovich], . . . the illness of and long separation from George [his brother], and finally, the incident in Otsu. All happened so fast, in such quick succession. Added to these great misfortunes has been the famine. I pray God that the year to come will not resemble the year just past."

Again it was March.

"5 March 1892. Mama says she hardly sees me, I gad about so much, but I do not think so, it seems to me at my age that is the way it should be.

"8 March. Woke up just before Mass. Sleeping so soundly that it drives even me to despair."

Thus passed this scattered life. Alix was far away, a myth, a dream, and nearby was this dear girl who was so well liked—by him, by Sergei, by his entire company of friends.

"25 March. Returned to Anichkov in falling flakes of snow. And this is spring? Dined with Sergei in my rooms, then went to visit the Kschessinskis, where I passed a pleasant hour and a half."

That day Nicholas ventured a step that was surprising for the indecisive young man.

The bold decision must have been made during the dinner he mentioned. The wine and the talk with his childhood friend Grand Duke Sergei Mikhailovich, who made no attempt to hide his own rapture over the young ballerina's charms. One might even guess what they talked about—after all, exactly two years had passed since Nicholas had first seen Mathilde. One might easily imagine what the lady-killer, the brilliant Petersburg dandy Grand Duke Sergei, advised him.

Nicholas came to a decision.

Kschessinska recalled that March Petersburg day. She was sitting at home, ill, with a bandaged eye. The romantic K. had been suffering from a mundane stye. When her maid informed her that a certain Guards officer, a Mr. Volkov, wished to see her, the surprised ballerina, who did not know Mr. Volkov, nevertheless told her to show him into the drawing room. She could not believe her eyes: standing in the drawing room was Nicholas.

They were alone for the first time. They made their declarations and . . . nothing! To Little K.'s astonishment, after "a pleasant hour and a half," he took his leave.

The next day she received a note: "Ever since our meeting I feel as if I am in a daze. I hope I shall be able to see you again soon. Nicky."

Now for her he was "Nicky." A charming (and what was amazing for the times) innocent game of love began. His fellows in the Corps brought flowers from her admirer, and the admirer himself was now a frequent visitor at Felix Kschessinski's apartment. But each visit coincided oddly with the absence of the rest of the family. Notes when he did not visit followed without letup. Now he called her *pannochka*, Polish for "young lady."

"Think of what Andrei, who adored a young pannochka, did."

He brought up Gogol's characters to no purpose: the story of the Cossack Andrei, who betrayed the behest of his father, the old Taras Bulba, for the love of his pannochka, was utterly inappropriate. Because the whole time, behind the scenes of his love story, stood the terrible Bulba—his father-emperor.

Actually, during his meetings with Mathilde he was always dreaming of another, whom his father opposed and with whom a union would indeed constitute a betrayal of the old Bulba. Kschessinska was merely the false pannochka. Hidden away as before in the depths of his soul was the true pannochka: Alix H.

In a strange way, he merged the two.

"31 March. Stopped in for a while at Uncle Misha's. . . . He led us through the rooms of his deceased wife—nothing had been touched." Here he is thinking about Alix. The touching love of the parents of his friends Sandro and Sergei—marital love—this is Alix H.

"Returned to Gatchina. Am in the most un-Lenten of moods. A

good thing am staying at Gatchina and 49 versts [30 miles] from the capital." This is Mathilde.

"1 April. . . . I note a very odd phenomenon in myself: never thought that two identical sentiments, two loves, could cohabit the soul simultaneously. Now it is over three years I have loved Alix H., and I constantly cherish the thought that God might let me marry her one day. . . . But ever since camp in 1890 I have loved little K. passionately. An amazing thing, our heart. At the same time do not cease to think of Alix, although it is true, one might conclude from this I am very amorous. To a certain extent, yes! I must add, though, that inside I am a harsh judge and extremely scrupulous—this is the mood that yesterday I called un-Lenten."

But for now a merry company gathered almost every evening in Little K.'s room. Nicholas came with his friends, the brothers Sergei, Sandro, and George. The three grand dukes and the heir had a good time in the fashionable ballet teacher's modest apartment.

Nicholas accompanied the emperor to Denmark, whence he sent Mathilde passionate letters. But simultaneously with these letters Nicholas cautiously resumed his discussion of Alix with his father.

The emperor was disturbed—his game had been to no avail. Was it not a direct consequence of this that the pannochka made her decisive thrust?

"At the time I was thinking more and more about intimacy," Kschessinska would recall in Paris. "I adored the tsarevich and wanted only one thing—my happiness, however brief it might be." Finally she was able to force Nicholas to come to a decision. He bought her a "ravishing palace" on the English Embankment, where their platonic love was finally to end. At one time Grand Duke Konstantin Nikolaevich had bought this palace for the dancer Kuznetsova. Little K. left her home and openly became the tsarevich's mistress. "This killed my father," she recalled. "He asked me: Did I realize I could never marry him? And that our idyll would be very brief? I replied: I understand, but I don't care. I want to experience all the happiness I am allowed."

That is how the old Kschessinska described the scene.

But it could be done more prosaically. Her father simply apprised her of the condition upon which the other father, who stood at the head of both the country and the family, had permitted the liaison: the tsarevich's marriage must mean an immediate finish to all their relations. In this game, too, the emperor remained a good family man.

So she had vanquished, but her victory was the beginning of the end.

"We arranged a housewarming. . . . The tsarevich gave me a water service—eight gold glasses encrusted with precious stones. . . .

"He brought me gifts quite often. I used to refuse to accept them, but he grieved so . . . so I had to accept them."

She had ceased to be a dream, and he pined more and more for his distant beauty. Life and dream: accessible Mathilde and the sublime, regal princess. Little K. disappeared from his diaries.

Yet another year of his life came to an end.

"31 December [1892]. Dear Anichkov sparkled with electricity. We went to mass at 7.30. At 12 the three of us, Papa, Mama, and I, greeted the New Year. God Grant it be just like this one."

Little K. was dancing part after part. But that was as it should be: the premier young man of Russia should have the premier ballerina for his mistress.

When the great ballet master Marius Petipa chose her to dance Esmeralda, he asked: "Are you in love?" "Yes." "Are you suffering?" "Certainly not!" Petipa explained to her that only an artist who has known suffering can dance Esmeralda. "I understood that later," Mathilde recalled sadly, "and then Esmeralda became my best role."

Her time would come to understand that. She was seeing Nicholas less and less often. But she still clung to her old ties: Nicky's dear friend Sandro and Nicky's sister Xenia held a merry engagement party in her home.

In April 1894 Nicholas went to Coburg to attend the wedding of Alix's brother Ernie. Soon after, the newspapers were writing about the tsarevich's engagement to Alix of Hesse-Darmstadt. After his return from Coburg he never went to see Little K. again.

They exchanged letters. Farsighted, she asked his permission to turn to him if necessary. He replied that the days he had spent by her side would ever be the most beautiful memories of his youth. She could always turn to him.

At his request Mathilde named a place for their last meeting: the main road between Petersburg and Krasnoe Selo. She arrived from town in a carriage; he, on horseback, from camp. "As always in such instances, I found it hard to say anything—choked with weeping and lost for the right words." She watched him recede into the distance, constantly turning around in the saddle. Thus she described the end.

But was this indeed the end? Although Kschessinska ceased to be Nicholas's mistress once he became engaged to Alix of Hesse-Darmstadt in 1894, she remained a presence in the Romanov family for the rest of her life, as she recounts in her memoir, *Dancing in Petersburg*.

Kschessinska very quickly turned to her longtime admirer Grand Duke Sergei Mikhailovich, who as head of the Theatrical Society and the Russian ballet could secure her former position in the ballet. For of all her lovers she remained faithful to only one: the ballet.

Kschessinska's shadow next crossed the palace threshold in May 1896 in conjunction with Nicholas's coronation, which was to be followed by a brilliant gala concert. The dowager empress, the new tsar's all-powerful mother, had no intention of allowing Little K. to perform, and her scandalous name was crossed off the list of performers. However, when the astonished public saw the program, there was the name: Mathilde Kschessinska, dancing the lead!

They had done everything—both his mother and the minister of the court—to convince Nicky not to permit this scandal, but Mathilde knew her old lover too well. She had gone to the aging Grand Duke Vladimir Alexandrovich, who pleaded her case with Nicholas. On Nicholas's other flank, his dear friend Sergei stepped forward. Nicholas ordered her name written in. Little K. had shown everyone her power—as she would continue to do in the years to come.

Kschessinska would bid the stage farewell many times but would continue to dance until 1917, and all the while she would keep the Romanov family around herself by whatever means necessary. When Sergei Mikhailovich and Kschessinska were accused of accepting huge bribes in arms deals during World War I, Nicholas refused to betray her, even to Alix.

For many years Sergei Mikhailovich remained by Little K.'s side. But when the frivolous grand duke became involved in a serious romance, Little K. immediately took an interest in a new Romanov: Grand Duke Andrei Vladimirovich came into her life. They went to Venice and then Provence, where he bought her a house by the sea. When they returned to Petersburg, Sergei Mikhailovich was by her side once more. Then she bore a son, Vladimir. Did she know whose son it was? Yes, indeed: the Romanovs'!

In February 1917, Kschessinska gave her last reception on the eve of the revolution. The following morning, as her housekeeper was checking the tea service and silver, she saw a vast crowd turning onto the bridge—toward the Winter Palace. Then she got a call from the chief of police: "The situation is critical, save whatever you can."

Vera Leonidovna: "In February 1917 I was in the apartment of a friend, the famous artist Yuriev. . . . That is where Mathilde hid out for a few days. She showed up dressed in a pathetic coat and some kind of kerchief with her little son, her dog, and a tiny reticule, which contained all that was left of her palaces and incalculable riches."

With her trembling, age-spotted hands, she showed me how Kschessinska had held her reticule.

Kschessinska had no faith in the stability of the situation in the capital. She decided to leave Russia and take her son with her. After her departure, the Bolsheviks occupied Kschessinska's palace. Cheap tobacco smoke permeated the upper rooms, endless people streamed up and down the trampled stairs, and sailors guarded the palace. In April 1917 a conference of Bolsheviks was held in her beloved hall, with its tall mirror over the mantel and its winter garden. And there, on her chairs, sat Filipp Goloshchekin, who was appointed to lead the Ural Bolsheviks. He would be the man to decide the fate of the two people who had been closest to her—Nicholas and Sergei.

Having escaped to Paris, Little K. would finally fulfill her dream: Grand Duke Andrei Vladimirovich married her. His brother Kirill became the Russian emperor in exile, and she became his relative.

$\mathcal{B}$Y THE WINDOW IN COBURG CASTLE
Early in 1894 it became clear that Alexander III was going to die, evidently as a consequence of the train wreck at Borki six years earlier. The tsar had received only a bruise, but that bruise developed into a fatal kidney disease. Now the heir's marriage had to be readied with all due speed.

The emperor's sudden mortal illness put an end to the game with Little K.

The diplomats earned their pay. Constant negotiations were conducted back and forth between Petersburg and Darmstadt.

In April 1894, Alix's brother Ernie was to marry his cousin the Saxe-Coburg Princess Victoria Melita, ("Ducky"), another granddaughter of Queen Victoria. Emperor Wilhelm II, Queen Victoria, and innumerable European princes were assembling in Coburg. One of the last brilliant balls of royal Europe was to be held at the brink of the terrible new century.

Russia was represented by a powerful phalanx of grand dukes. Even Father Ioann Yanyshev, confessor to the tsar's family, attended. His presence spoke clearly to the very serious intentions of those who had come: Father Ioann was supposed to instruct Alix in the fundamentals of Orthodox teaching. Also arriving in Coburg was Ekaterina Adolfovna Schneider, who had taught Russian to Ella, Alix's sister. Should the matter reach a favorable conclusion, she would teach Russian to the Hessian princess. And naturally, Alix's favorite sister, Ella (Grand Duchess Elizaveta Feodorovna), came too.

The engagement of Nicholas and Alix was to take place at the wedding of Alix's brother Ernie. Everyone knew it.

Nicholas's diary:

"5 April. . . . She has grown remarkably more beautiful, but she looked extremely sad. They left us alone, and then there began between us the conversation I have wished for and at the same time greatly feared for so long. We talked until 12, but with no result: she still objects to conversion. Poor thing, she cried a lot, and we parted more calmly."

Everything was drowning in lilac. It was a chilly, magnificent spring. That is how those days began. Despite her refusal, he was joyously calm. He knew that all his people were now in favor of this marriage, and most of all he knew she loved him. He had discovered a rule for himself, having twice found himself on the brink of death: trust the Lord in all things. He would be governed by this rule all the rest of his life, but during those Coburg days, in violation of this rule, he was quite persistent. The girl he wanted for a wife was deeply religious, and he ached for her, understanding what a change of religion meant. Loving her for her despair and her tears, he helped her with his tender persistence to shift responsibility for the decision onto him.

She, however, cried a lot during the interval. Subsequently she would write many times about how hard it had been for her to accept the idea of converting. Religion played an enormous role in her life. But her predecessor princesses of Hesse had set out for distant Russia many times and had converted. Even her sister Ella had accepted Orthodoxy and was happy in her new religion. No, something else was behind all this crying, but she could not put it into words. In decisive moments it is given to exalted, nervous natures to sense

the future. Is that not why she cried so bitterly and, virtually terrified, did her utmost to tell him no?

Nicholas's diary:

"7 April. Ducky and Ernie's wedding day. It began with me being
late for breakfast and having to walk like a cock past the crowd on
the square. At 12 everyone gathered upstairs, and after the civil marriage act was signed, we went into the church. Ernie and Ducky
make a fine couple. The pastor gave a good sermon, the point of
which was amazingly apropos to the essence of what I am going
through. At that moment had a terrible urge to look into Alix's soul.
After the wedding a family dinner. . . . The young people left for
Darmstadt. Went for a walk with Uncle Vladimir, climbed the hill,
and finally reached the castle. We viewed the weapons museum at
length and had dinner with Aunt Marie, in our uniforms, because of
the emperor [Wilhelm II], who will not wear civil dress. Then we
went, or rather ran, to the theater in a downpour. They gave the first
act of *Pagliacci*."

What a good time he had clambering up the hill to the castle and
then running across the street in the evening and sitting in a wet
uniform in the theater! He had a good time whatever he did then
because he knew it would all work out—and by tomorrow for sure.
He loved them all: dear Ernie, dear Ducky, dear Uncle Willy, and
dear Uncle Vladimir.

"8 April [he underscored the date three times in the diary]. A
marvelous, unforgettable day in my life! The day of my engagement
to my precious, beloved Alix. After our conversation we declared
ourselves to each other. So joyful to be able to gladden dear Papa
and Mama. Walked around the entire day in a haze, not fully con-
scious, actually, of what had happened to me. . . . Then a ball was
arranged. Didn't feel like dancing; walked and sat in the garden with
my fiancée. Can hardly believe that I have—a fiancée."

In a letter to his mother he described in more detail Alix's strange
despair and tears:

"She cried the whole time, and only whispered now and then:
'No, I cannot.' Still I continued to insist and repeat my arguments,
and though this conversation went on for two hours, it came to
nothing. . . . I gave her your letter [the letter of a Danish princess
who had converted happily], and after that she could no longer ar-
gue. . . . She joined us in the drawing room, where we were sitting
with Ella and Wilhelm, and then and there, right away, she agreed.
God Almighty only knows what that did to me. I was crying like a
baby, as was she. No, dear Mama, I cannot express how happy I am.
The whole world changed for me in an instant: nature, mankind—

they all seem so good, and dear, and happy. I cannot even write, my hands are trembling so. . . . She has completely changed—she is gay, amusing, and talkative."

He gave her a ruby ring and that brooch—the brooch he had given her at the children's ball long ago. She wore his ring around her neck, along with her cross, and the brooch was always with her.

From her letter on the twenty-first anniversary of their engagement:

"April 8th, 1915. Tenderly do my prayers & grateful thoughts full of very deepest love linger around you on this dear anniversary! . . . You know I have kept the grey princesse dress I wore that morning. And shall wear yr. dear brooch."

On their twenty-second anniversary:

"April 8th, 1916. . . . feel my longing to be held in your arms tightly clasped & to relive our beautiful bridal days. . . . That dear brooch will be worn today. I feel still your grey suite, the smell of it by the window in the Coburg Schloss."

A twelve-carat diamond would be found in the filthy campfire where their clothing was burned that morning of July 17, 1918. The remains of the brooch. It was with her until the end.

How happy he was then! She too tried to be happy. Nonetheless, she continued to cry even afterward. The people around them could not understand it. Observing her tears, a simple-hearted lady-in-waiting wrote in her diary exactly what she could have been expected to write: Alix did not love her future spouse. She herself did not understand her tears—after all, she loved him very much, as she would recall in her letter on the twenty-second anniversary of their engagement: "those sweet kisses wh. I had dreamed of & yearned after so many years & wh. I thought, I should never get . . . & when make up for sure mind, then it is already for always—the same in my love and affections. A far too big heart wh. eats me up."

He, however—he was deliriously happy. All his life he would gaily recall the orchestra playing at Coburg Castle and his Uncle Alfred, the Duke of Edinburgh, worn out from dinner, dozing off during the wedding ceremony and dropping his cane. What faith he had in the future then! And all those uncles and aunts (queens, an emperor, princes, dukes), who were still deciding the fates of nations, crowding in the halls of Coburg Castle and also believing in the future. If only they could have looked into the future then.

The newlyweds Ernie and Ducky, the "fine couple," would separate soon afterward, and Alix's sister Ella would perish at the bottom
of a mine shaft. Uncle Willy, who was so fond of his military uniforms and was looking forward to a military alliance with Russia,
instead would start a war with Russia. Uncle Paul, who was now
dancing the mazurka, would be lying with a bullet in his heart, and
Nicky himself. . . .

"Though thou exalt thyself as the eagle, and though thou set thy nest
among the stars, thence will I bring thee down, saith the Lord."

On April 9, Alexander Volkov was sent by his master, Grand Duke
Paul, to deliver a present on the occasion of the engagement. He
found Nicholas and Alix in the drawing room, sitting on the sofa,
holding hands. So swallowed up were they in each other that Nicholas did not notice Volkov right away.

"Oh, it's you, dear friend Volkov!"

Volkov, too, was "dear." Everyone was "dear" (Nicholas's favorite
word).

At that time Ekaterina Adolfovna Schneider was already tutoring
Alix in Russian. They were conjugating verbs, and Alix was recording
them neatly in notebooks. She liked to study.

I am leafing through her study notebooks. Alix learned the language
by conjugating three verbs: *forget, sing,* and *believe.* The unconscious: *forget!* Forget all her inexplicable premonitions. And *believe.*
And *sing.*

Ekaterina Schneider would become the court reader in the imperial palace and in 1917 would voluntarily go into exile with her former
pupil. In 1918, a thousand kilometers from Petersburg, en route to
the disposal pits, they would kill the old court reader.

These were their happiest days, after their betrothal. Poetic love à la
Goethe: he and Alix riding in a charabanc to gather flowers in the
countryside.

Easter. On Good Friday singers from Petersburg revealed to the
German-English princess all the triumphant goodness of the Orthodox service. With the singers came a courier from Petersburg, bringing presents, letters from the tsar and tsaritsa, and a medal—for Alix.

"20 April. . . . Went with Alix to the station and there said goodbye to her. How empty it feels now to go home. . . . So, we will have to spend a month and a half apart. Wandered alone to familiar places now dear to me and gathered her favorite flowers, which sent in a letter this evening. . . .

"21 April. Had breakfast. . . . By my place stood my old picture of Alix surrounded by familiar pink flowers."

Alix went to Windsor to see Queen Victoria. A month and a half later, the *Polar Star* approached the English shore. This was Nicholas's favorite yacht, and it would become the favorite of Alix and their children. The white yacht entered the Thames.

"We spent entire days together, rode on the boat, had picnics on shore—a true idyll. . . . But then we had to go to Windsor. Although cannot complain—her grandmother was very kind and permitted us to go out without chaperones. . . . Admit I never expected that from her."

All this time she was writing her favorite sayings in his diary: "They live through happiness and want together—& from their first kiss to their last breath sing to each other only of love." "Ever faithful & loving, devoted & pure, & strong, like death."

This word *death*, written in her hand, appeared in his diary.

"21 July. A sad day of parting, separation after more than a month of heavenly bliss. Received a letter from Alix on the *Polar Star*. Quite tired and sad."

Parting, they agreed to write one another. A tale out of the Brothers Grimm: a yacht, a castle, a princess, and a tsarevich.

The echo of this tale was preserved in the washroom—fouled by the guard and covered with obscene drawings—of their last home in Ekaterinburg. After their deaths in 1918, a little book was found in that washroom, behind the pipes. In it was a code and the inscription "For my own beloved Nicky to put to good use when he is far away from his *spitzbube*. From his loving Alice Osborne, July 1894."

This was the code book for their correspondence (she adored secrets), which "loving Alice" had given to him during their days of happiness in Osborne, the queen's home on the Isle of Wight.

———

"Nicky and Alice make a fine couple." Separated, they wrote each other letters almost every day.

These delicate sheets with small crowns—their letters. He wrote her from the castle at Spala, in Poland, where the Polish kings had had an ancient hunting lodge and where the Russian tsar loved to hunt. He wrote to her from the imperial train taking him to Livadia, where his father lay dying. Hundreds of his letters. And hundreds of her replies. Endless incantations of love.

Early in October, in Darmstadt, Alix received a telegram calling her urgently to the Crimea: Alexander was dying. In Berlin, her Uncle Willy saw her off at the station. He knew the firm but charming Alix's unforgiving nature and dear Nicky's softness. He had no doubt who would lead in this union, and he believed she would not forget her little homeland and her Uncle Willy. But Uncle Willy did not know the Hessian princess very well.

"Your people have become my people, and your God has become my God." This was the lesson of the beautiful Hessian princesses who had departed for distant lands in the past.

The emperor is dying.

The eminent Dr. Zakharin walks slowly into the dying man's bedroom. The doctor is short-winded and cannot take more than a few steps without sitting down. That is why chairs have been placed all through the hall leading to the bedroom.

In the emperor's bedroom is the tsar's confessor, the renowned priest Ioann of Kronstadt, Father Ioann Yanyshev. And the doctors. They have gathered around the dying man: powerless medicine and omnipotent prayer, which eases his final sufferings.

It is all over. The doors of the bedroom are opened. The dead emperor's body is drowning in his huge Voltairian armchair. The empress has her arms around him. A short distance away stands a pale-faced Nicky. The emperor has passed away in his armchair.

Chapter 2

DIARY OF THE NEW TSAR

"20 October, 1894. My God! My God! What a day! The Lord has called our adored, precious, fiercely beloved Papa to Him. My head is spinning. Don't want to believe it. It seems so unlikely, this terrible reality! We spent all morning around him. At about half past 2 he took Communion. Oh, Lord! I stood at the head of his bed for more than an hour holding his head. The death of a saint. . . .

"21 October. In our deep sadness, the Lord gives us quiet, luminous joy. At 10 my Alix was consecrated. There was an office of the dead, and then the other. . . . The expression on precious Papa's face was marvelous, as if he were about to laugh. It was cold and the sea howled.

"There was a fuss about where to celebrate my wedding. Mama and I feel it would be better to do it here, while dear Papa is under our roof, but all the uncles are against it, they say I have to do this in Peter[sburg]."

The uncles won out. No sooner had Alexander died than their voice was heard.

As always, the ascent to the throne was attended by rumors. According to one version, the dowager empress wanted to replace Nicholas with her favorite son, Michael, and tried to force Nicholas to abdicate.

But that was only a rumor. The renowned minister of her husband and, now, her son, Sergei Witte, recorded in his *Memoirs* his conversation with her about Nicholas before Alexander's death:

"You mean to say that the sovereign does not have the character of an emperor?"

"That is correct," replied Marie Feodorovna. "In the event that anything should happen, Misha must take his place, although actually he has less will and character."

Very soon something did happen. Alexander was younger than fifty when he died. This giant had seemed immortal, and when Nicholas suddenly learned about his father's illness, he was overcome with fright. His friend Sandro recorded Nicholas's exclamations of panic in his memoirs. So that, evidently, another rumor that emerged from inside the walls of the Livadia Palace was true: Nicholas begged to be allowed to abdicate. But Alexander was unbending: the law of succession must be observed. Nicholas must take the throne. And to his great joy, to strengthen his resolve, Nicholas was allowed to take the Hessian princess for his wife.

Petersburg, a gloomy autumn day. The funeral train arrived at the platform of Nikolaevsky Station.

Witte was among those meeting Alexander's coffin.

"The new emperor arrived in Petersburg with his fiancée, the future empress, whom they say he loves," wrote Witte.

Alix's general forebodings were beginning to take specific form: she rode into Petersburg behind a coffin.

The funeral lasted a long time. While the metropolitan was speaking, the dowager empress collapsed in a fit of hysterics, crying: "Enough! Enough! Enough!"

She buried the emperor in the Cathedral of Saints Peter and Paul. A year of mourning was proclaimed in the country, but the wedding had to take place within a week—on the dowager empress's birthday. Before the wedding they lived apart: she with her sister Ella, at the palace of Grand Duke Sergei Alexandrovich; he at his dear Anichkov with his mother.

"My wedding was the continuation of the funeral, only I was dressed in white," Alix would say later.

"13 November, 1894. Anichkov. At 11 we went to mass in our dear church. It was both sad and painful to stand there . . . knowing that one place would always remain empty. Words cannot express how hard it was and how sorry I feel for dear Mama! . . . Saw my dear Alix at tea. Then said goodbye to her at 8. We are not to see each other anymore! Until the wedding! It still seems as if all this were leading up to someone else's wedding. Odd under these circumstances to think about one's own marriage."

But why were they in such a hurry with the wedding? Why were they not even waiting out the usual forty days after his father's death?

November 14 was the last day before the start of a fast that would continue until the beginning of January. So otherwise they would have had to postpone the wedding for quite some time.

"14 November. My wedding day. After coffee with the others went to dress. Put on my hussar's uniform and at 11.30 went with Misha to the Winter Palace. Troops all along Nevsky. Mama and Alix. We all waited while they completed her toilette in the Hall of Malachite."

Finally she appeared: she wore a silver dress and a diamond necklace, and over her shoulders lay an ermine-lined, gold brocade mantle with a long train. On her head rested a tiara blazing with diamonds. The new empress.

"At 10 minutes after 12 the entrance into the Great Church began, whence I returned a married man. . . . We were presented with an enormous silver swan from the family. Alix and I changed clothes, got into a Russian carriage, and went to Kazan Cathedral. A sea of people in the streets. . . . An honor guard from the Uhlan Life Guard Regiment was waiting in the Anichkov courtyard when we arrived. Mama welcomed us with bread and salt. . . . All evening we answered telegrams. . . . Collapsed into bed early, since her [Alix's] head had begun to pound."

This rather crude, guardsmanly "collapsed into bed" concealed his embarrassment and fear before the mystery of her virginity. And she? It is no accident that he noted her headache. On her wedding night she decided to write of her happiness in his diary, but strange words appeared in her entry: "When this life ends, we shall meet again in another world and remain together always." She was tormented by the same sadness and odd fear. The young empress tried to explain it away by the recent funeral ceremonies —by this wedding mixed with grief.

"ALL IS FULL OF PEACE AND JOY"
The dowager empress did all she could to keep them with her: at first they lived in Anichkov Palace.

"15 November. So, a married man. . . .

"16 November. All morning saw dear Alix only for one hour. We went for a ride. . . . Strange sitting beside her in Peter[sburg].

"17 November. Am inexpressibly happy with Alix. It is a shame my duties take up so much time, which I would prefer to spend exclusively with her."

She was embarrassed by her poor Russian, and her active nature was tortured by the fact that she could only look on as the dowager empress and ministers managed her Nicky. But her voice was heard more and more frequently in his diary. She wrote admonitions: "First your duty, then rest and relaxation." "Do not fear danger, the Lord is near and protects you." The harmony of their union, his softness and her firmness. She thirsted to be at his side in everything. At his side—that is, to rule him. As yet she did so only in his diary.

A year of mourning: no balls or entertainments; they were left to themselves. He, after his duties, which "take up so much time"; she, all day long. At three o'clock, free after ministers' reports and other state duties, they would leave Anichkov and ride down Nevsky, then on to the Winter Palace, where their apartment was being readied, and then back to Anichkov Palace—and again they were together. In the evening, he read aloud to her, as his father used to do. When the first snow fell, they went to Tsarskoe Selo, and there for the first time they spent an entire week alone.

On the last day of the year they wrote in his diary.

He: "Along with this irreparable woe, the Lord has rewarded me with unimaginable happiness by giving me Alix."

She: "The last day of the old year. What happiness to spend it together. My love has grown so deep, so strong, so pure—it knows no bounds. May the Lord bless you and keep you." And a verse from Lermontov: "Transparent twilight, icon lamp. Bowed head and cross —symbol of holiness. All is full of peace and joy."

She had calmed down. Love filled her, and she longed to proclaim it. With him.

When he ascended to the throne, so much was expected of him. Russia's unfailing expectation of a good new tsar! His image had already been created: as heir he had tried to slip out of the palace to have a good time (he thirsted for freedom); he had been in love with a Jewess (he would not oppress national minorities); he had put a police chief in the guardhouse for twenty-four hours (an end to police tyranny). These hopes produced endless requests from local elected councils for all manner of reform.

Pobedonostsev decided it was time to put a halt to all of this. Nicholas had to deliver an appropriate speech (written for the tsar by Pobedonostsev himself).

On January 17 (!), 1895, the young emperor and the new empress (who was baptized in St. Feodor's Cathedral, becoming Alexandra Feodorovna) showed themselves to the country for the first time.

Representatives of the local councils, the cities, and the Cossacks gathered at Anichkov Palace. The sight of this multitude of people, who Pobedonostsev asserted harbored treason and whom Nicholas must now put in check, threw the timid Nicholas into confusion. The speech lay in the emperor's lambskin cap.

He begins reading too loudly, in a breaking falsetto: "Recently at certain meetings of local councils we have heard the voices of people carried away by senseless dreams." Out of his confusion and tenseness, he suddenly shouts this last sentence while staring at the representative of the Tver nobility. The tsar's shout startles the old man, so that the gold platter with bread and salt which, according to ancient custom, members of the local councils prepared to offer the new sovereign flies from his hands.

The platter rolls across the floor, clanging, the bread falls off, and the gold salt cellar embedded in it rolls behind the platter. The impeccably well bred tsar does what any young man should do when something falls from an old man's hands: Nicholas tries to pick the platter up, which embarrasses everyone dreadfully. The minister of the court, old Vorontsov-Dashkov, hastily chases after the platter, which is caught.

Aficionados of omens sigh grievously, anticipating sadness in the coming reign.

From the diary of Vladimir Nikolaevich Lamsdorf, a statesman who would become a minister to the tsar:

"January 19, 1895. In town they are directing harsh attacks against the emperor's speech of the day before yesterday, which made the most distressing impression. . . . They are also blaming the empress for holding herself as if she had swallowed a yardstick and for not bowing to the deputations."

Alix was just as shy as her spouse. She fended off embarrassment with her regal bearing.

"A DAUGHTER SENT BY GOD"

In the summer they went south, to the Crimea, to the Livadia Palace, where the dead emperor had so recently sat in his armchair. The dowager empress, Nicky's brother Misha, his childhood comrade Sandro, and Sandro's wife, Nicky's sister Xenia.

Both Xenia and Alix were pregnant.

"31 July, 1895. After tea I was busy when suddenly I learned that a daughter, Irina, had been born to dear Xenia. Alix and I flew to the farm immediately. We saw Xenia and my little niece. Praise God, it all ended for the best."

This Irina crying in her cradle would become the wife of Felix Yusupov, Grigory Rasputin's chief assassin.

In the fall they returned to Petersburg and Tsarskoe Selo. From 1895 until the end of his reign, Tsarskoe Selo would be his family's principal residence—"that charming, dear, precious place." In the park, set among small artificial lakes, not far from the opulent Catherine Palace, stood the smaller Alexander Palace half hidden by trees. Here they lived. On the night of November 3, the dowager empress was summoned there from Gatchina.

"3 November. Friday. A day forever memorable for me, during which I suffered much! At 1 in the morning dear Alix began having pains that would not let her sleep. All day she lay in bed in great torment, poor thing. I could not watch her calmly. At about 2 in the morning dear Mama arrived from Gatchina. The three of us—she, Ella, and I—were with Alix constantly. At exactly 9 we heard a child's squawk, and we all breathed freely! A daughter sent by God, in prayer we named her Olga. . . ."

"6 November. In the morning admired our enchanting little girl. She doesn't seem like a newborn at all because she's such a large child and her little head is covered with hair."

The Russian nanny (the assistant to the English nanny) said that "a head covered with hair" was a definite token of the little girl's future happiness.

In 1918 she would be lucky. She would be standing next to her mother in that half-cellar room. "The tsaritsa and Olga tried to shield themselves with the sign of the cross, but could not do so. Shots rang out" (from the testimony of one of the sharpshooters in the guard, A. Strekotin).

The little girl grew up. A photograph he took: Alix and, next to her mother, on spindly little legs, tiny Olga.

Childishly (to his death he would be sweetly infantile), he kept comparing her with his sister's daughter.

"21 March, 1896. After mass we brought our daughters to Holy Communion. Ours was perfectly calm, but Irina cried a little. . . .

"1 April. Xenia brought Irina to our little one's bath. They weigh the same, 20 pounds, but our little girl is chubbier."

The birth coincided with the end of the mourning period. A brilliant ball is held at the Winter Palace: thousands of guests, the orchestra plays a polonaise, the master of ceremonies strikes his staff three times, Arabs in white turbans throw the doors open wide, the brilliant hall bows—and Nicholas and Alexandra make their entrance.

Alix still spoke Russian poorly, and being among people was quite a task for her. In any case, she was completely taken up with her infant; Alix ruled the nest at Tsarskoe Selo.

Nicholas's mother and her people ruled the country There was a story about the flower that righted itself: crushed by her husband's iron will, the power-loving mother finally righted herself, and so on. In fact, it was all much more tragic and simple. The dowager empress (Aunt Minnie, as she was called in the Romanov family) knew her own son all too well. She feared that someone must inevitably come to influence the good Nicky (at that time she was not thinking of Alix)—perhaps Grand Duke Sergei Alexandrovich, an out-and-out retrograde, or the dead tsar's other brother Vladimir, as charming as he was stupid. Or Alexander's dear but foolish third brother, Paul. Any of them could be fatal for the empire. This pragmatic woman believed in herself; she had learned a great deal from Alexander III.

Witte's diaries contain a colorful description of this period: "Ask my mother"—that was Nicholas's response to Witte on the subject of naming another minister. And elsewhere, again in a difficult moment: "I shall ask my mother."

Marie Feodorovna demonstrated perspicacity by setting Nicky up with Sergei Yulievich Witte, her husband's minister of finance. Witte constituted an entire era in himself: a supporter of reforms, a liberal —or, rather, a conservative liberal, as he would have to be after the frost that raged under Alexander. Witte knew that in Russia one cannot change the temperature too quickly.

At first the empress-mother tried to appear everywhere at her son's side.

Vera Leonidovna:

"At that time the dowager empress suddenly seemed astonishingly young. All Petersburg was intrigued by this puzzle. People said that this stunning woman had decided to undergo an operation in Paris. She had heard about this operation from the future English Queen Alexandra—that is to say, she saw its fruits. Despite her age, Alexandra literally stunned everyone with her youthfulness. . . . It is a hideous operation: first the epidermis is removed from the face with a sharp spoon and the face is transformed into one great wound. The wound is moisturized and treated and a clear lacquer is applied to the face. This new, tender, pure face has to be treated very carefully so as not to spoil the lacquer. What comes next is even more painful: widening the hair follicles to insert long eyelashes. The entire operation demands heroism."

The poor woman had to reconcile herself to this pain: the young emperor must have a young mother by his side.

"ALL THAT HAS HAPPENED . . . SEEMS A DREAM" Russian sovereigns were crowned in the ancient Assumption Cathedral in Moscow.

On May 6 the imperial train, with the entire large Romanov family aboard, departed for Moscow.

"6 May, 1896. For the first time since our wedding we have had to sleep apart. Very tiresome. Arose at 9. After coffee answered telegrams. Even on the railway they do not leave me in peace. Met in Klin by Uncle Sergei [his former superior, Grand Duke Sergei Alexandrovich, who had become governor-general of Moscow]. Arrived in Moscow at 5, in dreadful weather: rain, wind, cold."

According to custom, before the ceremonial entry into Moscow for the coronation, the sovereigns had to stay in the old Petrovsky Palace located outside the Tver gate, at that time a verst (less than a mile) from Moscow. Here they spent three days in the castle with Gothic windows and romantic turrets that Catherine the Great had built to commemorate the victory over the Turks.

"7 May. Awoke to the same grim weather. . . . Received Henry's [the brother of Emperor Wilhelm] enormous suite, and the princes—of Baden, Wurtemberg, and Japan."

Royal Europe and all the rest of the world were converging for the coronation of the Russian autocrat.

On the day of the ceremonial entrance into Moscow, for the first time the sun came out, setting Moscow's countless golden cupolas and churches on fire.

Early morning. The young empress, golden hair to her waist, was standing by a Gothic window, looking out at the towers of the Petrovsky Palace—the continuation of the same fairy tale!

The magnificent procession set out for the Kremlin.

"9 May. The first hard day for us—the day of our entrance into Moscow. By 12 an entire gang of princes had gathered, with whom we sat down to lunch. At 2.30 the procession began to move. I was riding on Norma, Mama was sitting in the first gold carriage and Alix in the second, also alone."

There was one strange incident. They paid a visit to the holiest place in all of Russia: the Trinity-St. Sergius monastery. But when they got to the monastery, there was no one to meet them. No one remembered until the tsar had already set foot on the territory of the monastery. The mixup was due to poor coordination among those in charge of the coronation ceremonies; but some saw it as an omen: the most honored holy man in Russia, Sergii Radonezhsky, had not greeted the new tsar.

"13 May. Settled in the Kremlin. . . . We had to receive an entire army of suites of arriving princes. May the merciful Lord help us, may He strengthen us tomorrow and bless us for a peaceful life of work."

He followed his note with three exclamation points and a cross. The coronation, his marriage to Russia—for the religious Nicholas this was one of the greatest days in his life.

May 14, 1896. The procession from the Kremlin to Assumption Cathedral. The empress-mother wore a small diamond crown, and four generals bore her purple. Then, to cries of "Hurrah," they entered the cathedral—Nicholas and Alexandra.

"14 May, 1896. A great day, a triumphant day, but for Alix, Mama, and me, difficult in the moral sense.

"We were on our feet since 8 in the morning. The weather, happily, was marvelous. The Red Staircase presented a shining prospect. It all took place in Assumption Cathedral, though it seems a dream, I shall not forget it my whole life long."

Candles burned . . . the cherubic song a cappella. . . . He took the large crown from the metropolitan's hands and put it on his own head. She went down on her knees before him. He removed the crown and touched the crown of Empire to her head. And again the crown was on his head. A small diamond crown already sparkled on her golden hair. Four ladies-in-waiting fastened it with gold pins. Nicholas and Alexandra took their thrones in the ancient cathedral, and the empress-mother kissed Nicky four times. Then the former empress brushed Alix's cheek with two kisses.

How young, how happy they were.

They made three deep bows to the people from the Red Staircase.

"At 3 we went to the table in the Hall of Facets. . . . We had dinner with Mama, who bore up to this entire long trial excellently. At 9 we went to the upper balcony, where Alix lit the lamp on Ivan the Great. Then, afterward, the towers and walls of the Kremlin were illuminated."

The Hessian princess looked out on the golden cupola of the great cathedral: the capital of half the world, the lights of the ancient capital of Europe and Asia, sparkled.

The empress-mother did indeed bear up to this whole long trial excellently. Her endurance would stand her in good stead the next day as well.

"17 May. . . . At 1.15 we went to congratulate the ladies. We began with the grand duchesses, then the ladies-in-waiting, the ladies of the town. . . . My legs ached occasionally. . . .

"We went to the Bolshoi for the ceremonial performance. As usual, they were giving the first and last act of *Life for the Tsar* and a beautiful new ballet, *The Pearl*." This "beautiful new ballet" was the very one in which, to the public's amazement, Kschessinska appeared onstage.

The empress looked at the stage, at the detested Little K., and longed for revenge.

The next morning, on May 18, she wiped both the ill-starred ballet and triumphant Mathilde from her memory. May 18 became one of the most awful days in her son's reign.

According to custom, after a coronation there was an outdoor fête for the people, where free food, candies, cookies, and so on were given out. As if the tsar were feeding his people. A site for the fête was chosen outside the city limits on Khodynka Meadow. The ancient "bread and circuses"—Caesar and his people.

Gaudy tents had been set up with sweets on Khodynka Meadow. Mugs were to be given out as well, coronation mugs with seals—and all for free. But forgotten ditches lay between the tents and the crowd that had gathered on the evening of the 17th (the number 17 again!). Forgotten thanks to the sloppiness of those in charge. Many were those who had come for the free refreshments; at least half a million crowded around—the crush was so great a bullet could not have slipped through. Everyone was waiting for the present-giving to commence. Then shouts rang out—people were suffocating in the crowd. Someone thought the dainties were being passed out! They pressed in. As this mass of bodies began to move, they fell into the trenches, and the crowd trampled over their heads, crushed their rib cages.

At dawn the broken corpses were carted out.

Twenty-two years later, also at dawn, also in carts, the corpses of Nicholas and his family would also be carried away.

When Minister Witte got into his coach that afternoon to attend the continuation of the festivities, he had already been informed about the two thousand dead on Khodynka Meadow. But by the time the brilliant carriages approached Khodynka everything had already been carefully cleared away—there was no trace of the catastrophe. The sun was shining, all of Europe's aristocracy was in the pavilion, and a large orchestra was performing a cantata in honor of the coronation. The bedecked public milled around on the field. The sovereign was present as well. Constantly at his side was the governor-general of Moscow, Grand Duke Sergei Alexandrovich, organizer of the coronation ceremonies.

Nicholas was embarrassed and distressed. Everyone noticed.

"18 May, 1896. Until now all has gone smoothly, but today a great sin occurred: the crowd that spent the night on Khodynka Meadow waiting for the food and mugs began to press on the structures and there was a terrible crush, and I must add terribly that about 1,300 people were trampled. Learned of this at 10.30. . . . The news left a repellent impression. At 12.30 we had lunch, then left for Khodynka, to attend this 'sad national holiday.'

"From the pavilion we watched the crowd surrounding the stage, where they kept playing a hymn and 'Be praised.'

"We moved on to Petrovsky [Palace], where we received several deputations at the gates. . . . I had to give a speech. . . . Dined with Mama. Went to the ball at Montebello's."

Meanwhile, the empress-mother had a very clear understanding of what had caused the Khodynka catastrophe. She had mastered her husband's principles of rule. A command system (autocracy) functions only when the pyramid is crowned by Fear. With the death of the strong emperor, Fear had begun to wane. And just as an organism declares its illness with a high temperature, so with this terrible catastrophe the system had declared what was for her most ruinous: Fear had waned. Nicholas was a weak tsar.

His mother decided that Fear must return. The punishment must be harsh. Was Grand Duke Sergei Alexandrovich, her husband's own brother, guilty? All the better. It was he who must be punished as an example. Then Fear would return.

She demanded the immediate creation of a commission of inquiry and punishment for the guilty parties. Nicholas agreed. One other thing she demanded: the cancellation of all entertainments, including the evening ball being given by the French Ambassador Montebello.

This is the conversation concealed in his note "Dined with Mama."

"We left Mama's."

For the first time, Alix took a stand against his mother. She would not allow the husband of her beloved sister to be fed to the wolves. She would not allow the entertainments canceled. Sergei Alexandrovich was right: everything should go on as if nothing had happened. A coronation occurs once in a lifetime, the ball must take place. (In the depths of her soul she tried to drive out this new, bloody presentiment: first a wedding in the wake of a funeral, now these corpses on Khodynka Meadow. She hoped that the ball and the music and these triumphs would wipe them from her memory.) And again Nicholas consented.

"Went to the ball at Montebello's."

Yes, to the horror of the new emperor's friends, Nicholas and Alix danced at this ball.

As before, constantly at Nicholas's side was Grand Duke Sergei Alexandrovich: Moscow had already dubbed him the Duke of Khodynka.

Then, on the following days:

"19 May. At 2 went with Alix to Old St. Catherine's Hospital and toured all the barracks and wards where the unlucky victims from yesterday lay. . . .

"20 May. . . . At 3 went with Alix to St. Mary's Hospital, where we saw the second largest group of injured."

He contributed generously for the victims. But the country no ticed only one thing: "Went to the ball at Montebello's." His mother had been right.

There is a concept: a tsarlike nature is the sum of qualities that produces the impression of a powerful will. Nicholas did not possess those qualities. "Irresolute compassion," "paralysis of will"—this is what some said about him. Others objected: he was crafty. In actual fact, he was stubborn. His tragedy was that, although he was stubborn, he was also unable to say a clear no to a petitioner's face. He was too delicate and well bred to be crudely determinate. He preferred silence to rejection, and as a rule the petitioner took his silence for consent. Nicholas was merely waiting for someone to turn up with his point of view.

When he did, then Nicholas immediately made his decision. As a consequence, the first petitioner, who had taken silence for agreement, cursed the sovereign's perfidy and spinelessness. That is precisely what happened with Kschessinska. When his mother and the minister crossed the ballerina's name off the coronation program, he held his tongue—he could not insult his mother. But he waited. When his Uncle Vladimir came to intercede for Mathilde, Nicholas agreed on the spot.

It was the same with Khodynka. He was the one, understanding Alix's state, who decided to go on with the celebration, but he did not have the nerve to oppose his mother. Then, as if yielding to the demands of Sergei Alexandrovich. . . . But the legend about his spinelessness had been created, and it would run through his entire life. From the very beginning, his image was merged with an "un-tsarlike nature."

He appointed a commission of inquiry, headed by Count Pahlen, the dowager empress's protégé. At this point, however, a counterblow followed. Vladimir and Paul, the tsar's uncles, announced that they would quit the court immediately if Sergei Alexandrovich suffered as a result of the investigation.

It was a risk-free ultimatum. They knew they would not have to back down. Alix stood behind them.

Delicate Nicky was nodding tirelessly in opposite directions, trying to reconcile everyone: Pahlen's report disappeared into the bowels of the archives. But the Moscow police chief, Grand Duke Sergei Alexandrovich's man, was dismissed. And to his mother's horror, Nicholas set off for the estate of the Duke of Khodynka—Ilinskoe.

He had not wanted to be tsar, he had not wanted to distress his mother, he had not wanted anyone to be killed, he had not wanted Alix to be sad. Yet all those things had come to pass. That was what it meant to be tsar.

*F*EAST FOR THE SLAIN

Even now, outside Moscow, that broad *allée* with centuries-old trees leading up to the famous estate Ilinskoe is there. The plane trees, a hundred years old then, still stand in the park, as does the ancient church.

"3 June, 1896. The wedding anniversary of Uncle Sergei and Ella."

This day was celebrated noisily at Ilinskoe. Children ran around the estate: the new generation of the Romanov family.

The nineteenth century was drawing to a close, the sets for the terrible new century were being invisibly raised—and the cast was coming out onstage, the Romanovs who would live in the twentieth century.

Here was a five-year-old boy in velvet pants. This was Dmitry, son of the youngest brother of Nicholas's father, Grand Duke Paul. Dmitry was born here at Ilinskoe and he killed his own mother.

It happened in Ilinskoe before Nicholas's marriage to Alix.

Today, too, this path descends from the top of the hill to the Moscow River. At the river's edge you can find half-ruined wooden piers. It was here, in the hot summer of 1891, enjoying the sun and the morning, that the young woman, the Greek Princess Alexandra, the wife of Grand Duke Paul, ran down to the pier.

As she was getting into a boat she went into premature labor. Soon after, the dead Alexandra's body was laid out at the estate. But the boy came into the world and survived. He was called Dmitry.

Dmitry's father, Grand Duke Paul, would be exiled from Russia. After his wife's death he had a scandalous affair with the wife of Grand Duke Vladimir's adjutant. Paul decided to marry her, but the dowager empress was implacable, and Paul's brothers, Sergei and Vladimir, were forced to take her side. This was the first scandal in the Romanov family that poor Nicky had to referee. Nicholas was forced to send "dear Uncle Paul" out of Russia. But Dmitry remained in Russia and with his sister was raised in the family of Sergei Alexandrovich and Ella.

Unable to have their own children, Ella and Sergei Alexandrovich showered all their kindness on Dmitry and his sister.

During the revolution of 1905, the Socialist Revolutionary Kalyaev appeared with a bomb by the Bolshoi Theater. It had all been carefully calculated: as soon as the bright lanterns of the grand duke's carriage turned on in the storm, Kalyaev threw himself in front of the carriage—and saw Ella and the children in the carriage along with Sergei Alexandrovich. Kalyaev did not dare throw his bomb. An idealistic terrorist of the idealistic nineteenth century! The next time Sergei Alexandrovich went alone, however, Kalyaev did not miss.

After the murder of her husband, Ella devoted herself to the creation of a cloister, and Dmitry lived with his Uncle Nicky. "Papa and Mama"—that was what he called Nicholas and Alix.

Ella had been one of the most captivating women of that time long past. The French ambassador to Russia, Maurice Paléologue, recalled fondly:

"I remember dining with her in Paris . . . in about 1891. I can still see her as she was then. tall, stern, with shining blue, naive eyes, her tender mouth, the soft features of her face and her straight slender nose . . . the charming rhythm of her carriage and movements. In her conversation one intuited a marvelous feminine mind —natural, serious, and full of hidden goodness."

They were having a good time at Ilinskoe. Ioann and Konstantin, the Romanov sons of the poet Grand Duke Konstantin Konstantinovich (K.R.), were running through the meadow with Dmitry. The infant Igor, K.R.'s youngest son, was crawling by Grand Duke Paul.

Upstairs, in the house, Ella was singing K.R.'s "Lullaby" as her husband turned pages.

Downstairs, Nicky was watching the sporting children benignly; Alix, greedily. Oh, how Alix dreamt of a son.

At the bottom of a mine shaft, Ella would have the strength to tie a handkerchief around Ioann's smashed head. Konstantin and Igor would perish in the mine shaft too. And, by the way, Uncle Paul would be shot dead a few months later.

Their carefree life continued. They traveled.

Austria—a visit to the aged Emperor Franz Joseph, then visited Nicky's grandmother and grandfather (the Danish king and queen), and from there to England to another grandmother, Queen Victoria. The circuit of royal names ended in a republic—France.

Khodynka, which later would be held up to him so many times in Russia, had made no impression on Europe. In France he was received ecstatically: the beautiful empress, the young sovereign, and the enchanting little girl in the open carriage. This was the first visit to Paris of a Russian tsar since his grandfather's unfortunate visit, when the Pole Berezowski shot at him—in revenge for the oppression of Poland.

No one was shooting now. On the contrary: Nicholas was greeted by enthusiastic crowds and ovations. Only a free republic can get so excited about a monarch.

"On September 25, a bridge named after my papa was laid. We sat in a large tent. . . . Then the three of us went to Versailles. Crowds of people stood along the entire route from Paris to Versailles. My hand nearly dried up [he was in uniform and kept touching his hand to the brim of his cap].

"We arrived at 4.30 and took a ride around the beautiful park, viewing the fountains. . . . There truly is a similarity to Peterhof. The halls and rooms of the palace are interesting in this historical aspect."

He was stunned by the similarity to Peterhof, the tsar's summer palace on the Gulf of Finland, and by the "historical aspect." She stood on the balcony of the palace where during the Revolution the people had burst into Versailles and forced the royal couple out.

In Paris Alix was told about the former site of the pit where all those guillotined had been brought. She and Nicky pictured them together in the dark filth: Danton, Robespierre, the Girondists. They had dared execute their own king. Well, God punished them with madness, and they killed each other. She never forgot all this. Twenty years later, when she heard of Nicky's abdication, she repeated in French, *"abdiqué"* ("he has abdicated"). . . . The secret recesses of the soul.

The year 1896 was coming to an end. Alix was expecting a child, and she believed it would be a boy. How she longed for that boy.

"29 May, 1897. The second happiest day in our family's life. . . . At 10 in the morning the Lord blessed us with a little girl, Tatiana. She weighs 8 1/2 pounds and is 54 centimeters long. Read and wrote telegrams."

*T*HE IMPRACTICABILITY OF DREAMS

He was still ruling on the strength of his dead father, but an unseen volcano was already smoldering: upheaval in the army (which was not written about in the press; the army was always supposed to be loyal) and the terrible famine of 1898 (which was written about a great deal). But their carefree happiness continued. During those years he hunted a lot.

"20 September [1898]. Total game killed: 100 deer, 56 goats, 50 boar, 10 foxes, 27 hares—253 in 11 days."

Such was the tsar's hunt. But another hunt had already begun in his country—a hunt in which the trophies would be much more serious: a hunt for people.

It began as soon as the twentieth century was under way. In February 1901 the minister of education was killed by a former student. The student explained that Moscow University was dissatisfied with the minister's reactionary views. A year later Sipyagin, the minister of internal affairs, was killed. The Finnish governor-general perished, and then Nicholas's new minister of internal affairs, Vyacheslav Plehve. Thus the Socialist Revolutionaries' terrorist organization began its operations.

The young tsar was behaving rather strangely. He scarcely mourned. It was as if he immediately forgot about his dead ministers.

The solution to the riddle was in his diary: "We must endure the

trials the Lord sends us for our good with humility and steadfastness" (after the murder of Sipyagin).

"Thus is His sacred will" (after the murder of Plehve).

One and the same principal feature in his outlook: God deter-
mines everything in this world, the fate of nations and men. It is not
for us to guess at God's intent or the good that each of His actions
conceals.

This belief helped Nicholas reconcile himself to the strange impracticability of all his beginnings. He was already getting the feeling
that no matter what he did, no matter what he undertook, no matter
how good his intentions, it would all either come to naught, turn
into its opposite, or simply go to rack and ruin.

As his father had instructed, immediately after his ascent to the
throne Nicholas passed a law against drunkenness. Drunkenness—
the "Russian disease," as it was called in Europe. The law was good,
but drunkenness did not disappear. People simply paid more for
vodka. They continued to drink and ruin themselves as before. The
next law was proposed by the irrepressible Witte, who put the Russian ruble on the gold standard so that Russian currency would rise
to a level with European currencies (which it did). Now rich Russians created a furor in Europe, losing their fortunes and squander-
ing their estates in Parisian restaurants: "Russian beluga began to
spawn gold." But as a result, many people of good birth, scions of
the best families, were ruined. And those same gold coins on which
Nicholas's profile was stamped came to rule his country more and
more.

T HE RUSSIAN TSAR GOES TO THE PEOPLE

It was at this time that Alix developed her mistrust for the rich.
Then, on the threshold of the century, he had an idea: "the tsar and
the people—and no one between them." On the threshold of the
century his strange preoccupation with truth seeking first manifested itself.

One day in conversation with one of the grand dukes he learned
of an impoverished Novgorod landowner with a very funny name,
Klopov—"Bedbugson." This Klopov was always writing the grand
duke eloquent letters about the embezzlement of public funds in the
flour milling business. These first letters naturally did not reach
Nicholas, but the indefatigable truth seeker continued to write.
Nicholas told Alix about him, and they read the letters aloud,
amazed at the purity of this unknown, simple man. Perhaps he was

found, the man of the people, perhaps he had come to them himself? The people and the tsar—and no one between them!

The titular councilor was brought to the tsar. The quiet, shy little Klopov, with his gentle eyes, was very much like the not very tall, shy man who met him in his office. Indeed, they were alike—the pathetic titular councilor and the ruler of one-sixth of the world.

Nicholas sent Klopov on a secret mission, giving him broad, confidential authorities. Klopov was going to inspect Russia. He was to understand the reasons for the crop failures, clarify officials' abuses, and bring the tsar back the truth. Moreover, not the "governor's truth"—the truth of the bureaucracy—but the genuine, popular truth they were hiding from the tsar. So Klopov went.

"In Russia, everything is a secret but there is no secrecy." Very soon afterward the whole country knew about the mysterious Klopov. Crowds of people besieged the tsar's emissary with petitions.

But Klopov was after all merely a minor landowner who knew the flour milling business. High officials chatted courteously with him and promised to see to all the problems in the flour milling business. Klopov, deeply moved, brought back to his patron this truth from the depths of Russia: "Minister of Internal Affairs Plehve and his entire ministry are instilled with the very best intentions."

Thus began Nicholas's perilous truth seeking. After Klopov's truth he could tell himself yet again: the impracticability of dreams. . . .

So it was in everything. His fearsome father had aptly been called the "Peacemaker" because he was adept at avoiding war. Nicholas ascended to the throne with the same intention. At the turn of the century he read the essays of I. Bloch, an industrialist and philosopher who wrote about the impossibility of waging a limited war in the new Europe. War in the twentieth century, if it happened, must necessarily become global. "The victor will be unable to avert the most dreadful havoc; therefore every government that is now preparing for war must prepare too for social catastrophe." Bloch predicted that war could be a graveyard for the great European monarchies. Nicholas received Bloch, and their conversation made an impression on him.

It was then that Nicholas's "Appeal to the Rulers" was conceived. Nicholas proposed to Europe a universal peace.

Witte wrote about the basic idea for the "Appeal" in his *Memoirs*: "All of Europe will be united and peaceful, Europe will not be spending great sums on the rivalry between the various countries; it will not represent an armed camp, as it does now. Europe is deteriorating under the weight of mutual enmity and international wars

. . . soon the other nations of America and Japan may be treating Europe with respect, but the kind of respect . . . due an aging beauty."

The idea of universal peace would soon end, however, in war with Japan.

In 1899 a third daughter, Marie, was born. They still did not have their long-awaited son. The tsar's family entered the twentieth century with three daughters. In 1899 Nicholas's brother George died of tuberculosis, and now his youngest brother, Michael, became heir to the throne.

*S*ORCERERS AND SAINTS

In the fall of 1900 Nicholas fell seriously ill in the Crimea. It was typhus.

He was dying. The question had already been raised as to who would inherit the throne, a strange question for Alix: their oldest daughter, Olga, naturally. As in England, where her grandmother, Queen Victoria, ruled. If you thought about it, the Russians themselves had had quite a few empresses. But Witte explained that Michael must rule. Such was Paul I's law on succession, which embodied all of Paul's hatred for his mother, Empress Catherine the Great: a woman must not occupy the Russian throne. A delicate point arose, however: Alix was pregnant, and this time she was certain a son would be born. The law, though, did not care. Whoever was heir to the throne at the moment of the monarch's death would rule.

Witte was now a daily guest at the Livadia Palace. The ministers took up residence in a Yalta hotel. They shuttled between Yalta and Livadia, like crows anticipating their spoils, it seemed to Alix.

But Nicholas recovered—cheating death a third time. After his illness the dream of a son consumed Alix's entire being. It was at this moment that the Montenegrin princesses appeared.

The daughters of the prince of Montenegro had been educated in Russia at the famous Smolny Institute for Well-Bred Young Ladies.

Militsa and Stana, those were the Montenegrins' names (although at court they were sarcastically referred to as Montenegrin No. 1—Stana—and Montenegrin No. 2—Militsa). Both married grand dukes: Militsa the weak-chested Peter Nikolaevich and Stana his brother, Nicholas Nikolaevich, or Nikolasha, as he was called in the large Romanov family. Nicholas the Long, as he was called in the army and at court, ironically by some, admiringly by others. Big, shrill, the army's favorite: Grand Duke Nicholas Nikolaevich.

With the Montenegrins Alix felt like a tsaritsa. They showed her deference and admiration instead of the icy civility of the court. The Montenegrins surrounded her with deft servility. When she was stricken with a stomach ailment, they tended her like the lowliest of servants.

From their mysterious homeland the Montenegrins brought an unshakable belief in the supernatural. Witches and sorcerers had always lived there, in the high mountains grown up in wild forest, and some people there could talk with the dead and predict the fates of the living. All this was new to the granddaughter of the skeptical Queen Victoria; this mysterious new world intrigued her. But the main thing was that the Montenegrins promised the fulfillment of a dream. Alix longed for an heir? Nothing could be easier. It was merely a matter of finding the right person, someone who possessed the *power*. Alix, the exalted romantic, was drawn into the new game with all her being. The dark blood of Mary Stuart had stirred. They began with a foreigner, someone less exotic to the Hessian princess: a certain Monsieur Philippe from Lyons, who was famed in France for his miracles (the Montenegrins had learned about him in Paris from the military attaché at the Russian embassy).

It was Alix's nature: if she believed in something, then she believed with all her heart, without reservation. She believed that this was the way she would get her wished-for son.

The Russian church condemned such perilous escapades with wizards and sorcerers, but the Montenegrins explained: "Monsieur Philippe is not a sorcerer. A sorcerer is a renegade from God, he is dangerous, he does not make the sign of the cross, he does not go to church. Through him the devil reveals his power. But a *znakhar* is something altogether different. A znakhar is a Christian. So he creates from God, not himself." No one in the court could speak out against this not-so-innocent lie. Philippe arrived in Petersburg. Despite his dubious education and the warnings from the French authorities, Philippe received the title of doctor of medicine and the rank of full state councilor. At court an amusing story went around: Monsieur Philippe had moved into the tsar's bedroom, ostensibly to hasten the birth of an heir with his prayers. The empress-mother was forced to have a talk with Nicky and demand that the Frenchman be sent away. As always, Nicky agreed, but Philippe remained. He could not deprive his beloved Alix of hope. Philippe continued to play doctor.

And joy: Alix felt she was pregnant. She did not want to see the doctors for fear of breaking Monsieur Philippe's spells. But the pregnancy was proceeding so oddly that she had to consult the doctors. It turned out to be a false pregnancy: she was pregnant with her dream. So much did she long for a son! But then, finally! And the doctors confirmed it: she was pregnant. Philippe predicted a boy.

On June 5, 1901, she gave birth to a fourth daughter, Anastasia. The Frenchman declared that this was a special sign: the birth of a daughter instead of a son, which the stars had promised, only proved the girl's unusual destiny.

But the Frenchman was too civilized. The Montenegrins understood they needed something more mysterious and strange.

Mitka the Fool was brought to court. The Montenegrins explained to Alix: "fools for Christ's love" existed only in this country. Feigning insanity, they engaged at times in indecent conduct and went around in rags and even naked to mock the pathetic visible world and extract alms from people. They revealed the contradiction between God's profound truth and worldly, superficial common sense. One was to seek the word of God on their lips, in their indecipherable speech. They were blessed, given to prophecy and miracle working. But Alix had not yet been made over into a Muscovite tsarevna: she found Mitka's incoherent speech irksome.

Daria Osipova appeared.

Vera Leonidovna:

"At that time everyone lived for miracles. This mystical feeling is probably common at the end of a century. Perhaps it was a premonition of Atlantis's collapse. . . . We adored séances, we sniffed cocaine. . . . At that time we had taken up with Daria Osipova. . . . This Osipova writhed on the floor—and then exclaimed her prophecies. We wrote down her exclamations; I still have them somewhere. . . . Swimming in the river 'during a storm and the new moon'— that was her recipe for conception. . . . She also talked about how to prepare a potion to turn into a witch and fly at night. I remember the simple, ordinary way she talked about this: 'Ramson . . . thorn apple . . . witch's grass.' . . .

"By the way, it was she who predicted that under the last three Russian tsars Russian history would take a sharp turn every twelve years. Judge for yourself, my friend: 1894, Nicholas ascended to the throne; in the twelfth year of his reign the constitution of October 17, 1905, put an end to Russian autocracy; and another twelve years later, in 1917, the empire came to an end. Another twelve years later, in 1929, a new tsar came to power at last: Stalin. In 1941, the war began. In 1953, Stalin died and Khrushchev came to power. How interesting it would be for me to live long enough to find out what happens to us twelve years after that."

Vera Leonidovna did not live that long. Twelve years later Khrushchev was overthrown and Brezhnev came to power, but he was not a tsar. He was a parody, a puppet. And with him, evidently, the twelve-year rule of the last Russian tsars ceased to apply.

Revelations stretching back into pagan Russia. The weighty mutterings of a znakhar would teach Alix to find meaning later on in the mutterings of Rasputin, and the vague stories about fools' indecent conduct would become the justification for Rasputin's debauch. All these magicians were preparing her for the coming of the "Holy Devil."

The whole pernicious game alarmed Ioann of Kronstadt.

Father Ioann of Kronstadt told them about a true saint and his miracle working, about Serafim of Sarov, whose posthumous glory was already thundering across Russia.

Serafim was a holy man who died in 1833 in the Sarov wilderness. "Fortifying himself in devout thought, in ceaseless incantations of God, and in readings of holy books, Serafim was granted many spiritual visions," Ioann wrote. "He healed and prophesied."

At age eighteen, Serafim (at that time he was still Prokhor Moshnin; he became Serafim after he entered the cloister) left his home and went to worship in the great city of Kiev, at the Holy Monastery of the Caves. Afterward he lived for a long time in the Sarov wilderness under a vow of silence. He taught: "The soul must be given the Word of God—the bread of angels. It is this that nourishes the soul."

The holy man was meek and filled with light and joy.

"The soul replete with despair goes mad; he who conquers passion conquers despair as well." Sadness and despair are sinful.

Serafim went about surrounded by nuns, those happy brides of Christ.

But there were rumors about Serafim and the nuns. The secular authorities grew concerned and instructed the spiritual authorities to question Serafim —and the mystery of holiness became the object of a police investigation. Soon after, the case was put on hold for lack of evidence, but Serafim apparently said at that point: "This event signifies that the end of my life is near." He quietly passed away.

This is how, in connection with the investigation, Father Serafim's prophecies found their way to the Department of Police.

Alix believed immediately: Serafim the holy man, standing by God's throne, would intercede for them, and Holy Russia would get its heir. Meek Serafim had entered their life.

Alix did everything in her power to get him canonized. She succeeded, and it was decided that the entire family would travel to Sarov for the canonization ceremony. How Alix believed in that trip! She would bow to the powers of the saint and pray for a son, for the continuation of the line.

On July 16, 1903, the imperial train pulled into the Arzamas station, and from there the family set out for the Sarov wilderness and the monastery.

The Ministry of Internal Affairs, under Minister Plehve, had been preparing for this trip for a long time. As usual in Russia, the secret police turned everything into a gigantic farce. Orders were issued to the inhabitants of the settlements along the tsarist family's route: "Decorate the entrances to the settlement with arches, your houses with flags, line up along both sides of the road to greet . . . and so on." Huts were immediately painted, covered with boards and even iron. The strictest security measures were taken. Even the welcome had been carefully conceived. During the formal ceremony at the station, a loaded revolver "accidentally" fell out of Minister Plehve's coat, which his servant was carrying, and a shot rang out. The scheming Plehve had played it exactly right. The sound of the shot was supposed to evoke terrible memories, so that the tsar would properly appreciate the precautionary measures undertaken by the concerned minister.

The police games went right past the imperial couple, though. They saw only the ecstatic crowds lining the road and the sea of people—150,000—who had gathered at the monastery. These people were not driven away. The people who had come to worship Serafim were inclined to be especially devoted to Nicholas. He saw the enthusiasm of the immense crowd that greeted him.

The Sarov trip made an enormous impression on Nicholas and Alexandra.

They spent three days in prayer on the Sarov grounds.

At night the empress bathed in the holy pond, imploring Serafim for the birth of a son, while Nicholas sat on the bank. Her body was white in the silver water.

A sense of quiet well-being at the saint's grave and these peaceful days in Sarov.

At Sarov Alix grasped the astounding concept of the "holy man." A holy man is your intercessor before God. You entrust your will to him, your cunning reason, and he, sensing the continuous link with Him, guides you. The holy man is your guide; he delivers the bread of the angels to your soul. Serafim the holy man was at their side; they could sense his presence and hear his quiet voice speaking to them in his teachings: "Man corporeal is akin to a lighted candle: it must burn and he must die. But his soul is immortal, and our concern must be the soul, not the body."

Venerable Serafim was proclaimed the protector of the tsar's family.

They say when Serafim was dying he asked that his body be tossed out like carrion—for the wild animals to eat, so meek and humble was he.

In 1920 his relics were unearthed and confiscated. Thus after death, he, along with the entire Russian church, "accepted insult and humiliation." The trail of his relics was hopelessly lost—they were believed to have been destroyed. Yet seventy years later, they were discovered in the cellar of the Museum of Atheism, which is housed in Kazan Cathedral, a once renowned Russian Orthodox church.

One museum worker noticed a large rectangular object encased in canvas standing in a corner heaped with tapestries. When they opened the canvas, under it they saw a wooden box, where under the gauze and cotton wool the astonished workers of the Museum of Atheism laid their eyes on unrotted relics. It was the complete frame of a man: the beard and hair were preserved, as were bits of muscle. On the skull was a monk's cowl, on his chest a bronze cross, on his crossed arms satin gauntlets embroidered in gold: "Holy Father Serafim, pray God for us."

Seventy years after his death Serafim was canonized.

Seventy years after his outrage, his relics were returned. And all this he had prophesied.

Prophecies. . . . In Sarov Nicholas learned several of the saint's amazing prophecies. Witte recounted them in his *Memoirs*. When

Witte was leaving to conclude the peace treaty with Japan in Portsmouth, an infuriating message was sent after him: he should not worry but know that Saint Serafim had *prophesied* that the peace treaty would be concluded.

The Department of Police, too, presented the tsar with Serafim's prophecies.

Among them was one that stunned Nicholas. Here is what the amazing elder prophesied about Nicholas's rule: "At the beginning of this monarch's reign there will be national disasters, there will be an unsuccessful war, and great confusion will ensue within the government. Father will rise up against son and brother against brother. But the second half of his reign will be bright, and the sovereign's life long."

What did Nicholas feel when just a year later the prophecy began to come true: first an unsuccessful war, then great confusion. Was it because he knew the holy elder's prophecy that the mystical tsar was so calm during the very worst calamities?

When did he cease to believe in the prophecy? And when did he understand that those last words had simply been added by the Department of Police for his benefit?

We do not know what Serafim of Sarov in truth prophesied for him—and we never will.

*H*IS FIRST WAR

His first war—the Russo-Japanese War—began in 1904. The Peacemaker's son, who so hated war, found himself at war. Subsequently Witte recalled that Nicholas was pushed into seizing lands in Manchuria, having been assured that little Japan would not dare attack Russia.

Witte and his mother explained to him the risk involved. Nicholas agreed and instructed Witte to write a proposal for normalizing relations with Japan. The tsar left for Poland and his hunting lodge.

Witte wrote a memorandum that disappeared in the depths of the archives. The negotiations with Japan that his mother and Witte had fought for fell through.

Nicholas's diary:

"26 January, 1904. . . . Went to the theater at 8—they were doing *Rusalka*. Very good. Returning home, received a telegram from Alexeyev with the news that that night Japanese torpedo boats had carried out an attack against the *Tsesarevich*, *Pallada*, etc., which were at anchor, and put holes in them. Is this undeclared war? Then may God help us! . .

"27 January. This morning a telegram arrived about the bombardment of Port Arthur. Everywhere there are manifestations of a unanimous upsurge of spirit."

Calm entries. He was assured that the Japanese did not know how to fight. His ministers argued over how many Japanese soldiers it took to equal one Russian soldier—two or one and a half.

Very soon, though, he was writing in his diary: "It is painful and hard."

There followed unprecedented defeats for the Russian army and the destruction of the fleet.

CAMARILLA

So, Nicholas was pushed into seizing lands in Manchuria. But who stood behind this unattributed "push"?

When Minister of Interior Affairs Plehve (the Department of Police was part of his ministry) was killed by a bomb, in his archives were discovered copies of *all* the papers relating to the Far East. "To hold back revolution, we need a small, victorious war." This, it turns out, was a statement Minister Plehve had made to one of his high officials on the eve of war.

"We need." . . . But who were "we"?

In his *Memoirs* Witte recounted a curious episode: during his tenure as prime minister he struggled against Jewish pogroms. Naturally, he had to help the Department of Police, and he did. Witte was shocked to discover from a department official that while fighting against Jewish pogroms the Department of Police was simultaneously preparing proclamations inciting the population . . . to Jewish pogroms! These proclamations were sent secretly, in bundles, to the provinces. The terrible pogrom of Jews in Gomel had begun with these very proclamations. Forces existed whose actions even the prime minister was not given to control.

Here is an amazing story from Vera Leonidovna Yureneva:

"My friend at the time [her pronunciation of 'friend' was captivating, and she smiled at the ancient memory] . . . he was very close to Count Witte. . . . He tried to prove that many of the events that occurred during Nicholas's reign were connected with

the secret actions of the *camarilla*. This is a forgotten word now that
Count Witte liked a lot. . . . a Spanish word referring to a group of
influential court intriguers under the Spanish King Ferdinand. It
became pejorative. . . . The camarilla in Russia involved distinguished but degenerate families. . . . They were afraid of losing
their wealth and power and hated the new times—this incomprehensible capitalism. It was they who formed the inner circle, the court
of Nicholas and Alexandra. My friend felt that in Russia, as in any
country where age-old traditions of conservatism persist, a secret
alliance had been formed a long time ago between the extreme right
—that is, the camarilla—and the secret police. That is why when
Alexander II was preparing the constitution the police failed to 'keep
an eye' on him—and he was killed. . . . My friend used to talk
about how back under Alexander III terrorists' notes with threats
against the tsar were always turning up at the carefully guarded
Gatchina Palace. In this way they confirmed the tsar in his hatred
for liberals, by planting these notes through the secret police. . . .
My friend used to say that the Department of Police slipped the
tsar's leash at the end of the century, when the secret police began
to place provocateurs in the revolution. . . . This allowed the police to shroud everything in the greatest secrecy. That was when the
sinister practice began of provocateurs throwing the bombs of unsuspecting revolutionaries at tsarist officials the camarilla didn't
like.

"It was at that time, my friend used to say, that the camarilla and
the secret police carried out an entire series of dangerous intrigues
against the tsar and society.

"One of them was the Japanese war."

"COMFORT HEAVEN-SENT"

The war began—and immediately the Russian bureaucracy's
steadfast rule went into effect: when something clever is conceived,
the result will be its direct opposite. The war, contrived to avert
revolution, encouraged it instead.

This was when—in the aftermath of terrible defeats, in the confusion of advancing revolution—it happened.

Alix's sacred belief that Serafim would intercede with God in
heaven had not been in vain.

It happened at the Alexandria Palace, that small summer palace
where he, the fourteen-year-old Nicholas, had heard the song of the
old hag death and where once they—a boy and a girl in love—had

etched their names in the glass. And so, on the afternoon of July 30, 1904. . . .

"The empress," Anna Vyrubova recalled, "had scarcely gone upstairs from her little study when the heir was born."

Nicholas's diary:

"30 July. For us a great, unforgettable day on which God's goodness was so clearly visited upon us. At 1:15 this afternoon, Alix gave birth to a son, whom in prayer we have named Alexei. Everything happened remarkably quickly, for me at least. There are not words to thank God properly for the comfort He has sent us in this year of hard trials."

General Raukh, who commanded the Cuirassiers, recalled his conversation with Nicholas: "The empress and I have decided to give the heir the name Alexei. We must do this to break the chain of Alexanders and Nicholases," so the happy father and honorary chairman of the Russian Historical Society joked.

Indeed, tsars with the names Nicholas and Alexander had ruled Russia for an entire century.

But it was not all that simple.

The name Alexei was out of favor in the Romanov family. Ever since Peter the Great had ordered his son and heir Alexei secretly murdered, the Romanovs had avoided giving this name to heirs to the throne. There was even a story about a curse on the Romanov line that the stricken Tsarevich Alexei managed to cry out before his death. But Nicholas was set on this name, since he had long been attracted by the image of another Alexei, the Romanov Tsar Alexei Mikhailovich.

Shortly before the heir's birth, several grand historical balls had been held. The halls of the Winter Palace had been filled with boyars and their ladies from the times of the first Romanovs. Nicholas appeared in a costume from Tsar Alexei Mikhailovich that glittered with gold and gems. Alix wore a jewel-strewn dress from Alexei's wife, Tsaritsa Natalia Kirillovna. For Nicholas this was not simply a costume ball but a remembrance of his favorite tsar. By his religiosity, goodness, and exemplary behavior, Tsar Alexei had earned the sobriquet "the Quietest." He had done a great deal for the state—not with cruelty or fierce will, as Peter the Great had, but with meekness and gradual reforms. So Nicholas gave his son this name.

"Christening began at 11. The morning was clear and warm. In front of the house, along the sea road, appeared golden carriages, and in the convoy platoon—hussars and Cossack chieftains."

There was a convoy at Alexei's birth— and there would be another at his death.

The Swiss Pierre Gilliard, Alexei's future tutor, was giving lessons to Alexei's sisters. The tsaritsa brought the boy into the room where Gilliard was working with the girls. The heir was a month and a half old, a fairy-tale prince with platinum locks and big gray-blue eyes. Alexandra bathed the boy herself and had been inseparable from him since his birth.

But after that the Swiss rarely saw the magical boy. Dark rumors about some sort of illness were roaming the palace.

Once the boy ran into the classroom, and right behind appeared the sailor who watched after him. The boy was scooped up and carried away, and his indignant shouts were heard in the halls. Again he disappeared for months.

The mystery was revealed to Gilliard when the tsar was hunting at Spala in Poland. The family was staying at the lodge. Hunting, endless entertainments. At one such celebration Gilliard walked out of the ballroom into an inner passageway.

He found himself standing in front of a door where he heard desperate moans. A moment later the Swiss saw Alix approaching at a run, clutching her long dress, which was getting in her way. She was so upset she did not notice him.

This was the secret the family was keeping: soon after their son's birth the doctors established what Alix had feared most in the world —her child had inherited a disease that was in her maternal line and that was transmitted only through females almost exclusively to their male offspring (to the heirs to thrones—fate's joke on kings). Terrible and incurable—hemophilia. When Gilliard was later entrusted with Alexei's education, the heir's physician, Dr. Derevenko, explained the symptoms in detail: the walls of hemophiliacs' arteries are so fragile that any blow or intense pressure can cause the blood vessels to burst and can mean the end. A fall or a cut can be the beginning of that end.

She had given birth to a son. She had dreamed of him for so long, yet she was the cause of his advancing, irrevocable death. Herein lay the reason behind her quickly progressing hysteria. Now they could only wait for a miracle, which Alix believed in with every fiber of her being: the disease would be cured. No one need know of this temporary illness. Because it was temporary. Saint Serafim would not abandon them. The Guardian would certainly send their family someone to save the heir to the great throne.

The image of Serafim of Sarov hung in the sovereign's office.

The family left Petersburg and shut themselves up in the tsar's residences on the outskirts of the capital, guarding the boy's illness, which became a state secret. All their hopes were pinned on a Deliverer.

At that time magical rumors began to reach her: somewhere in the backwoods of Siberia, on the broad river Tobol (Nicholas recalled his youthful journey), in the small village of Pokrovskoe, *he* lived—the Holy Man.

Thus, on the threshold of the First Revolution, in the fire of a lost war, Grigory Rasputin appeared.

Chapter 3

DRESS REHEARSAL FOR THE COLLAPSE OF HIS EMPIRE

The revolution began with a mysterious event known as Bloody Sunday.

In 1881 the socialist Colonel Zubatov, shaken by the assassination of Alexander II, had rejected his socialist ideas and joined the police. During Nicholas's coronation, Zubatov was already head of the Moscow secret police. The former socialist had devised a fantastic experiment: fight the socialists for influence over the workers with the aid of the police! So the police began to create workers' unions.

Now during strikes the police tried to support the workers, and Zubatov forced the capitalists to make concessions, which they did. In 1902 thousands of workers filled the old squares of the Kremlin chorusing "God Save the Tsar." They prayed for the health of their sovereign emperor—on their knees, in silence, heads bared. The governor-general of Moscow, Grand Duke Sergei Alexandrovich, thanked the workers for their loyalty to the throne. The newspapers of Europe wrote in astonishment of the unprecedented spectacle— police socialism. As always in Russia, the reformer Zubatov was eventually dismissed. His organization, however, lived on.

In 1905, in Petersburg, in the midst of these Zubatov-inspired workers' unions, Father Georgy Gapon appeared. During these difficult years of military defeats and shortages, Gapon called on the workers to take a petition to the tsar to tell him about the problems of the simple people and the oppressions of the factory owners.

A workers' march was slated for January 9. Carrying banners, portraits of the tsar, and holy icons, thousands of loyal workers under Gapon's leadership went to their tsar.

The very idea of this demonstration was the embodiment of Nicholas's cherished dream—"the people and the tsar"—which had brought him to call upon Klopov. Now it had come true: the simple people themselves were seeking protection from the autocrat. It had come true!

And then suddenly, on the eve of the march, the tsar left the capital for Tsarskoe Selo.

An unsettling event had occurred just three days before the planned march. It was Epiphany. "Jordan" had been erected on the Palace Embankment as the site for the annual consecration of the water. Under an elegant canopy—blue with gold stars topped by a cross—Nicholas assisted the metropolitan in the ceremony, after which, according to tradition, the cannon of the Fortress of Peter and Paul, located directly opposite the "Jordan" on the other side of the Neva, was supposed to fire ceremonial blanks. To the horror of those gathered, the cannon turned out to be loaded with live ammunition. By a miracle the tsar was not hit, but a policeman was injured, and his name was Romanov!

The police, who would normally have exaggerated something like this, declared the incident an annoying accident. But someone's intended effect had been achieved: Nicholas was reminded of his grandfather's terrible end, and the policeman's name resounded like an omen. The shot gave Nicholas a good scare.

The Department of Police was extremely well informed about the loyal inclinations of the march because Gapon, who had arranged the demonstration, was a department agent (he would be unmasked subsequently by the Socialist Revolutionaries' terrorist group). The secret police was beginning to frighten the tsar. The police leaked dark rumors: during the demonstration there would be bloody riots prepared by the revolutionaries, perhaps a seizure of the palace. Grand Duke Vladimir, who commanded the Petersburg garrison, was talking about the beginning of the French Revolution.

Nicholas left to join his family at Tsarskoe Selo.

The night before the march they started to pass out bullets in the barracks. The route Gapon had devised made the march an extraordinarily convenient target. First aid stations were readied, and Gapon gave his final speech to the workers. The police provocateur called on the workers to go to the palace.

Thus was readied Bloody Sunday.

In the morning, thousands of people set out for Palace Square. Portraits of the tsar floated over the crowd, which included many children. In the lead was Gapon. Troops waiting on the approaches to the square ordered the march to disperse. But the people did not believe them. Gapon had promised that the tsar was awaiting them. So they stepped onto the square. Shots rang out. More than a thousand were killed and two thousand wounded. Children's corpses lay in the snow. In the afternoon sledges dispersed throughout the city with corpses tied down by ropes.

The night after the firing Gapon addressed the workers: "Blood brothers. Innocent blood has been shed! The bullets of the tsar's soldiers . . . have riddled our portraits of the tsar and killed our faith in him. We must take revenge for our brothers on the tsar, cursed by the people, and on all his wicked breed, the ministers, and all the plunderers of the unhappy Russian land. Death to them. . . ."

"The tsar, cursed by the people"—this is what the Police Department provocateur had written. Bullet-riddled portraits of the tsar.

At Tsarskoe Selo the police reported to Nicholas that he had been spared mortal danger, that the troops had had to fire in defense of the palace, as a result of which there had been casualties—two hundred people.

That is how the police version of the event and official figures were created for the tsar. He recorded in his diary:

"9 January, 1905. A difficult day! In Petersburg there were serious disturbances . . . as a consequence of the workers' desire to get to the Winter Palace. The troops had to fire, and in various places in the city many were killed and injured. Lord, it is so painful and hard!"

Later two dozen workers were brought to Tsarskoe Selo. They spoke loyal words to the tsar. Nicholas uttered a speech in response, promising to satisfy their needs and wants. He was very distressed over the two hundred victims on Palace Square.

He never did find out what happened.

In a single morning a new image of him was created: Nicholas the Bloody. From then on, that is what lovers of freedom would call him.

"Any child's cap, or mitten, or woman's scarf pitifully abandoned that day in the Petersburg snows became a reminder of the fact that the tsar must die, the tsar would die" (the poet Osip Mandelshtam).

Bloody Sunday was one of the chief causes for the future vengeance of the revolution, a prologue to the murder of the tsar's family.

What had happened?

*O*NE VERSION

Vera Leonidovna:

"Everything in those days was mixed up with politics. . . . It was fashionable. . . . Everyone used to talk about how dissatisfied they were. I've had the thrill of recalling everything my freethinking friend who was close to Witte explained to me. . . . To understand Bloody Sunday you have to understand the situation. . . . Russia was on the verge. Everyone knew that. . . . And the 'rights' were nervous. . . . They'd tried to play the Japan card. It hadn't worked out. The Jewish card got tossed in then, of course. They had always looked on the Jews as a pressure valve for popular tension, by organizing pogroms. . . . At our estate outside Kiev we had a servant. . . . She had come to us after a pogrom: the crowd had burst into her house and ripped open her master's stomach, all the while laughing and joking. . . . They had tied his wife to his bloody corpse and heaped them with feathers. She recounted all this while crossing herself incessantly and muttering, 'God will punish them!' And He did: the stupid anti-Semitic policy not only was vile but also proved dangerous. The revolution was advancing. Only for a short period—under Alexander II—had Russian Jews felt like human beings. . . . Nicholas's father had brought back state anti-Semitism. Jews had been driven into the Pale of Settlement and encouraged to emigrate. Tens of thousands of highly enterprising people had left Russia. My father had a brilliant physician's assistant working for him who left for America, where he became a celebrity. But millions remained. My husband, the Jew Koltsov, used to say, 'The non-suckling breasts of their own mother'—that is how they perceived their homeland. The Jews were a vast, underutilized store of intellect, energy, and obsessiveness. The revolutionary party took that reserve into their service. My sister was a terrible revolutionary, and we were daughters of a general. But her friend underground was the daughter of a poor Jewish tailor. . . . My friend used to say that Witte frequently tried to explain to Nicholas's father the danger of the Jewish situation for the country's future."

(The matter was actually somewhat more subtle than this. Witte reports this interchange in his *Memoirs:*

"Are you right to stand up for the Jews?" asked Alexander III. In reply Witte asked permission to answer the question with a question: "Can we drown all the Russian Jews in the Black Sea? If we can, then I accept that resolution of the Jewish question. If not, the resolution of the Jewish question consists in giving them a chance to live. That is, in offering them equal rights and equal laws."

But Witte was a brilliant courtier if he responded to the despot-tsar so boldly; it means he sensed that the tsar wanted to hear that kind of answer from him. Evidently, the zealous master Alexander III was considering how best to make use of the state's four million Jews. But he never went beyond thinking, and Witte recorded the terrible result on the eve of the revolution: "From among the phe-nomenally cowardly people that nearly all Jews were thirty years ago, people have appeared who are sacrificing their lives for the revolu-tion, who have made themselves over into bombers, assassins, and rioters. No one nation has given Russia such a percentage of revolu-tionaries as the Jewish nation.")

Vera Leonidovna:

"So, in response to the actions of the Jewish revolutionaries, on the eve of the revolution, the camarilla decided to play the Jewish card a different way. In Europe the 'Will and Testament' of Peter I was going around. This was a forgery created, apparently, by the French during the time of Napoleon. . . . From this document it followed that Peter the Great, dying, left to the Russian tsars his will and testament: conquer the world. Following this model, the Rus-sian secret police started to publish books, only instead of the words 'Russian threat' they substituted 'Jewish threat.' This is how the *Pro-tocols of the Elders of Zion* saw the light of day. The book was written like a mystery: the story of mankind as a series of calamities attribut-able to the Jews and the Masons, whom they controlled. . . . The charm of it lay in the fact that in Russia the most distinguished Russian families belonged to Freemasonry. In their day Field Mar-shal Kutuzov, Alexander I, and Tchaikovsky had all been Masons. Nicholas II's friend Grand Duke Alexander Mikhailovich and his older brother Nicholas Mikhailovich were Masons. I myself was in-terested in Freemasonry. My idols—Mozart and Goethe—were Ma-sons. Masons were always liberals. There was a constant struggle in Russia between the liberals and the nobility, and the nobility was an

*E*mpress Marie Feodorovna with her son Nicholas, 1871.

*T*he heir to the throne Nicholas Alexandrovich, St. Petersburg.

*T*he family of Emperor Alexander III, St. Petersburg.

*N*icholas Alexandrovich,
St. Petersburg, 1888.

*N*icholas and Princess Alix of Hesse
Darmstadt at Coburg Castle on the day of
their engagement, April 8, 1894.

*C*oronation Day procession
from Assumption Cathedral
to the palace, Moscow,
May 14, 1896.

*N*icholas, Alexandra, and their first child, Grand Duchess Olga, at Grand Duke Sergei Alexandrovich's estate, Ilinskoe, 1895.

*N*icholas and Alexandra on the Kremlin walls.

*T*he ballerina Mathilda Kschessinska, 1897.

Nicholas in the costume of Tsar Alexei Mikhailovich, Winter Palace Ball, 1903.

Alexandra in the costume of Tsaritsa Maria Ilinichna, Winter Palace Ball, 1903.

*T*sarevich Alexei
Nikolaevich and his
nurse with a goat, 1906.

*A*lexei with his sailor-companion
Nagorny on the tsar's yacht *Standart*.

*T*he grand duchesses with ladies-in-waiting
at the beach, Livadia, Crimea.

Alexandra and the grand duchesses. Clockwise from top: Tatiana, Alexandra, Anastasia, Marie, Olga.

Nicholas and Alexandra playing tennis, Germany, 1910.

A picnic during a hunt at Spala in Poland, 1912.

*T*rophies from the tsarist hunt in Belorussia, 1912.

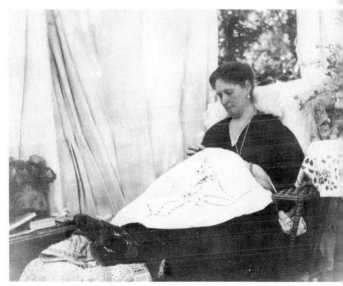

*A*lexandra embroidering in her lilac study at Tsarskoe Selo, 1912.

*T*he tsar's family on the train platform at Borodino, 1912, during the centennial of the Russian victory over Napoleon's forces on September 7, 1812.

Nicholas, Alexandra, Grand Duke
Michael Alexandrovich, and his
future wife Countess Natalia
Sheremetievskya frolicking on the
deck of the *Standart*.

Alexei with his playmates and his companion Nagorny.

Tsarevich Alexei.

obstinate, dark force. . . . The camarilla was trying to discredit the liberal segment of the nobility by associating it with the Jews. By the way, my friend . . . he too was a Mason and belonged to a glorious noble family. He was incensed by the baldness of their intentions. . . .

"The *Protocols* were presented to Nicholas. Everything had been calculated faultlessly: Nicholas had been raised since childhood in 'state anti-Semitism.' . . . 'Those abominable Jews,' 'enemies of Christ'—that was the vocabulary of the court. . . . In his book, my husband Koltsov wrote a devastating portrait of Nicholas, but he didn't understand him. I called the tsar a man from a Chinese play in which the evildoer lies to the good man—who for a moment believes. The intrigue builds on this. That is how they dealt with Nicholas. To the tsar, the pogroms organized by the police seemed like a holy outburst of popular indignation against the revolutionaries. A mob of coachmen and ignorant rabble, the Union of the Russian People was proclaimed a national movement—simple people defending their tsar. And he believed it. Childlike faith is an enchanting quality in an ordinary person—and a fatal quality in a ruler. What was even more amazing, the tsar didn't believe in the *Protocols!* And that disappointed them greatly."

The revolutionary Burtsev, who scarcely loved the tsar, confirmed this in his research on the *Protocols:*

"If in the beginning, when the *Protocols* first appeared, Nicholas II regarded them in good faith and was even delighted over them, he quickly recognized them as an obvious provocation."

Vera Leonidovna:

"In short, before the revolution they had done everything in their power to push the tsar to the right, and suddenly he started to dig in his heels. There was even talk of reforms. That was when they realized that the weak tsar could not withstand a revolution—and he had decided to abdicate. All this forced the camarilla to act. My friend felt that by the end of 1904 there was a secret plot at court—and Bloody Sunday was a part of it."

(Indeed, Zubatov passed on to Witte the secret conclusions of the Department of Police: a storm was brewing in the country. Anticipating that storm, the rightists were indeed greatly annoyed with the tsar.)

Beginning in 1904, Nicholas began to change—suddenly and recklessly. After the death of the reactionary Plehve, he named as his new minister of internal affairs Prince Svyatopolk-Mirsky, a landowner, an aristocrat, and a liberal. During the final months of 1904, Svyatopolk-Mirsky persuaded the tsar to discuss measures for assuaging public opinion. Before when public opinion had been mentioned, Nicholas had answered just as the autocrat of all Russia would be expected to: "What do I care for public opinion?" Now he was taking the problem seriously. The events of the Japanese war had changed him. He understood the peril of the storm. Instead of trying to return to the ruthless ways of his father, as the camarilla had expected, he decided on something else. He liked this new minister, who instead of suppressing the people was proposing reconciliation. Accord was dear to Nicholas's heart. At the end of the year Nicholas convened a broad meeting of all the leading statesmen of Russia. Both Witte and Pobedonostsev were there. Nicholas gave a speech about the revolutionary trend that kept intensifying each year in Russia. He posed what was for him a new question: Do we need to meet society's demands?

The question was rhetorical, for he had already made his decision. As usual, however, he wanted others to force him to make it. One after another the officials rose and demanded concessions. Pobedonostsev was isolated. Now Nicholas was more or less compelled to agree and go against both his teacher and his father's behests. A decision was made to work out a law "on designs and improvements for governmental procedure." Everyone understood that this was the beginning of reforms. Perhaps a constitution. Witte was instructed to write the law—it was a total victory for the liberals. Everyone was moved: The minister for communications, Prince Khilkov, could not hold back tears. In the name of those present, the chairman of the State Council thanked Nicholas: Russia had been saved by peaceful means.

Then came the response of the rightists: on January 1, in protest against the policy of Svyatopolk-Mirsky, one of their leaders, Dmitry Feodorovich Trepov, the Moscow police chief, quit.

A week later this strange, bloody bacchanalia occurred: Bloody Sunday.

Let us assume that a camarilla plot did indeed exist. Then why this bloody slaughter? Perhaps they had gotten the idea of simply frightening the tsar to nudge him, at last, to the right, and at the same time put all society in its place.

Or was it all actually much more serious? A weak tsar, a lost war, an advancing revolution, and on top of it all the mirage of a detested constitution. Did they decide enough was enough? And in the best traditions of the secret police use a bloody provocation to discredit the weak tsar at a single blow? And then? Then Bloody Sunday was a beginning that should have led to replacing Nicholas in the future.

Destabilization for the sake of future stabilization: the advent of a strong monarch?

As Vera Leonidovna suggested, one can find a strange link—an intrigue—through subsequent events.

Bloody Sunday bore its fruits: Svyatopolk-Mirsky stepped down. Nicholas conceded: on January 11 the reactionary Trepov was named governor-general of Petersburg.

But this was only a beginning. After Petersburg a blow against Moscow followed. In Moscow was Nicholas's chief adviser and support—Grand Duke Sergei Alexandrovich.

"A dreadful crime has been committed in Moscow: at the Nikolsky Gate Uncle Sergei, riding in his carriage, has been killed by a bomb and his driver mortally wounded. . . . Unhappy Ella! God bless and help her! . . .

"On February 4, on Senate Square in the Kremlin, the Socialist Revolutionary Kalyaev lay in wait for Sergei Alexandrovich. He hurled a bomb into the carriage."

From prison, Kalyaev described it in his last letters:

"At me—I smelled smoke and fragments coming right at my face, my cap was ripped off. . . . Then about five paces away I saw shreds of the grand duke's clothing and his naked body."

The viceroy of Moscow (as he was called at court) had been blown up by a bomb: his head was gone; all that was left was a hand and part of a foot.

Ella ran out of the palace and threw herself on the bloody bits, crawling on her knees among the remnants of her husband. What the revolutionary Kalyaev did not know was that the bomb with which he had killed the grand duke had been prepared with the help of a workshop belonging to the Department of Police. The actual assassination had been organized by a secret agent of the department, head of the Socialist Revolutionaries' terrorist group, the provocateur Azef.

Again the shadow of the secret police behind the event?

From the diary of Konstantin Romanov, the poet K.R.:

"5 February. . . . Thunderstruck, for the first minute I could not think at all, only as I came around did I understand what I had been deprived of and begin to cry. I had to prepare my wife—she loved Sergei very much. Both she and I felt that I should go to Moscow to see my poor friend's body, to see poor Ella, who has no family around her. . . .

"9 February. . . . The sovereign and both empresses are inconsolable that they cannot pay their final respects to the deceased. It is too dangerous for them to leave Tsarskoe. All the grand dukes have been informed in writing that not only can they not go to Moscow, but they are forbidden to attend the funeral at Kazan and St. Isaac's cathedrals [in St. Petersburg]."

Meanwhile in Moscow a majestic tragedy was being played out.

Ella spent all the days before the burial in ceaseless prayer. On her husband's tombstone she wrote: "Father, release them: they know not what they do."

She understood the words of the Gospels heart and soul, and on the eve of the funeral she demanded to be taken to the prison where Kalyaev was being held. Brought into his cell, she asked, "Why did you kill my husband?"

"I killed Sergei Alexandrovich because he was a weapon of tyranny. I was taking revenge for the people."

"Do not listen to your pride. Repent . . . and I will beg the sovereign to give you your life. I will ask him for you. I myself have already forgiven you."

On the eve of revolution she had found a way out: forgiveness! Forgive through the impossible pain and blood—and thereby stop it then, at the beginning, this bloody wheel. By her example, poor Ella appealed to society, calling upon the people to live in Christian faith.

"No!" replied Kalyaev. "I do not repent. I must die for my deed and I will. . . . My death will be more useful to my cause than Sergei Alexandrovich's death."

Kalyaev was sentenced to death. "I am pleased with your sentence," he told the judges. "I hope you will carry it out just as openly and publicly as I carried out the sentence of the Socialist Revolutionaries' party. Learn to look the advancing revolution right in the eye."

Kalyaev met death fearlessly.

Nicholas had lost Moscow.

The camarilla knew what came next in their intrigue: Nicholas

must soon be deprived of his chief adviser. The empress-mother was
leaving for Denmark, where her father was mortally ill. Now one last
figure remained by the tsar, Uncle Vladimir Alexandrovich. But the
third blow was known. The Department of Police had been informed
that the son of Vladimir Alexandrovich, Kirill, had broken up the
marriage of the tsaritsa's brother Ernie (that "fine couple"). Victoria
Melita had divorced her husband, and now Kirill had decided to
marry her and create an open family scandal. This would provoke
harsh countermeasures; he would be punished, which meant that
his father, Vladimir Alexandrovich, would have to step down as commander of the Petersburg garrison.

From a letter of Nicholas to his mother in Denmark:

"This week there was a drama in the family over Kirill's unfortunate marriage. You certainly remember my conversations with him,
as well as the consequences he would necessarily suffer: exclusion
from the service, being forbidden to enter Russia, deprivation of all
crown monies, and loss of the title of grand duke. Last week I
learned that he has married. . . . I had a very unpleasant talk with
his poor father, and no matter how he defended his son, I insisted.
We left it that he would ask to leave the service. In the end, I agreed.

"At the same time I have been overtaken by doubt. Is it good to
punish someone publicly several times in a row? . . . After long
thought, which gave me a headache, I decided . . . to telegraph
that I am returning Kirill his lost title. . . . Ugh! What tiresome,
unpleasant days these have been. Now it is as if a mountain has
fallen from my shoulders."

WHO PULLED THE STRINGS?

If we suppose that the camarilla did intend to replace Nicholas with
a strong tsar, then who would that have been? After all, by law, in
the event of abdication, the minor Alexei would ascend to the
throne. But Alexei was mortally ill; Alexei could be avoided. The next
legal pretender was Michael. But he had no more the nature of a
tsar than his brother.

The intriguers knew they could avoid Michael as well, for Michael was romantically involved and thinking about marrying, moreover marrying a certain Mrs. Wulfert, who was anything but of royal
blood. Naturally, the Department of Police was informed of the affair. According to the law on succession, by marrying he would for-
feit his title of grand duke.

"My dear mama! . . . Misha wrote that he is asking my permission to marry. That he can wait no longer. Naturally, I shall never consent to this marriage. I feel with all my being that our dear papa would have acted in the same way. I feel it is quite impossible to change the law in this one case during such a dangerous period. Help me, dear Mama, to restrain him. May the Lord protect you."

For whom, then, was all this plotting?

Grand Duke Nicholas Nikolaevich—Nikolasha, Nicholas the Long—who was so similar in build to his cousin the deceased emperor.

The young Romanovs called him the "terrible uncle." Those who saw him in military parades could never forget him, so imposing was his presence.

Hussars on jet black horses wearing black helmets topped by a horsehair comb gallop toward the small mounted figure—toward the tsar, who is reviewing the parade. And amid this terrible avalanche is Nicholas the giant, who has merged with his horse. . . . Just a few steps from the emperor, the commander's magnificent leonine roar: "Halt!" And in an instant the inexorable avalanche halts. There is only the heavy breathing of people and horses.

Yes, he had the look of a tsar. He was known for his right-wing views. Nicholas Nikolaevich was being led to their goal: he was replacing all the uncles. He, not the retired Vladimir, was now in command of the Petersburg garrison. Alix, who was linked by friendship to the wife of Nicholas Nikolaevich, was also favorably disposed toward him.

Did Nicholas Nikolaevich himself know? Or, as sometimes happens, did "he know but not know"? Just as his ancestor Alexander I "knew but did not know" that they wanted to kill his father Emperor Paul and put Alexander himself on the throne? In any event, Nicholas Nikolaevich served the tsar honestly during all these days of upheaval. It all went right past him.

This is a seductive version of Bloody Sunday, but dreadfully romantic. Russians love a good plot—camarillas, Masons, whatever—where in fact there is usually just plain sloppiness. Someone mistrusted someone else; someone failed to warn someone else. So someone decided to take out more insurance, called up the troops, and removed the tsar from Petersburg. Great and terrible events in Russia are usually due to someone's stupidity or laziness.

"*L*EARN TO LOOK THE ADVANCING ENEMY RIGHT IN THE EYE"
From the very start, the wave raised by Bloody Sunday was more like a tsunami.

From the diary of K.R.:

"February 6, 1905. . . . I simply cannot believe how quickly we are moving toward unknown, exotic calamities. There is mischief everywhere, all are confused. . . . The government has yet to feel a strong hand. Not that there is one."

All the elements would be there: barricades out of overturned trams, a general strike, mutiny in the army. In the Crimea an insurrectionist cruiser would approach the shores, and at their estates the horrified grand dukes would wait for the firing to begin. The red rooster of arson—the "light show"—would rampage through the landowners' estates.

In Petersburg, in the noisy crowd at the World of Art exhibit, arms crossed haughtily, stood the famous terrorist Boris Savinkov. Openly. No one dared turn him in.

Vera Leonidovna:

"Absolutely everyone went on strike. It was like a holiday. At the Mariinsky Theater the ballet struck, and even the brother of his [Nicholas's] mistress Mathilde, Iosif Kschessinski, struck. . . . I knew him well. By the way, after the revolution this participation in the strike became his indulgence, his safe conduct. Kschessinski even became an honored artist of the Russian Republic, this brother of the tsar's mistress. The last time I saw him was on the eve of the war. He starved to death in blockaded Leningrad. A habitué of good restaurants, a gourmand who feasted on silver platters—he starved to death!"

"*D*EAR MAMA, YOU CANNOT IMAGINE HOW MUCH I HAVE SUFFERED"
By the fall of 1905, the tsar's family, cut off by the general strike, was living in Peterhof, and their sole means of communication with Petersburg was by steamer. "Even if you have to swim to get here," the tsar joked sadly. The issue of Nicholas's fall seemed decided.

Returning from abroad, Witte, who reached the tsar by steamship, listened to Benckendorff, the sympathetic marshal of the court, about how difficult it was going to be for the tsar's family, with the five children, to find a safe haven among their royal relatives in Europe. Still, Nicholas sailed the ship of state out of this storm.

In the summer of 1905, as the revolution gathered steam, the tsar, who outwardly clung to the rightists, had made an unexpected move. In June American President Theodore Roosevelt offered his services to help Russia and Japan reach an accord. To America the tsar sent the liberal Witte. At first the rightists were jubilant—Witte's mission appeared hopeless. The Japanese had won too much; it was inconceivable that he would conclude a peace on honorable terms. But he did. And on the best possible terms, given the circumstances. Witte returned to Russia triumphant. Nicholas rewarded him with the title of count.

Two choices remained to the tsar: proclaim Nicholas Nikolaevich military dictator (and himself gradually withdraw, as, evidently, the camarilla intended) or decide in favor of what his father had instructed him to fight—reforms and a constitution.

The latter is what the returned Witte proposed to him: "Russia has outgrown its existing governmental forms. "There is still a chance—you must give the people their constitution, otherwise they will wrest one away."

Nicholas possessed sufficient flexibility. He agreed to a constitution.

And hesitated. Behind Witte's back, Nicholas continued to importune Grand Duke Nicholas Nikolaevich to become dictator. Witte was angry; he saw in this a pathetic spinelessness. Nicholas did not want to understand: the world had fallen apart. Like the prodigal son, Nicholas was ready to part with everything his forefathers had created. The great autocratic empire was to end with him.

Once again he wanted others to beg him to do what he himself had long since decided on.

It fell to Nicholas Nikolaevich to do the begging. Even if he knew about the intrigue, he could not have profited from its results. The army was at the front in Manchuria (everything was as it would be in 1917, when the army was fighting on the fronts of the world war). There was no one to crush a revolution. Agreeing to become dictator was tantamount to finishing off the dynasty.

On the day Nicholas signed the constitution, he had a terrible headache. He thought of the Japanese who had once sliced his brow. The minister of the court, Count Fredericks, told Witte when he arrived that the tsar had again asked Nicholas Nikolaevich to become dictator, whereupon Nikolasha had pulled out a gun and said: "Either I shoot myself right now, or you sign."

Now Nicholas had the right: he signed.

"17 October [!]. . . . Nikolasha and Stana had breakfast. We sat and talked, waiting for Witte to arrive. I signed the Manifesto at 5 o'clock. Since that day my head has been very heavy and my thoughts confused. Lord, save Russia, and bring her peace."

On the returning steamer, Nicholas Nikolaevich embraced Witte triumphantly: "Today, October 17th, is an important date. Exactly seventeen years ago, also on the 17th at Borki, God saved the dynasty. I think that now the dynasty is being saved from a no lesser danger."

He was right. The 17th was an important date for their family.

October 17: the train wreck at Borki, when by a miracle Nicholas survived.

January 17: Nicholas appeared for the first time, so disastrously, before the Russian public.

October 17, 1905: The end of the autocracy. That day Nicholas signed a manifesto granting the first Russian constitution.

December 17: The death of Rasputin.

And 1917: The end of Nicholas's empire.

In the early morning hours of July 17: His own death and that of his family.

All this time Nicholas remained calm and silent, as always. In his letters to his mother, though . . .

"Peterhof. 19 October, 1905. . . . It feels as though I have not written you for a year, so many difficult and unprecedented events have we experienced. You of course remember those days we spent together at Tsarskoe in January. . . . But they are nothing compared with now. The railway strikes that began around Moscow overtook all of Russia immediately thereafter. Petersburg and Moscow have been left cut off from the inner provinces. . . . The only contact with the city is by sea—which is quite convenient at this time of year! After the railways the strike spread to factories and plants, and then even to municipal institutions. . . . Imagine the shame! We have just had news of strikes, of policemen, Cossacks, and soldiers slain, of riots, disorders, and upheavals. . . . The gentlemen ministers have been arguing like wet hens . . . instead of acting decisively. There have been 'meetings'—a fashionable new word—where armed insurrection was openly debated and approved, which I learned about immediately. . . . The use of arms was prescribed in the event of troops being attacked. Quiet, ominous days set in. It was like the feeling you sometimes get in the summer before a powerful storm. *Everyone's* nerves were stretched beyond the limit. Of course, this situation could not last very long. During those terrible days I saw Witte constantly. Our conversations began in the morning and ended in the evening in full darkness. It seemed we could choose one of two paths: either appoint an energetic military man and do everything in our power to suppress the sedition. Or else present the population with civil rights, freedom of speech, press, assembly, and unions, and so on. . . . That would also entail an obligation to pass all kinds of legislation through the State Duma. . . . This is for all intents and purposes a constitution. Witte insisted heatedly on this path. And everyone I turned to answered me exactly as Witte had. The Manifesto was written by him and Alexei Obolensky. We discussed it for two days, and eventually I said a prayer and signed it. . . . Dear Mama, you cannot imagine how much I have suffered. My only comfort is that such is God's will, and that this difficult decision will lead my dear Russia out of this unbearable, chaotic state in which it finds itself for nearly a year."

Pierre Gilliard, the grand duchesses' tutor, saw the empress on the day the manifesto was signed. She was sitting like a sleepwalker, staring at one point. Her world had fallen apart. Her son had been snatched in his cradle. He would not be the autocrat. She decided to fight.

In November the second capital rebelled. Barricades went up in Moscow. Trams were overturned. Nicholas felt the anger of a man deceived. He had given them a constitution, he had outdone himself. And in response, it all continued!

His troops pacified Moscow.

At Christmas Nicholas wrote his mother a letter, his usual tender letter, but there was already bloodshed in it. He was growing more and more inured to blood.

"22 December. Dear sweet Mama! All my prayers for you will be especially fervent during this holiday. . . . It will be very sad around the tree without you. It has been so cozy at Gatchina upstairs. . . .

"In Moscow, as you know, thank God, the uprising was crushed, thanks to the loyalty and steadfastness of our troops. . . . The revolutionaries' losses were enormous, but it is hard to get precise information, since many of those killed burned up and the wounded were carried away and hidden."

While the revolution was being put down, Alix instilled in Nicholas —with all her faith and passion—the idea of Witte's evil intentions. The manifesto had led to nothing. The uprisings had continued anyway. Great shadows loomed behind him—his Romanov ancestors and his heavenly protector, Serafim of Sarov. With him, they had crushed the revolution, not the pathetic manifesto, which he had been forced to sign during a grave crisis.

Witte was Nicholas's mother's man. In struggling against him Alix was removing his mother from power. For good.

By then it was all clear. Nicholas had dealt with the Revolution. Having lived through that storm the rightists evidently gave up on the idea of replacing the monarch on the throne, but they were contemplating a change in the guard by the throne: the time had come to sweep away the liberals. As always: "Witte has done his deed."

Not coincidentally, soon afterward Nicholas Nikolaevich joined forces with Alix. Yesterday he was embracing Witte and praising the manifesto; now he was its enemy. The tsar was avid to believe in this new stance. The fury of battle had changed him. A knight and his sword defending his God-given rights, a warrior for his people and his dynasty—Nicholas liked that image.

Now in his letters to his mother there was a pervasive martial tone:

"I want to see my regiments and shall begin, in turn, with the Semyonovsky." "There was a review of my favorite Nizhegorodsky." "A review of the officers of the Cavalry Guards." "A review of the Marine of the Guard."

Soon after Nicholas informed his mother:

"I have never seen a chameleon, someone who changes his convictions, the likes of [Witte]. Thanks to this quality of character, almost no one believes him anymore."

In April 1906 Witte handed Nicholas his letter of resignation, and Nicholas replied with satisfaction:

"Count Sergei Yulievich! Yesterday morning I received your letter in which you asked to be relieved of all the positions you now hold. I hereby express my consent to your request. Nicholas."

Vera Leonidovna:

"The revolution was dying. . . . Darkness and despair had set in. The intelligentsia had run into error, into anarchism. . . . Now, looking back, I understand: this was the despair of people who had looked revolution in the face for the first time. The intelligentsia had seen the bloody face of popular revolt and shuddered. . . . The revolution was not a celebration of freedom but a natural disaster, like a tornado. . . . The most terrifying part, though, was that we had a feeling, perhaps unconscious, but still: it would return."

Witte was huge, corpulent. The tall Witte was replaced by the giant Peter Arkadievich Stolypin. Nicholas's two most famous ministers were tall. Here lay his hidden complex: his large father had always been a reliable and strong defense. He had confidence in tall people.

Late in April in the Winter Palace throne room, Witte, now removed from affairs of state, observed the meeting between his own off-spring—the State Duma—and the tsar. "Nicholas is pale," Witte noted in his diary. "He gave a speech. 'May my fervent hopes be fulfilled to see my people happy and to bequeath to my son a stronger, better, and more enlightened state.'"

Witte must have chuckled when he heard these words about the heir. The old minister understood everything.

A son robbed by a manifesto—this was Alix's pathos. Nicholas declared to the uncomprehending Russian parliament that the heir would receive what belonged to him—the old autocracy without a constitution. In other words, Nicholas told the Duma that he intended to disband it.

Later the tsar received the first Russian parliamentarians: in black frock coats, like jackdaws, they jostled among the brilliant uniforms of the tsar's suite.

Witte foresaw an inevitable conflict between the tsar and the Duma, and he believed that, as always, in a moment of disaster, Nicholas would come running to him. Witte wrote mockingly:

"It has reached society's consciousness that despite my strained relations with His Highness . . . despite my total disfavor, as soon as the situation becomes critical my name will immediately come up." He added sternly: "But they are forgetting one thing: there is a limit to everything."

This was a weighty statement: a powerful new figure had already appeared on the horizon.

Peter Arkadievich Stolypin, the new prime minister, was Witte's direct opposite. From an old noble line, he was "one of them." Considered a liberal, he was nevertheless a liberal-landowner. Stolypin knew and loved the muzhik, as well a landowner should. In the muzhik, he saw the country's future. That was why he immediately appealed to the tsar. Stolypin could appreciate Nicholas' long-held dream: "the people and the tsar."

The First Duma was disbanded and a second elected, but to his astonishment Nicholas saw that nothing had changed. The calmest people, as soon as they stepped out on the dais, became rebels. Speaking before the Duma seemed to intoxicate them.

There was Alexander Ivanovich Guchkov, for example, an honorable man, a full state councilor, a councilor of the Petersburg Municipal Duma. Stolypin offered him a ministerial post, and not only did he refuse, but in the new Duma he reviled all the grand dukes at one fell swoop.

The assassinations continued: General Min, the subduer of Moscow, was shot.

A bomb exploded on Aptekarsky Island, at Stolypin's dacha. It was a Saturday, Stolypin's at-home day, and many visitors were waiting for him in the first-floor rooms. On the second floor of the dacha were the family's rooms, where Stolypin's children, a daughter and a son, were playing.

Three men dressed in military uniforms entered the house. The guard immediately noticed a defect in their uniforms and tried to restrain them, but with a shout—"Long live the revolution!"—one of them threw a bomb. Everyone in the room, including the terrorists themselves, died. The force of the explosion was such that trees on the Neva embankment were torn up by the roots. Stolypin himself was knocked to the ground by a shock wave but was not harmed. Injured people stirred under the fragments of the demolished house, bits of human flesh lay about. Among the fragments they found Stolypin's injured daughter. Stolypin himself pulled his four-year-old son out from under a heap of rubble.

At the same time the Tsar of All the Russias was made a hostage in his own home. Nicholas learned that terrorists had turned up in Peterhof, where he spent the summers. "We sit here virtually locked up," he informed his mother. "What a shame and disgrace to speak of this. . . . Those anarchist scoundrels came to Peterhof to hunt for me, Nikolasha, Trepov [Moscow police chief]. . . . But you understand my feelings: not to be able to go horseback riding, not to go out beyond the gates anywhere at all. And this at my own home in ever peaceful Peterhof! I blush to write you of this."

His life was under guard. No walks. In constant terror for the safety of Alix and the children. Like a rehearsal for a future life—twelve years hence.

"Sunshine," "Baby," "Little Man"—they had many pet names for their sick son. Nonetheless, Nicholas—father and tsar—could not protect him from a bomb in his own home. He underwent a sea change. He had to repay all the suffering and humiliation, and he had to preserve his rule—subdue the rebels, give the country peace. That is what his father's shadow demanded; that is what Alix and his mother demanded. "The monsters must be exterminated!" the dowager empress wrote him.

So he tried to be merciless.

He could hardly have managed it, however, were it not for the powerful figure of Stolypin by his side. Stolypin, a firm, indomitable, power-loving man, had something in common with the gentle Nicholas: he adored his family and was very dependent on his beloved wife. The suffering of their injured children had hardened both wife and husband. Now Stolypin was prepared to punish and to execute. "Stolypin's tie"—that's what the revolutionaries would call the nooses around their necks.

In June 1906 the Duma repealed the death penalty. But while Europe was sending congratulatory telegrams, Nicholas was passing a law on field courts-martial.

The hangman set about his work. Not since the time of Ivan the Terrible had Russia seen so many executions.

When Witte reminded the former liberal Stolypin of his previous views, the minister replied: "Yes, that was how I used to feel. Before the explosion on Aptekarsky Island."

On August 26, 1907, the sovereign "royally saw fit to instruct that troop commanders be informed" that they must "see to it" that the tsar not receive any telegrams requesting pardons.

In the time of Nicholas's father, Alexander Ulyanov had been hanged for attempting to assassinate the tsar. This punishment was instrumental in shaping the character of his brother, the future leader of the revolution, Vladimir Ulyanov: Lenin. Execution and blood infiltrated his subconscious.

Under Nicholas, brothers and sisters of the slain all across Russia swore their hatred for the tsar.

"I don't want to die at all: at night they're taken out into the back courtyard, even in the wet, in the rain. By the time they get there they're soaked through, and that's how they're hanged, wet. . . . You get up in the morning and you're as happy as a child to be alive, to have an entire day ahead of you to enjoy life"—these were the kinds of letters families were reading.

In blood he became heir, in blood he was tsar, this gentle man. Bloody Sunday. Bloody Khodynka. The blood of the First Revolution. Like an omen of what was to come: his unlucky son's strength was draining away with his loss of blood.

The First Revolution ended. They had had a remarkable rehearsal for the future, for what would happen twelve years later. But the warning passed them right by.

He and Alix never did understand that the revolution had been subdued not by bullets but by the words on the paper that his minister had written and that Nicholas had signed. They imagined a different lesson for themselves instead: force is necessary.

Wise Witte realized then that this would be their ruin. Sitting in his study and contemplating the events of the era, the old man wrote these terrible words:

"Much blood may be shed, and you yourself could perish in that blood. . . . And it may kill your own firstborn, your pure infant, your son and heir. . . . God grant this not be so. In any event that I never see such horrors."

God did: Witte died in January 1915. Before his death the old man wrote Nicholas a letter and instructed that it be given to the sovereign after his death. Thus Nicholas received Witte's message from beyond the grave.

In his letter, Witte asked the tsar to give his title of count to his "most beloved grandson, L. K. Naryshkin. Let him be called Naryshkin, Count Witte." But this was only a pretext. The most important part came after his request. It was a rundown of Nicholas's greatest deeds, which also happened to be linked with the name of Witte. In first place stood the constitution: "This is your undying service to your people and to humanity."

The dying old man had no intention of wounding Nicholas or reminding him of his own services by his mention of the constitution. Even then, in 1915, the great politician sensed the current situation's uncanny similarity to the eve of the tragic year 1905. He realized the storm would soon break. So he decided to prompt the tsar once more with the chief lesson of 1905: know how to yield!

But that year Alix and Nicholas were caught up in another battle with the Duma. Nicholas was angered by this reminder of his "past sin" (as he now referred to the constitution). He did not grant his former minister's small request: Naryshkin never did become Count Witte.

Vera Leonidovna:

"I don't agree with Count Witte. The mysterious lesson of 1905 lay elsewhere. A certain church historian explained this to me: During the Time of Troubles, in the seventeenth century, when the ancient dynasty of tsars was broken and widespread troubles ensued, when the noble boyars handed Russia over to foreigners, it was the ecclesiastical authority—the patriarch—that preserved Russia. There is good reason why, under the first Romanovs, patriarchs bore the title Great Sovereign. Peter the Great, in an effort to strengthen secular authority, did away with the patriarchate. Two centuries without a patriarch weakened the church. Under Nicholas talks were initiated on reviving the patriarchy, but matters never progressed beyond talks. When the events of the First Revolution began, the tsar must have understood: he was weak. The Lord in his mercy had given him a warning that he had not understood. In the event of major new disasters, he must establish a second center—by bringing back the authority of the patriarch. Only a strong church could keep Holy Russia from eventual catastrophe. But he had not understood the warning."

Chapter 4

A MIGHTY PAIR

"THANKS BE TO GOD; HE HAS SENT ME A FRIEND"
The revolution in Russia coincided with a revolution in the tsar's family. At just this time, two people appeared at Tsarskoe Selo who are little reflected in Nicholas's diaries, although they occupied an important place in his life. And in the life of the family. And the country. Grigory Rasputin and Anna Taneyeva Vyrubova.

In her memoirs, Anna Taneyeva writes about her family. Her father, Alexander Sergeyevich Taneyev, was a marshal of the court and director of the imperial chancellery. His grandfather and great-grandfather had held the same post under previous emperors, and his other great-great-grandfather was the conqueror of Napoleon, Field Marshal Kutuzov. True, she fails to mention in her book one other ancestor, whom society rumor plausibly ascribed to the Taneyevs: Emperor Paul I. The blood of this mad emperor (or rather, his illegitimate child) flowed in Anna Taneyeva's veins. Yes, she too was of the Romanov clan.

As a young lady, intoxicated by her first encounter with society, she danced at twenty-two balls and was presented to the empress. Alix had noticed her.

Very soon after, a footman conveyed the empress's invitation to Anya, as she was called, over the telephone.

Their first conversation. Anya Taneyeva told Alix that as a child she had contracted typhus and was at death's door when her father summoned Ioann of Kronstadt, who raised her from her sickbed with prayer. The story must have made an impression on the unhappy empress. The miracle of healing. That was all Alix could think of when she looked at this lovely woman: her son.

Anya was quite musical. From the very beginning she managed to pick the right note.

In 1907 she was invited to join the family on their yacht to their favorite place, the Finnish Skerries.

In the sun-filled stateroom they played piano four-handed. Later Anya would tell Alix of how her hands had turned to stone, she was so agitated. Then they sang duets. Alix was a contralto, Anya a soprano, so their duet meshed instantly.

When Anya disembarked, Alix said, "Thanks be to God; He has sent me a Friend."

Anya was often taken on walks in the Skerries. Bright, tranquil evenings on the tsar's yacht. Peaceful lights burning onshore. The smell of the water and of the cigarettes in the sovereign's hands. The white yacht *Polar Star* slipped through the fallen night.

In 1918, the arrested Anya Taneyeva would find herself once again on the *Polar Star,* where the Central Baltic staff would convene and the yacht's new masters—the revolutionary sailors—would take her. Everything would be spat upon, befouled. They would put her in the filthy hold, which teemed with parasites, and then lead her across the familiar deck to be interrogated. And she would remember those other nights.

What was the main reason behind the young lady's success?

"The most ordinary Petersburg young lady, who had fallen in love with the empress and was always gazing at her with her ecstatic eyes and saying 'Ach, ach, ach!' Anya Taneyeva herself is not pretty and looks like a blob of fancy pastry," Witte wrote in his *Memoirs*.

After the fall of the tsarist regime in February 1917, the "Special Commission of Inquiry on the abuses of tsarist government ministers and other high officials of the overthrown regime" was created. Assigned to it was a typical liberal figure, a comrade procurator of the Ekaterinoslav district court, a certain V. M. Rudnev. Subsequently he recalled questioning the arrested Anya: "I was . . . frankly speaking, hostilely inclined toward her. . . . I was immediately struck by the unusual expression in her eyes, an expression full of unworldly meekness." Guileless Anya had brought to the tsar's family sincerity, devotion, and adoration, which were so lacking in the cold court. That was the investigator's conclusion. He added: "Mrs. Vyrubova could not have exercised any political influence whatsoever. The empress's intellect and will were far too strong a counterweight."

Simple-hearted, stupid, and ugly?

Vera Leonidovna:

"She was quite pretty. . . . A beauty but in a very Russian manner: ash blond hair, great big blue eyes, a luxuriant body. . . . I remember seeing her for the first time. I was walking down Nevsky after a rehearsal. Atlantis was still alive: smart carriages raced past, and coachmen in tight-fitting indigo coats drove cheap droshkies. I often hear that sound now—the sound of a vanished life. . . . Here was the magnificent plume of a horse guardsman dashing by. With his back to the coachman and a greatcoat draped over his shoulders, the mayor of Petersburg went flying past surrounded by bicyclists; evidently the sovereign himself was to drive through shortly. It was two o'clock, and I saw the most elegant turnouts.

"That was when I saw the carriage: a young woman half-reclining, lazily, the feathers of her hat dangling over her beautiful, rather full face, her legs draped with a fur coverlet. 'There she is,' said my friend. There was a great deal of talk about her then. If rumor had Rasputin for the tsaritsa, they gave the tsar to Anya as a lover as well. By the way, she always told very sweet stories about herself and always funny things. Only intelligent people know how to make fun of themselves. . . . She was intelligent. She was also a great actress. This woman, who participated in all of Rasputin's political games, appointed and ousted ministers, and carried out the most complex intrigues in the court, could look like an utterly artless Russian dolt. Was it a mask? Or had the mask become her face once and for all?"

Yes, Anya immediately grasped "Sana's" nature. Russia's mistress was shy. Her ingenuousness clashed with the icy chill of the court. Seeing herself misunderstood, she turned inward. She mastered reserve and distance, which were perceived as arrogance. Anya found the key to Sana's heart: ecstatic, constant, and unbounded adoration.

Could she really have remained by Alix's side for twelve whole years playing such a monotonous game, though? Oh no, she was

constantly thinking up dangerous, intriguing new games for her imperial friend.

Anya's games

Among the papers Yurovsky brought out after the family's execution
were many letters. All through World War I, breathless with love,
Alix and Nicky inundated each other with letters, letters that contained puzzling lines. For instance, once Alix added this enigmatic
postscript: "Lovy, you burn her letters so as that they should never
fall into anybody's hands?"

Whose letters? Why mustn't those letters fall into anybody's
hands? Who is this person anyway, this "she"?

Elsewhere: "If we are not both firm, we will have lovers' scenes &
scandals. . . . You will see when we return she will tell you how
terribly she suffered without you. . . . Be nice & firm. . . . She
always needs cooling down." So "she" would dare pursue lovers'
scenes and scandals and, evidently, letters to Nicholas?

Not mincing words, Alix brands this unknown woman: "quite
hardened already . . . nothing of the loving gentle woman." "She is
boring and very tiresome." And so on.

Here is quite a nasty caricature—testimony to Alix's infinite jealousy: "She is full of how thin she has grown, tho I find her stomach
& legs colossal (& most unappetising)—her face is rosy, but the
cheeks less fat & shades under her eyes." In her letters Alix refers to
her as "the Cow."

But now we have nearly a cry: "No one dare call you 'my own.'
You are mine, all mine, not hers. . . . Anya wants to come see us
tomorrow & I was so happy that we are not going to have her in the
house for a long time."

Yes, "she," "the Cow"—this is all Anya. What about "naive" and
"meek"? Does this mean the rumor was right? And there was no
idyllic love between Alix and Nicky? Was Anya the tsar's mistress?
But here is Investigator Rudnev:

"The facts of the medical certificate for Mrs. Vyrubova drawn up
in May 1917 at the instruction of the Special Commission of Inquiry
establish beyond a doubt that Mrs. Vyrubova was a virgin." Does this
mean, again, that there was nothing going on? But what *was* in fact
going on? Where are these curses of the tsaritsa coming from?

Meanwhile, almost simultaneously, Alix was writing her husband: "Perhaps you will put in your telegram to me that you thank
her for the inclosed letter & send love or messages?" And in another

letter: "Ania talks about her loneliness—that makes me angry. She visits us twice a day & spends 4 hours every evening with us,—you are her life." Does this mean the home wrecker calmly visited every day and they allowed her to spend long hours at court?

What was going on?

"THE OTHER MAN"

On September 2, 1915, Alix wrote Nicholas: "I went with Ania to Orlov's grave." On October 4 Alix wrote again: "Then we fetched Ania & drove . . to the cemetery as I wanted to put flowers on poor Orlov's grave." She informed Nicholas of each visit to "poor Orlov's" grave. This is amazing, for rumor proclaimed Orlov to be Alix's lover. Moreover, society gossip named him Alexei's father.

Alexander Afinogenovich Orlov was a major-general of the imperial suite, a brigade commander, and namesake of the famous Alexei Orlov who put Catherine the Great on the Russian throne. Alexander Afinogenovich liked to play up his connection to that handsome rake of the gallant eighteenth century, but with a dash of the twentieth century—cocaine and other such pleasures. Everything changed completely with the arrival in Petersburg of the young Hessian princess. Orlov offered up to her his sincere, chivalrous respect. His crude hussar ways disappeared, leaving only the ecstatic admiration of a knight encountering his Beautiful Lady. When Alix was rejected by Nicholas's parents, Orlov remained constant in his admiration. We underscore—admiration. When she became empress, Alix never forgot the faithful Orlov.

Orlov was assigned to a regiment whose chief was the Beautiful Lady herself. Now he rightfully carried the empress's colors. The medieval romance continued.

Jack London wrote a story about two people who decide to trick God and make their passion eternal: they come up with the idea of not allowing a final embrace. Alix did not want her romantic passion with Nicky to extinguish in the prose of life. Her instinct as a loving woman told her that it would require "another man" to keep the fire going. And Orlov's love—the respectful love of a poor knight for an unattainable princess—was the love of that other man.

The court reacted as would be expected: an artless rumor about the tsaritsa's amorous intrigues was born. The result was a conversation between the empress-mother and Nicholas. But Alix would not allow this exciting game canceled. She thought up something with her friend: Orlov could marry Anya, to forestall gossip. But the handsome general declined, and this, evidently, was his downfall. Orlov was sent abroad, and en route he died suddenly. Possibly the omnipotent secret police was concerned with the family's reputation.

There was no "other man" now. Would Alix and Nicky's love actually die of familiarity? Anya took on the role of the other woman. Orlov had adored the tsaritsa platonically. Now Anya would adore the tsar platonically. Now she was the other, creating the necessary tension in the eternal love game between Alix and Nicky. At the same time, she adored the tsaritsa as before . . . and now the tsar as well! Like a schoolgirl who falls in love with her girlfriend, she idolized the object of Alix's affections. No, of course she did not allow herself to vie with her sovereign mistress, she merely let herself languish from unrequited love for her chosen one—she even staged scenes, but ridiculous, naive ones. At the center of the new love tension was Nicky the supernumerary, and circling him the two leading actresses in this subtle love play.

Anya was already starting to worry. Voices were beginning to be heard in the large Romanov family: get rid of this friend. But Anya managed to hang on with the help of an amusing new game.

One day she announced to Alix that she had decided to go away. Sacrifice her love for them to calm the court. Soon afterward, to general astonishment, omnipotent Anya married the modest naval officer Boris Vyrubov. Witte commented nastily: "The poor empress wails like the wife of a Moscow merchant marrying off her daughter." But Anya knew the finale to this marriage in advance—she possessed precise information about her groom—and soon she fled her marital bed, for her husband turned out to be a sexual deviant and drug addict. Anya could tell the mystically inclined tsaritsa that this was her punishment for betraying her predestination. Her lot, having given up on the possibility of a family of her own, was to serve Russia's first family.

So who was she? Simple-hearted, good, serene, candid? Yes. And also—sly, secretive, cunning, intelligent. A dangerous woman who devoted herself to a single passion. Witte wrote: "The entire inner circle pays court to Anya Vyrubova, as do their wives and daughters. Anya arranges various indulgences for them and influences which political figures get close to the sovereign."

This was her passion: power. The power that immediately suited the young lady and to which she subsumed her entire life. The secret blood of Emperor Paul. Anya was the invisible mistress of the most brilliant court in Europe.

Then suddenly, in 1914, this unexpected hurricane of insane jealousy from the empress. Everything was in jeopardy!

What had happened? Had Anya overplayed her hand? Were the southern nights to blame—those maddening nights in the white Livadia Palace?

None of them are alive now. They have long since departed this world. We are still trying to re-create the scenes, but the shaky figures dissolve in the darkness. The curtain falls. They are behind the curtain, and we are not going to disturb them.

Actually, it is all quite clear: in 1914 (at the start of the war between her new and former homelands), Alix was on the verge of hysteria, and this combined in her with the strange, carnal quality that had been introduced into the palace with the "Holy Devil," Grigory Rasputin. Although the palace made the devil over into a saint, the half-mad tsaritsa could not help but sense the invisible field of his lust, the electrical charge of his unbridled power. Hence her passionate, carnal dreams in her letters to Nicholas. No, this was no longer comfortable marital love but a frenzied challenge that found an outlet in the insane jealousy that engulfed her then. Now, as in years past, Anya was energetically playing her part of the safe other woman. But one day Alix saw herself in the mirror: tormented, aging . . . gray hairs had appeared. And next to Nicky this young, blooming woman with ecstatic eyes riveted to him as if she were begging to be petted. Delusion was born.

Anya behaved wisely. Trying to justify herself would have meant fanning suspicion, so she responded with the offended coolness and contempt of the unjustly insulted. And with rudeness. This last was new for Russia's mistress, but it proved the best medicine. Soon Alexandra was complaining to Nicky: "her humour towards me has not been amiable this morning—what one would call rude." To rudeness Anya added yet another kind of medicine. "She flirts hard with the young Ukrainian," the empress wrote querulously, but "misses & longs for you." The storm was already abating, however. And soon: "I only dread Ania's humour"—and, humbly—"I will take all much cooler now and don't worry over her rudeness . . . we are friends & am very fond of her & always shall be, but something has gone."

Everything fell back into place.

In battling Alix's jealousy, Anya could be perfectly calm. Next to her stood someone who would never allow her to be insulted, her strongest partner in these games with Alix: Rasputin.

Anya had heard of Rasputin from the Montenegrin princesses. When she saw him, she appreciated him immediately.

"A FANTASTIC MAN"

Rasputin had been long awaited in the palace. At the very beginning of Nicholas's reign, as the family searched in vain for popular truth seekers and the Montenegrins seduced the Anglo-German princess with the mysterious world of sorcerers and holy fools, he was approaching.

When they went to the canonization ceremonies at Sarov and the mysterious wilderness—here, indeed, the devil took on the guise of the saint: the image of the wise, meek Serafim would be adopted by the Holy Devil—Grigory Rasputin.

"In the village of Pokrovskoe there is a pious Grigory. Like Saint Serafim, and the prophet Elijah, he is given to shutting the sky—so that drought befalls the land until he commands the heavens to open and pour down life-giving rain." Thus recounted Father Feofan, rector of the Petersburg Theological Academy, to his admirers the Grand Dukes Peter and Nicholas Nikolaevich. And here were the Montenegrins, the grand dukes' wives, bringing news to the palace: just like the Venerable Serafim, Grigory walked about his village surrounded by innocent girls, and just like him he preached humility, love, and kindness and healed the sick.

Late in 1903, Rasputin appeared in the halls of the St. Petersburg Theological Academy wearing a greasy jacket, oiled boots, and baggy trousers that hung down in back like a torn hammock, his beard tangled and his hair parted like a tavern waiter's. He had hypnotic gray-blue eyes, first gentle and kind, then fierce and angry—but usually guarded. His speech was strange, too, almost incoherent, lulling, somehow primordial.

While the Montenegrins were passing on to Alix their ecstatic tales of the Holy Man, Anya decided to bring him to the palace. Like a brilliant director she staged her scene: the appearance of the Holy Man before the empress.

It is late at night, she and the tsaritsa are playing Beethoven four-handed. At about midnight, on Anya's instruction, Rasputin is led silently into the half-lighted room. The empress is seated with her back to him. She continues to play with Anya. The clock strikes midnight.

"Don't you feel something happening, Sana?"

"Yes, yes," answers the empress, a little frightened.

Then Anya slowly turns her head, and the poor tsaritsa, obediently, does as well. When the nervous Alix sees the vague figure of a muzhik in the doorway, like a vision, she is struck by hysterics. Rasputin comes to her, hugs the tormented woman to his chest, and strokes her quietly, gently murmuring, "Be not afraid, my dear. Christ is with you."

Rasputin is one of the most popular myths of the twentieth century. The madness of Russian debauch, the sexual power that vanquished Petersburg society, the diamonds and luxurious furs thrown at the oiled boots of the devil-muzhik, and this muzhik, who defiled the marital bed of Russia's first family in full view of the country—all this has sold millions of books.

Rudnev, the investigator of the Special Commission of Inquiry, later compiled a very interesting memorandum: "One of the most valuable materials for illuminating the personality of Rasputin was the observations journal kept by the surveillance established for Rasputin by agents of the secret police. The surveillance was both external and internal, and his apartment was under constant watch. . . . Since the periodic press paid inordinate attention to Rasputin's unruliness, which became synonymous with his name, the investigation has given this issue proper attention. The richest material for illuminating this aspect of his personality came from that permanent secret surveillance of his apartment, which made it clear that Rasputin's amorous exploits did not go beyond nighttime orgies with young women of frivolous conduct and chanteuses, as well as with several of his suppliants. . . . As for his proximity to ladies of high society, in this respect the surveillance and investigation obtained no positive materials whatsoever."

So, there were no "ladies of high society"! But what was there?

Grigory Rasputin was born in the village of Pokrovskoe, in Siberia, the son of the peasant Efim Novykh. His father was a terrible drunkard who suddenly saw the light, stopped drinking, and saved up a sufficiency. Then his wife died and his muzhik despair kicked in again: he began drinking and lost all his money. His son Grigory was well known at this time for his own dissolute life. As Rasputin he went to Tobolsk, worked as a waiter in a hotel, there married the servant Praskovye, and she bore him three children: a son and two daughters.

Grigory himself described this dissipated beginning to his life poetically and tenderly: "When I was fifteen in my village in the summertime and the sun warmed me and the birds sang their heavenly songs I dreamed of God. . . . My soul yearned for the distance. . . . Dreaming many times I wept and did not know myself where these tears had come from or why. . . . So my youth passed. In a kind of contemplation, a kind of dream. And later, when life brushed me, touched me, I ran into a corner and prayed secretly. I was not content and could not find the answer to many things; I was sad. I began drinking."

What sweet speech. The gift of seduction.

Until the age of thirty he smoked and fornicated and even worse —he stole. But just as he was about to turn thirty, it happened: a novice monk met him on the road and their conversation set the errant soul on the correct path. The mysterious life of the holy man Grigory began with that moment. During the threshing, when the servants laughed at his holiness, he thrust his shovel into a heap of grain and set out for holy places. He walked for more than a year, came home, dug out a cave under his cattle shed, and prayed there for two weeks. Then he went off again to wander, praying at holy places. He was in Kiev, like Venerable Serafim, and then in the Sarov wilderness itself, then on pilgrimage in Moscow, and on through Russia's endless towns and villages.

He returned home after long wanderings, and as he was praying in church, in front of the people, he beat his brow on the floor in his zeal. From that time he was given to prophecy and healing.

Vera Leonidovna:

"This was a fantastic man. When the fashionable restaurant Vienna opened, I was taken there by Artsybashev, the author of the play *Jealousy*. What a success I was in that play! Also with us was an incredible man well known throughout Petersburg, Manusevich-Manuilov. There were rumors that he was an agent of every possible intelligence service at one and the same time. It was he who made the suggestion: 'Let's go see Rasputin.' It was right next door to the Vienna, on Gorokhovskaya Street. Artsybashev refused, but I'm a daredevil. Rasputin was sitting in the dining room between two girls, his daughters. His eyes bore into me—I have a physical memory of the sensation. The table was laden with flowers and across sat the young, pale blond Munia—Maria Golovina, the empress's lady-in-waiting. People kept calling and stopping in constantly. Women came by. Maria kept running to open the door, as diligent as a servant, and then he said to her: 'Write.' And he began to speak. It was all about meekness, about the soul. I tried to remember it and later, when I got home, I even wrote it down, but it wasn't the same thing. Everyone's eyes had ignited. There was an ineffable flow of love. It was intoxicating."

I was reminded of this story in the archive. The empress's dark blue notebook. On the inside cover of the notebook is written its owner's name: "Alexandra." Next to this elegant signature is Rasputin's scribble. Grigory wrote without punctuation: "Here is my peace my glory the source of light in the world a present to my dear Mama Grigory." He called her "Mama"—the Mother of the Russian Land. Nicholas was "Papa."

"A present to my dear Mama"—these are his oral teachings, painstakingly recorded in Alix's elegant hand.

She took them with her to Tobolsk and Ekaterinburg. She would keep rereading them until the day she died.

Here are some of them:

"Whosoever cares only for himself, he is a fool or a torturer of the Light, the ministers we have in general care only for themselves —Ach! That is not the way! Our homeland is broad, we must make room for people to work, but not the leftists or the rightists; the leftists are stupid and the rightists are fools. Why? Because they want to teach with the stick. I have lived fifty years already, my sixth decade is beginning, and I can say: Whosoever thinks he is learned and has studied—wise men speak the truth—he is a fool.

"The Mother of God was intelligent, though she never wrote about herself. . . . But her life is known to our spirit. . . .

"Never fear releasing prisoners or resurrecting sinners to a just life. Through their suffering prisoners . . . come to stand above us before God. . . .

"Love heaven, it comes from love, wheresoever the spirit, there are we. Love the clouds—for that is where we live. . . ."

The inordinate influence of a semiliterate muzhik on the mistress of all Russia. Because he ministered not only to the unfortunate son's body but also to the tormented empress's soul.

From his lips poured a stream of great Christian truths, with which she cleansed herself from the day's trials. An aficionado of religious books and, of course, a hypnotist, he was able to become the longed-for "holy man" of whom she had dreamed in the Sarov wilderness. Saint Serafim resurrected. To Grigory she entrusted her soul.

In the beginning when he first entered the palace, Rasputin was meek and radiant. Later, when he was already settling into his role of holy man, he would be by turns familiar, ferocious, mocking, and threatening with the tsarist couple. There was no pose in this. He was stupefyingly simple and natural.

THE MYSTERY OF RASPUTIN

Rasputin's mystery lay not in his power of miracle working. That power is indisputable, and it saved Alix's son repeatedly. He did not even necessarily have to be physically close to Alexei. A twentieth-century sorcerer, he was already using the telephone and telegraph.

The stories have been told a multitude of times.

A call from Tsarskoe Selo to Rasputin's apartment: the boy is suffering. His ear hurts; he cannot sleep.

"Have him come here," the holy man addresses the empress over the phone. And very tenderly to the boy who has come to the phone: "What is it, Alyoshenka, burning the midnight oil? Nothing hurts, your ear does not hurt anymore, I'm telling you. Sleep."

Fifteen minutes later, a call comes from Tsarskoe Selo: his ear does not hurt, he is sleeping.

In 1912 the heir is dying at Spala. He has a bruise, and he is getting a blood infection. But Alix, her face racked by night vigils, triumphantly shows the doctors Rasputin's telegram: "God has gazed on your tears and accepted your prayers. Be not sad. Your son shall live." The distinguished doctors can only shake their heads sadly: the terrible finale is inevitable.

But the boy . . . the boy soon recovers.

During the war Nicholas takes the heir with him to Headquarters at Mogilev. Alexei gets chilled and catches an ordinary cold. But the boy is not ordinary: as he is blowing his nose the blood vessels burst and the blood begins to gush—and this blood the doctors can no longer stop. Alexei is sent to Tsarskoe Selo on the imperial train along with Gilliard and the powerless Dr. Derevenko. The tsaritsa awaits him at the platform in Tsarskoe Selo.

"The blood has stopped!" Gilliard announces triumphantly.

"I know," Alix replies calmly. "When did this happen?"

"Somewhere around six-thirty."

Alix holds out Rasputin's telegram. GOD WILL HELP YOU, BE HEALTHY. The telegram had been sent at six-twenty in the morning.

In 1914 Anya Vyrubova incurs life-threatening injuries in a train wreck between Petersburg and Tsarskoe Selo. She is lying unconscious in the railroad guard booth with broken legs and a fractured skull. Rasputin approaches Anya. He is standing over her bed, his eyes are popping out of their sockets from the terrible strain, and suddenly he whispers gently: "Anyushka, wake up, look at me." She opens her eyes.

How must Alix have felt about the person who resurrected the dead right before her very eyes! The only person who could save—and so many times already *had saved*—her son! Could Nicholas deprive her of her son's healer? And her soul's? Getting rid of Rasputin would mean killing her. And the boy.

So he suffered all of it. He even played along.

He acquiesced to Alix's request to eat a miracle-working crust of bread from Rasputin's table and comb his hair with his miraculous comb. Alix had a sacred belief in their miraculous power. He had to pretend that he too believed.

But Nicholas was not simply playing along. For him Grigory was the result of his own truth seeking, which began with Klopov, the destitute landowner who had become for a time Nicholas's "man of the people," and was now finding its culmination in a genuine muzhik in the palace. The union of "people and tsar" had come to pass. Naturally, he knew of Grigory's debauchery. Unlike Alix, he did not try to construct any mystical justifications for him. He accepted it as the debauchery of the real people, proving yet again that his people were not ready for a constitution. Through this wildness he glimpsed in Grigory common sense, goodness, and faith. For him Grigory's voice was the voice of the people.

"This is merely a simple Russian man, very religious and believing," he explained to Count Fredericks, minister of the court. "The empress likes his sincerity, she believes in the power of his prayers for our Family and Alexei, but after all this is our own business, completely private. It is amazing how people love to interfere in all that does not concern them."

People were interfering. In society people spoke with horror about the astounding ritual that had become the norm in the tsar's palace: the Siberian muzhik kissed the hand of the tsar and tsaritsa and then they—the autocrat and empress—kissed the rough hand of the muzhik. This exchange of kisses was entirely evangelical: Christ had washed his disciples' feet. And here they were, the rulers of Russia, humbly kissing the hands of a Siberian muzhik. The people. The tsar's religious family and an increasingly atheistic society were finding they understood each other less and less.

Rasputin indisputably possessed a supernatural gift. For our century, accustomed to the dark miracles of parapsychologists, there is no mystery in this whatsoever. Still, Rasputin's mystery did exist.

The mystery began with his strange behavior. His endless debauches, drinking, unbridled lust—all this became the talk of the town. Petersburg and Moscow saw him boozing outrageously in smart restaurants.

But why? He had an apartment guarded by the police where he could have indulged in drink and depravity to his heart's content without provoking gossip or widespread indignation. But he preferred to carry on in full view of the entire country.

Perhaps there was a challenge in this: I, a simple muzhik, am above your official Petersburg magnificence, above all your proprieties. I'm dancing a mad dance, committing every kind of obscene act. Burn! Burn! What I want—I get!

This was a wholly self-conscious attempt to exploit the alleged mystery of the Russian soul for his own ends. Tolstoy plus Dostoevsky, a kind of banal Tolstoevsky—the symbol of the West's perception of Russia.

There was something wrong with this image. A cunning muzhik with a stinging, guarded gaze. Everyone remarked on the intense *guardedness* of his eyes. So why this recklessness? What was his mystery?

One of his noisiest scandals occurred in 1915. He went to Moscow, fulfilling a vow: to worship in the Kremlin at the holy grave of Patriarch Hermogen. His praying culminated, however, in a wild debauch at the Yar, a well-known restaurant. The police report was intriguing:

"On March 26 of this year at about 11 P.M. the well-known Grigory Rasputin arrived at the Yar restaurant in the company of Anisia Reshetnikova, who is the widow of a man of a respected family, an associate of the Moscow and Petrograd newspapers, Nikolai Soedov, and an unidentified young woman. The entire party was already in high spirits. Once they had occupied a room, the arrivals called up the editor-publisher of the Moscow newspaper *News of the Season,* Semyon Kugulsky, and asked him to join them. They also invited a women's chorus, which performed several songs and danced the matchish. . . . Drunk, Rasputin danced the russkaya afterward and then began confiding with the singers this type of thing: 'This caftan was a gift to me from the "old lady," she sewed it, too.' Further, Rasputin's behavior became truly outrageous, sexually psychopathic: he bared his sexual organs and in that state carried on a conversation with the singers, giving to some his own handwritten notes, such as 'Love unselfishly.' "

What curious company Rasputin kept: to witness his binge, this cunning, cautious muzhik invited not one but two journalists! And in the presence of these journalists, one of whom worked for the tabloids, he orchestrated this obscene spectacle.

There is only one way a man would act like this: if for some strange reason he wanted everything that went on at the Yar to become common knowledge immediately.

Indeed, that is what he wanted—for everyone to know of his excesses. A sinister detail: at the Yar he told tales about the tsaritsa that they did not even dare include in the report.

"I do with her what I want," he proclaimed in the journalists' presence. This was not the only time such statements were heard during his public drinking bouts.

There was a paradoxical move involved in this as well that the clever muzhik had discovered. If Nicholas and Alexandra could not believe in his debauches in the palaces, then neither he nor she herself, of course, could believe those filthy words about the tsaritsa he idolized. As if the lips of the man whose devoted love for "Mama" they had known so many years could actually utter such a thing! In the family's eyes, the mere recounting of such words immediately stripped the rest of its veracity. It all became yet another plot against the poor muzhik whom the devil had beguiled into drinking, a fact his enemies were exploiting.

One more thing: Rasputin knew that the tsaritsa could not get on without him. She would do anything not to believe his enemies. And to avenge him.

This was Rasputin's mystery: his drunken orgies and dirty stories about the tsar's family were wild provocations. He put a weapon into the hands of his own enemies, but as soon as they used it they inevitably disappeared from the palace. It was a paradox, but his debauches destroyed his influential enemies. Lady-in-waiting Tyutcheva, granddaughter of Feodor Tyutchev, the great nineteenth-century poet, and teacher to the grand duchesses, waged a war against the holy man. After yet another one of his escapades she demanded that Rasputin be forbidden to associate with the grand duchesses. As a result, Tyutcheva was forced to leave Tsarskoe Selo.

The all-powerful head of state Stolypin compiled a list of Grigory's adventures and gave it to Nicholas. Nicholas read it, made no comment, and asked Stolypin to proceed to current affairs. Soon the minister found himself preparing for retirement.

Finally, Grand Duke Nicholas Nikolaevich, Rasputin's former admirer, who understood the terrible danger looming over the dynasty, came out against Rasputin. So, the man the tsar had named commander-in-chief at the outset of the war, the man closest to the tsar, and the Siberian muzhik. . . . The muzhik won out.

Until Rasputin's murder, his enemies would continue to fall into his trap each time they brought out the usual accusations of revelry and lust. They did not know that he had provided a marvelous and conclusive explanation for Alix and his loyal admirers, revealing the secret reason for his strange conduct.

Felix Yusupov, his future murderer, learned of this astonishing interpretation of Rasputin's escapades from his friend Maria Golovina, the tsaritsa's lady-in-waiting: with tender sympathy, she explained to Felix as she would to a not very bright child: "If he does this, then it is with a special purpose—to temper himself morally."

The holy man, taking on the sins of the world and through his fall subjecting himself to a voluntary flogging by society, as the holy fools did back in ancient Russia—that is how Rasputin mystically explained his escapades. "The tsaritsa had a book, *Holy Fools of the Russian Church,* with her comments in places where it talked about the manifestation of idiocy in the form of sexual degeneracy," recalled Father Georgy Shavelsky, the archpresbyter of the imperial army and navy.

Rasputin and Anya were the two people closest to the family. Two people who gave birth to terrible myths on which the coming revolution would feed: the spineless, pathetic cuckold of a tsar, and the tsaritsa in the brazen embraces of an adventurist muzhik, a tsaritsa who rumor asserted gave her friend as mistress to the tsar.

A great number of obscene drawings circulated throughout Russia right up until the revolution. One of these "graffiti": a bearded muzhik (Rasputin) and in his arms two broad-hipped beauties (the tsaritsa and Anya), and all this on the background of brazen virgins (the tsaritsa's daughters) dancing zestfully.

Chapter 5

THE TSAR'S FAMILY

✛

*M*eanwhile, the family lived in nearly idyllic seclusion. Few knew of their real life. An enchanting portrait of them was left in the memoirs of one of those few, the woman who had done so much toward the family's ruin—Anya.

It is early morning. The family is waking up. Alix's dream has come true: it is all as it was in her childhood, when she had just such a large family as this. Through her "tireless labor of love" a family has been created. And she—wife and mother—is its shelter and support.

The Alexander Palace has long been cramped for five children. Next door, the enormous Catherine Palace stands empty. But she does not want to change quarters. This is not merely habit for the old hearth but an awareness: our life together, in this small palace, unites us, bonds us.

Her daughters. We know very little about them: shadows in the bloody reflection of impending tragedy.

Her Victorian education, the legacy Alix received from her English grandmother Victoria, she passed on to her daughters: tennis, a cold bath in the morning, a warm one in the evening. This was for the good of the body. And for the soul—a religious education: reading books pleasing to God, strictly observing church rituals. "Olga and Tatiana were at mass for the first time and bore up for the entire service excellently," a gratified Nicholas would record in his diary.

When Olga was quite tiny, the older girls teased her: "What kind of grand duchess are you if you can't even reach the table?"

"I don't know myself," Olga answered with a sigh, "but you ask Papa, he knows everything." "He knows everything"—that was how Alix raised them.

Wearing white dresses and colored sashes, they descend noisily to the empress's lilac (Alix's favorite color) study: there was a huge rug, so cozy to crawl over, and on the rug a huge box of toys, which were passed down from older to younger.

They were growing up.

"Olga has turned 9—quite the big girl."

Olga and Tatiana—these names frequently appear together in their diaries and, later, when Nicholas went to Headquarters, in his correspondence with Alix. Here they are quite little: "Olga and Tatiana rode their bicycles side by side" (Nicholas's diary).

"Olga & Tatiana returned only at about 2." "Now O. & T. are at Olga's Committee" (from letters of the tsaritsa).

And so on.

Olga was a snub-nosed blonde, enchanting and impetuous. Tatiana was more focused, less spontaneous, and less talented, but she made up for this lack with her equanimity. Tatiana was like her mother. The gray-eyed beauty was the conduit of all her mother's decisions. The sisters called her "the Governor."

And the two younger girls, so tenderly devoted to one another, both merry, a little plump—broad in the bone, like their grandfather: Marie, a Russian beauty, and good-hearted Anastasia. For her constant readiness to serve everyone they called Anastasia "our good, fat Tutu." They also called her *schwibzik*—little one.

They did not like to study very much (this is evident from the many mistakes in their diaries). The sharpest was Olga, who did have an aptitude for learning.

"Ah, I understand: the helping verbs are the servant of the verbs. Only one unlucky verb, 'to have,' must serve itself," she told her teacher Gilliard.

The sentence of a girl surrounded by servants from the cradle.

They slept in large children's beds and on cots, practically without pillows, two to a room.

They would take those cots with them into exile, all the way to

Ekaterinburg; they would sleep on them that very last night. Then their murderers would spend the night on those beds.

Like the whole family, they kept diaries. Subsequently in Tobolsk, when the commissar came from Moscow, they would burn those diaries. Only a few notebooks would remain.

I am looking through the diaries of Marie and Tatiana, in the traditional scrapbooks, with gold bindings and a moiré lining (their father had started his diary as a boy in just such books). Marie's faceless enumeration of events: "This morning church, supper in the evening with Papa and Alexei, in the afternoon tea with Ania."

Tatiana kept exactly the same kind of diary.

Again in Olga's diary (in a plain black notebook; she wanted to be like her father even in this): "We had tea. . . . We played tiddly-winks." And so on. But one thing is surprising: it is always "we" in the diaries. They were together so much that they even thought of themselves collectively.

An enchanting detail: dried flowers remained in the girls' diaries. Flowers from the park at Tsarskoe Selo, where they had been so happy. They took them along into exile and preserved them between the pages of their notebooks. After burning nearly all their diaries, they put the flowers in the remaining notebooks. Souvenirs of a destroyed life.

I turn the pages cautiously. If only they don't crumble into dust, these flowers, dried once upon a time by little girls in the last carefree summer of their life.

There is a photograph in the empress's album.

She is lying on a couch, her head flung back, her disturbing, tragic profile. Around her on little benches sit her daughters and on a pillow on the floor—Alexei. The girls are gazing at him with adoring smiles. The delicate oval of his face, the light chestnut, curling hair with a streak of bronze, and his mother's gray eyes—the little prince. The chronically ill prince.

"Give me a bicycle," he asks his mother.

"You know you cannot."

"I want to play tennis like my sisters."

"You know you dare not play."

And then, breaking their hearts, he cries, repeating: "Why aren't I like everyone else?"

The girls witnessed and helped their mother during his endless suffering. During the war they, like their mother, would be good nurses.

Pages from their life. Brilliant balls, the noisy life of society—how little of all this there was in the life of these first young ladies of Russia.

But then, one summer. . . .

Aboard the imperial yacht *Standart,* they approached a pier in Crimea. Dressed in enormous white hats and long white dresses they were seated in open carriages, which set out in a brilliant string.

Alix's dream had come true: on the site of the unhappy palace where Alexander III had died, where Nicholas himself had nearly died, they had erected a miracle. A white Italianate palace to replace the old wooden one; the sea stretched out from the rooms. They would remember this paradise in their Siberian imprisonment, in their freezing house.

At Livadia they took many photographs of each other: here is Alexei and next to him his favorite spaniel, Joy.

They all had their favorite dogs. Anastasia had a tiny King Charles, which a wounded officer had given the sisters in the hospital. It could be carried in a muff.

Mikhail Medvedev, the son of a guard who took part in the family's execution, told this story: "My father used to tell us—when they loaded the corpses onto the truck, he was in charge of the loading—the corpse of a tiny dog fell out of the sleeve of the outfit of one of the grand duchesses."

Here, in Livadia, Olga turned sixteen. She was appointed colonel-in-chief of the Hussar Regiment. In the evening there was a ball. An orchestra of military trumpeters played. Blond, wearing a long pink dress, she stood in the middle of the hall, and all the Hussar officers at the ball were in love with her.

That evening she put on her diamond jewelry for the first time.

Every birthday, the thrifty Alix gave her daughters one pearl and one diamond. So that when they were sixteen they could have two pieces of jewelry made.

The family spent the winter at Tsarskoe Selo, in their beloved old Alexander Palace. Everything followed Alix's regular routine.

At two o'clock she emerged from the room with the children: an outing in the carriage. She did not like to walk; she had weak legs. She drove to some distant church where no one knew her and there prayed earnestly, kneeling on the stone slabs. At eight o'clock, dinner. Nicholas came out as well. Alix appeared in an open dress with diamonds. At nine they went upstairs to the nursery and prayed with Alexei, and then Nicholas went to his study to write in his diary. In the evening, the traditional reading aloud.

In the golden cage where the family lived, nothing had changed for centuries. Anya described it: the furniture in the palace smelt of the same perfume as it had under her great-great-grandmother Catherine the Great, and there was the same gilt furniture, and the same footmen in feathered caps.

The Alexander Palace floats out of nothingness. Now we see it through the eyes of the French ambassador to Russia, Maurice Paléologue:

"The Alexander Palace appears before me in its most ordinary aspect, . . . my suite includes a footman . . . wearing a little cap decorated with red, black, and yellow feathers. They lead me through the formal drawing rooms, through the empress's drawing room, down a long corridor onto which open the rooms of the sovereign. There I encounter a lackey wearing a very simple livery and bearing a tea tray. Further on a small internal staircase opens up leading to the rooms of the most august children: the parlormaid runs up it to the next floor."

This parlormaid running to the upper floor may have been Elizaveta Ersberg.

*T*HE PARLORMAID ELIZAVETA ERSBERG
One day I received a letter.

"Writing to you is Maria Nikolaevna Ersberg."

I confess, I shuddered. That was the last name of the imperial family's parlormaid who shared their exile.

"My grandfather Nikolai Ersberg was the palace stoker under Alexander III. He stoked the furnaces in Anichkov and Gatchina palaces, as well as the Winter Palace. He suffered a blow in the wreck of the imperial train near Borki and died in 1889. *His daughter, my father's younger sister, Elizaveta Nikolaevna Ersberg (born September 18, 1882, died in the blockade, March 12, 1942), graduated from the Patriotic Grammar School and was chosen by Nicholas' mother Maria Feodorovna for a parlormaid.* She served with faith and truth from 1898 until May 1918. . . . When the family was forced into exile in 1917, the tsaritsa gathered together all the servants and announced that she would be pleased if any of them wanted to serve them in exile as well. Inasmuch as the situation was altogether uncertain, however, she could promise no salary. Elizaveta, moved by a sense of duty and by her devotion to the girls, decided to go. In the blueprint of the Alexander Palace at Tsarskoe Selo, all the quarters are marked as to whom they belonged to. On it there is the room of my Aunt Elizaveta.

"When I was in the palace for the first time in 1932, accompanied by my father, everything there was just as it had been 'at the moment its owners departed' (as my father said). The bedroom of Nicholas and Alexandra with its oriel and hydrangeas, Alexandra's favorite flower. Iron beds with wrought decorations at the head, just like we had in our house. Over the head of the bed there were a great many icons ranging from ordinary (household) size to the tiniest medallions and porcelain Easter eggs with depictions of the saints. Upstairs in the nursery was Alexei's rocking horse. . . .

"My aunt used to tell us that one of her responsibilities was cleaning the children's rooms and putting together their wardrobe, and when the little girls were growing up she taught them handwork. My aunt was inseparable from the girls even on the family's trips to the Crimea. . . . When the war began, Elizaveta taught the girls to care for the sick. The girls worked in a hospital as nurses and aides, and all the maids and parlormaids worked with them. This collective of amateur medics was headed up by the tsaritsa. . . .

"According to Aunt Elizaveta's stories, the children were modest and diligent. Olga, the eldest, was a little spoiled and capricious and could be lazy, but Tatiana and Anastasia were always busy—all of them sewed and embroidered, they even cleaned their own room. Their father paid the children more attention than their mother did. Alexandra Feodorovna often lay in bed with a migraine, or quarreled with the parlormaids, or was busy with antique buyers from the Alexander Market (the tsaritsa ordered old and unfashionable items sold to the antiquarians, although she changed mother of pearl buttons for ivory or glass before selling). . . . In about 1905 Elizaveta acquired a helper, another parlormaid, Anna Stepanovna [Stefanovna] Demidova. She became very friendly with Elizaveta and her family. She even became my father's fiancée. At that time he was an official for the State Railway Inspection Control. He served under State Councilor Vladimir Skryabin, the brother of Vyacheslav Skryabin-Molotov, future prime minister under Stalin.

"The parlormaids were permitted to invite guests to visit. The tsaritsa was very frugal with the housekeeping. If the girls had to offer their guests something, they did so at their own expense. Moreover, all were warned to save their money while they were working, since they would receive no pension. Parlormaids, maids, and lackeys had to be unmarried. In the event of marriage they were dismissed or moved to other jobs.

"At our house we kept a cherished box with photographs of the Family with dedicatory inscriptions to my aunt. Simple inscriptions like 'To Liza as a memento from a grateful father,' 'To Liza in gratitude for her loyalty' (Alexandra). And children's like 'To dear Liza from Tania' and the uneven letters of childish scribbles. 'Liza, sew on my button,' and so on. In 1932 my father brought this box out, it was opened, and my whole family looked through them all—and burned them, to my aunt's sobs as well as mine. They were destroyed because of the general searches being made then of 'formers.' They were looking for gold, digging up cellars and attics. My father was extremely cautious and decided to be rid of the dangerous burden."

Yet another view from the "people."

"People"—that's what Nicholas called his servants in his diaries.

The girls were growing up, and Alix was giving increasing thought to their marriages.

"Oh, if only our children could be as happy in their married life," she wrote him.

In 1912 everyone began to talk about a marriage between Olga and Nicholas's cousin Dmitry, who had been taken in by the tsar many years earlier. She was in love. Dmitry was a charming rake, her father's favorite. Even the evil-tongued Grand Duke Sergei Mikhailovich said that he was "as elegant as a Fabergé statuette."

In the happy year 1912, on August 26, on the centennial of the victory over Napoleon at Borodino, a cavalcade of grand dukes, with the tsar in the lead, rides a circuit around the famous field of Borodino. There is a fence ahead.

"Hey, show us what you can do, Olympian!" (that summer Dmitry had participated in the Olympic Games in Stockholm), Grand Duke Kirill Vladimirovich says to Dmitry. "Show us how to jump?"

Immediately Dmitry, playful, sails over the high fence. Later, in the forest, where the imperial train is waiting, Dmitry gallops right up the embankment to the train car. Alix is smiling out the window. So is Olga.

Then all of a sudden the engagement is off. Behind the scenes of the break is that same smiling Alix. The mistress of the family does not want Dmitry.

She is looking for another match for her daughter: the Romanian heir. But Olga is true to her feelings, as her father once was. She thinks up a patriotic justification: "I am Russian and wish to remain Russian."

But the engagement must take place, so the family sails to Constanta on the *Standart*.

A ceremonial welcome on the wharf, in the evening an official dinner. Olga sits next to the prince and chats with him with her usual delicate graciousness. Meanwhile the remaining grand duchesses make a show of being deadly bored.

Yes, the roles have been passed out—and the sisters are playing them well. The next morning no one is talking about a wedding anymore.

Why did the empress not want the marriage to Dmitry? Did she dream of seeing her eldest daughter a queen? Or had a terrible premonition already settled in her nervous soul then, and had she decided to remove her eldest daughter from the country no matter what the cost?

Chapter 6

DIARY OF THE SUCCESSFUL MONARCH

"*J*T SEEMS STRANGE TO THINK I HAVE TURNED 45"
The idyllic prewar decade. The family and royal Europe were living their own special life. They visited one another, corresponded, and married. These people, who had the lengthiest of titles, were to each other Georgie and Nicky, Alix and Minnie—simply, sisters, aunts, brothers, uncles, fathers, and sons.

All these years he kept in his diary a chronicle of the royal families' social life.

In 1908, the Swedish King Gustav paid a visit. (During the reception for the Swedish king, Nicholas pointedly did not introduce Count Witte to him——Alix's idea.) A meeting with the French President Falière, another with the English King Edward VII.

The royal family came—the new king and queen of Denmark. (After the death of Nicholas's grandfather, the Danish king, Nicholas's uncle took the throne.) At the ceremonial dinner the empress-mother did not pass up the opportunity to demonstrate her power, or, rather, what was left of her power. At her request, Count Witte was seated next to the high table where both royal families sat.

Vanity Fair continued: in late July the *Standart* went to France, then England. This was his return visit to Edward VII.

And again, the Crimea, the Livadia Palace. And from the Crimea, he went to see the king of Italy.

(On the eve of this farewell, Alix was sitting with Anya in the blooming Livadia park when Anya heard a familiar whistle. As always at that sound, Alix jumped up from the bench, blushing like a young girl, and said: "That's *him* calling me." And she rushed off, ran. It was all just as it had been in 1894.)

But it was already 1909.

On the return trip Nicholas circumvented Austria (thus expressing his protest to the Austrian emperor over Austria's annexation of Bosnia and Herzegovina. This gesture was widely noted by the newspapers of the world and in it the prelude to the future world war was already sounded.)

Grand Duke Michael Nikolaevich, the father of Sergei, Sandro, and George, Nicholas's closest childhood friends, died. The people of his youth were leaving him behind.

The priest Ioann of Kronstadt died. His prophecies and his miracle working were famous to all Russia. He had not taken the vows of schema, he was not a monk, and he had not given up conjugal life, but the people considered him a saint. The only man who could have stood up to Rasputin was dead.

Another year passed. The years were slipping by. The English King Edward VII, one of the principal founders of the Russo-Anglo-Franco alliance, passed away. Nine monarchs and innumerable princes converged for the funeral. They thought they were burying the English king, but they were actually burying peaceful monarchical Europe. Only a few years remained until the great upheavals of world war. George, the same George who so strikingly resembled Nicholas, became King George V.

On the return trip Nicholas stopped at Uncle Willy's residence in Potsdam. The arrow of the Russian political compass had to stand exactly halfway between England and Germany.

In December 1910 Tolstoy died. On learning of Tolstoy's death, Nicholas wrote that Tolstoy was a great artist and that God was his judge.

In February 1911 they celebrated the fiftieth anniversary of the freeing of the serfs. Only fifty years before, people in his country had lived as slaves. There were celebrations in Kiev and the unveiling of a monument to Alexander II.

During these festivities in honor of the slain reformer another great reformer was killed: Stolypin. The minister was shot before

Nicholas's very own eyes. The mortally wounded Stolypin managed to make the sign of the cross over his tsar.

Thus his children witnessed murder for the first time. Once again the "police had failed to keep an eye out," and again the assassin turned out to be a revolutionary enlisted as an agent of the Department of Police. The shadow of the omnipotent secret police?

An inquiry was made about this in the Duma on October 15: "It can be proven that in the last decade we have had a series of analogous murders of Russian officials that implicate the political police. They are everywhere setting up illegal publishing houses, bomb workshops, and terrorist acts. . . . [The political police] have become a weapon of internecine war between individuals and groups in governmental spheres."

The tsar preferred not to think about these terrible surmises. He knew: life and death—everything was predetermined. Everything was God's doing.

Evidently, Alix laid out these thoughts of his to Stolypin's successor, Count Vladimir Kokovtsev: "There is no need to pity so much those who are gone. If someone is no longer among us, then that is because he has already played his role. Stolypin died to make way for you."

The year 1913 began—the pinnacle of his empire's flowering, the year of the great jubilee: his ancestors had ruled Russia for three hundred years, and Russian history was marked off by their names. God had willed that he greet the triumphal date in prosperity.

Prosperity? Yes, after Stolypin's reforms an unprecedented upswing began. Europe watched in amazement as the giant picked itself up. The government of France sent to Russia the economist Edmond Terry, who in his book *Russia in 1914* wrote: "None of the European peoples is achieving these kinds of results. . . . By midcentury Russia will dominate Europe." There was an intellectual explosion going on in the country. The homeland of Tolstoy and Chekhov became a laboratory for the future art of the twentieth century: Malevich, Kandinsky, Chagall, Khlebnikov, Mayakovsky, Rachmaninoff, Scriabin, Stravinsky, Stanislavsky, Meyerhold.

All these joyous changes scared Nicholas, though. Until very recently, Moscow, the ancient capital, had been permeated with the smell of the past he so cherished. But now, right before his eyes, the garden city had vanished: factory stacks puffed, huge new buildings were threatening to become skyscrapers, money men now ruled in the capital of the Muscovite tsars. "Manchester has invaded the City of the Tsars," as the Russian newspapers wrote in those days. Petersburg, too.

The greater his country's prosperity, the lonelier he felt. Educated society amiably termed tsarist rule Asiatic and dreamed of uniting Russia and Europe. A troubled, worrisome future was upon them—and both Witte and Stolypin had created it. Could he love his own great ministers?

As before, he believed that all this was the intelligentsia's error: the muzhik feared Europe. Distrust for the "mutes" (as foreigners had been called in Russia since way back when) and holy tsarist rule were in the people's blood.

(Who turned out to be right? Yes, soon the people's revolution would destroy tsarist rule. But ten years later, new revolutionary tsars would come, and for many decades Russia would cut itself off from Europe once again.)

On the day of the dynasty's tricentennial, *Life for the Tsar* was performed as usual at the Mariinsky Theater. During the service in Kazan Cathedral, two doves circled under the cupola. Nicholas stood beside his son, gazing up at this beautiful omen. The Sarov saint had been right after all: the second half of his reign would see a flourishing.

Everything seemed so stable!

"21 February, 1913. Thursday. The day of the celebration of 300 years of rule was bright and very springlike. At 12.15 Alexei and I in a carriage, Mama and Alix in a Russian coach, and finally, all the daughters in a landau set out for Kazan Cathedral. Ahead was a company in convoy, with another company behind."

During the ceremonies, Alix was persecuted by headaches and her ineffable, recurrent sadness.

"I'm a wreck," she told Anya.

"There was a service at the cathedral and a manifesto was read. We returned to the Winter Palace the same way. . . . We were in a happy mood that reminded me of the coronation. We had lunch with Mama. At 3.45 everyone gathered in the Hall of Malachite. And in the concert chamber we received congratulations until 5.30. About 1500 people filed by. Alix was very tired and went to bed. . . . I read and sorted through the sea of telegrams. . . . I looked out the window at the lights and searchlights from the Admiralty tower. A strong southwest wind was blowing."

But "We were in a happy mood" is not what sticks in the mind. What sticks in the mind is "Alix was very tired and went to bed" and the silent, lonely man gazing out the window at the holiday lights.

"It made me so sad to see your lonely figure," she would write him in a letter.

Loneliness. Only the family. Alix, the children, and he. The friends of his youth were rarely invited now. Sergei Mikhailovich was still with the aging Mathilde (that "awful woman"—a taboo theme in the family). Nicholas Mikhailovich, the liberal historian, was chairman of the Russian Historical Society (of which Nicholas himself was honorary chairman). Author of a monumental biography of Alexander I, he was especially interested in the mysterious legends surrounding the strange death of that emperor and in the holy man Feodor Kuzmich who appeared in Siberia shortly after the tsar's burial. He tried to find clues to the puzzle in the Romanov family archives. The possible secret departure from the throne of his grandfather's brother and the tsar's transformation into a holy man were very disturbing to Nicholas himself, too, but it was hard for them to talk. Nicholas Mikhailovich was a mystic, a Mason, and a freethinker. In Petersburg he lived all alone in his palace among his books and manuscripts. He livened up only "at home"—in Paris, where he painstakingly tried to explain to his friends the principles of Nicky's rule.

In the family he was called "Monsieur Egalité." As the eighteenth century once called the liberal Duke of Orléans.

To complete the resemblance: the liberal Duke of Orléans was guillotined by the French Revolution; the liberal Nicholas Mikhailovich would be shot in the Fortress of Peter and Paul by the October Revolution. Meanwhile, this mysterious man predicted his own death and even described it: "one dark, raw night, a few paces from the ponderous graves of my ancestors."

The year 1913 was drawing to a close. It was fall at the Livadia Palace. But the paths of the beautiful park were deserted. Once a frequent visitor, Dmitry no longer showed his face here. Now the favorite cousin was no longer allowed access to Livadia, but in Petersburg's salons the brilliant guardsman must have heard the wild gossip about his lost bride and the dirty Siberian muzhik. Nor was Nicholas's brother Misha there on the Livadia park *allées*. He had persisted in his romance with the twice-divorced Mrs. Wulfert, a commoner, and had in fact defied Nicholas's order that he not marry her. He had quit Russia to be with his beloved.

An encoded telegram to the Russian embassies in 1911:

"The bearer of this, Major-General of Gendarmes A. V. Gerasimov, is commanded at His Highness's behest to travel abroad with the assignment of taking all possible measures to avert the marriage abroad of Mrs. Wulfert and Grand Duke Michael Alexandrovich."

Michael had done all he could to prevent his reigning brother's learning about what had happened. He had gone abroad, he was circling Europe, in search of a secluded spot for a secret wedding.

Another encoded telegram in 1911: "In conducting my investigation, I have the honor to report the circumstances of and specific time at which the ceremony in which His Imperial Highness entered into marriage took place. . . . On October 29 he told his companions that he was going out with Mrs. Wulfert in his automobile through Switzerland and Italy to Cannes, and the individuals and servants accompanying them would travel by train through Paris to Cannes. . . . That day, October 29, they rode in the automobile only as far as Wurtzburg, where they boarded a train continuing on to Vienna, where His Imperial Highness arrived on the morning of October 30. . . . That same day in four hours and by midday the grand duke and Mrs. Wulfert drove to the Serbian church of Saint Savva, where they performed the marriage ceremony. . . . For those individuals surrounding the grand duke and Mrs. Wulfert, their trip remained utterly secret. . . . During the grand duke's sojourn, foreign secret service agents accompanied him everywhere in a special car."

Such was the picture—motor races at the beginning of the century. A car with agents of the secret police following a car whose driver was a grand duke and whose passenger was his mistress. The entire journey was recorded by the agents his brother had sent.

Nicholas received the news of the "shocking marriage" during a particularly acute attack of his son's illness.

Alix demanded that Nicholas remain implacable, as his father had known how to be. Taking pity on his brother would have meant allowing the further collapse of the Romanov family.

September 3, 1911. The embassy in Paris. More telegrams: "According to information received, the sovereign emperor's aide-de-camp appeared in Cannes to inform the grand duke in the name of His Highness that he was prohibited to enter Russia. . . . The grand duke is very depressed and does not go out anywhere."

After the birth of the tsarevich Alexei, Michael had lost the title of heir and had received that of state regent. Now he was deprived of that as well.

Of those who witnessed the inception of Nicholas and Alexandra's happy marriage, Ella was one of few who remained. Still a beauty, she walked through the park dressed in a gray nun's habit. After mourning her husband, Sergei, Ella had disbanded her court, moved into rooms on Ordynka, and founded a religious community, the Cloister of Martha and Mary. The order was named for the Gospel's Martha and Mary, sisters who lived in the house of Lazarus and were friends of Jesus. The nuns of the cloister cared for sick and abandoned children, the poor, and the dying.

Wise Ella understood that speaking about Rasputin with Alix meant sundering relations and leaving her sister completely isolated. All that remained for Ella was to pray for her. And be patient.

Also next to Nicky was his childhood friend Prince Peter Alexandrovich of Oldenburg—Petya in Nicholas's diaries.

The Oldenburgs came from an ancient line famous for its savage cruelty. European chroniclers wrote with horror about them. In the eighteenth century this line merged with the Romanovs. So here was Petya, a descendant of those horrible Oldenburgs—a very good and very ungainly, tall man. In his spare time he wrote sweet, sentimental stories about nature. He was married to Grand Duchess Olga, the sister of his reigning comrade. But Petya was a homosexual, and unhappy Olga could not decide whether to leave him.

Petya would survive the terrible revolution and the companion of his childhood games. After the revolution, at an émigré party, he would meet the writer Ivan Bunin. Bunin later would recount with a smile how Peter of Oldenburg, having listened to a conversation among old revolutionaries, exclaimed: "Oh, what dear, charming people you all are and how sad that Nicky never was at your parties! Everything, everything would have been different had you known one another."

The pages of the diary were turning quickly. Life went on.

"6 May, 1913. It seems strange to think I have turned 45. . . .

The weather was marvelous, unfortunately Alix felt poorly [this was often the case now]. Mass, congratulations, just like in the old days, only with the difference that they were all daughters."

This was his forty-fifth birthday, the saint's day of Job the Long-Suffering. From her letter: "You were also born on the day of Job, my long-suffering darling." He was calling himself Job more and more often.

From the memoirs of the French ambassador Maurice Paléologue:

"One day Stolypin proposed to the sovereign an important domestic policy measure. Nicholas II listened to him thoughtfully and made a gesture, skeptical, offhand, as if to say: that or something else, does it really matter. Finally he declared in a sad voice: 'Nothing I undertake ever works out. I am unlucky . . . and moreover the human will is so weak. . . . Do you know when my birthday is?'

" 'How could I not know?'

" 'May 6th. And what saint is celebrated on that day?'

" 'Forgive me, sovereign, I do not recall.'

" 'Job the Long-suffering.'

" 'Glory be to God, Your Highness's reign shall culminate in glory, just like Job, who endured the most terrible trials and was rewarded by God's blessing and prosperity.'

" 'No, believe me, Peter Arkadievich, I have more than a premonition. I am profoundly certain of this. I am doomed to terrible trials, but I will not receive my reward here, on earth. . . . How many times have I applied to myself Job's words: "For the thing which I greatly feared is come upon me, and that which I was afraid of is come unto me" ' [Job 3:25]."

Forty-five years old—an old man already. Job. . . . And a feeling common to people in their forties: life was becoming more and more like a dream. Such moods were especially strong in him during these years of relative peace. There was still calm in Europe, there was still peace, friendly visits were still being exchanged with Uncle Willy (it was en route to Berlin that Nicholas started this notebook of his diary).

Strange photographs were already pasted into his diary: his son in a military uniform saluting. The tsaritsa and a grand duchess, both of them in the uniforms of the regiments they served as colonel-in-chief.

A strange martial accent appeared in this notebook.

It also appeared in their life.

A nervous Alix felt a foreboding and melancholy. She was plagued by horrific headaches—that is why she was weeping at the tricentennial ceremonies.

The year 1913, the year of greatest well-being for his empire, came to a close.

On December 31 he wrote in his diary: "Oh Lord, bless Russia and us all with peace and quiet and piety."

On January 6, 1914, as if concluding an era, the last Epiphany parade was held in the Winter Palace. Platoons of the Guards and the military institutes formed up. The empress-mother wore a silver Russian sarafan with the blue ribbon of St. Andrew. Alix was dressed in a deep blue, gold-embroidered sarafan with an enormous sable-trimmed train. Her headdress was crowned by a diamond diadem with a pearl. The legendary Romanov jewels!

In the cramped stuffiness of Ekaterinburg imprisonment, they would recall the endless cold marble hall, the Guards in formation with their backs to the Neva, giant Nicholas Nikolaevich surrounded by his giant Grenadiers . . . and how they emerged from the palace onto the Palace Embankment . . . and how the metropolitan descended to the ice-bound Neva to sanctify the water in an ice hole.

*H*IS SECOND WAR ("A MAGNIFICENT IMPULSE HAS GRIPPED ALL RUSSIA")

The year was 1914. That hot July day they left with the children as usual for the Finnish Skerries on the yacht. In the afternoon a launch carrying a courier from Petersburg moored to the yacht. Nicholas read the two telegrams and hurriedly went into his drawing room–cum–study. On June 14, in the Bosnian town of Sarajevo, the heir to the Austro-Hungarian throne, Franz-Ferdinand, and his wife were killed by shots fired from a revolver. Sarajevo had been inundated with Serbian nationalists, and the coach for some reason had been driving slowly without any guard. Like a target. The assassin was the Serbian nationalist Gavril Princip. In the language of the politicians of the day, this event meant one thing: war.

The second telegram was possibly connected with the first. In Siberia, in the village of Pokrovskoe, Grigory Rasputin had been severely wounded. A former admirer, Fyonia Guseva, had attacked him with a knife. Rasputin was a supporter of the German party, an active enemy of war with Germany.

So, simultaneously, grounds appeared for the future war, and the only person who had any influence over the tsar and who might have attempted to avert it was eliminated. Now Alix was helpless. When the yacht moored at Peterhof, she quickly proceeded to the palace. Locking herself in her study, the empress wept.

What was this? Coincidence? Or a game of the secret police, be it Russian (many in the camarilla wanted this war; actually, so did Grand Duke Nicholas Nikolaevich) or German (bellicose Uncle Willy had long dreamed of this war).

In July 1914, French President Raymond Poincaré approached Russian shores aboard the battleship *France*. The president had come to negotiate an alliance in the impending war.

A reception was in progress in the palace at Peterhof. The most brilliant court in Europe was greeting the French president.

The ladies' toilettes were a stream of jewels. The French president's black suit stood out among the uniforms of the imperial suite. The minister of the court, magnificent old Count Fredericks, who even now had a captivating bearing and noble features; the chief marshal of the court, Prince Vasily Dolgorukov, a tall man with the elegant manners of the old aristocracy; the polished marshal of the court, Count Benckendorff—they made an amazing trio, reminding the French president of the magnificence of the court of the various Louises.

During this noisy reception, French Ambassador Paléologue, who was seated across from Alix, observed with astonishment the strange scene, which he recorded in detail in his diary: "In the course of the dinner I observed Alexandra Feodorovna. . . . Her head gleaming with diamonds and her figure in a décolleté dress of white brocade were still quite beautiful. . . . She was trying to engage Poincaré, seated to her right, in conversation, but quickly her smile became convulsive, her cheeks covered in spots. She kept biting her lips, and her feverish breathing infused the diamond net covering her breast with flames. While the dinner, which went on for a long time, was in progress, the poor woman evidently struggled with an attack of hysterics. Her features suddenly smoothed out when the emperor stood to pronounce a toast."

Poor Alix. She knew that the president's arrival meant war.

Everyone knew it. At a dinner in the home of Grand Duke Nicholas Nikolaevich, his wife, the Montenegrin Princess Stana, kept exclaiming as if inspired: "Before the end of the month we will have war. Our armies will meet in Berlin. Germany will be destroyed." Only a look from the tsar interrupted this prophecy.

War. This was her trap. Now Alix constantly had to demonstrate her patriotism and her hatred for Uncle Willy and Germany.

Her brother Ernie lived in Germany, though, and he was going to have to fight her husband. Her homeland would send its sons to fight her new country. And of course, war would give her enemies, her many enemies, a terrible ace. She was already hearing the future whisper "German!" behind her back. But all this was in the inmost recesses of her soul. The only person who could read her soul was the Siberian muzhik, who understood immediately. He was the chief opponent of war with Germany. Over and over again he repeated the potential misfortunes and whispered terrible prophecies.

Rasputin had one other secret: he always said what she wanted to hear. Including what she kept deeply hidden and did not dare utter even to herself. He said it for her.

Rasputin was the sole figure who could have averted war at that time. She could have cited him as the voice of God and the people. She could have entreated Nicholas to listen to him.

Rasputin, however, lay wounded in a distant Siberian village.

The day after the state dinner with the French president, under a hot, threatening sky, 60,000 men engaged in military exercises. In the evening there was a farewell dinner on board the *France*, and a military orchestra played marches. With a convulsive smile Alix listened to the frenzied allegro. Once again, the French ambassador described the scene in his diary: With a suffering, somehow pleading face, she begged the ambassador, "Couldn't you possibly. . . ." Paléologue guessed and with a gesture of his hand asked the orchestra to stop. She was on the verge of hysterics. Olga rushed over to her.

The Gulf of Finland was lit by the moon, and the battleship's shadow lay on the water.

From Nicholas's diary:

"19 July, 1914. After breakfast summoned Nikolasha [Nicholas Nikolaevich] and informed him of his appointment as commander-in-chief until I could join the army. . . . At 6.30 went to vespers. Upon my return I learned that Germany had declared war on us. . . .

"20 July. A good day in particular in the sense of an upsurge of spirit. At 2.30 set out on the *Alexandria* to Petr[ograd] and took a cutter directly to the Winter Palace. Signed the declaration of war. From the [Hall of] Malachite, we went out into St. Nicholas Hall, in the middle of which the declaration was read. Then public prayers were said. . . . The entire hall sang 'Save Us, Lord' and 'Many Years.' I said a few words. Upon our return the ladies rushed to kiss our hands and rather wore Alix and myself out. . . . Then we went out on the balcony on Alexander Square and bowed to the enormous mass of people. . . . At about 6 we went out onto the embankment to the cutter through a large crowd of officers and public. We returned to Peterhof at 7.15 and spent a quiet evening. . . .

"23. In the morning learned good news: England has declared war on Germany. . . .

"24. Austria has finally declared war on us. Now the situation is quite clear."

Thus began the war that destroyed an empire.

On December 31, he looked back as usual on the year just past:

"We prayed to the Lord God to give us victory in the coming year and a quiet, tranquil life after that. Oh Lord, bless and strengthen our incomparable, valorous, and uncomplaining host for further victories."

What about Rasputin? Once recovered from his wound he sent telegrams. Subsequently a great deal would be written about a certain mysterious telegram to the empress in which Rasputin predicted ruin and misery in war.

Alix herself later believed this and in Tobolsk talked of the mysterious telegram. But in the notebook of the holy man's utterances, I found some very different telegrams from those days:

On July 19, the holy man wrote a telegram predicting peace: "I believe in, I hope for, peaceful rest. A great crime is being undertaken, we are not participants."

But the prediction did not come true; war began—and Grigory predicted victory. Yes, as always, he predicted what his masters wanted to hear.

July 20, 1914: "The criminals shall receive all evil and cunning a hundredfold. . . . Strong is the Lord's grace, beneath its shelter we shall remain in greatness."

But when he returned to Petersburg and sensed Alix's casting about, Rasputin attempted to revive his apocalyptic predictions. Nicholas forbade him to visit the palace. As always, the Holy Devil did a turnabout just in time. Now he was declaring to his admirers: "I am glad about this war. It will rid us of two great evils: drunkenness and German friendship."

Chapter 7

A NOVEL IN LETTERS

The German embassies were burned. The Literary and Artistic Circle expelled anyone with a German name. The future Prime Minister Boris Sturmer considered changing his German name. Petersburg was renamed Petrograd.

All debates in the Duma were forgotten. Unity, unity! All discord in the large Romanov family was forgotten.

To his joy, now, during this national war, Nicholas gained the right to pardon—and his brother Misha returned to Russia. Only to perish there a few years later. Unity, unity!

The story of his great-grandfather flickered before him: like the war with Napoleon, this would be a patriotic war. The entire people. Unity, unity! He set out for Moscow, the ancient capital, the symbol of the Fatherland.

The Kremlin. The emperor and the family entered the white marble St. George Hall, Alexei (as usual he was sick, having hurt his leg) carried by his sailor-companion; alongside the tsaritsa was her sister Ella.

Maurice Paléologue recorded the emperor's inspired words: "A magnificent impulse has gripped all Russia, without distinction for tribe or nationality. Hence, from the heart of the Russian land, I send my valiant warriors fervent greeting. God is with us!"

Outside Assumption Cathedral, by the bell tower of Ivan the Great, there were immense crowds. The bell chimes drowned out their ecstatic cries, and the marshal of the court, Count Benckendorff, gazing at the smiling crowd, spoke triumphantly and mockingly: "Here's the revolution they promised us in Berlin!"

Yes, warnings had come from Berlin: if there is war, it may well end in revolution in Russia. Actually, there had been many such warnings earlier as well, at the very start of Nicholas's reign. But now all was forgotten: smiling shouts the people were greeting the tsar's family. There was joy on Alix's face, for the first time in many months. Her dream had come true. How unexpectedly it had been achieved, this long-awaited unity—the people and the tsar!

In the golden dusk of the ancient Assumption Cathedral, the trembling flames of candles, court singers in silver garments from the sixteenth century, the source of the Romanov dynasty. The Divine Liturgy was read, and the precious stones on the brocade of the clergy's vestments flickered in the candlelight.

In just three years, lost in wintry Siberia, they would recall this ringing of bells, this ecstasy of the people at the sight of their emperor.

"Official and private information reaching me from all over Russia is one and the same. The same popular exclamations and reverential zeal, the same rallying around the tsar. . . . No dissent whatsoever. The difficult days of 1905 seem to have been crossed out of their minds. Holy Russia's collective soul has not expressed such power since 1812," wrote the French ambassador.

On what a triumphant note this epilogue began.

"Everything has been closed up, all the revolutions have hidden themselves away, everyone's thoughts are of common service to the Homeland. One breathes very easily in this pure atmosphere, which has become almost unknown among us," wrote a Duma deputy.

In 1914 sadness bordering on despair reigned among the Bolshevik revolutionaries.

The Bolshevik leaders were scattered across the world: Lenin, Zinoviev, and Trotsky were in hopeless emigration. Actually, no one in Russia gave them the slightest thought now, except maybe the police.

Apathy and hopelessness had gripped the exiled revolutionaries. A most curious company gathered that year in Turukhansk exile: a certain young Georgian spent entire days on his cot, his face to the wall. He had stopped taking care of himself, had even stopped washing his dishes, and the dog licked his plate. His name was Joseph, and one of his party names was Stalin. In just four years he would be living behind the Kremlin Wall, right where the tsar and his family were now.

Here was another resident of Turukhansk exile. He too had fallen into a severe depression. Then, in September 1914, another exiled Bolshevik, Sverdlov, ran into him here. Sverdlov was linked with him not only by a commonality of views but also by an old and fond friendship. It was with chagrin that Sverdlov wrote his wife: "I spent a few days with George. He's not doing very well. . . . It is absolutely impossible for him to live away from turbulent activity. We need to find some outlet for his energy."

"George" was one of Goloshchekin's party names. Thus two old friends met in Turukhansk—Goloshchekin and Sverdlov, the two future organizers of the execution of the tsar and his family.

And Ekaterinburg, where the last tsar parted with his life, would be renamed Sverdlovsk after one of these two friends now in exile.

Grand Duke Nicholas Nikolaevich became commander-in-chief, and soon afterward the Tsar of All the Russias set out for the front to join the army, to Headquarters at Baranovitchi.

The tsar went to war, and the tsaritsa wrote him letters. "The tsar went to war"—that is how fairy tales used to start. Once upon a time, in another century, preparing to become the rulers of the country, they had written each other endless letters. Now, on the eve of his farewell to the throne, everything was repeating itself. Between these two streams of letters lay their entire life. A life that did not require them to resort to the pen, for in twenty years of marriage they had rarely been apart. And here it was: war.

As once before, they wrote each other in English. Many years had passed since she had come to Russia, but she still thought in the language of her grandmother Victoria. She placed a cross at the end of her letters: "Save and protect."

"*J* REREAD YOUR LETTERS AND TRY TO IMAGINE IT IS MY BELOVED TALKING TO ME"
In their letters, they carried on a conversation. Here I take snatches from their vanished speech.

She: "Ts[arskoe] S[elo], Sept. 19th 1914. My own, my very own sweet One. I am so happy for you that you can at last manage to go, as I know how deeply you have been suffering all this time—yr. restless sleep has been even a proof of it. . . . Except all I go through with you & our beloved country & men I suffer for my 'small old home' & her troops & Ernie. . . . egoistically I suffer horribly to be separated—we are not accustomed to it & I do so endlessly love my very own precious Boysy dear. Soon 20 years that I belong to you & what bliss it has been. . . .

"Sept. 20th 1914. Oh, my love! It was hard bidding you goodbye and seeing that lonely pale face with big sad eyes at the waggon-window—my heart cried out, take me with you. . . . I came home and then broke down, prayed—then lay down and smoked to get myself into order. When eyes looked more decent I went up to Alexei and lay for a time near him on the sopha in the dark."

He: "Headquarters, 22 September, 1914. . . . How terrible it was parting from you and the dear children, though I knew that it was not for long. The first night I slept badly, because the engines jerked the train roughly at each station. I arrived here the next day at 5.30; it was cold and raining hard. Nicolasha met me at the station at Baranovitchi. . . .

"[The officers] made a long and interesting report to me in their train, where, as I expected, the heat was terrible! . . .

"Beloved mine, I kiss you again and again. . . . I am quite free and have time to think of my Wify and my family. It is strange, but it is so."

She: "Sept. 24th, 1914. . . . Sweetheart, I hope you sleep better now, I cannot say that of myself, the brain seems to be working all the time and never wanting to rest. Hundreds of ideas and combinations come bothering one—I reread your dear letters several times and try to think its Lovy speaking to me. Somehow we see so little of each other, you are so much occupied and one does not like to bother with questions when you are tired after your reports and then we are never alone together. . . .

"25th. . . . This miserable war, when will it ever end. William, I feel sure must at times pass through hideous moments of despair, when he grasps that it was he, and especially his antirussian set, wh. began the war and is dragging his country into ruin. All those little states, for years they will continue suffering from the aftereffects. It makes my heart bleed when I think of how hard Papa and Ernie struggled to bring our little country to its present state of prosperity. . . . Prayers and implicit trust in God's mercy alone, give one strength to bear all. And our Friend helps you carry yr. heavy cross and great responsibilities—and all will come right, as the right is on our side." ("Our Friend," "Gr.," or "He"—this is what she called the Holy Devil in her correspondence. This third party was constantly present. She would mention him hundreds of times in her letters.)

Nicholas returned to Tsarskoe Selo. And soon again—"the tsar went to war." As always, in the train car he found her letter. It was a ritual.

She: "Oct. 20th. . . . Twenty years to-morrow that you reign & I became orthodox! How the years have flown, how much we have lived through together. . . .

"Oct. 22nd 1914. . . . How vile one having thrown bombs from aeroplans on to King Albert's [the Belgian king] Villa. . . . thank God no harm was done but I have never known one trying to kill a sovereign because he is one's enemy during the war!" (They were still living in the nineteenth century, and the new iron age shocked them.)

"Oct. 24th 1914. . . . There were many wounded . . . one officer had been 4 days in Olga's hospital and said there was not such a second sister."

Now the empress was working in the hospital alongside her daughters.

"Oct. 27th 1914. . . . Oh this miserable war! At moments one cannot bear it any more, the misery & bloodshed break one's heart. . . . All over the world losses! Well, some good must come out of it, & they wont all have shed their blood in vain. Life is difficult to understand—It must be so—have patience; that is all one can say— One does so long for quiet happy times again! But we shall have long to wait."

He: "27 October, 1914. . . . At last I am able to write a few lines. . . . I found old Petyusha [Prince Peter of Oldenburg, husband to the tsar's sister Olga]. . . . They spent three hours under the fire of the Austrian heavy artillery. . . . Petya conducted himself with the utmost coolness and requests an award for himself; I therefore gave him the Arms of St. George, which made him nearly mad [with joy].

. . . I had the pleasure of spending the whole of Saturday with Misha, who has become quite his old self and is again charming."

Yes, Michael Alexandrovich and his wife, who now bore the title Countess Brasova, were back. Misha would receive the Cross of St. George, commanding an irregular cavalry. They were alike, Nicky and Misha. They both loved their wives very much, and Misha, like Nicky, worried about his wife's nerves; Countess Brasova had not forgiven her humiliation. Her salon would open the doors wide to the Duma's left-wing deputies. "In court circles she is even accused of betraying tsarism. . . . She says things for which someone else would have been sentenced to twenty years in Siberia," wrote Paléologue.

Again Nicky is at Tsarskoe Selo, only soon, once again. . . .

She: "Nov. 17th 1914. . . . Once more the hour of separation has come—& always equally hard to bear . . . when you are gone . . . a bit of my life gone—we make one. . . . You always bring revival as our Friend says . . . comforting to know His prayers follow you—It is good you can have a thorough talk with N[icholas Nikolaevich] & tell him your opinion of some people & give him some ideas."

News had already reached "our Friend" that the commander-in-chief was gathering evidence against him. He complained to "Mama"—and now Alix asked Nicholas to suggest "a few ideas" to the commander-in-chief.

She: "Our last night together, its horribly lonely without you—and so silent—nobody lives in this story. Holy angels guard you."

He: "18 November, 1914. My beloved Sunny and darling Wify. . . . I have read your sweet, tender letter with moist eyes. This time I succeeded in keeping myself in hand at the moment of parting, but it was a hard struggle. . . . My love, I miss you terribly—more than I can express in words. . . . I shall try to write very often, as, to my amazement, I have come to the conclusion that I can write while the train is in motion. My hanging trapeze has proved very practical and useful. I swing on it many times and climbed up it before meals. It is really an excellent thing for the train, it stirs up the blood and the whole organism."

From the letter of Konstantin Sheboldaev, a pensioner who had worked for the Ministry of Internal Affairs:

"When I arrived in Sverdlovsk I was shown the Ipatiev house. At that time it was already a special attraction, for the select—visit the house where the tsar's family was shot. By the way, near the fence they showed me the place where he had his trapeze. When he arrived he immediately hung it and began swinging. His feet went high over the fence. At that moment they immediately decided to put up a double fence."

She: "No. 19. . . . Nov. 20th 1914. There is a belated gnat flying around my head whilst I am writing to you. . . . Dearest Beloved— I kiss yr. cushion morn and evening and bless it and long for its treasured master. . . . It's quite mild weather. Baby is going in his motor and then Olga . . . will take him to the big palace to see the officers who are impatient for him. I am too tired to go and we have at 5 1/4 an amputation . . . in the big hospital. . . . My nose is full of hideous smells from those blood-poisoning wounds."

"*H*OW CLOSE DEATH IS ALWAYS"
General Samsonov's army perished in the swamps. The terrible defeats and losses were cooling popular enthusiasm. The wounded, the refugees, the sweat, blood, and dirt. All Europe was heaped in this.
    She: "Nov. 24th 1914. . . . The news from out there make one so anxious—I don't listen to the gossip of town which makes one otherwise quite serious, but only believe what Nicolasha lets know. Nevertheless I begged A[nya] to wire to our Friend that things are very serious and we beg for his prayers. . . .
    "Nov. 25th 1914. . . . In great haste a few lines. We were occupied all morning—during an operation a soldier died—it was too sad —the first such time it had happened to the Princess . . . the girlies were brave—they and Ania had never seen a death. . . . It made us all so sad as you can imagine—how near death always is."

At that time he was on his way to the Caucasus via the larger Cossack villages.
    He: "25 November, 1914, in the train. My beloved, darling Sunny! . . . We [he had taken with him on his journey Nikolai Pavlovich Sablin, his aide-de-camp and one of the closest members of his retinue] are passing through picturesque country which is new to me, with beautiful high mountains on one side and steppes on the other. . . . I sat for a long time at the open door of the carriage and

breathed in the warm fresh air with delight. At each station the platforms are crowded with people, especially children . . . they are charming with their tiny *papakha* [fur caps] on their heads. . . . The train is jolting terribly, so you must excuse my writing. After the hospitals I looked in for a minute at the Kouban Girls' Institute and at a large orphanage dating from the last war, all of them Cossack girls. . . . They look well and unconstrained, here and there a pretty face. . . . This country of the Cossacks is magnificent and rich; a large number of orchards. They are beginning to be wealthy, above all they have an inconceivably high number of small infants. All future subjects. This all fills me with joy and faith in God's mercy; I must look forward in peace and confidence to what lies in store for Russia."

She: "Nov. 28th 1914. My very own precious One! [I am] glad you two sinners had pretty faces to look at—I see more other parts of the body, less ideal ones!!"

Again he returned and left.

She: "Dec. 14th 1914. . . . Sunbeam [Alexei] has just gone out in the donkey sledge—he kisses you—he can put the foot down. . . . How horrid it was saying goodbye to you in Moscou, seeing you stand there amongst heaps of people. . . . I had to bow and look at them too and smile and could not keep my eyes fixed on you as should have wished to. . . .

"Dec. 15th 1914. My beloved Darling, . . . and now Botkin got the news from the regiment that his son was killed as he could not surrender—a German officer, prisoner told the news; poor man is quite broken down. . . . My heart is still enlarged and aches, as does my head. . . . I press you to my heart and kiss you over and over again."

Evgeny Sergeyevich Botkin was the son of the very famous Sergei Botkin, physician to Alexander II and Alexander III, whose sons also became doctors: the famous Sergei and the much more modest but unusually good and sincere Evgeny Sergeyevich.

The empress was complaining more and more of her sick heart. She spent hours in bed trying to vanquish the dull pain in her heart. The most famous European luminaries were summoned to the palace. They did not find heart disease in the tsaritsa, but they did diagnose nervous ailments and ordered a change of regimen.

Alix could not stand it when anyone disagreed with her. This applied to diagnoses of her illness as well. That is why the easygoing Evgeny Sergeyevich was invited to become her personal physician. On one hand, this continued the tradition of Botkins as personal physicians; on the other, the obliging Evgeny Sergeyevich immediately prescribed for the tsaritsa familiar medicine: lie undisturbed. He did this not because he did not understand her condition. The familiar diagnosis *calmed* her; contradicting Alix meant increasing what was for her perilous agitation.

"THE OLD COUPLE SELDOM GET A CHANCE OF BEING TOGETHER"

The year 1914 had come to an end. Petrograd's winter sun was pale— outside the palace windows it sparkled on the blindingly white snow of Tsarskoe Selo. A string of carriages and an auto (the twentieth century!) were waiting at the entrance to the Great Palace. In the mirror gallery, the diplomatic corps had lined up. Nicholas, accompanied by his suite, walked among the diplomats. He had a long conversation with the French ambassador: "The journey I have just completed all the way across Russia has shown me that I am in spiritual accord with my people." And suddenly, in a completely different voice full of worry, he added: "I know of several attempts . . . to spread the idea that I am dispirited and no longer believe anymore in the possibility of crushing Germany and that I even intend to conduct peace negotiations. These are rumors spread by nogoods and German agents."

After ushering in the new year at Tsarskoe Selo, the tsar left for the front at the end of January.

She: "Jan. 22nd 1915. My beloved One, Baby . . . begins to complain a little of his leg & dreads the night. . . . Ania begs me to tell you what she forgot giving over to you yesterday from our Friend, that you must be sure not once to mention the name of the commander-in-chief in your manifest—it must solely come from you to the people. [Her war with Nicholas Nikolaevich was heating up.] . . . Sweet treasure, I am writing in bed, after 6—the room looks big & empty, as the tree has been taken away."

He: "26 January, 1915. . . . I visited Nicolasha and inspected his new railway carriage; very comfortable and practical one, but the heat in it is such that one cannot endure it above half an hour. We discussed thoroughly several important questions and, to my joy, came to an entire agreement. . . . I must say, that when he is alone and in a good humour he is sound . . . a great change in him since the beginning of the war. Life in this isolated place, which he calls his 'hermitage,' and the sense of the crushing responsibility which rests on his shoulders, must have made a deep impression upon his soul; and that, if you will, is a great achievement too."

He dreamed so of accord. He needed to calm her, so he reported: Nikolasha was alone, that is, without those dreadful "Montenegrin women"—Rasputin's enemies.

He: "28 February, 1915. My beloved darling! . . . I was so happy to spend those two days at home—perhaps you noticed it, but I am foolish, and never speak of what I feel. What a nuisance it is to be always so busy and not to have an opportunity for sitting quietly together and having a talk! After dinner I cannot stay indoors, as I long to get out in the fresh air— and so all the free hours pass, and the old couple seldom get a chance of being together."

She: "March 8th 1915. My own beloved One, I hope you get my letters regularly, I write and number them daily, also in my little lilac book. . . . Just heard that Irene [Irina, Sandro and Xenia's daughter, married to Felix Yusupov] had a daughter (thought it would be a girl)."

Reading this letter he must have sighed: how time flies. He well remembered the day when Irina herself was born, it was all so recent, and here Irina was already having. . . .

Vera Leonidovna:

"Handsome Felix had what are called 'grammatical errors,' that is, he was bisexual, plain and simple. . . . Gossip outlives people. But the two of them—they were an amazing couple—they were so attractive. What bearing! Breeding!"

She: "March 9th 1915. . . . What happiness to know, that the day after tomorrow I shall be holding you tight in my arms again, listening to your dear voice and looking into your beloved eyes. . . . I enclose a letter from Masha (from Austria) which she was asked to write to you, for peace's sake. I never answer her letters, of course, now."

In 1915, lady-in-waiting Maria Vasilchikova (Masha) was staying at her villa in Austria. One day, as she later explained, three strangers appeared at her house and proposed that she send the sovereign the following message: "Your Imperial Highness's love of peace is well known throughout all Europe. . . . Austria and Germany are already sufficiently convinced of the force of Russian arms," and so on. In short, the strangers appeared with a proposal from Germany (as yet unofficial) that the three representatives—of Austria, Russia, and Germany—meet secretly to begin talks on a separate peace. It was suggested that the meeting be arranged in Stockholm.

He understood that the story of the letter would engender all the same abominable rumors. When he read "the letter from Masha,"

Nicholas immediately passed it on to his minister of foreign affairs. He wanted everyone to know that he was making no secret of these proposals, for they were unacceptable to him. Nicholas was in a hurry. A paradox: twenty years before, when the straightforward Wilhelm parted with Alix in Berlin, he had been certain that she would become a loyal support for Germany in Russia. However, precisely because she was a German princess, Alix had to be above suspicion in any peace initiative, in any attempt to conclude a peace with Germany. Appreciating the whole horror of the war, dreaming of peace with her homeland, and possessing the most enormous influence over Nicholas's decisions, she was compelled to be silent. To suffer in silence and thereby demonstrate her adherence to all-out war.

Masha was instructed to return to Russia immediately.

Again the tsar was staying at Tsarskoe Selo, only to leave very shortly.

She: "April 4th 1915. . . . Once more you are leaving us, and I think with gladness, because the life you had here, all excepting the work in the garden—is more than trying and tiring. We have seen next to nothing of each other through my having been lain up. Full many a thing have I not had time to ask, and when together only late in the evening, half the thoughts have flown away again."

Indeed, he was not talkative, and when they were together they did not talk. Only separation engendered this spate of affection.

She: "Every possible tender word for to-morrow [their beloved April 8, the anniversary of their engagement, was coming up]. The first time in 21 years we dont spend this anniversary together—How vividly one remembers all! Ah my beloved Boy, what happiness & love you have given me all these years. . . .

"April 8th 1915. . . . How the years go by! 21 already. You know I have kept the grey princesse dress I wore that morning. And shall wear yr. dear brooch."

At about that time Vasilchikova returned to Petrograd—and evidently brought with her letters from Germany.

She: "April 17th 1915. . . . I had a long, dear letter fr. Erni—I will show it you upon your return. He says that 'if there is someone who understands him (i.e., you) & know what he is going through, then it is me.' He kisses you tenderly. He longs for a way out of this dilemma, that someone ought to begin to make a bridge for discussion. So he had an idea of quite privately sending a man of confidence to Stockholm, who should meet a gentleman sent by you (privately) that they could help disperse many momentary difficulties. He had this idea, as in Germany there is no real hatred against Russia. So he sent a gentleman to be there on the 28. . . . So I at once wrote an answer . . . & sent it the gentleman, telling him you are not yet back, so he better not wait—& that tho one longs for peace, the time has not yet come. I wanted to get all done before you return, as I know it would be unpleasant for you."

How she hoped he would suddenly say, "The time has come." In vain.

May 6 was approaching.

She: "May 4th 1915. . . . So sad we shall not spend your dear birthday together—the first time! . . . It is not an easy nor light cross He has placed upon yr. shoulders—would that I could help you carrying, in prayers & thoughts I ever do. I would yearn to lessen yr. burden—so much you have had to suffer in those 20 years—& you were borne on the day of the long-suffering Job too, my poor Sweetheart."

"*I* T IS EASIER FOR ME TO PUT IT DOWN ON PAPER— OWING TO STUPID SHYNESS''

She: "June 13th. . . . I am sad that your dear heart does not feel right, please let Botkin see you upon yr. return. . . . I feel so awfully for those who have anything with the heart, suffering from it myself for so many years. Hiding ones sorrow, swallowing all, makes it so bad. . . . Your eyes seemed like it at times. Only always tell it me, as I have after all enough experience with heart complains & I can perhaps help you. Speak about all to me, talk it out, cry even, it makes it phisically too, easier sometimes. . . .

"June 14th 1915. . . . Then he [Grand Duke Paul] mentioned another thing to me wh. tho' painful its better to warn you about— namely, that since 6 months one speaks of a spy being at the Headquarters & when I asked the name, he said Gen. Danilov [one of Russia's most talented generals]. . . . Try & have an eye upon the man & his doings."

Defeats at the front compelled him to look for scapegoats, and he found a way: spies. Spy mania began—a spy hunt. At first they wanted to make Jews into spies. A field court-martial in Dvinsk hung

several for espionage. Subsequently it turned out that they were
innocent and were posthumously vindicated, but by that time Grand
Duke Nicholas Nikolaevich had already hatched a different plan: the
commander-in-chief decided to go hunting for much bigger game.

So arose the famous affair of the German spy Colonel Myasoedov. With the help of Myasoedov's testimonies, Nikolasha got
his main enemy, War Minister Vladimir Sukhomlinov. In June
Sukhomlinov resigned from his ministerial post. From Sukhomlinov
a thread stretched, via his wife, to "our Friend." And that meant to
Alix. The "German spy"—what could be simpler!

Alix decided to show that she too was taking part in this universal
occupation of spy catching. She found her own: Quartermaster General Danilov, one of the most talented and evil-tongued generals at
Headquarters, and her "Friend's" natural enemy.

She: "June 15th 1915. . . . I am eagerly awaiting your promised
letter. . . . I went to Mavra for an hour [the wife of Grand Duke
Konstantin Konstaninovich, K.R.], she is calm & brave—Tatiana
[K.R.'s daughter] looks awful & yet thinner & greener."

In early June, K.R. passed away at his palace in Pavlovsk. Not
long before, the youngest and most brilliant of his sons, Oleg, had
been mortally wounded at the front during an attack. K.R. himself
had shut the young man's eyes. The death of his favorite son had
hastened K.R.'s own end. The poet was the last Romanov to be
buried with ceremony in the Cathedral of Saints Peter and Paul.

She: "June 16th 1915. . . . Your sweet smelling jasmine I put in
my gospel—it reminded me of Peterhof. . . . The afternoon I remained on the balkony—I wanted to go to Church in the evening,
but felt too tired. The heart is, oh, so heavy & sad—I always remember what our Friend says & how often we do not enough heed His
words. He was so much against yr. going to the Headquarters, because people there get round you & make you do things, wh. would
have been better not done. . . . When He says not to do a thing &
one does not listen, one sees ones fault always afterwards. . . .
That can mean no good. He [Nikolasha] grudges no doubt
Gr[igory]'s visits to our house & therefore wants you away from him,
at the Headquarters. If they only knew how they harm instead of
helping you, blind people with their hatred against Gr.! You remember *dans Les amis de Dieu* it says a country cannot be lost whose
Sovereign is guided by a man of God's. Oh let him guide you more."

He: "16 June, 1915. My beloved Sunny, I thank you with all my
heart for your sweet, long letter. . . . With regard to Danilov, I
think that the idea of his being a spy is not worth an empty eggshell."

She: "June 17th 1915. My very own darling, . . . Wify ought to send you bright & cheery letters, but its difficult, as am feeling more than lowspirited & depressed these days—so many things worry me. Now the Duma is to come together in August, & our Friend begged you several times to do it as late as possible. . . . Here they will try to mix in & speak about things that do not concern them. Never forget that you are & must remain an authocratic Emperor—we are not ready for a constitutional government. N[ikolasha]'s faults & Wittes it was that the Duma exists, & it has caused you more worry than joy. . . . Forgive my writing all this, but I feel so utterly miserable, & as tho' all were giving you wrong advises & profitting of your kindness. Hang the Headquarters. . . . You are remaining still long away, Gr. begged not—once all goes against his wishes my heart bleeds in anguish & fright;—Oh, to keep & protect you fr. more worries & miserys, one has enough more than the heart can bear."

She had already received news: Nikolasha was planning to bring charges against Rasputin. Good Nicky might not understand, he might believe him!

Meanwhile, the spy business had already reached Rasputin's vicinity. Was he really a German spy? Of course not. He served the family loyally. But he had a problem: Alix kept demanding new predictions, and he could not err. Therefore Rasputin put together his own think tank in his apartment on Gorokhovskaya: sharp operators and industrialists—"smart men." He was sharing military information with them that came from the tsar, which he discussed with them, whereupon the cunning man grasped what his next prophecy should be. Of course, since one of those "smart men" could have represented German intelligence on Gorokhovskaya, proof was evidently not impossible to find. But the commander-in-chief took the usual route: instead of patiently preparing an espionage case, he bit at what the Holy Devil had held out to him—the scandal at the Yar restaurant—and fell into Rasputin's trap. Familiar with the peripeteiae of the Moscow scandal, the commander of the Gendarme Corps, Dzhunkovsky, prepared a report on Grigory's escapades, which Nikolasha rushed out.

She: "June 22nd. . . . My enemy Dzhunkovsky . . . has shown that vile, filthy paper (against our Friend) to Dmitri who repeated all to Paul. . . . Such a sin; & as tho' you had said to him, that you have had enough of these dirty stories & wish him to be severely punished. . . . You see how he turns your words & orders round— the slanderers were to be punished & not he [Rasputin]—& that at Headquarters one wants him to be got rid of (this I believe)—ah, its so vile. . . . If we let our Friend be persecuted we & our country shall suffer for it. . . . Ah, my Love, when at last will you thump with your hand upon the table & scream at Dzhu[n]kovsky & others? . . . One does not fear you . . . they must be frightened of you. . . . If Dzhunkovsky is with you, call him, tell him you know . . . he has shown that paper in town & that you order him to tear it up & not to dare speak of Gregory as he does & that he acts as a traitor & not a devoted subject, who ought to stand up for the Friends of his Sovereign, as one does in every other country. Oh my Boy, make one tremble before you. . . . You are always too kind & all profit. It cannot go on like that."

Indeed, the commander-in-chief made a long report to the tsar. Big, ferocious Nikolasha shouted in the red-hot heat of his train car. At first all his accusations were quite familiar to the tsar: Rasputin's debauchery and so on.

But then the commander-in-chief's speech became frightening: German agents had access to Rasputin's home, everything being done at Headquarters was becoming known in the Gorokhovskaya apartment through the trusting empress—and then. . . .

"I never knew about any of this. . . . I could never even have imagined"—was all the distraught tsar could say. Then Nikolasha proposed bringing Alexandra Feodorovna to Headquarters to show her the report and put an end to the Friend. "Resolve the matter within the family"—here at Headquarters!

Nicholas agreed. Right now he wanted only one thing: to escape from this train and go home, to Tsarskoe Selo. He was already beginning to fear that they might simply not let him go. En route, calmer, he understood that all this was emotion and conjecture, that there was no real proof of treason. All that remained were stories about their Friend's dissipation.

When she found out the whole story of what had happened at Headquarters, she fell into a febrile delirium and kept begging to let her keep Baby and not shut her up in a monastery. What did Alix's cry not to shut her up in a monastery mean? "Is the Sovereign indeed powerless to shut up in a monastery the woman who is ruining him and Russia, the evil genius of the Russian people and the Romanov dynasty?" That is what the monarchist Purishkevich would write in his diary a year later (so this was not merely the fruit of Alix's sick imagination).

Evidently, Nicholas had received an important report at Tsarskoe Selo. More than likely Rasputin collected the information; he had direct links to the secret police. As Alix would later write: "If [the tsar] had not taken N. N.'s place, he would have been dashed from the throne." The report told Nicholas that there was in fact a plot.

Was this all Rasputin's idea? Alexandra Feodorovna's idée fixe?

Or, indeed, had the camarilla, sensing as in 1905 impending catastrophe, decided to replace Nicholas with Nikolasha again?

The diary of Grand Duke Andrei Vladimirovich, looking back on events of the previous years, includes this note for December 29, 1916: "Then Dehn [the tsaritsa's friend Lili Dehn] conveyed the portion of her conversation with Alix that had to do with Nikolasha. Alix had assured Dehn that she had documents in her hands proving that Nikolasha wanted to sit on the throne. That was why he had to be removed."

It was clear to the tsar that this time at Headquarters things would come to no good. The commander-in-chief would demand that Rasputin be removed, which would kill Alix. Perhaps even the harshest measures for Alix herself, knowing that Nicholas would never consent to that. He would fall into a trap, though: they would not let him leave Headquarters, and he would be left with no choice but to abdicate. This secretive man did not want to insult Nikolasha with his suspicions. He simply announced to the ministers: "At this critical moment, the country's supreme leader must stand at the army's head." This decision seemed insane to everyone. He had no other solution, though. Soon after, rumors circulated in Petrograd that the tsar had deposed Nikolasha and made himself commander-in-chief. This was a shock. Nicholas Nikolaevich had authority; the weak tsar was not any more popular in the army than in society at large, but even in the army there were rumors about the German tsaritsa, about her dealings with the enemy, about the dirty holy man.

His mother realized that Nicholas's actions were a catastrophe.

Little K.'s gentle friend Grand Duke Andrei Vladimirovich wrote in his diary on August 24, 1915:

"This afternoon I was at Aunt Minnie's [Empress-Mother Marie Feodorovna] and found her terribly despondent. . . . She believes that the removal of N[icholas] N[ikolaevich] will lead to N[icholas II]'s inevitable ruin. . . . She kept asking, 'Where are we going? Where are we going? It isn't Nicky, he is . . . he is sweet, and honest, and good—it's all her doing. . . . She alone is responsible for all that is going on. It was not my dear boy who did this!'

"When Mama went to see her, she added as well that she was

reminded of the times of Emperor Paul I, who in his last year began removing everyone loyal, and our great-great-grandfather's sad end haunts her in all its horror. . . . Not once in history since the times of Peter I has a tsar himself stood at the head of his armies. All such attempts, both under Alexander I in 1812, and under Alexander II, have yielded instead a sorry result."

Nicholas left for Headquarters. This was the most difficult departure for him. He had to announce his decision to the commander-in-chief, the enormous Nikolasha, before whom he was unwillingly shy, in his red-hot train car.

On the train, a letter awaited him as always:

She: "Aug. 22nd 1915. . . . Never have they seen such firmness in you before . . . proving yourself the Autocrat without wh. Russia cannot exist. . . . Forgive me, I beseech you, my Angel, for having left you no peace . . . but I too well know yr. marvelously gentle character. . . . I have suffered so terribly, & phisically overtired myself these 2 days, & morally worried (& worry still till all is done at the Headquarters & Nikolasha goes) only then shall I feel calm. . . . You see they are afraid of me & so come to you when alone—they know I have a will of my own when I feel I am in the right—& you are now—we know this, so you make them tremble before your courage & will. God is with you & our Friend for you. . . . His holy angels guard & guide you. . . . I am near & with you for ever & ever & none shall separate us."

Nikolasha understood immediately: the game was lost. The former commander-in-chief conducted himself impeccably.

He: "25 August, 1915. . . . Thank God it is all over, and here I am with this new responsibility on my shoulders! But God's will be fulfilled. . . . The whole morning of that memorable day, Aug. 23, while coming here, I prayed much and read your first letter over and over again. The nearer the moment of our meeting, the greater the peace that reigned in my heart. N[ikolasha] came in with a kind, brave smile, and asked simply when I would order him to go. I answered in the same manner that he could remain for two days; then we discussed the questions connected with military operations, some of the generals, and so forth, and that was all. The following day at lunch and dinner he was very talkative and in a very good mood, such as we have not seen him in for many months. . . . The expression on his adjutant's face was of the gloomiest—it was quite amusing."

Thus Nicholas II became commander-in-chief of a retreating army.

From that moment on, with all her energy, with all her passion, her invincible, hysterical will, Alix began to help him lead the country and the army.

She: "Aug. 30th 1915. My own beloved darling. . . . [Duma member] Guchkov ought to be got rid of, only how is the question, war-time—is there nothing one can hook on to have him shut up? He hunts after anarchy & against our dynasty, wh. our Friend said God would protect."

At that time vile drawings, shameful conversations about the commander-in-chief's wife and about the country's ruler became commonplace.

She: "Botkin told me that a certain Gorodinsky (Anna's friend) overheard a conversation on a train between two gentlemen saying nasty things about me. He slapped them both."

He: "31 August, 1915. . . . How grateful I am to you for your dear letters! In my loneliness they are my only consolation, and I look forward to them with impatience. . . . Now a few words about the military situation—it looks threatening in the direction of Dvinsk and Vilna, grave in the centre towards Baranovitchi, and good in the South. . . . The gravity lies in the terribly weak condition of our regiments, which consist of less than a quarter of their normal strength; it is impossible to reinforce them in less than a month's time, as the new recruits will not be ready, and, moreover, there are very few rifles. . . . We cannot rely on our worn-out railway lines, as in former times. This concentration will only be accomplished towards the 10th or 12th of September. . . . For this reason I cannot decide to come home before the dates indicated. . . . Your charming flowers, which you gave me in the train, are still standing on my table before me—they have only faded a little."

She: "Sept. 4th 1915. My own beloved darling. . . . Why don't we have a telephone run from your room to mine, as Nikolasha and Stana do. It would be fantastic & you could tell me good news or discuss a question. . . . We would try not to pester you, since I know you do not like to talk—but this would be for our exclusive, private conversation, & we would be able to speak without concern that someone was listening in. This could be useful in an extreme instance, to say nothing of how comforting it would be to hear your tender voice!

"Sept. 7th 1915. . . . Cold, windy, & rainy. . . . I have read through the newspapers—nothing written that we left Vilna—again very mixed, success, bad luck. . . .

"Sept. 9th. . . . only don't send Dmitri, he is too young & it makes him conceited—wish you could send him off! Only don't say its I who ask this."

She either loved or hated. Whichever it was, it was total.

"Sept. 11th 1915. Sad to think summer is over & endless winter awaits us soon. . . . Is it true that they intend to send Guchkov & some others from Moscou as deputation to you? A railway accident in wh. he alone wld. suffer wld. be a real punishment fr. God. . . . Show yr. fist . . . be the master & lord; you are the Autocrat & they dare not forget it, when they do, as now, woe into them. . . . I fear Misha [Nicholas's brother] will ask for his wife to get a title—she cant—she left two husbands already. . . .

"Sept. 13th 1915. . . . The leaves are turning very yellow and red, I see it from the windows of my big room—Sweetheart, you never give me an answer about Dmitri, why you dont send him back to his regiment. . . . It does not look well, no Granddukes are out, only Boris from time to time, the poor Constantins boys always ill."

He: "14 September, 1915. . . . The weather continues to be lovely. I go out every day in a car with Misha, and we spend a great part of my leisure together, as in former years. He is so calm and cheery—he sends you his very heartiest greetings."

How he wished there were peace in the family.

She: "Sept. 15th 1915. . . . Remember to keep the Image in yr. hand again & several times to comb yr. hair with this comb before the sitting of the ministers. Oh how I shall think of you & pray for you more than ever then, Beloved One. . . . I find [Nikolasha] is taking far too big a suite. . . . its not good coming [to the Caucasus, where the former commander-in-chief had been appointed governor-general] with such a court & clique & I very much dread that they will try to continue making messes,—God grant only that nothing shld. succeed in the Caucasus, & the people show their devotion to you & allow no playing of a grand part."

Again the tsar left Tsarskoe Selo, but this time she sent their son with him.

She: "Oct. 1st 1915. . . . Well there we are again separated—but I hope it will be easier for you whilst Sunbeam is near you—he will bring life into your house & cheer you up. How happy he was to go, with what excitement he has been awaiting this great moment to travel with you alone. . . .

"Oct. 2th 1915. . . . Goodmorning, my precious ones, how did you sleep, I wonder! . . . Oh, how I miss you both! The hour for his prayers . . . please ask whether he remembers them daily.—What will it be to you when I fetch him! . . . It seems to me as tho' you were already gone ages ago, such yearning after you!"

He: "Mogilev. 6 October, 1915. My warmest thanks for your loving letter; I am in despair at not having written once since we left, but really, I am occupied here every minute from 2.30 to 6. And Little One's presence takes up part of my time, too, for which, of course, I am not sorry. . . . It is very cosy to sleep side by side. I say prayers with him every night since the time we were on the train; he says his prayers too fast, and it is difficult to stop him. He was tremendously pleased with the review; he followed me, and stood the whole time while the troops were marching past, which was splendid. Before the evening we go out in a car . . . either into the wood or on the bank of the river, where we light a fire and I walk about nearby. . . . He sleeps well, as I do, in spite of the bright light of his [icon lamp]. He wakes up early in the mornings between 7–8, sits up in bed and begins to talk quietly to me. I answer him drowsily, he settles down and lies quietly until I am called."

Later they returned to Tsarskoe Selo, only to leave together again. He had come to enjoy taking the boy along to Headquarters.

He: "2 November, 1915. When we arrived here by train in the evening, Baby played the fool, pretended to fall off his chair, and hurt his left arm. . . . Yesterday he spent in bed. I explained to every one that he had simply slept badly, and myself as well."

The boy's illness remained a state secret. This was ruinous, for they still could not explain to the country what Rasputin was doing in the palace.

She: "Nov. 5th 1915. . . . How charming Alexei's photographs are. . . . Fredericks asked my opinion, whether to permit that cinema of Baby and Joy [his setter] . . . to be shown in public. . . . Baby told Mr. Gilliard, that it was silly to see him . . . and that the dog looked cleverer than he—I like that."

He: "31 December, 1915. . . . My warmest thanks for all your love. . . . If you only knew how it supports me and how it rewards me for my work, responsibilities and anxieties, and so forth? Indeed, I do not know how I could have endured it all, if God had not decreed to give you to me as a wife and friend! I speak in earnest. At times it is difficult to speak of such truths, and it is easier for me to put it down on paper—owing to stupid shyness."

She: "Dec. 31st 1915. My own Sweetheart, This is the last time writing to you in the year 1915. . . . I don't know how we shall meet the new Year—I likes being in Church—it bores the children. . . . And yr. rooms without our Sunbeam, poor angel!"

Thus began 1916, the last full year of their reign. Alexei spent New Year's at home, at Tsarskoe Selo.

She: "Jan. 4th 1916. . . . Baby seriously writes his diary, only it so funny about it,—as little time in the evening, . . . writes in the afternoon about dinner.—Yesterday as a treat he remained long with me, drew, wrote and played on my bed—and I longed for you to be with us."

I am leafing through the first diary of the heir to the Russian throne. An heir who never did become tsar. It is "The Book of Souvenirs for 1916"—a yellow silk cover, gold edging, and on the back an inscription by the empress: "The first diary of my little Alexei."

Alexei's first entries are written in large, comical letters, almost scribbles. He was already eleven. Because he was always sick, he had gotten a late start on his studies.

"January 1. Got up late today. Tea at 10. Then went to see Mama. Mama doesn't feel good and so she lied all day. Stayed home with a cold. Had lunch with Olga, Tatiana, Marie, and Anastasia. In the afternoon was at Kolya's [Dr. Derevenko's son, Alexei's best friend] and played there. It was a lot of fun. Had dinner at 6, then played. With Mama at dinner at 8. In bed at 10."

And so on—faceless narration, a precise reflection of his father's diary: most important, brevity and no reflection.

"July 8. Bath in the morning. Then a walk and play, before lunch Mama and sister arrived. In the afternoon a ride in the motor. Ran over a dog. Tea with Mama. After dinner in the city garden. Children playing there."

He did not play with them. He could only watch. Any movement was dangerous for him. The days passed steadily. As usual. Everything for him was "as usual."

"February 27. Got up as usual. Was at Nizhnyaya Church. We took Communian [sic], then—as usual. . . .

"February 15. Everything as usual. Papa left at 12. Saw him off. . . .

"March 3. Everything as usual. . . .

"April 7. The same. Confession in bed. . . .

"April 8. The same. Communion in bed."

"The same"—bed, walks, food, prayer, and bed again. The trip to Headquarters was his dream, a fantastic event in his monotonous life, in his "as usual."

She: "Jan. 28th 1916. . . . Once more the train is carrying my Treasure away, but I hope not for long—I know I ought not to say this, & for an old married woman it may seem ridiculous—but cannot help it.—With the years love increases. . . . It was so nice you read to us & I hear your dear voice now always! . . . Oh, could but our children be equally blessed in their married lives. . . . Oh, the lonely night! . . .

"March 5th 1916. . . . I had a collection of English [books] brought me to-day, but I fear there is nothing very interesting amongst them. No great authors already since a long time & in no other country either, nor celebrated artist, or composer—a strange lack. One lives too quickly, impressions follow in rapid succession—machinery & money rule the world & crush all art; & those who think themselves gifted have ill minds.—I do wonder what will be after this great war is over. Will there be a reawakening and new birth in all—shall once more ideals exist, will people be more pure & poetic, or will they continue being dry materialists? So many things one longs to know! I had a vile anon. letter yesterday—happily only read 4 first lines & at once tore it up. . . .

"April 6th 1916. . . . Baby was awfully cheery and gay all day and till he went to bed—in the night he woke up from pain in his left arm and from 2 on scarcely got a moment's sleep, the girls sat with him a good while. Its too despairing for words and he is already worrying about Easter—standing with candles tomorrow in Church. . . . It seems he worked with a dirk and must have done too much —he is so strong that its difficult for him always to remember and think that he must not do strong movements."

In this same letter the tsaritsa wrote about a wounded Jew who was in her hospital. "Tho' in America, he never forgot Russia & suffered much from homesickness & the moment war broke out he flew here to enlist as soldier to defend his country. Now that he has lost his arm serving in our army, got the St. George's medal, he longs to remain here & have the right to live wherever he pleases in Russia, a right the Jews don't possess. . . . One sees the bitterness, & I grasp it . . . one ought not to let him become more bitter & feel the cruelty of his old country."

Thus she complained of her husband's laws.

He: "7 April, 1916. . . . I have made a note on the petition of the wounded Jew from America: 'to be granted universal domicile in Russia.' "

She: "April 8th 1916. Christ has risen! My own sweet Nicky love, On this our engagement day, all my tenderest thoughts are with you. . . . That dear brooch will be worn today."

In July 1916 she traveled to see him at Headquarters, where Alexei was staying with him. For the first time she traveled with the entire family—for a few days.

They "relished their vacation," and again the train carried them back to their beloved Tsarskoe Selo. Once again father and son remained at Headquarters.

He: "13 July. . . . It is I who ought to thank you, dear, for your coming here with the girls, and for bringing me life and sun in spite of the rainy weather. . . . Of course I did not succeed in telling you half of what I had intended, because, when I meet you, having been parted for long, I become stupidly shy, and only sit and gaze at you, which is by itself a great joy to me."

At that time Alix fell into a trap. The case of the spies was dragging on. Along with Sukhomlinov they had already implicated Manusevich-Manuilov, the former agent of the Russian Ministry of Internal Affairs, and the stockbroker Rubinstein, both of whom were close to Rasputin. But this was not the full extent of the situation. Through Rubinstein, Alix had transferred money to her impoverished relatives in Germany unbeknownst to Nicky. How her enemies could twist things! Now she needed a loyal minister of internal affairs who could free them all and finally put an end to this affair, which was so awful for her Friend as well as for her.

"Sept. 7th 1916. My own Sweetheart, . . . Gregory begs you earnestly to name Protopopov [minister of internal affairs]. You know him & had such a good impression of him—happens to be of the Duma (is not left) & so will know how to be with them. . . . He likes our Friend since at least 4 years & that says much for a man."

So a new ruinous name appeared: Protopopov.

She: "Sept. 9th 1916. . . . Went . . . to town . . . to see poor Countess Hendrikov [Gendrikova], who is quite dying—utterly unconscious, but I remembered she had asked me to come when she wld. die. . . . Nastinka [the countess's daughter] very brave only cried when I went away."

A charming lady-in-waiting, Nastenka Gendrikova was devoted to the empress. Only a few months later, when they were deciding who was to accompany the family into exile, Nastenka would be among the first to answer the call.

He: "9 September, 1916. Headquarters. . . . It seems to me that this Protopopov is a good man. . . . Rodzianko has for a long time suggested him for the post of Minister of Trade. . . . I must consider the question, as it has taken me completely by surprise. Our Friend's opinions of people are sometimes very strange, as you know yourself—therefore one must be careful, especially with appoint ments to high offices. . . . This must be thought out very carefully. . . . All these changes make my head go round. In my opinion, they are too frequent. In any case, they are not good for the internal situation of the country, as each new man brings with him alterations in the administration. I am very sorry that my letter has turned out to be so dull."

This ministerial leapfrog continued throughout 1916—until the empire's collapse. Goremykin, Stürmer, Trepov, and Golitsyn succeeded one another at the head of the government.

He was looking for a figure who could reconcile him and the Duma. He did not want to admit that finding such a figure was impossible. What he actually needed was not a new figure but a new principle: a ministry responsible to the Duma. That was what the Duma demanded, but he could not accede. It seemed like a return to the terrible year 1905. Alix was fervently opposed, as was their Friend (who ably echoed his mistress's opinion, as always).

The figure of Alexander Protopopov seemed felicitous to Nicholas. Only recently Protopopov had emerged at the head of the Duma delegation and had enjoyed great success abroad, and Mikhail Rodzianko, Duma chairman, approved of him. It seemed a name had been found that would reconcile him and the Duma. But once the Duma found out that the tsaritsa and Rasputin approved of him, Protopopov's fate was decided. He became detested by all.

Nicholas's fury knew no bounds: he even banged his fist on the table: "Until I appointed him he was fine for them; now he is not because I appointed him."

She: "Sept. 22nd 1916. . . . I scarcely slept at all this night—saw every hour, 1/2 hour . . . on the watch (don't know why, as had spent a lovely, soothing evening). . . . We spoke [with Protopopov] for 1 1/2 hour . . . very clever, coaxing, beautiful manners, speaks also very good French & English. . . . I spoke very frankly to him, how yr. orders are constantly not fulfilled, put aside, how difficult to believe people. . . . I am no longer the slightest bit shy or afraid of the ministers and speak like a waterfall in Russia!!! And they kindly don't laugh at my faults. They see I am energetic & tell all to you I hear & see & that I am yr. wall in the rear . . . eyes & ears. . . .

"Sept. 26th. . . . There—you will say—a big sheet, means she is going to chatter a lot again!—Well, Protopopov dined with A[nya]— she knows him already a year or two. . . . Protopopov has asked to see—wont you tell him to let Sukhomlinov out. . . . Protopopov quite agrees with the way our Fr[iend] looks upon this question. He will tell of Justice, write this down to remember when you see him and also speak to him about Rubinstein to have him quietly sent to Siberia. . . . Prot[opopov] thinks it was Guchkov, who must have egged on the military to catch the man, hoping to find evidences against our Friend. Certainly he had ugly money affairs—but not he alone."

In October 1916, Protopopov was called before a meeting of influential Duma members. A stenographic record was made of the meeting:

" 'We do not want to talk with you, a man who received his appointment through Rasputin and freed the traitor Sukhomlinov.'

" 'I am the personal candidate of the sovereign, whom I now have come to know better and to love,' Protopopov responded, exaltedly. 'All of you have titles, good positions, connections, but I began my career as a modest student giving lessons for fifty kopeks, I have nothing besides the personal support of the sovereign.' "

But this time all of society had united in their hatred for the new minister. The Duma and Russia had been shaken by the speeches of the great Duma orators. Pavel Milyukov, for instance, the leader of the Cadets (Constitutional Democrats), spoke from the Duma rostrum:

"From one end of the country to the other, dark rumors have been spreading about betrayal and treason. These rumors have reached high and spared no one. The name of the empress comes up more and more often along with the names of the adventurists that surround her. What is this—stupidity or treason?"

Milyukov wanted to prove that all this was the government's stupidity, but the country kept repeating: "Treason!"

"The rumors of treason played a fateful role in the army's attitude toward the dynasty," wrote General A. Denikin, the tsarist general who took command of the White forces in the south of Russia after General Kornilov's death.

"More than once I had a horrible thought about the empress plotting with Wilhelm," Grand Duke Kirill Vladimirovich would say after the revolution in an interview for a Petrograd newspaper.

She: "Sept. 28th 1916. . . . What a joy to meet soon—in 5 days!!! Seems incredible. Eating in the fresh air is very healthful for Baby & shall bring 2 camp chairs and folding table for him—then I can sit outside too. We plan to leave Sunday at 3 to be in Mogilev for tea— at 5 on Monday. Alright? After your walk, then I can lie down a while longer."

She: "Oct. 12th 1916. . . . Its with a very heavy heart I leave you again—I hate these goodbies. . . . You are so lonely amongst this crowd—so little warmth around. How I wish you cld. have come for 2 days only, just to have got our Friend's blessing, it would have given you new strength—I know you are brave & patient—but human—& a touch of His on your chest would have soothed much pain & given you new wisdom & energy from Above—these are no idle words—but my firm conviction. . . . I too well know & believe in the peace our Friend can give & you are tired, morally, you cannot deceive old wify!"

"MY POOR FRIEND"
She was right. He was exhausted.
She: "Nov. 1st 1916. My own beloved treasure. . . . So Olga will marry on Saturday—& where will that be?"

This was yet another scandal in the family: after her divorce from Peter of Oldenburg, the tsar's sister Olga married Nikolai Alexandrovich Kulikovsky, a cavalry captain in the Cuirassier Regiment, whose colonel-in-chief was the empress dowager.

Converging on Kiev for the wedding, the large Romanov family closed ranks—the situation in the country was disastrous. The family saw one way out: Nicholas must yield to the Duma's demands and give it the right to appoint ministers. Such an action would free the government from the pernicious influence of Alix and Rasputin and good Nicky from responsibility at this critical moment. And of course, it would mean the immediate removal of the Holy Devil. A family council decided to send Grand Duke Nicholas Mikhailovich, the historian Nicholas Romanov, to see Nicky.

He: "2 November. . . . My precious. Nicolai M. has come for one day; we had a long talk together last night, of which I will tell you in my next letter.—I am too busy to-day. God preserve you, my dearly beloved Sunny, and children. . . . Eternally your old Nicky."

He was being cunning. He simply did not know how to tell her about this conversation. So he decided to send her the letter the family's emissary had given him:

"You have told me many times that you can trust no one, that you are being deceived. If this is so, the same phenomenon must also hold true for your spouse, who loves you ardently but has been led astray thanks to the malicious and utter deception of the people who surround her. You trust Alexandra Feodorovna, which is understandable, but what comes out of her mouth is the result of clever juggling and not the actual truth. If you are not competent to remove this influence from her, then at least guard against those constant interferences and whisperings through your beloved spouse. . . . I have long hesitated to reveal the whole truth, but after your mother and sisters convinced me to do this, I made my decision. You are on the eve of an era of new upheavals—even more, I would say an era of assassination attempts. Believe me: if I urge you thus to free yourself from the chains that have been forged . . . then it is only out of my hope and desire to save you, your throne, and our dear homeland from the most difficult and irreparable consequences."

In conclusion, Nicholas Mikhailovich suggested that the tsar grant "the much desired ministry responsible to the Duma and do so before outside pressure is brought to bear," that is, not in the way the memorable act of October 17, 1905, had come about.

They were threatening him with a new revolution. And reminding him of the last.

She: "Nov. 4th. . . . I read Nikolai's & am utterly disgusted. Had you stopped him in the midle of his talk & told him that, if he only once more touched that subject or me, you will send him to Siberia—as it becomes next to high treason. He has always hated & spoken badly of me since 22 years. . . . But during war & at such a time to crawl behind yr. Mama & Sisters & not stick up bravely . . . for his Emperor's wife—is loathesome & treachery. . . . You, my Love, far too good & kind & soft—such a man needs to be held in awe of you—He & Nikolasha are my greatest enemies in the family, not counting the Montenegrin women—& Sergei. . . . Wife is your staunch One & stands as a rock behind you."

Postscript:

". . . I dreamt I was being operated on: th' my arm was cut off I felt utterly no pain. After a letter came from Nikolai."

Now she began her struggle against the entire Romanov family. She remained intact.

He: "5 November. . . . I am so sorry that I have upset you and made you angry by sending the two letters of N., but as I am in a constant hurry I had not read them, because he had spoken exhaustively of the matter for a long time. But he never once mentioned you, discussing only the stories about spies, factories, workmen, disorders, Ministers, and the general internal situation. Had he said anything about you, you do not really doubt that your dear hubby would have taken your part!"

She: "Nov. 12th 1916. . . . I am but a woman fighting for her Master & Child, her two dearest ones on earth--& God will help me being your guardian angel, only dont pull the sticks away upon wh. I have found it possible to rest [i.e., Rasputin and Protopopov]. . . . What joy to rest to-morrow in your arms to kiss & bless you. . . . True unto death."

Postscript:

"Darling, remember that it does not lie in the man Protopopov or x.y.z., but its the question of monarchy & yr. prestige. . . . Dont think they will stop at him, but they will make all others leave who are devoted to you one by one—then ourselves. Remember, last year yr. leaving to the Army—when also you were alone with us two [her and Rasputin] against everybody, who promised revolution if you went. You stood up against all & God blessed your decision."

She: "Dec. 4th 1916. . . . Show to all, that you are the Master & your will shall be obeyed—the time of great indulgence & gentleness is over—now comes your reign of will & power, & obedience they must be taught. . . . Why do people hate me? Because they know I have a strong will & when am convinced of a thing being right (when besides blessed by Gregory), do not change my mind & that they can't bear. . . . Remember Mr. Philipps [the charlatan mystic Monsieur Philippe from France] words when he gave me the image with the bell. As you were so kind, trusting & gentle, I was to be yr. bell, those that came with wrong intentions wld. not be able to approach me & I wld. warn you. Should Motherdear write, remember the Michels [the Mikhailovich brothers] are behind her.—Don't heed & take to heart—thank God she is not here, but kind people find means of writing & doing harm."

The bell rang and rang. . . . And then the family played its trump: her sister Ella went to Tsarskoe Selo and attempted to explain to her beloved Alix as kindly as possible the horror of the situation, by which she meant Rasputin. But Alix immediately shut her out and cut the conversation short.

Alix saw her sister off at the train, but they parted in silence. Ella would never reappear at Tsarskoe Selo. They would not see each other again.

He: "10 December, 1916. . . . Things do not look too bright in Roumania. . . . In the Dobrudja our troops had to retire to the very Danube. . . . By the 15th of Dec. the concentration of our forces will, I hope, [be] more or less accomplished and perhaps toward Christmas we shall begin our offensive. As you see, the position there is not a happy one."

What was the extent of his participation in the war? An ignorant, weak-willed executor of the wishes of his hysterical wife and Rasputin—that was the answer given by the coming revolution.

But here is another widely known opinion. Winston Churchill wrote about it in *World Crisis:* "Surely to no nation has Fate been more malignant than to Russia. Her ship went down in sight of port. . . . Every sacrifice had been made; the toil was achieved. . . . The long retreats were ended; the munition famine was broken; arms were pouring in; stronger, larger, better equipped armies guarded the immense front. . . . Alexeiff directed the Army and Kolchak the Fleet. Moreover, no difficult action was now required: to remain in presence: to lean with heavy weight upon the far stretched Teutonic line: to hold without exceptional activity the weakened hostile forces on her front: in a word to endure—that was all that stood between Russia and the fruits of general victory. . . .

"The brunt of supreme decisions centred upon him. At the summit where all problems are reduced to Yea and Nay, where events transcend the faculties of men and where all is inscrutable, he had to give the answers. His was the function of the compass needle. War or no war? Advance or retreat? Right or left? Democratise or hold firm? Quit or persevere? These were the battlefields of Nicholas II. Why should he reap no honor for them? . . . In spite of errors vast and terrible, the regime he personified, over which he presided, to which his personal character gave the final spark, had at this moment won the war for Russia."

He: "I am so glad that you were pleased with Novgorod. . . . You saw more there than I did in 1904."

In Novgorod Alix had been to see the famous prophetess, the holy woman Maria Mikhailovna, who lived in the Desyatinna Convent. He hoped her trip would divert her indomitable energy into a new channel, so he could pause for breath.

Subsequently Alix would repeat the legend: Maria Mikhailovna was lying in the darkness when Alix appeared. Then the holy woman suddenly rose up on her bed, climbed down to the floor, and bowed to the ground before the empress. And she said: "You, beautiful lady, shall know suffering." But what was the point of legends if Alix herself described the meeting?

She: "She lay in bed in a small dark room, so they brought a candle for us to see each other. She is 107, weares irons . . . generally always works, goes about, sews for the convicts & soldiers, without spectacles—never washes. And of course, no smell, or feeling of dirt, scraggy grey hair standing out, a sweet fine, oval face with lovely young, shining eyes & sweet smile. She blessed us & kissed us. . . . To me she said: 'And you the beautiful one—dont fear the heavy cross' (several times)—has grey hair and a sweet, delicate, oval face —'for your coming to visit us, two churches will be built in Russia.' . . . Said not to worry about the children, will marry, & could not hear the rest."

Or maybe poor Alix didn't understand what marriage she was talking about. Old-style Russian was hard for the Hessian princess. Her friend Anya preferred "not to hear" it either. The holy woman was speaking of Alix's daughters' being wed to death.

He: "3 December, 1916. . . . Endless thanks for your long interesting letter with the many details of your trip to Novgorod. . . . Well now, about Trepov [in 1916 Alexander Feodorovich Trepov was appointed prime minister]. He was quiet and submissive and did not touch upon the name of Protopopov. . . . He unfolded his plan concerning the Duma—to prorogue it on the 17th of December and reassemble it on the 19th of January so as to show them and the whole country that, in spite of all they have said, the Government wish to work together. . . . I went to pray before the ikon of the Mother of God before this conversation, and felt comforted after it."

She: "Dec. 14th. . . . Scarcely slept this night again. . . . Trepov was very wrong in putting off the Duma now & wishing to call it beginning of January again, the result being . . . nobody goes home & all will remain, fomenting, boiling in Petrograd. . . . Lovy, our Friend begged you to shut it 14th . . . & you see, they have time to make trouble. . . . Be Peter the Great, John [Ivan] the Terrible, Emperor Paul—crush them all under you—now don't laugh, naughty one—but I long to see you with all those men. . . . 'Do not fear,' the old woman said & therefore I write without fear to my agoo wee one."

Her constant pressure had kept him on the brink. Now she had gone too far.

He: "14 December, 1916. . . . Tender thanks for the severe written scolding. I read it with a smile, because you speak to me as though I was a child."

She: "Dec. 15th 1916. . . . Please, forgive me for my impertinent letters, but writes from deepest love—& sometimes driven to exasperation, knowing one cheets you & proposes wrong things. . . . Wish the telephone were not so bad."

He: "16 December, 1916. . . . No, I am not angry with you for the other, written by you. I perfectly understand your desire to help me! But I cannot change the day for the reassembly of the Duma, because the day is already fixed in the Proclamation. . . . Tender greetings and kisses sends to you Your 'poor, weak-willed little hubby.'"

Yes, this time he was implacable.

She: "Dec. 17th 1916. . . . Again very cold & gently snowing. . . . Heart is not famous & don't feel well. You see my heart for some time was bad again. . . . The moral strain of these last trying months on a weak heart of course had to tell . . . the old machine broke down. . . . Has Baby's 'worm' quite been got rid of? Then he will get fatter & less transparent—the precious Boy!"

The end of her letter was finished in pencil—after she learned of what was for her the most dreadful event possible:

"We are sitting together—you can imagine our feelings—thoughts—our Friend has disappeared. Yesterday A[nya] saw him & he said Felix [Prince Yusupov] asked him to come in the night, a motor wld. fetch him to see Irina.—A motor fetched him (military one) with 2 civilians & went away. This night big scandal at Yousupov's house—big meeting, Dmitrii [Pavlovich, Nicholas's cousin], Purishkevich [Vladimir Mitrofanovich Purishkevich, extremely right-wing Duma member], etc. all drunk. Police heard shots, Purishkevich ran out screaming to the Police that our Friend was killed. Police searching & Justice entered now into Yusupov's house—did not dare before as Dmitrii there. Chief of police has sent for Dmitrii. Felix wished to leave to-night for Crimea, [I] begged Protopopov to stop him. Our Friend was in good spirits but nervous these days & for A[nya] too, as Batiushin [the military investigator handling the case of the German spies] wants to catch things against Ania. Felix pretends he never came to the house & never asked him. Seems quite a paw. I still trust in God's mercy that one has only driven Him off somewhere. . . . We women are alone with our weak heads. Shall keep her [Anya] to live here—as now they will get at her next. I cannot & wont believe He has been killed. God have mercy. Such utter anguish. . . . Come quickly—nobody will dare to touch her or do anything when you are here."

They had been plotting Rasputin's murder for a long time. The large Romanov family saw it as the sole means of saving the dynasty. And the Holy Devil knew about it. When the clouds had thickened, he made a brilliant move, as always. He composed a will and prophecy, which he showed to the tsaritsa.

The "Spirit of Grigory Rasputin Novykh" promised:

"Russian Tsar!

". . . Know, that if your relatives commit murder, then not one of your family, i.e., your relatives and children, will live more than two years. . . . The Russian people will kill them. . . . They will kill me. I am no longer among the living. Pray. Pray. Be strong. Worry about your elected family."

Rasputin transmitted it to the empress through his secretary. Imagine what poor Alix felt! She did not show the letter to Nicholas, but the holy man's guard was strengthened. The tsaritsa and her daughters themselves went to ask Rasputin not to receive any guests without her knowledge. They locked up his clothing and so on.

But the cunningly artless holy man outwitted the "accursed aristocrats."

Vera Leonidovna:

"It was a puzzling intrigue in the spirit of my favorite play, *Masquerade*. Dmitry and Felix dreamed it up. Felix was an old enemy of the holy man. Through Mania Golovin he let it be known he was looking to reconcile with the holy man. It was all done very realistically. The holy man knew that Felix wanted to join the Guards; but the tsar, who did not want homosexuals, opposed it. So through poor, unsuspecting Mania, who was certain she was going to reconcile the holy man and her friend Felix, Felix asked the holy man to put in a word for him with Alix, which Rasputin agreed to do. That fateful evening, Grigory was going to see Felix in his palace for a complete reconciliation. He had been promised wine and dancing, of which he was passionately fond. One day I'll tell you how marvelously he danced. That evening he had promised to heal Princess Irina. . . . The legend about the holy man lusting after Irina was created later by the assassins themselves: 'Grigory's filthy intentions toward the daughter of Sandro himself.' All this was supposed to vindicate the assassins. Subsequently there was a legend about how Rasputin had been poisoned with potassium cyanide, but it wasn't poison that took him. In fact, the person who gave him the poison didn't want to take a sin on his soul, so he gave him a harmless powder. . . . When Felix realized the poison wasn't working, he shot him and Rasputin fell. A second legend arose that Felix killed him and he rose up. In fact, he was only wounded. Felix wasn't a murderer, and he was nervous. Rasputin was lying motionless on the pelt of a white bear, and Felix was with him in the room. Rasputin evidently came to and hurled himself on Felix to strangle him, bellowing horribly, like a wounded beast. Imagine what Felix must have felt when the 'corpse' fell on him! Horrified, Felix froze, and Rasputin was able to flee the cellar for the courtyard. He was killed right by the gate, with a revolver, and evidently not completely, because when they rolled him onto a portière to load him into Grand Duke Dmitry's automobile he opened his eyes—and none of them ever forgot that inexpressible look. They had tried to kill Rasputin in the half-cellar."

She (telegram): "Dec. 18th 1916. In your name I order Dmitrii forbidden to leave his house till yr. return. Dmitrii wanted to see me today, but I refused. Mainly he is implicated. The body still not found. When will you come?"

I am leafing through the diaries of the grand duchesses. Olga's diary: "December 17. . . . Father Grigory has been missing since last night. They are looking everywhere. It is terribly hard. The four of us slept together. God help us! . . .

"December 18. . . . Ania is staying with us, since Mama is afraid for her. . . . We have finally learned that Father Gregorii was killed, probably by Dmitrii, and thrown from the bridge by Krestovskii. He was found in the water. No words can say how hard it is. We sat and drank tea, and the whole time we felt that Father Gregorii was with us."

Did Dmitry kill him? This was the end to all her hopes. This is why "No words can say how hard it is."

He (telegram): "18 Dec., 1916. . . . I have only just read your letter. Am horrified and shaken. In prayers and thoughts I am with you. Am arriving to-morrow at 5 o'clock."

Was Rasputin's prediction only a muzhik's cunning or was it dictated by the Holy Devil's dark power? Or both? This drunken, insanely debauched muzhik who had trampled the luxurious floors of their palaces truly was a precursor. The precursor of those hundreds of thousands of terrible muzhiks who would trample their palaces and murder them—and throw their corpses, like carrion, without burial, into the warm July earth.

At first Rasputin's corpse was placed in a crypt at St. Feodor's Cathedral. Then he was buried secretly—not far from the park and palace, under a chapel that was being built. Right under the altar. He was close by as before.

Nicholas's diary:

"December 21. Wednesday. . . . At 9 the whole family went past the photography building and turned right toward the field, where we assisted at a sad scene: the coffin with the body of the unforgettable Grigory, murdered on the night of December 17 by monsters in the home of F. Yusupov, had already been lowered into the grave. Father Alexander Vasiliev finished the eulogy, after which we returned home. The weather was gray with 12 degrees of frost. Walked until reports. . . . In the afternoon took a walk with the children."

Nicholas was firm: The decision was made to banish "the monsters Dmitry and Felix" from Petrograd. His wife's sufferings were not all that forced him to be firm. For a Christian, murder is blasphemous—not only that, the tsar's own relatives had killed the muzhik! The rest of the Romanov family honored the "monsters." At the station Felix was seen off by his father-in-law, Grand Duke Alexander Mikhailovich. How poor Dmitry envied everyone who remained in his beloved Petrograd. How many of his relatives—of those who remained in "beloved Petrograd"—would be killed! Felix and Dmitry, though, the "monsters" banished from the capital, would survive.

For the next few days it was as if Alix had turned to stone. At first she had been violent, shouting "Hang them!," but later she became ominously calm, almost indifferent. She understood that this was the end. The end that the holy man had predicted. Alix showed Nicky the holy man's will, and he tried to calm her: Grigory's behests were being carried out. Trepov, whom the empress (and consequently Grigory) did not like, was being driven out. The decrepit Golitsyn was being appointed prime minister, which for all intents and purposes meant that Protopopov, the holy man's favorite, was to head the government.

Society rebelled. Endless meetings were held—municipal, district, noble—and all against the new government. While everyone was waiting for the revolution, it had already begun. The holy man was right: it began immediately upon his death!

Part II

THE DEATH OF NICHOLAS AND ALEXANDRA

Verily, verily, I say unto you, Except a corn of wheat fall into the ground and die, it abideth alone: but if it die, it bringeth forth much fruit.

JOHN 12:24

Chapter 8

THE FALL OF ATLANTIS

✛

_N_EW YEAR 1917

Frost, the sun secreted behind the clouds. The pure snow of Tsarskoe Selo glittering as if splashed with quicksilver. The sovereign's annual grand entrance in the Great Palace. Another New Year's in the long line of years of his reign.

"1 January. Sunday. The day passed gray, quiet, and warm. . . . At about 3 Misha arrived, and he and I left for the Great Palace to a reception of the Ministers, Suite, and diplomats."

In early 1917 no one had the slightest doubt about the coming revolution. Plots were being hatched in luxurious Petrograd apartments. And in the palaces.

The plot of the grand dukes—here, of course, the name of the army's favorite immediately surfaced: the former commander-in-chief, Grand Duke Nicholas Nikolaevich. Sixteen grand dukes sent an emissary to Tiflis to the out-of-favor Nikolasha. Duma plotters, too, began open negotiations with Nicholas Nikolaevich. In the name of Duma member Prince Georgy Lvov, it was already being openly proposed to Nikolasha that he replace the other Nicholas on the throne. Nicholas Nikolaevich hesitated—and refused. He remained a loyal subject.

The sons of Vladimir Alexandrovich went into action and called the monarchist Purishkevich to the palace of Grand Duke Kirill Vladimirovich. "Still under the impression of my conversation with them, I left the grand duke's palace with the firm conviction that he, Guchkov, and Rodzianko were plotting something inadmissible . . . with respect to the sovereign," Purishkevich wrote in his diary. In fact, this never went beyond seditious conversations either. Many in the large Romanov family at the time could have repeated the words that burst from Grand Duke Nicholas Mikhailovich: "He [the tsar] infuriates me, yet I still love him!"

Endless meetings in Duma members' apartments. General Krymov arrived from the front and told of the tragic situation in the army—the rumors of treason and the numerous defeats. The conclusion: a coup was inevitable.

At this time, as once before in the nineteenth century, the opposition was allying itself increasingly in secret Masonic lodges, which flourished in Russia after the 1905 revolution. By 1917 they had united society's liberal elite, which was fed up with the Rasputin business. The paradox of the situation was that on the eve of 1905, when the police had frightened Nicholas with Masons, Masonry scarcely existed in Russia. Now, on the eve of 1917, when Masonry had become a real force, the police knew little about it. Meanwhile, the Masonic lodges included among their members tsarist ministers, generals, members of the State Council, Duma figures, prominent diplomats, industrialists: P. Balk, minister of finance; N. Pokrovsky, minister of foreign affairs; N. Polivanov, minister of war; Generals V. Gurko, A. Krymov, and N. Ruzsky; K. Dzhunkovsky, the chief of police, and so on. No, they did not want revolution—but they did want changes. Even in the lodges, then, activity was limited to seditious conversations. "Quite enough was done to get someone hanged, but not enough actually to carry out any plans," one of the chief opposition leaders, Duma member Guchkov, would later say. Guchkov was trying to take practical steps: he was beginning to prepare a coup for March, when military units loyal to the Duma would be moved up toward Petrograd. To avoid bloodshed, he was planning to seize the tsar's train and force the tsar to abdicate then and there. But none of the prominent military men (other than Krymov) joined in his plot. "I will never enter into a plot, I have sworn an oath." Many could have repeated this statement by Duma Chairman Rodzianko.

At that time the head of the Petrograd secret police was submitting endless reports to Internal Affairs Minister Protopopov.

January 9: "Alarming mood among the revolutionary underground and widespread propagandization of the proletariat."

January 28: "Events of extraordinary importance, fraught with exceptional consequences for Russian statehood, are not beyond the hills."

February 5: "Animosity is mounting. . . . Spontaneous demonstrations by the popular masses will be the first and last stage on the path to senseless and merciless excesses of the most horrible thing of all—anarchical revolution."

Protopopov blithely shelved the reports. After all, the empress had said: "There is no revolution in Russia, nor could there be. God would not allow it."

Nicholas's diary:

"29 January. Sunday. . . . In the afternoon took a walk and worked in the snow a while. . . . At 6 received old Klopov."

Yes, this was the same Klopov who had come to see Nicholas at the dawn of his reign. Then Klopov had wanted to tell Nicholas the people's truth. He came now one more time, to save his beloved tsar.

After the revolution Klopov worked quietly as a bookkeeper, and he died in 1927. Klopov left a note among his papers about his 1917 audience with Nicholas. He talked to the tsar about the court's egoism, about the government's criminal actions. Nicholas listened with a strange smile on his face, as if he were absent. Klopov left frightened by the incomprehensible equanimity of the tired man who had sat before him.

At this time Nicholas's childhood friend Sandro, Grand Duke Alexander Mikhailovich, wrote Nicholas a letter. He wrote it at several sittings, decided to send it, and then changed his mind.

Nicholas's diary:

"10 February. . . . Sandro arrived at 2 and had a long talk with Alix in my presence in the bedroom."

Alix lay in bed for Sandro's visit, as she was unwell. Sandro kissed her hand, and her lips grazed his cheeks. Sandro wanted to talk with her alone, but Nicky remained. She feared a tête-à-tête.

Later Alexander Mikhailovich told all about his conversation with Alix in his memoirs. But we are all strong in hindsight. It would be more accurate to draw on his own letter, which he wrote to Nicholas at the time and never sent:

". . . We are living through a most dangerous moment in Russia's history. . . . Everyone senses it: some with their mind, some their heart, some their soul. . . .

"Certain forces inside Russia are leading you, and consequently Russia as well, to irrevocable ruin. I say 'you and Russia' wholly consciously, since Russia cannot exist without a tsar. One must remember, nevertheless, that the tsar alone cannot rule a state such as Russia. . . . The current situation, in which all responsibility lies on you and you alone, makes no sense.

". . . Events have shown that your advisers are continuing to lead Russia and you to certain ruin," Sandro repeated. "It leads one to utter despair that you do not care to heed the voices of those who know the state Russia is in and advise you to take the measures necessary to lead us out of chaos.

". . . The government today is the organ preparing the revolution. The people do not want it, but the government is taking every possible measure to create as many dissatisfied people as possible and is succeeding completely at it. We are assisting at an unprecedented spectacle of revolution from above, rather than below."

In his conversation at Alix's bedside, Sandro begged Alix to confine herself to family matters, and Alix cut him off. He persisted. She raised her voice; so did he. During their stormy exchange Nicholas smoked silently. Sandro left, promising that one day Alix would recognize his truth. He kissed her hand in parting but received no parting kiss in response.

The entire conversation with Sandro made Alix see one thing: they wanted to remove Protopopov, whom the holy man had bequeathed to them. She was furious. What they needed was to disband the Duma, not remove devoted people from the throne.

That day Nicholas was forced to listen to a great deal more. He recorded in his diary, laconically and in order as always, the day's chain of events.

"Took a walk with Marie, Olga's ear hurt. Before tea received Rodzianko."

His conversation with the Duma chairman was ominous. The usually restrained Rodzianko was unrecognizable.

Rodzianko: "A change of faces and not only faces but the whole system of government is imperative."

Nicholas: "You keep demanding the removal of Protopopov. But he was your comrade in the Duma. Why do you all hate him so now?"

Rodzianko: "I do demand it. Before I asked, now I demand. Your Excellency, we are on the eve of great events whose outcome we cannot foresee. I have been reporting to you for an hour and a half, but everything tells me you have already selected the most dangerous path—disbanding the Duma. I am convinced that before three weeks are out a revolution will ignite that will wipe away everything, and you will not be able to rule."

When Rodzianko had entered the study to see the tsar, he had run into Alexander Volkov and asked him to note how long he stayed in the sovereign's study.

When the agitated Duma chairman walked out of the study, Volkov said: "You were with His Excellency for exactly twenty-six minutes."

Rodzianko handed his briefcase to the footman who was waiting to carry it to his carriage, waved his hand hopelessly, and said, "It doesn't matter now, it's finished."

But Rodzianko was wrong. This conversation did make an impression. Nicholas yielded.

On the twentieth of February the prime minister, old Golitsyn, returned home from Tsarskoe Selo unusually happy and cheerful. Nicholas himself had suddenly expressed a wish to discuss the question of an accountable ministry. He announced to Golitsyn that he was preparing to appear before the Duma and proclaim his will: to give Russia a ministry that would answer to the Russian parliament.

But on the evening of the same day Golitsyn was called to the palace again. Nicholas informed the astonished prime minister that he was leaving for Headquarters.

Between these two events, of course, there had been a conversation with Alix. That vigilant warrior would not allow him to repeat the concessions of 1905.

By that time Nicholas was very tired. Old Golitsyn sensed his desperate weariness. Subsequently he explained Nicholas's departure for Headquarters, which stunned everyone, as the sovereign's desire "to avoid more reports, meetings, and conversations."

Yes, he was running away—running away from everything: her hysteria, fat Rodzianko, the Duma's fury. From the demands of his mother, his relatives, his friends, and his country.

"Long the weary slave, I conceived a flight."

Rodzianko described in his memoirs how one time Nicholas, having heard his report, walked over to the window.

"Why is it like this, Mikhail Vladimirovich? I was in the woods today—it's quiet there and you forget everything—all these squabbles . . . the human bustle. I felt so good deep down. It's closer to nature there . . . closer to God."

Once in his diary Nicholas wrote, "Dangled my foot in a stream." A tired, lonely man, childlike, splashing his foot in the water.

She was right: his profound loneliness.

Now he wanted to run away from everyone to his loneliness. So he ran to the woods, taking long walks down an empty road.

He explained to her that he would be away for a short time and would be back by March 1, so he was not even taking Baby with him. But she felt a horror at his trip. The empire had exactly ten days to live.

She: "Feb. 22nd 1917. . . . Such deep sadness and alarm at letting you leave without dear Baby—such terrible times for us now!—and even harder apart, I can't stroke you so tired & worried. God truly has sent you a terrible & heavy cross. . . . Our dear Friend in another world prays for you, too now even closer to us, but I would so love to hear His consoling & heartening voice. . . . Lovy, be firm, because the Russians need you to be—at every turn you show love & kindness—now let them feel your fist, as they themselves ask. So many of late have told, that we need the knout. Its strange, but that is the Slav nature. . . . They must learn to fear you, love is not enough. Tho' a child adores his father, he must fear his anger. I embrace you tight and hug your tired head. Oh the lonely nights to come—no Sunny or Sunshine with you. Feel my arms hold you, my lips press tenderly to yours. Eternally together, always inseparable."

Russia was the fist and the knout. These were all very old ideas. Here is the monologue of a Russian monarchist quoted by French Ambassador Maurice Paléologue:

"The tsars founded Russia, and the harshest and cruelest were the best. Without Ivan the Terrible, without Peter the Great, without Nicholas I, there would be no Russia. The Russian people are the most submissive of all when they are sternly mastered, but they are incapable of ruling themselves. No sooner is the bridle loosened than they lapse into anarchy; they need a master, an unlimited master; they walk a straight path only when they feel an iron fist over

Nicholas and the grand dukes on parade at Krasnoe Selo.

Grand Duke Sergei Alexandrovich, uncle of Nicholas II.

*T*he imperial family: Olga, Marie, Nicholas, Alexandra, Anastasia, Alexei, and Tatiana.

*G*rigory Rasputin.

*G*rand Duchess Marie, photographed by Alexandra, Tsarskoe Selo.

*P*rocession of the tsar through Red Square and ceremonial greeting during celebrations for the tricentennial of the Romanov dynasty, Moscow, May 24, 1913.

*R*eligious procession during the Romanov tricentennial, Kostroma, 1913.

$\mathcal{N}$icholas emerging from a coach at the entrance to the Romanov house on Varvarka Street, Moscow, during the Romanov tricentennial, May 25, 1913. The Romanov coat of arms can be seen on the house.

$\mathcal{K}$ostroma Mayor N. K. Shelashinov performs the ritual offering of bread and salt to the tsar, Romanov tricentennial, 1913.

$\mathcal{T}$sar Nicholas II, 1914.

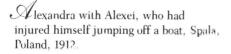
*T*saritsa Alexandra Feodorovna, 1914.

*A*lexandra with Alexei, who had
injured himself jumping off a boat, Spala,
Poland, 1912.

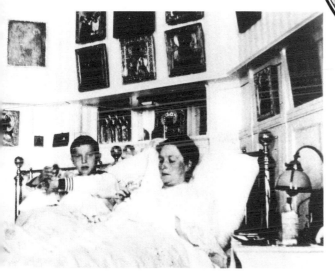

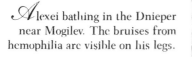
*A*lexei bathing in the Dnieper
near Mogilev. The bruises from
hemophilia are visible on his legs.

*A*lexandra, Olga, and Tatiana after completing their nursing course and receiving diplomas from the International Red Cross Society, 1914.

*W*orld War I: a ward for wounded officers in the Winter Palace, Petrograd, 1916.

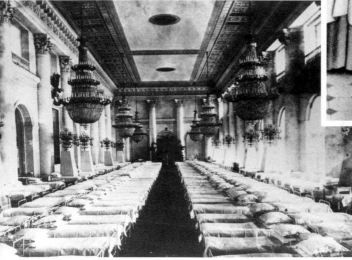

*N*icholas and his family preparing for a meeting with representatives of a town in the south of Russia during World War I.

$\mathcal{N}$icholas before a map of military operations, the western front, World War I.

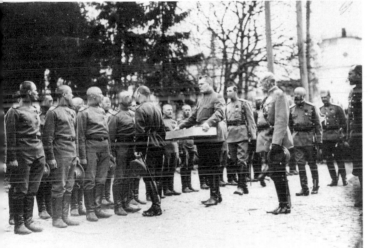

$\mathcal{T}$he tsar exchanges Easter salutations with officers, imperial headquarters, Mogilev, April 11, 1916.

$\mathcal{N}$icholas at headquarters with military representatives of the Allied powers: Colonel Marsengo (Italy), Baron B. de Ricquel (Belgium), General Sir John Hanbury-Williams (England), Nicholas, Marquess de Laguiche (France), and Colonel Londkijevic (Serbia), 1916.

*T*he parlor car on the imperial train in which Vasily Shulgin and Alexander Guchkov accepted Nicholas's abdication in March 1917.

*T*he grand duchesses with shaved heads, under arrest of the Provisional Government, Tsarskoe Selo, 1917.

*N*icholas on a bicycle, in captivity, in Tobolsk, Siberia, 1917.

their head. . . . The knout, we owe it to the Tatars, and it is the best thing they left us."

He (telegram): "Feel again firm, but very lonely. Thank you and Baby for telegrams. Am terribly sad. Kiss you all tenderly."

She: "Feb. 23rd. . . . Well now, Olga & Alexei both have measles & Olga's face is all covered with rash. Baby suffers more in the mouth—a bad cough and sore eyes. They lie in the dark. . . . We are all in summer skirts & white robes, and when we receive somebody (not afraid) we put on dresses. If the others are not to avoid this, I hope they get it quickly. That way is more fun for them & does not last so long."

Alexei had caught the measles from a little cadet who had been excused from school especially to play with the heir. Many there had already had the measles, but the empress did not know that. Now, in her white robe, the empress was rushing among her sick and soon to be sick children and Anya. The measles cut her off from the not very distant capital. She now received reports through the valet Volkov. The fall of the empire began with this illness.

He: "Headquarters. 23 February, 1917. . . . The day was sunny and cold and I was met by the usual public with Alexeyev [the chief of staff] at the head. . . . We had a good talk together for about half an hour. After that I put my room in order and got your telegram telling me of Olga and Baby having measles. I could not believe my eyes—this news was so unexpected. . . . In any case, it is very tiresome and disturbing for you, my darling. Perhaps you will cease to receive so many people?"

He was hoping that the measles would put a damper on her temperament and she would cease getting so fired up about affairs and putting such steady pressure on him.

". . . You write I should be a firm master—that is quite true. Rest assured I have not forgotten, but it is not at all necessary to snap at people right and left each minute. Often a calm, sharp comment or reply is quite enough to show whoever it is his place."

She: "Feb. 24th. Strikes now in Petrograd—80,000 workers have struck, lines of the hungry have formed outside the bakeries. Not enough bread in town."

He: "Headquarters. 24 February. . . . I am sending you and Alexei Orders from the King and Queen of the Belgians in memory of the war. . . . He will be so pleased with a new little cross!"

She: "Feb. 24nd. My precious one. . . . There were riots yesterday, on Vasilievsky Island and Nevsky Prospect because some poor people stoned a bakery, tearing Filippov's bakery to pieces & the Cossacks were called in. I learned all unofficially. . . . At 10 went to see Ania (she probably has measles too). . . . Am going from room to room, from sick bed to sick bed. . . . Went out for a minute to light candles for everyone."

He: "Headquarters. 24 February. . . . And so we have now three children and Anya ill with measles! . . . Moreover, the rooms in Tsarskoe must be disinfected, and most likely you will not want to go to Peterhof—where can we live then? We shall think this out in peace on my return home, which I hope will be soon! My brain is resting here—no Ministers, no troublesome questions demanding thought, I consider that this is good for me, but only for my brain. My heart is suffering from the separation."

In Petrograd, on the morning of February 25, 1917, Duma Chairman Rodzianko went to see Prime Minister Golitsyn and demand his resignation. The offended Golitsyn showed him the decree disbanding the Duma, which the tsar had signed beforehand. Golitsyn could use it at any time.

Both Golitsyn and Rodzianko realized, however, that the Duma would not obey, for the government's power no longer existed.

On Znamenskaya Square crowds had already gathered, shouting, "Long live the republic." Cossacks had driven out the police. The crowd was fraternizing with the troops.

She: "Feb. 25th. My precious, beloved treasure, The city's strikes and riots are more than provoking . . . its a movement of hooligans, boys and girls running around shouting about no bread—just to stir up excitement—as are the workers preventing others from working. If the days were very cold, they would probably all be sitting home, but all this will pass & calm down, if only the Duma behaves. . . . I had a feeling when you were leaving things would go badly. . . . Write me a greeting for Ania—it would be nice for her. . . . Forgive this gloomy letter, but all round are so many tiresome requests."

Only on the evening of the twenty-fifth did Nicholas learn about the riots that had been going on in the city for three days.

On the twenty-sixth he received a telegram from the war minister: the soldiers were refusing to fire on the rioters and were going over to the insurrectionists.

Nicholas sent a telegram to Khabalov, commander of the Petersburg Military District, ordering him to put an immediate halt to the riots.

Nicholas's diary:

"26 February. Sunday. . . . Mass at 10. Report ended promptly.

. . . Wrote Alix and walked down the Bobruisky Road to the chapel. The day was clear and frosty. . . . In the evening played dominoes."

Everyone remarked on his strange indifference at that terrible time.

She: "Febr. 26th. . . . What joy to receive your letter, covered it with kisses and will kiss it often. . . . Much talk about the riots in town (I think more than 200,000 people . . .), but I already wrote this yesterday, forgive me, I am silly. A coupon simply must be brought in for bread (as it is now in every country; after all, it is already set up for sugar and everyone is calm and gets enough), we have idiots. . . . The whole trouble is this bawling public, those well-dressed people, wounded soldiers, & so on, girl students & the like, inciting the others. Lili [Lili Dehn, the wife of an aide-de-camp and naval officer, was the empress's friend and, unlike Anya, the soul of good sense and order] talks to drivers to find out news & they have told that students have come and said if they go out in the morning they will be shot at—what rotten types! Naturally the drivers & carters are striking, but they say its not like 1905 because everyone adores you & only wants bread. . . . What warm weather vexing that the children cannot even go for a ride in an open car. It seems though that all will be well. The sun is shining brightly—I feel such peace at His dear grave. He died to save us. . . . Baby is one great rash, covered like a leopard, Olga has large flat spots. Ania too is covered with rash. All their throats & eyes hurt—I have to go back to them in the dark. I bless & kiss you over & over."

He: "Headquarters. 26 February. . . . Please do not overtire yourself, running about among the sick ones. . . . Yesterday I visited the ikon of the Holy Virgin and prayed fervently for you, my love, for the dear children, for our country, and also for Anya. . . . This morning, during the service, I felt an excruciating pain in the chest, which lasted for a quarter of an hour. I could hardly stand the service out, and my forehead was covered with drops of perspiration, I cannot understand what it could have been, because I had no palpitation of the heart; but later it disappeared, vanishing suddenly when I knelt before the image of the Holy Virgin."

On February 26 Rodzianko sent the tsar a desperate telegram: "There is anarchy in the capital. The government is paralyzed, transportation, food, and fuel have reached a pathetic state. Military units are firing on each other. There is random shooting on the streets. You must immediately name someone who has the country's trust to form a new government. . . . Any delay is akin to death. I pray God that in this hour accountability does not fall on the wearer of the crown." The telegram arrived in the night, but Chief of Staff Alexeyev decided not to wake the tsar, not showing him the telegram until morning.

On the morning of February 27, Rodzianko addressed a second telegram to the tsar: "The situation is growing worse. You must take measures immediately, for tomorrow will be too late. The final hour has come when the fate of the Homeland and the dynasty shall be decided."

In Petrograd the offices of the secret police were in flames, and the crowd would not let the fire be put out; regiments were on their way to the Tauride Palace, where the Provisional Committee of the Duma was in session. To furled flags and music they were swearing an oath to the new government. At that point General Khabalov decided, finally, to post notices declaring a state of siege in the city —but the authorities were unable to obtain paste or brushes.

The district court was burning, and they were already hunting down policemen.

What strange entries at this time in Nicholas's diary. If Alix got her information "from the drivers Ania spoke with," then he, who had all the information and read Rodzianko's desperate telegrams—what was his excuse for his astounding inaction? Weary indifference? But then what was the meaning of "the excruciating pain in the chest"?

It does make sense, of course.

As he was leaving Tsarskoe Selo that last time on February 22, he assumed a storm was possible—a storm everyone was promising him. And he decided in advance *not to fight the storm.* He could not and would not make war on society anymore. He knew, though, that she would not let him concede peacefully. Just as they would not accept his concessions if she remained. Rasputin and the rumors of treason had compromised her too badly. He was left with only one choice: either her or the throne. He chose her. He chose his private life with his family, so that his unhappy, half-mad wife would not be driven even more insane, so that he could openly seek treatment for his mortally ill son. He decided to give up the throne—and this decision almost killed him. His "excruciating pain in the chest" was the result of that decision, the result of the torture he had repressed within himself.

Subsequently, discussing the activities of Nicholas's chief of staff, Alexeyev, who oddly was in no hurry to familiarize the tsar with the panicky information from the capital, people have suspected Alexeyev of complicity in a plot. A strange figure, this chief of staff. He had come from simple people, had earned everything for himself, and under Nicholas was the actual commander-in-chief. He was Rasputin's enemy and forbade him to come to Headquarters—but Nicholas did not give him up to Alix's fury. They were similar in their temperaments, the chief of staff and the tsar, reserved and taciturn. And they liked each other. They understood. That was why Alexeyev was in no hurry with the alarming telegrams: he had figured Nicholas out, and he was tacitly supporting him.

Nicholas did not manage to carry his decision through to completion. He had expected that the Duma would control the situation, that the coup everyone was so certain of had been readied. He would find out, however, that the mob had gone out into the street. From the telegrams he realized with horror that in fact the Duma's big talkers were not in control of the situation. That was when he got scared—for Alix and the children. Riots in the city could spread to his beloved Tsarskoe Selo. Nicholas was forced to act.

On Monday, February 27, he wrote in his diary:

"Riots began in Petrograd several days ago. To my regret, troops have begun to take part in them. It is a hateful feeling to be so far away and receive such poor, fragmentary news! Was not long at report. In the afternoon took a walk down the road to Orsha. After dinner decided to go to Tsarskoe as soon as possible and at 1 moved into the train."

He (telegram): "Am starting to-morrow at 2.30. The Cavalry Guards have received orders to leave Nov[gorod] for town immediately. God grant that the disorders among the troops will soon be stopped."

Nicholas's diary:

"28 February. Tuesday. Went to bed at 3.15, having spoken at length with N. I. Ivanov [General Nikolai Iudovich Ivanov], whom I am sending to Petrograd with troops to establish order. Slept until 10. Left Mogilev at 5 in the morning. The weather was frostily sunny. In the afternoon traveled through Vyazma, Rzhev, and Likhoslavl at 9."

But he never did get as far as his beloved Tsarskoe Selo.

A DREADFUL PLAY

Lermontov's *Masquerade* is a play with dreadful associations. On the day war was declared in 1941, *Masquerade* premiered in Moscow. *Masquerade* also premiered then, at the end of February 1917, during the empire's fall.

The street lamps were no longer burning. Only a searchlight on the Admiralty side beat down on Nevsky, and in this dead light, people were walking to the theater. There was shooting in the streets. A murdered student lay in the lobby. There were a great many rumors about the readied performance. All theatrical Petrograd had gathered at the Alexandrinsky Theater. Indeed, it was a fantastic spectacle. On the stage, improbable luxury no one had ever seen in a theater: huge mirrors, gilded doors. The stage presented a glittering palace hall. The apotheosis of luxury. A hymn to a palace. It was a theatrical set of the world that was drowning on that February street, moving off into nonbeing. In the Tauride Palace the Duma was in permanent session. Hoarse, ecstatic speakers. . . .

On February 28, the last day of winter, the garrison at Tsarskoe Selo rebelled: 40,000 soldiers with antiaircraft guns.

Rodzianko, as chairman of the Duma the sole authority in the mutinous capital, made a call on the palace. Rodzianko spoke with Benckendorff, marshal of the imperial court, and asked him to tell Alix to flee the Alexander Palace as quickly as possible.

"But the sick children—" said Benckendorff.

"When a house is on fire, sick children are carried out," Rodzianko replied (his voice said: if only you had listened to me earlier!).

"I am not going anywhere! Let them do what they wish," the empress answered Benckendorff.

By now the station at Tsarskoe Selo had been taken by the rebels. The trains were not running. So she sent two Cossacks from the convoy to Petrograd by rail. Their fur coats hid the uniform they had recently worn so proudly.

The Cossacks returned with news: the city was firmly in the hands of the rebellion. The mobs had opened the prisons and were storming the police stations and picking up policemen. The center was overflowing with people, and there were flags everywhere. The city was awash in blood-red calico.

In the palace all day February 28 they heard disorderly firing. It was the mutinous soldiers of the Tsarskoe Selo garrison shooting ecstatically (so far still in the air). Bands were thundering the "Marseillaise." All day—that music. Half a kilometer from the palace, the first victim: a Cossack was killed. But the 40,000 insurrectionists were not yet threatening the palace.

Along the iron fence of the palace, astride their magnificent horses, were the mounted Cossack patrols of His Imperial Highness's Convoy.

She called in Generals Resin and von Groten, in whose hands she now placed the palace's defense.

The many faces of Alix: the obedient granddaughter of Queen Victoria, the eternal Sweetheart, the sequestered Muscovite tsarevna, the insane fanatic of autocracy. And finally Alix, in March 1917. The heroine of an antique tragedy: overthrown but ever the warrior. The blood of Mary Stuart.

At nine o'clock the palace trumpeters sounded the alarm, and the inspection of her troops began.

They formed up before the main entry of the palace: the Life Guards Second Kuban and Third Tersk companies. Two companies of the Convoy's Cossacks lined up.

Next to the Cossacks, having come from the barracks, was a battalion of the Marine of the Guard under the command of Grand Duke Kirill. (The Marine had thinned out, some daring sailors having already begun to disappear mysteriously in the night.)

Finally, a battalion of a mixed infantry regiment and an antiaircraft battery—two guns on motorized platforms.

Here was all her army surrounded by a sea of gray greatcoats—the garrison of Tsarskoe Selo.

Lanterns burned by the palace entrance. Several hundred defenders stood silently in the freezing night. Commands were heard: "From the Convoy—constant mounted patrols along the railway between the station and the barracks. Anti-aircraft batteries and the Marine's machine-guns—take a position suitable for opening fire, down the streets leading to the palace." Midnight, when she would emerge from the palace, was drawing nigh.

Across the crunching snow, in the fierce frost, a fur coat draped over her shoulders, she walked down the rank. Her proud bearing. The leading tragic actress in the drama of the revolution. Beside her was Grand Duchess Marie, her only healthy daughter. Together they passed down the rank. Alix gathered the officers in the palace's guard room: "Gentlemen, please, there is no need to shoot. No matter what happens. I do not want blood shed because of us."

She had realized: one shot and everything would go up in a puff of smoke. Gray coats fanned out around the palace.

The next day, when she awoke, a new blow awaited her. The palace's pride and glory, the Marine of the Guard, under the command of Grand Duke Kirill, had left the barracks. A red ribbon on his high-collared jacket and the tsar's monogram on his epaulets, the tsar's cousin had taken his unit to the Tauride Palace—to swear allegiance to the Duma. Kirill had not forgotten the humiliations of 1905. Nor had he forgiven Nicholas and Alexandra the filthy muzhik who had soiled the dynasty.

That same morning, a company of the railway battalion left for Petrograd in the Marine's wake. Two companies of Cossacks, two guns, and an infantry battalion—such was her army then.

She realized that the palace could be stormed at any moment— the mutinous garrison no longer had anyone to fear.

As before, though, they did not approach. This was an ominous calm, however. Rumors were going around the palace—the rebels' cannons were already aimed at the cathedral and palace. They had to wait from hour to hour.

By the afternoon she had nearly forgotten the inevitable threat rushing between her sick children and sick friend.

That night she could not sleep. She went down to the palace's half-cellar, where the Convoy's Cossacks were resting in the warmth of the furnace, and tried to encourage them, to strengthen their spirit through prayers. Later, before dawn, she talked with Lili Dehn. And all this time she kept sending him telegrams, which returned with the mocking comment: "Place of residence unknown." The place of residence of the Autocrat of All the Russias was unknown! She could not stand it—she sent for Paul, who had not been called to the palace since his son killed Rasputin. He came and told her that Nicky's train had been held up, but Nicky was alive and well.

She begged Paul to do something. Catastrophe was imminent. He did not try to explain to her that the catastrophe had already occurred; he pitied her. He informed her that he, Kirill, and Misha had written a draft manifesto, which they intended to take to the Duma and in which the tsar granted a ministry accountable to the Duma. Yes, yes, she now understood: concessions were needed. (No one paid any attention to the manifesto signed by the three grand dukes. The Duma was waiting for a very different manifesto.)

On the night of March 1, Alix received yet another blow. At about one in the morning General Ivanov appeared at the palace—the same man whom Nicky had sent out with a crack detachment of highly decorated men.

In her lilac study, the old general told Alix how the railway had been seized and the echelon surrounded by rebels. And propagandized. Those men with their St. George's Crosses refused to leave their train cars—no one would come to the aid of the palace. Again her delusions emerged: she begged the old man to try to get through to Nicky.

After the general's departure she realized she was totally defenseless. The mutineers could come at any moment. Again she sent a Cossack lieutenant from the Convoy for Paul. The emissary walked up to the gate of the grand duke's palace and rang for a long time. Receiving no response, he scaled the fence and was amazed to see the formal entry to the palace open. He wandered through the endless halls of the empty palace and realized the servants had fled. Finally he came to Paul's bedroom. At the door slept Paul's valet, all that remained of a great many servants.

He explained to Paul that the palace was expecting the mutineers at any moment. The grand duke started making phone calls, negotiating. Finally he asked the lieutenant to tell Alix that the Duma guaranteed the palace's safety and Alix should not worry. He would sooner part with his own life than let . . . and so on.

On the morning of March 2 Alix wrote two long letters to Nicky. Two Cossacks from the Convoy sewed the tiny envelopes under their trouser stripes.

She: "My heart breaks from the thought of you living through all these tortures & upsets totally alone—& we know nothing of you, & you know nothing of us. I am sending Soloviev & Gramotin to you, giving each a letter, & hope at least one shall reach you. I wanted to send an aeroplan, but all have vanished. The young men will tell you all so I have nothing to tell of the state of affairs. It is all hateful, & events are progressing with colossal speed. I firmly believe, though— & no one shall shake this belief—that all will be alright. . . . Clearly they dont want to let you see me so above all you must not sign any paper, constitution, or other such horror—but you are alone, without your army, caught like a mouse in a trap, what can you do? This is supremely base and mean, unprecedented in history, to detain one's sovereign. . . . What if you show yourself to the troops in other places and gather them around? If you must make concessions, under no circumstances are you obliged to honor them since they were obtained in ignoble fashion. . . . Your little family is worthy of their father. I gradually explained the situation to the Older Girls and the Cow [Anya]; before they were too ill. . . . It was very difficult to pretend before them. I have only told Baby half, he has 36.1 [his body temperature: 97°F] & is quite merry. Only everyone is in despair that you are not coming. . . . Last night was with Ivanov from 1 til 2.30. . . . I think he could go through Dno to see you, but could he get through? He had hoped to pull your train behind his. [Count] Fredericks's home was burned down, and his

family now in the Cavalry Guards hospital. The two movements—
the Duma and the revolutionaries—are two snakes & I hope they
bite each others heads off, which would save the situation. I feel that
God will do something. What bright sun. If only you were here!
There is only bad, even the Marine has abandoned us. They absolutely do not understand a thing, some microbe has implanted in
them. . . . When people find out they have not let you go, the
troops will be outraged & will rise up against them all. . . .

"Well then let them bring order & show that they are good for
something in the Duma. They have ignited too great a fire, tho'—
how is it to be put out now? . . . The children are sleeping peacefully in the darkness, the elevator has not worked for 4 days, the
cable broke. . . . Right now am going out to greet the soldiers
standing in front. . . . I can advise you nothing, only be yourself,
my precious one. Should you have to submit to circumstances, God
will help you free yourself from them. Oh my holy sufferer.

"Postscript: . . . Wear his [Rasputin's] cross, even if it is un-
comfortable, for my peace of mind."

The children began to recover in their darkened bedroom.

Anya awoke from her illness and high temperature. She had
fallen ill in a world where she was the omnipotent friend of the most
powerful woman in Russia; she woke up in a disgraced, besieged
palace.

There were horrifying, maddening rumors beginning on March 2:
Nicholas had abdicated!

Again she appealed to Paul.

Paul brought her the newspaper with the text of the abdication
manifesto. "No, no, I do not believe it, these are all rumors, newspaper slander." She said something else that made no sense: she did
not want to read the manifesto. She fell prostrate, whispering in
French: *"Abdiqué! Abdiqué!"* Her life was over. They had stolen her
Little One's legacy. All was lost. She remained, however, the Beautiful Lover. She did not blame him—not for a second, not in a word.

"March 3rd. My beloved, Soul of my soul—Oh, how my heart
bleeds for you. I am going mad not knowing anything at all other
than the vilest rumors which are enough to drive one insane. I would
like to know whether the two young men I sent with my letters ever
reached you today? . . . Oh for the love of God, at least a line. An

officer's wife will give you this letter. I know nothing about you, only heart-rending rumors. You are doubtless hearing the same.

"My heart is breaking with pain for you and your total isolation. I shall only write a little, since I do not know whether my letter will get to you, whether they will search her en route—so crazy have people become. This evening Marie & I are making a tour of the cellar to see the men—very heartening. . . . In town, Ducky's husband [Grand Duke Kirill] is behaving repulsively, though acting as if he were toiling for the good of the monarch and the Homeland. . . . My love, my love! We had marvelous prayers & acathistus at the ikon of the Mother of God, which was brought into the green bedroom, where they were all lying—very encouraging. Everything shall —must—be alright. I shall not waver in my faith. Oh, my dear angel, I love you so much, I am with you always, night & day. I realize what your poor heart is experiencing now. God shall have mercy & send you strength & wisdom. He shall help & reward you for these mad sufferings. . . . We shall all fight for you, we are all in our places. . . . One could go mad, but we shall not for we believe in a bright future.

". . . Paul was just here—and told me everything. I wholly understand your action, oh my hero. I know that you could not have signed anything that contradicted what you swore at your coronation. We know each other to perfection, we have no need of words, we shall see you again on your throne, restored by your people and troops to the glory of your realm."

She did not force herself to read the manifesto until the following day. Then for the first time she heard his voice again. The telephone was working—he was calling from Headquarters. She spoke tender words of encouragement. Soon after the conversation a telegram was brought.

"Headquarters. 4 March, 10 o'clock in the morning. Your Highness [he called her that, as before, and would continue to call her that to the very end]. Thanks, my dear. . . . Despair is passing away. May God bless you all! Tender love."

On the evening of March 4 she wrote him her last, 653rd letter:

"March 4th 1917. My dear, beloved Treasure! What a relief & joy to hear your dear voice, only it was very hard to hear, & anyway they listen to all our conversations now!—and your dear telegram today. . . . Baby has leaned across the bed & asks to send you a kiss. All 4 girls are lying in the green room in the darkness. Marie & I are writing, tho' we can see almost nothing, since the curtains are lowered. Only this morning I read the manifesto. . . . People are beside themselves with despair, they adore my angel. Movement is beginning among the troops. . . . Ahead, I feel, I foresee the sun shining. I am extremely angry with Ducky's husband. . . .

"People are being arrested right & left now, officers naturally. God knows what is going on: the riflemen are choosing their own commanders & acting abominably to them—show no respect, smoke right in the officers' faces. I do not want to write all that is going on —so repulsive. The sick upstairs & down do not know your decision, I am afraid to tell them, & for the time being no need. . . . God! Of course He will repay you a hundredfold for all your sufferings. My beloved, angel dear, I am afraid thinking what you are enduring, am going mad. I must not write of this more, I cannot! How they humiliated you, sending those two swine! I didnt know who that was until you told me. I feel the army will rise up."

The novel in letters had come to an end. Captivity commenced.

He had spoken briefly of the abdication in that first telephone conversation. She would learn the details upon his return.

"CAUGHT LIKE A MOUSE IN A TRAP" On the night of February 28 he was on the train to Tsarskoe Selo.

Nicholas's diary:

"1 March, Wednesday. Last night . . . turned back because Lyuban and Tosno have been taken by the rebels and went to Valdai, Dno, and Pskov, where the train stopped for the night."

When he awoke in Pskov the next morning, he learned that there was nowhere for him to go.

"Gatchina and Luga have been taken too. The shame and disgrace! We could not get to Tsarskoe, but my thoughts and feelings are there always. So distressing for poor Alix to endure all these events alone! Help us, Lord."

Gatchina was his childhood, the garden where at the beginning of his life they built bonfires . . . their constant, unshakable world. And now. . . .

"2 March. Thursday. This morning Ruzsky [commander of the northwestern and northern fronts] came and related his very long telephone conversation with Rodzianko. According to him, the situation in Petrograd is such that now the Duma ministry will be powerless to do anything since they are being opposed by the Social Democratic Party in the guise of the workers' committee [the Petrograd

Soviet of Workers' and Soldiers' Deputies]. My abdication is necessary."

Everything did occur very quickly. As sometimes happens, though, once he had what he had decided on in a moment of weakness and exhaustion, he did not want it anymore. He cursed his weakness and detested his helplessness and the entire horror that would not pass: Alix, alone with their sick children, and he himself locked in a train at the Dno station! (Such was its name, Dno, or "Bottom.") He declared to Ruzsky that he was prepared to sign the abdication, but first all the commanders at the fronts must say whether or not he should abdicate.

Nicholas's diary:

"2 March [continuation]. Ruzsky transmitted this conversation to Headquarters and Alexeyev to all the chief commanders. By 2.30 replies had come from all of them. The essence is that, to save Russia and keep the army at the front quiet, this is a necessary step. I agreed."

That afternoon he learned that the Duma in Petrograd had already sent for his abdication

"*H*OW THEY HUMILIATED YOU, SENDING THOSE TWO SWINE"

The hour is late. Nicholas walks out on the platform to stretch his legs. It is cold—the frost is hardening. All the lights are on in the imperial train. The "gentlemen"—as he teasingly refers to his suite— are not sleeping; they are waiting.

Several tracks away, a locomotive emerges from the darkness pulling a single car.

Two men get out and walk over to his train; one is Vasily Shulgin, whom Nicholas knows: a monarchist who once pleased him with a speech in the Duma. But the other—the other is Guchkov, his life-long enemy. His despised enemy!

It is the seventh decade of the twentieth century, Leningrad. A documentary is being readied for the fiftieth anniversary of the October Revolution. The floodlights are off on the set at Lenfilm studios. In the grimy dimness an old man sits on a chair—a bald skull, a prophet's beard, and a young man's flashing eyes. I have come over from the set where they are shooting my film to look at this old man, who spent time in Stalin's camps and later, according to legend, worked as a doorman in a restaurant in Vladimir. After Khrushchev's Thaw, the decorated Soviet director Fridrikh Ermler got the idea of shooting a documentary about this old man. Today on the set the director and the old man are discussing an episode in *Abdication of the Tsar*. In his book, the old man described the scene in the train car. Now he is recalling once again how they entered the car. Where each man stood. How the tsar entered. The old man bears a name once known to all of Russia: Vasily Shulgin.

It is a parlor car. Green silk on the walls. An old general with loops of gilt cord hanging from his shoulders—the minister of the imperial court, Count Fredericks.

They sit at a small table: the tsar, wearing a gray Circassian coat, across from Guchkov and Shulgin.

Guchkov launches into a long, bombastic speech. Nicholas listens in silence, his elbow propped against the wall. Shulgin is watching the tsar: there are bags under his eyes, brown, wrinkled, singed-looking skin from hard, sleepless nights.

Finally Guchkov speaks of the abdication, his voice trembling. When he finishes, Nicholas says calmly, indifferently, with his particular guardsman's accent: "I have taken the decision, gentlemen, to renounce the throne. . . . Until three o'clock today I thought I could abdicate in favor of my son, but at that point I changed this decision in favor of my brother Michael. I hope, gentlemen, that you will understand a father's feelings."

Rising from the table, he picks up the Duma's draft manifesto, which Guchkov had brought, and walks out.

While he is gone, Guchkov and Shulgin learn that the tsar is consulting with Dr. Feodorov—who tells him definitively that there is no hope for Alexei's recovery.

So everything is the way Nicholas himself had wished all along. Michael will rule, and they—Alix and the family—will remain at liberty. For some reason, though, he now feels . . . not even sadness, but horror!

He returns to the train car and places on the table the text of abdication that he had written that afternoon, typed on telegraph blanks.

"How pitiful the sketch we brought seemed," recalls Shulgin, "and how noble his parting words."

*T*HE MANIFESTO

"In these times of great struggle against an external enemy who for nearly three years has been trying to enslave our homeland, the Lord God has seen fit to send down upon Russia yet another difficult trial. Popular domestic upheavals threaten to reflect calamitously on the further conduct of a sustained war. The fate of Russia, the honor of her heroic army, the good of her people, the entire future of our dear Fatherland demand that this war be waged to a victorious conclusion no matter what. . . . During these decisive days in the life of Russia, we have deemed it a matter of conscience to facilitate for our people the close unity and serried ranks of all our popular forces for the speedy attainment of victory and, in agreement with the Duma, have recognized it as a good to abdicate the Throne of the Russian State and disencumber ourselves of supreme power. Not wishing to part with our beloved son, we transfer our legacy to our brother Grand Duke Michael Alexandrovich and bless him on his ascension to the Throne of the Russian State. . . . We command our brother to rule state affairs in full and inviolable unity with the representatives of the people. . . . On those principles which they shall establish. . . . May the Lord God help Russia."

Although they are touched, they immediately ask him to bend the truth so that no suspicion should arise that the abdication was torn from him: they ask him to put down not the true hour when he signed it but when he *himself* came to this decision. And he agrees. He signs: "March 2, 15:00"—although by the clock it is already midnight.

Later there is another lie: they propose that the new prime minister, Prince Lvov, be appointed by the sovereign himself. "Ah, Lvov? Well, all right, so be it, Lvov." He signs that as well. He is doing almost everything mechanically. All his thoughts are at Tsarskoe Selo.

Nicholas's diary:

"2 March [continuation]. . . . They sent the draft manifesto from Headquarters. In the evening Guchkov and Shulgin arrived from Petrograd. Spoke with them and gave them the signed and revised manifesto. At 1 in the morning left Pskov with the heavy sense of what I had been through. Am surrounded by betrayal, cowardice, and deceit."

Having signed the manifesto, he could leave immediately for Tsarskoe Selo. To everyone's surprise, though, he returned to Headquarters, to Mogilev.

It may have been too much for him to see her and the children right after his downfall. He may have wanted to give them time to get used to the situation. Also, he had to say goodbye to the army. There was a war in progress, and he discharged his duties as commander-in-chief to the end.

In the very depths of his soul, though, he may still have held out hope. She might suddenly turn out to be right: loyal troops could rise up and a miracle could happen. He did not want to return to Tsarskoe Selo like this, laid low.

Also, he had to say goodbye to his mother.

On March 3 he returned to Headquarters. No one knew how he should be met or indeed whether he should be met at all. Naturally, though, Alexeyev decided to greet him as usual. His generals formed up in the special pavilion for meeting the tsar's trains. They waited in silence. Only the sarcastic Sergei Mikhailovich spoke, discussing the conduct of another grand duke, Kirill, "calling things by their proper names."

The imperial train approached. No one got out. Finally, one of the servants emerged and called to Alexeyev, who disappeared after him into the train car. Everyone waited.

Then Nicholas appeared—with a new face: yellow skin stretched across his temples, distinct bags under his eyes. Behind him was Count Fredericks: carefully clean-shaven and erect as always. The tsar (the former tsar now) began his review by greeting each and every one of them as usual.

"3 March. Friday. Slept long and hard. Woke up long past Dvinsk. The day was sunny and freezing. . . . Read a lot about Julius Caesar. At 8.20 arrived in Mogilev. All the staff officers were on the platform. Received Alexeyev in my car. At 9.30 moved to the house. Alexeyev came with the latest news from Rodzianko. Misha, it turns out, has abdicated. His manifesto ends with a four-line addendum about elections for a Constituent Assembly in 6 months. God knows who gave him the idea of signing such rot! The riots have stopped in Petrograd—if only things would continue like this."

A new world was drawing near.

The abdication in favor of Michael did not work out. Nor could it have: the new world did not want the Romanovs. The workers nearly dismembered Guchkov when he dared make the announcement about Tsar Michael Romanov.

On March 3, Guchkov and Shulgin were driven by car to obtain the new abdication from Michael. Soldiers lay on the automobile's front fenders holding bared bayonets.

On February 27, Rodzianko had summoned Michael from Gatchina to Petrograd. At Rodzianko's request, Michael had got on the phone directly with Headquarters and asked Nicholas to cede to the Duma —to form a government of confidence. Nicholas refused. But Michael did not make it back to Gatchina—the railway was seized by rebels. He spent the night in the Winter Palace and in the morning found himself right in the thick of things. Generals came over from the Admiralty building to the Winter Palace (among them War Minister Belaev) and proposed that Michael head a detachment to save Petrograd. Michael refused. He preferred hiding on Millionnaya Street in the apartment of Prince Putyatin.

In that apartment on Millionnaya Street, the expensive fur coats of Duma figures were tossed down in the entryway (this was still the overthrown regime—soon, very soon, both the fur coats and their owners would disappear).

Michael came in, tall, pale, his face very young. They spoke in turn.

Socialist Revolutionary and Duma member Alexander Kerensky:

"By taking the throne you will not save Russia. I know the mood of the masses. Right now everyone feels intense displeasure at the monarchy. I have no right to conceal the dangers taking power would subject you to personally. I could not vouch for your life."

Then silence, a long silence. And Michael's voice, his barely audible voice: "Under these circumstances, I cannot."

Silence, and almost distinct sobbing.

Michael was crying. It was his fate to end the monarchy. Three hundred years—and it all ended with him.

And Kerensky's happy shout: "I deeply respect your gesture! As does all Russia."

The new world sent congratulatory telegrams to Michael Romanov, a congratulatory telegram came even from Turukhansk, where the Bolsheviks were in exile.

Nicholas was living in the governor's house in Mogilev. Daily he walked to the quarters of the general staff, where Alexeyev reported to him and read agents' telegrams. As if nothing had happened.

"4 March. Saturday. . . . Just before 12 went to the platform to meet dear mother arriving from Kiev. Brought her to my place and had lunch with her and our people. Sat and talked for a long time. . . . Just before 8 went to dine at Mama's and sat with her 'til 11."

A new world was walking around the city: clerks, drivers bedecked with red armbands and ribbons, red cockades on their caps. Endless meetings, speeches by "the freest citizens of the freest country in the world" about "the damn regime."

Gathered in the train car of the dowager empress, however, were "his people": Grand Duke Boris Vladimirovich (now simply Boris Romanov), Prince Alexander of Oldenburg (now simply Alec), and simply Sergei . . . and simply Sandro. At the time they still believed that Nikolasha would come soon and take over as commander-in-chief. Alexeyev, the generals—they all wanted him.

But the new world did not. Nikolasha had to refuse. He was already on his way to Headquarters when he was informed in the name of the Provisional Government: "Popular opinion has expressed itself decisively and insistently in opposition to members of the house of Romanov occupying any position whatsoever. . . . The Provisional Government is convinced that you, in the name of love for your Homeland," etc. His reply to the telegram did not lack sarcasm: "I am happy once again to prove my love for my Homeland. Of which Russia has yet to have any doubt."

Popular opinion. When to the question "What is your name?" one of the grand dukes answered "Romanov," the clerk said sympathetically: "What an ugly name you have."

The new rule was beginning—the rule of the victorious crowd, the rule of Nicholas's former soldiers. The Soviet of Workers' and Soldiers' Deputies. Those once bold talkers of the Duma and the Provisional Government—how they feared that power now and tried to ingratiate themselves with it.

Once he was back at Tsarskoe Selo Nicholas would observe with a certain malicious pleasure the once terrible orators of the Duma becoming increasingly helpless to do anything about the natural disaster they had provoked.

Alexeyev was negotiating the departure of the tsar's family. Through Murmansk, it was assumed, to England. Nicholas wanted it all arranged before his return to Alix.

But something else happened. The new world did not want his departure. On March 3, immediately after his abdication, the Petrograd Soviet of Workers' and Soldiers' Deputies passed a decree "On the arrest of Nicholas II and the other members of the Romanov dynasty."

The Provisional Government was forced to yield, so much did they fear this new world, despite the fact that he had met all their conditions without a murmur and had signed the manifesto.

"The journal of the Provisional Government's sessions of March 7.

"Considered: The incarceration of the abdicated emperor and his spouse.

"Resolved: To approve the incarceration of the abdicated Emperor Nicholas II and his wife and to remove the abdicated emperor to Tsarskoe Selo."

Kerensky later explained the reasons for the arrest:

"The extremely agitated state of the soldiers at the rear and the workers. The Petrograd and Moscow garrisons were hostile to Nicholas. . . . Recall my speech of March 20 at the plenum of the Moscow Soviet—demands for execution were heard then, addressed directly to me. I said I would never take on the role of Marat, that an impartial court would examine Nicholas's guilt before Russia."

The Provisional Government had more or less defended him from the Soviets' arbitrariness. But this arrest "tied the knot later broken in Ekaterinburg" (V. Nabokov, administrator of affairs for the Provisional Government).

True, Alexeyev informed him of what the government had implied: all this was temporary, for purposes of placating the crowd's fury. A special commission of inquiry was being created—it would prove the tsar's innocence and the nonsense of the rumors about Alix's treason. And then—bon voyage—to England!

Nicholas's diary:

"8 March, Wednesday. Last day in Mogilev. At 10.15 signed a parting decree to the army."

He wanted good and reconciliation for Russia. That was why he ceded power and asked his people to serve the new government loyally: "I address you for the last time, my ardently loved troops. Do your duty—defend our valorous homeland, obey the Provisional Government, heed your leaders: may God bless you and the great martyr St. George the Conqueror lead you to holy victory." At that moment Nicholas fell for good in monarchists' eyes as well.

Meanwhile, no one dared publish the decree—its author was too unpopular.

Nicholas's diary:

"8 March [continuation]. . . . At 10.30 went to the Guards

building, where said goodbye to all the officials of the staff and administration. At home said goodbye to the officers and Cossacks of the Convoy and Mixed Regiment—my heart nearly burst. At 12 went to see Mama in her train car, had lunch with her and her suite, and sat with her 'til 4.30. Said goodbye to her, Sandro, Sergei, Boris, and Alec."

He was seeing them all for the last time.

"At 4.45 left Mogilev. A touching crowd of people saw me off. Four members of the Duma are accompanying me in my train. . . . It is hard, painful, and miserable."

"Accompanying"—his delicate way of noting his arrest.

*D*IARY OF THE PRISONER
According to the government's resolution:

1. The family and everyone who remained with them were to be isolated from the outside world.

2. An inside and outside guard was formed.

3. The family was permitted to move about only within the confines of the Alexander Palace.

4. Papers were confiscated from the tsar and tsaritsa, to be handed over to the conduct of the Special Commission of Inquiry.

On March 8, General Kornilov's automobile drove up to the Alexander Palace. Lavr Kornilov, a distinguished military general—with his peaked martial mustache—left his automobile at the main gates of the palace and was met by the empress's secretary, Count Apraxin, and taken to see Alix.

"Your Highness, it has most burdensomely fallen upon me to inform you of your arrest."

After Kornilov's departure Alix called in Lieutenant Zborovsky of the Convoy. Her words were worthy of the moment.

"Beginning with me, we are all going to have to submit to fate. I knew General Kornilov before. He is a knight, and I am at peace now for my children."

(Exactly one year later, in March 1918, Kornilov would perish on the field of battle in the Civil War. His corpse would be dug out of its grave and burned by the Red victors on the outskirts of Ekaterinoslav.)

The surrender of posts at Tsarskoe Selo was set for 4:00 P.M. His Imperial Highness's Convoy had to quit the palace. The tragic play continued: they acted out the parting scene wonderfully, the empress and the Convoy. She gave them small icons and gifts from the family. Accepting an icon, each officer dropped to one knee. Then she led Lieutenant Zborovsky into a darkened room—to say goodbye to the sick grand duchesses (Marie too had fallen ill by that time). Zborovsky bowed low to the tsar's daughters, but he thought they seemed bewildered. No, they still did not know everything.

The empress gathered her "people" and suite in a hall. "Anyone who does not leave the palace by four o'clock this afternoon will be considered under arrest," she told them. "The sovereign is arriving tomorrow morning."

The hardest of all now remained: to tell *them*. She told her daughters herself. It was a dreadful conversation. "Mama was grieving, and I was crying, too. . . . But later we all tried to smile at tea," Marie told Anya.

Gilliard took on the task of informing his pupil.

"You know, Alexei Nikolaevich, your father does not want to be emperor any longer."

The boy looked at him with astonishment, trying to read what was happening on his face.

"He is awfully tired and he has had many difficulties of late."

"Oh, yes! Mama told me that they stopped his train when he wanted to come here, but father will be emperor again, won't he, later on?"

Gilliard explained that the sovereign had abdicated in favor of Michael, but Uncle Michael had refused the throne.

"In that case, who will be emperor?"

"Now—no one."

Alexei flushed furiously and said nothing for a long time, but did not ask about himself. Then he said: "In that case, if there is not going to be a tsar anymore, who is going to rule Russia?"

This question seemed naive and childish to the good Swiss, but millions of others, too, were asking: Who will be tsar? The new tsar in a country that had always had tsars.

The revolution could not wipe out autocracy because it was in the people's blood. And he would come again—a new tsar. A revolutionary tsar. But a tsar.

"If there is not going to be a tsar anymore, who is going to rule Russia?"

At four o'clock the revolutionary soldiers replaced the Tsar's Convoy. But they were not protecting the family; they were guarding it. Lieutenant Zborovsky looked on with horror at this new sentry with their red ribbons. The world had fallen apart. "We had it . . . we had it . . . and now it is gone. This is something savage . . . incomprehensible." So he wrote in his diary.

Alix's first night under arrest, the last night before the arrival of the overthrown emperor.

A cruel frost, and the snow in the Tsarskoe Selo park sparkling under the moon. In the nighttime silence, Lili Dehn went downstairs with a blanket and linens to the boudoir next to the empress's bedroom. The grand duchesses had asked her not to leave Alix alone.

Alix, with enthusiasm, made Lili's bed on the couch: "Oh, Lili, Russian ladies don't know how to make their own beds. When I was a girl, my grandmother showed me how it is done."

The bed "in the style of Queen Victoria" was ready; she had played the role of concerned mistress. Alix left her bedroom door open so Lili "would not be lonely." Both were left alone with their thoughts in the moonlit rooms. Neither slept. Lili listened to the empress's coughing and a new sound: the steps of the sentry in the hallway—back and forth, back and forth.

On March 9, at eleven o'clock in the morning, automobiles drove out of the palace garage to the station—to the imperial pavilion. The train pulled in, and Nicholas emerged wearing a Caucasian fur cap and soldier's greatcoat, his yellow skin taut across his temples. Behind him the members of his suite began to jump off the train and run away down the platform. Not looking back—they fled. This was not only the effect of banal fear. This was the first demonstration of the camarilla's true attitude toward Nicholas.

The tsar got in the automobile. Next to him was Marshal of the Court Dolgorukov. In the front seat was his orderly, Pilipenko, a sergeant-major in the convoy. (Dolgorukov would be shot in 1918, Pilipenko in 1920.) The order was given: "Open the gates for the former tsar."

The gates opened and the automobile of living corpses drove in to Tsarskoe Selo.

By this time the empress had burned her papers in her beloved lilac study. In Vyrubova's room she destroyed all her letters to her friend. She probably burned her brother Ernie's letters as well. And her diaries. Given her passion for the pen, one can imagine what quantity this amounted to! She did decide to preserve the memory of these days, though, so she invented a style for keeping a new diary. Only events and times. That was all, not a single opinion—a canvas for future reminiscences.

That was how she transmitted to us everything that happened from the early part of the terrible year 1917. That was how her diary of the empire's collapse was created. English words in this diary are interspersed with Russian. She often joined individual letters—Russian and English—to make it harder to read if it were ever confiscated.

"March 1. 11:00. Benck. Tea."

This means Count Benckendorff had been invited for tea and on that day they discussed the latest news from Petrograd.

"O. 38 and 9, T. 38, A. 36 and 7, Ania 38"—these are the temperatures of her sick children and her friend.

"Ivanov—1–2.5 night."

This was a notation about that tragic nighttime conversation with General Ivanov, when she understood the full extent of their defenselessness.

Here is the day that interests us especially:

"March 9. O. 36.3, T. 36.2, M. 37.2, An. 36.5, A. 36.2.

"11:45—N. arrived." Yes, this was Nicholas arriving.

When the car drove up with the sovereign, she was sitting in the playroom with Little One.

"She ran down the corridors of the palace like a fifteen-year-old girl," Anya would write. The perpetually youthful girl was greeting her perpetual sweetheart. The two young people embraced passionately.

The valet Volkov observed this meeting: "The empress rushed to meet him, smiling. And they kissed."

The parlormaid Anna Demidova observed her as well:

"When they were left alone together, they began to cry."

More precisely—he cried. Her other boy.

"Lunch with N. . . . Alexei in the playroom."

Afterward, when he was again calm and steady, Alix led him to the playroom to see Alexei. At lunch they talked cheerful nonsense with their son, and neither he nor she nor their son spoiled this new game. Nothing had happened, everything was as before.

Yes, everything was as before. After he saw his daughters in their darkened room, he left the palace for his cherished long walk.

Out the window, Alix saw the soldiers pushing the former tsar back toward the palace, jostling him with their rifles: "You can't go there, colonel sir, go back, that's an order."

He returned to the palace in silence.

Nicholas's diary:

"9 March, Thursday. Arrived quickly and safely at Tsarskoe Selo at 10.30. But Lord, what a change! There are guards outside and around the palace, and ensigns of some kind inside the entry. Went upstairs and there saw my sweetheart Alix and my dear children. They looked cheerful and healthy, but they were all lying in a dark room. They all feel good except Marie, who got the measles only recently. Had lunch and dinner in the playroom with Alexei. Took a walk with Valya Dolgorukov and worked with him a bit in the garden, since we are not allowed to walk any farther. . . .

"10 March. Slept well, despite the conditions we now find ourselves in. The thought that we are together gladdens and consoles me. . . . Looked through papers, put them in order, and burned them. . . .

"11 March. . . . In the morning received Benckendorff, learned from him that we shall be staying here quite a while. A pleasant thought. Continued burning letters and papers."

Did he assume the possibility of his diary's confiscation? Undoubtedly. But he did not stoop to concealment.

He "burned papers"—that was it!

Indeed, soon after, a portion of their papers would be taken away by the Provisional Government's Special Commission.

"14 March. . . . Now plenty of time to read for my own pleasure. Although also enough time to sit upstairs with the children."

A peaceful life in their beloved Tsarskoe Selo. But the life of prisoners.

"March 21. . . . This afternoon Kerensky, the current minister of justice, came quite unexpectedly. Walked through all the rooms, wanted to see us, spoke with me for about 5 minutes, introduced the new commandant of the palace, and then left. . . . He ordered poor Anya put under arrest and taken to town along with Lili Dehn."

A parting of friends. The valet Alexander Volkov brought Alix in a wheelchair. She and Anya managed an embrace and practically had to be torn apart. But Sana managed to tell her friend something sublime:

"There"—she pointed to the sky—"and in God we are always together."

A car took Anya away to Petrograd, to prison.

She kept looking back at the palace disappearing behind the trees. Tsarskoe Selo's park, the white statues, St. Feodor's Cathedral —all would become a dream. The house of this family. . . . For twelve years it had been her home as well. She would recall the large semicircular window, the sovereign's study. That was how she would now refer to Nicky. Sana too would disappear and remain the empress who had bestowed friendship on modest, devoted Anya. There she was, a little girl, catching a glimpse of the empress at Ilinskoe; tall, with thick golden hair to her knees. And there was the empress in the first days of their friendship—dressed in dark, fur-trimmed velvet and a long pearl necklace. An Abyssinian in a white turban was at the table. And there was the war. And the tsaritsa's face in the kerchief of a Sister of Mercy—thin lips pressed, gray eyes sorrowful.

Meanwhile, events were unfolding.

Nicholas's diary:

"27 March. . . . Kerensky came and asked me to limit my meetings [with Alix] to mealtimes and to sit separately from the children. As if he needed this to keep the famous Soviet of Workers' and Soldiers' Deputies quiet. Forced to obey to avoid any kind of violence."

Their correspondence and personal papers were gathered up for the "Special Commission of Inquiry examining abuses of the ministers of the tsarist government and other high officials of the overthrown regime."

The commission was supposed to respond to the persistent rumors current in society about the tsar's family's treason and dealings with Germany.

All this time the commission was slaving away. As secretary of the commission, the great poet Alexander Blok went every morning to the Fortress of Peter and Paul to record interrogations. The fortress's cells made him think of the brilliant receptions at the Winter Palace. It was as if all of Petersburg society had moved into the fortress: prime ministers, department heads, the war minister, secret service chiefs.

At night the poet was writing his *Notebook*.

"Manasevich-Manuilov is loathsome, undersized, and smooth-shaven. . . . Prime Minister Sturmer is a large, melancholy ruin, old man's rubber-soled boots. . . . The other prime minister, Goremykin, is an utter wreck, quite feeble—about to die. The director of the Police Department, Beletsky, has stubby fingers and greasy hands . . . an oily face, talkative. . . . Unusual eyes—narrow, as if tear-filled—a steady glimmer."

Blok also gave a portrait of Anya in her cell.

"We went to see Vyrubova in her cell. She was standing by the bed with a crutch propped under her broad (misshapen) shoulder. She had done something with her chamberpot—broken it or thrown papers into it perhaps. She was still speaking helplessly, shooting pleading glances at me. She had all the givens for a Russian beauty, still, somehow distorted, irreparably and long ago, hackneyed."

"Helpless"? "Pleading"? While "helpless Anya" had managed to set up a correspondence from the fortress with the most dangerous woman in Russia, the empress?

Blok recorded her interrogation as well.

"Chairman: 'And did you know that Rasputin was a degenerate and nasty man?'

"Vyrubova: 'That is what everyone said. I personally never saw anything. Perhaps he was afraid in my presence. He knew that I was close to the court. Thousands of people came with many many petitions about him, but I never saw anything.'

" 'And you yourself never were involved in politics?'

" 'Why would I be involved in politics?'

" 'Do you mean you never tried to place ministers?'

" 'No.'

" 'But you brought the empress together with ministers?'

" 'I give you my word of honor. There was never anything of the kind.'

" 'You can give no better than your word of honor.' "

Thus Anya mocked them.

But what did the Special Commission finally say about the tsar's case?

Romanov (another bearer of that name), a member of the commission's presidium, wrote: "The only thing the sovereign can be accused of was his inability to take men's measure. . . . It is always easier to mislead a pure man than a bad one capable of deception. The sovereign was indisputably a pure man."

In the interests of the family, however, the commission did not publish these thoughts—about the pure man—so as not to fan already inflamed passions and avoid a collision between the government and the Soviet. A month later Nicholas was simply allowed to be together with his family again, and Kerensky declared: "Thank God, the sovereign is innocent."

No one made any effort to let society hear that, though. The Romanovs were much too unpopular!

That is why the famous actress Vera Leonidovna Yureneva was so surprised when, that same year, they decided to do Konstantin Konstantinovich's play *King of the Jews* at the Nezlobin Theater and she was offered the role of the Christian Anna. The play had been performed once at the Hermitage Theater. Nezlobin, an entrepreneur, had bought the whole luxurious set for peanuts. Three young men came to each performance, K. R.'s sons: Ioann, Konstantin, and Igor. The extras in the performance were people with magnificent posture, "formers": officers who had fled Tsarskoe Selo. Now they exchanged their brilliant uniforms for the costumes of theatrical slaves of the first century of our era.

At this time something terrible happened to Alix at Tsarskoe Selo: there was a rumor that soldiers searching for jewels had found Rasputin's grave under the chapel. The garrison ordered Rasputin's corpse removed from Tsarskoe Selo. Poor Alix did the impossible: the head of the guard, Colonel Kobylinsky, got in touch with the Provisional Government and asked them to prohibit the grave being dug up.

She was on the brink of hysteria, and Kerensky, who sympathized with them more and more (a common feeling of revolutionary rulers toward genuine tsars) sent a tank to guard the ill-fated grave—but it arrived too late.

The coffin with Rasputin's body was already on the truck. The lid was lying on the ground by the wheels, and the holy man's awful made-up face and disheveled beard were looking up at the sky.

A meeting was being held beside the coffin, and a soldier was speaking. To the delight of those gathered, he showed them a small wooden icon that had been removed from the coffin. Inscribed on the back were the initials of the tsar's entire family.

Later the truck with the coffin set out from Tsarskoe Selo. At a deserted spot on the Vyborg road where the luxurious mansion of Rasputin's friend, the Tibetan doctor Badmaev, had once stood (an angry mob had burned the mansion down), the truck came to a halt. An enormous fire was laid, into which they threw the zinc coffin and

Grishka's gasoline-doused body. The salvaged icon was sent to the Petrograd Soviet.

The Soviet's voice was being heard more and more.

Soon after the holy man was incinerated, Alix had a dream—much more terrible than the one with the amputated arm she had once written about to Nicky.

Grigory came to her, and his entire body was covered in terrible wounds. "They will burn you all in bonfires. All of you!" he shouted. Immediately the room was set ablaze. He beckoned to her to run and she rushed toward him, but it was too late. The whole room was lit up in flame, and the fire had already enveloped her—when she woke up, choking on her scream.

The Provisional Government was weakening. The voice of the new world was growing louder and louder, the Petrograd Soviet stronger and stronger.

In April 1917, Lenin and about three dozen Bolsheviks left Switzerland and traveled through a Germany that was at war with Russia—the émigrés were hastily returning to Petrograd.

Germany was allowing them to cross its territory in a sealed train car. Later Karl Radek, a passenger on that train, wrote that the car was not sealed at all—they were simply obliged not to leave it, and two German officers sat inside. For all this there remained the train's puzzling delay of many hours on German territory.

From quiet Switzerland Lenin would land in turbulent Russia. At the beginning of the year he had still not believed in the possibility of any kind of revolution in Russia in his generation's lifetime. Scarcely having set foot on Petrograd soil, however, Lenin proclaimed the path to a new, socialist revolution. Power must transfer from the hands of the Provisional Government to the Soviets. Lenin talked about a peaceful transfer of power, a peaceful revolution. But he was taken from the station to Kschessinska's mansion—Bolshevik headquarters—by a tank of armed sailors.

In July, to demonstrate the Bolsheviks' strength, the sailors of Kronstadt entered the city.

From her prison fortress, Anya observed this new calamity with horror: "No one slept that night, parades of sailors marched down our street toward the Tauride Palace. It felt terrible, disastrous. They marched by the thousands, dusty, tired, with horrible, brutalized faces, carrying enormous placards: 'Down with the Provisional Government,' 'Down with the War.' The sailors, including women, were riding in trucks with set bayonets. General Belaev and the imprisoned naval officers were rushing around the house of detention in horror. Our head guard announced that if the sailors approached the prison, the guard would go out to meet them and surrender their arms, since they were on the Bolsheviks' side."

Although the government put down this July demonstration, one could already catch a glimpse of the future in this ominous element.

But no one did.

A peaceful life. He "cultivated his own garden," as Rousseau taught. He cleaned paths, sprinkled ditches, and burned downed trees. A return to childhood. As he had once worked in the garden with his father. Only now his children were working alongside him.

"6 May. Turned 49, not far from half a century."

But the new world's hatred kept breaking through the palace fence more and more often.

"3 June. . . . Sawed up some tree trunks. That was when the incident with Alexei's bayonet happened: he was playing with it, and the riflemen walking in the garden saw it and asked an officer to take it to guard quarters. . . . Fine officers who lack the nerve to refuse the lower ranks!"

In Petrograd rumors were going around that the tsar and his family had fled.

A representative of the Soviet, Socialist Revolutionary Mstislavsky, appeared at Tsarskoe Selo wearing a dirty sheepskin coat (as revolutionaries are supposed to show up at hated tsarist palaces) with a revolver poking out of his holster. He took out a warrant and demanded to be allowed to hand it personally to the emperor, for rumors about the flight of Nicholas the Bloody (as he was called now more and more often) were alarming the workers and soldiers.

The guard was indignant: "Do you think we're guarding empty rooms?" But Mstislavsky was implacable. He needed this revolutionary theater: let the tsar stand before him, the emissary of the revolutionary workers and soldiers, as arrested revolutionaries once stood at checks in his tsarist prisons.

They yielded to the Soviet. It was decided to take Mstislavsky into the inner rooms; he would stand at the intersection of two corridors, and Nicholas would walk past.

In the inner corridors the same three-hundred-year-old life continued: Abyssinians in gold-embroidered crimson jackets and turbans, footmen in tricorner hats, lackeys in frock coats. And among them Mstislavsky, the new world, with his dirty sheepskin coat and his automatic pistol. The door bolt clicked and Nicholas appeared wearing the uniform of the Life Guard Hussar Regiment. He pulled at his mustache (as always when he was nervous), walked past, and looked indifferently at Mstislavsky. But the next moment Mstislavsky saw Nicholas's eyes ablaze with fury. The man who had ruled Russia for twenty-two years had yet to learn humility.

FAREWELL TO TSARSKOE SELO

Newspapers, those reliable scandalmongers, were spreading rumors about their escape. In fact, all these months of their confinement so near to Petrograd, there was not one authentic plot, not a single attempt to liberate them! There were boasting, drunken conversations of young officers—but that was all.

On July 4, E. A. Naryshkina, the empress's lady-in-waiting (Madame Zizi, as Alix called her), wrote in her diary: "Princess Paley [Grand Duke Paul's wife] just left. She told me in confidence that a group of young officers has devised an insane plan to take them away at night by motor to one of the ports, where an English ship would be waiting. I am unspeakably worried."

Why worried? Why was the plan insane? Because both Zizi and Paley knew that feelings about the family were such that they would never make it to any port—they would be captured and killed en route. Fortunately, these were all cock-and-bull stories. There was no English ship, nor would there be one.

During this period Alexander Blok wrote in his *Notebook:* "The tragedy has yet to occur, it will either not happen at all or it will be horrible, and they shall stand face to face with the enraged people."

What were their royal relatives doing at the time?

For instance, the English Georgie, King George to the rest of the world, Nicholas's ally in war who looked so like Nicky.

It all began quite reasonably. Immediately after the tsar's arrest the British ambassador warned the Provisional Government that every measure must be taken to ensure the family's safety. The Provisional Government readily entered into talks with George's government about their departure for England. Agreement was reached in a few days. After the arrest, they informed the British ambassador on March 23. Ambassador George Buchanan wrote that "the representative of His Highness and the King will be pleased to receive," etc.

That was in March, and it was already July—and they were still at Tsarskoe Selo. Why?

Subsequently British Prime Minister Lloyd George would blame the Provisional Government for being unable to overcome the resistance of the Petrograd Soviet. But there is another point of view: "Prime Minister Lloyd George himself advised King George to decline the Romanovs' arrival in order to buy popularity among leftist England at the price of his own relatives' lives." For from the very beginning of the revolution Russian society had pronounced an implicit sentence on the tsar's family. That is why the Special Commission, which investigated the accusations against the tsar and tsaritsa of betraying the homeland and their allies' interests, was created. How could George provide a haven for those whom his own country was getting ready to accuse of being traitors in their common struggle? How could Kerensky release this family, which embodied "treason" and the "damned old regime"? So all these talks were just a game—a game of good intentions for the purpose of salving consciences.

"We sincerely hope that the English government does not have any intention of providing a haven for the tsar and his wife. . . . This would profoundly and justly hurt the feelings of the Russians, who have been forced to bring about a great revolution because of being constantly betrayed to our present enemies," wrote the *Daily Telegraph* at the time.

The tsar's family was becoming an increasingly dangerous card in the struggle between the Soviet and the Provisional Government. A decision was finally made: remove the family from Petrograd. They dreamed they would be sent to sunny Livadia, but the Provisional Government did not dare. Kerensky found an effective solution: send the tsar's family to Siberia—to the same place where the tsar had exiled the revolutionaries. They chose Tobolsk, where their fateful favorite, the holy man, had been from. Herein lay both a hidden joke and a cunning trap. Kerensky understood that she would take this as an omen and would submit without a murmur.

The departure date and destination were kept secret; Kerensky was afraid of the Soviet and the crowd—their hatred for the family was too great.

On July 30 they sat for the last time at the formal table in the deserted palace.

Nicholas's diary:

"30 July, Sunday. Today dear Alexei turned 13. May the Lord grant him health, patience, and strength of spirit and body in our present trying times! We went to Mass and after breakfast to prayers, where we brought the icon of the Znamenskaya Mother of God. Somehow it felt especially warm to pray to her holy face with all our people. . . . Everything is packed, and only paintings remain on the walls."

Their departure was set for the following day. But the hour was kept secret. Toward evening a car arrived at the palace—Kerensky had brought Michael.

"31 July. . . . Our last day at Tsarskoe Selo. Marvelous weather. . . . After dinner waited for the departure hour to be set, which they kept postponing. Unexpectedly Kerensky arrived and declared that Misha would arrive soon. Indeed, at about 10.30 dear Misha walked in accompanied by Kerensky and the chief of guards. It was very nice to see him, but awkward to talk in front of outsiders."

During the meeting with Misha, Kerensky was sitting in the corner, demonstratively shutting his ears to show that he was not listening to the conversation.

There was no conversation, though: "awkward to talk in front of outsiders." They stood facing each other in silence, shifting from leg to leg, holding hands for some reason, touching each other's buttons —as if they were trying to remember for all time, as if they felt that they were about to vanish from each other forever.

As he was leaving, Misha asked to say goodbye to the children, but Kerensky would not allow it. And he tried to make the fact known: it was popular to persecute the Romanovs.

Nicholas's diary:

"31 July [continued]. . . . When he left, the riflemen from the guard staff began hauling our baggage into the circular hall. Already sitting there were Benckendorff, the ladies-in-waiting, the girls, and our people. We walked back and forth, waiting for the trucks to arrive. The secret of our departure was observed to the point that both the cars and the train were ordered after the appointed departure hour. We were colossally exhausted. Alexei wanted to sleep, and he kept lying down and getting up, there were several false alarms when we got on our coats, went out onto the balcony, and again returned to the halls."

Between the vacant walls Alix wrote to Anya. Leaving Tsarskoe, she thought about her and about the holy man. Alix knew how to be a friend.

"They aren't telling us where we are going or for how long—we shall only find out on the train, but we think its where you just went —the Holy Man is calling us there, our Friend. . . . Dear one, what suffering our departure is; all is packed, empty rooms—it hurts so much: our hearth for 23 years, but you, my angel, have suffered much more."

Nicholas's diary:

"31 July [continued]. . . . It got quite light, we drank tea, and finally, at 5.15, Kerensky appeared and said we could go. We got into our two cars and drove to the Alexander Station. A cavalry unit galloped behind us from the park."

The car stopped in a field by the Alexander Station. By the tracks stood three or more companies of soldiers—the detachment being sent along to guard and protect the tsar and his family. These were all St. George's Cross holders, brave lads all, riflemen from the First, Second, and Fourth Guards regiments. All in new tunics and new greatcoats. For their future service they had been promised pay as well as travel compensation. At the head of the entire detachment was Colonel Evgeny Kobylinsky of the Life Guard Keksgolmsky Regiment, a fighting officer who had been at the front since the war's outset, had been wounded many times, had returned to the front, and had been taken to the hospital again by wounds. He had lain in the hospital at Tsarskoe Selo in September 1916, when the "most august Sisters of Mercy"—Alix and her daughters, the grand duchesses—made the injured colonel's acquaintance for the first time. "We visited him in hospital & took our picture together." Later he was a "true soldier"—so Alix wrote to her friend. Now the former wounded officer was master of their fate.

Among the guard's riflemen was Sergeant-Major Peter Matveyev. His "Notes and Reminiscences About Nicholas Romanov" are kept in the Sverdlovsk Party Archives.

From Matveyev's Notes:

"We saw that from the tsar's branch line a train of international cars, with 'Red Cross Mission' written on them in red letters, was pulling in. . . . We still didn't know where we were going or where we were taking them."

Two trains were made up. In the breaking sun a string of people walked over to the train cars.

One train carried the guard, the other the family, the guard, their "people," and the suite. The "people and suite" comprised forty-five people. More "people"—their servants—and many fewer of the suite had agreed to share their exile. Even then, in early March, their closest friends had made themselves scarce at the Tsarskoe Selo station—K. Naryshkin, head of the imperial chancellery; von Grabbe, commander of the imperial convoy; Nikolai Sablin, an aide-de-camp and one of the tsar's and tsaritsa's closest friends; the Prince of Leuchtenberg; and Colonel Mordvinov. Their loyal suite took to their heels.

"How they all betrayed him," Nicholas Romanov said biliously and curtly.

Traveling with them were Valya (Marshal of the Court Prince Dolgorukov), the tsar's aide-de-camp General Tatishchev, and several of the tsaritsa's ladies-in-waiting—all that remained of their brilliant court—and their "people."

Kerensky was nervous. He himself was directing the loading— the endless trunks, suitcase, and boxes, the furniture. Commissar Makarov entered the car; he was to accompany the family into exile for the Provisional Government (he already had experience, having brought the arrested Nicholas from Headquarters to Tsarskoe Selo in early March).

Two trains under the Red Cross flag. They would pass through large stations with curtains drawn, and at each of them Commissar Makarov would have to send a telegram to Prime Minister Kerensky. Even the riflemen of the guard did not yet know the direction of their route.

Nicholas and Alexandra were walking along the tracks to their car. The recession from Tsarskoe Selo was almost complete.

A certain Colonel Artabolevsky was present at this recession and recorded in detail how they walked to their train across the approach tracks, along the rails, how he led her, supporting her, toward the car (she had weak legs), how he helped her climb the high step, supporting her by the elbow, how she struggled up and how easily and boldly (a guardsman!) yesterday's tsar jumped up to the step of the train car.

This was the sleeping car of the same Chinese-Eastern Railway for which countless years before, while still heir to the throne, he had helped lay a foundation stone in Vladivostok. Now he was taking this route into exile.

As dawn was breaking, they were still loading the many suitcases into the cars.

Aide-de-camp General Ilya Leonidovich Tatishchev; Marshal of the Court Vasily Alexandrovich Dolgorukov; the children's tutor Pierre Gilliard; Alexei's English teacher Charles Gibbes; Court Physician Evgeny Sergeyevich Botkin; the tsaritsa's personal lady-in-waiting Anastasia Gendrikova; her reader Ekaterina Schneider; her lady-in-waiting Baroness Buxhoeveden; the two friends, the parlor-maids Anna Demidova and Elizaveta Ersberg; the children's servant Ivan Sednev; the heir's companion, the sailor N. G. Nagorny; the cook Kharitonov; and the valet Alexander Volkov entered the car. Servers, lackeys, scribes, a hairdresser, a wardrobe attendant, a wine steward—the string of retainers took their places in the train.

Nicholas's diary:

"The sunrise that saw us off was beautiful. . . . Left Tsarskoe Selo at 6.10 in the morning."

The entire family stood at the windows of the train and looked at Tsarskoe illuminated by the rising sun.

Tsarskoe vanished—and along with it their entire past life.

From Matveyev's Notes:

"Only when we turned away from Petrograd did we realize from the station names that we were following the direct northern route and taking the former tsar into the forests and steppes of Siberia."

Chapter 9

THE PRISONER'S
SIBERIAN DIARY

"*T*HANK GOD WE ARE SAVED AND TOGETHER"
The two trains, their windows gleaming in the rising sun, inexorably
linked, were heading toward Siberia.

Nicholas's diary:

"1 August. The whole family got settled in a fine sleeping car.
. . . Quite stifling and dusty—26 degrees [79°F] in the car. Took a
walk in the afternoon with our riflemen—gathered flowers and ber-
ries. . . .

"2 August. . . . At all stations have had to draw the curtains, at
the commandant's request—stupid and boring. . . .

"4 August. Crossed the Urals and felt a substantial cooling.
Passed Ekaterinburg early morning. All these days the second echelon with the riflemen has frequently overtaken us—we meet like old
friends."

The children and Alix slept, but he did not. Behind the curtained
windows was a station. There had been so many stations in his life,
but this was destined to be his last.

"4 August. Dragged along incredibly slowly to arrive at Tyumen
late—at 11.30. There the train pulled in almost to the platform, so
that we only had to go down to the steamer. Ours is called the

Russia. The loading of our things began and went on all night. . . . Poor Alexei again went to bed God knows when!"

They were met in Tyumen.

From Matveyev's Notes:

"I was watching and the doors of the Romanovs' car opened. Nicholas appeared before them all. I turned toward the gathered military authorities and saw that Romanov was still only thinking about leaving the car and they were all standing, strung out in a line, maintaining a salute. . . . How many people there are who have absolutely not been permeated by the revolutionary spirit!"

At six in the morning they left Tyumen on the *Russia*. Two steamers sailed behind the *Russia*—the *Kormilets* and the *Tyumen*, which carried the servants and baggage. The caravan of vessels sailed down the river Tur.

On August 6 they entered the river Tobol.

"The river is broader and the banks higher. The morning was fresher, and in the afternoon it got quite warm when the sun showed itself. . . . Forgot to mention that yesterday before dinner we went past the village of Pokrovskoe—Grigory's home."

At the very beginning of their journey toward death, they were near him again, the immortal holy man.

Volkov heard Alix say with feeling: "Here lived Grigory Efimovich. In this river he caught the fish he brought to us in Tsarskoe Selo." There were tears in her eyes.

They were approaching Tobolsk.

A quarter of a century before, so young and happy, he too had sailed on a steamer.

Nicholas's diary:

"6 August [continued]. . . . Many people were standing on shore, so they knew of our arrival. I remembered the view of the cathedral and houses on the hill."

From Matveyev's Notes:

"Literally the entire town, I am not exaggerating, spilled out onto the shore."

The crowd gazed at the short man wearing a khaki shirt with regimental stripes, a forage cap with a cross-shaped cockade, his shirt belted by an ordinary soldier's belt with a gleaming brass buckle, on his chest the silver Cross of St. George, wide trousers with a crimson stripe, and folded-over boots. Next to him was a boy dressed in a soldier's greatcoat with epaulets, a lance corporal's stripes, and a soldier's forage cap. And she—in a black coat—and the four girls in navy traveling costumes.

Bells were ringing in all the churches. The commissars of the

Provisional Government took fright that a monarchist demonstration had begun in the town, but it was the Feast of the Divine Transfiguration.

Nicholas's diary:

"6 August [conclusion]. . . . As soon as the steamer landed they began unloading our baggage. Valya [Dolgorukov], the commissar, and the commandant [as he called the guard commander, Kobylinsky] went off to inspect the houses designated for us and the suite. Upon his return Valya told us the lodgings were empty, unfurnished, dirty, and unfit to move into. So we remained on the steamer and began to wait for them to bring back the necessary baggage for us to retire. We had supper, joked about people's astonishing inability to arrange even for lodgings, and went to bed early."

So they remained on the steamer. But they were happy at this liberty and this new, unfamiliar place.

Only on August 6, after their commissar reported that the family had arrived in Tobolsk, was the official announcement about their departure published: "Due to considerations of state necessity, the government has resolved to move the former emperor and empress, now under guard, to a new location. Designated as such is the town of Tobolsk, where the former emperor and empress have been sent in accordance with all measures pertaining to their protection. Along with the former emperor and empress under the same conditions their children and individuals close to them have at their own wish gone to Tobolsk."

The governor's house, where they were to live, was called Freedom House after the February Revolution, which brought the Provisional Government to power, and the street where this house was located was called Freedom Street. The word *freedom* was very popular then.

Freedom House became the first home of their Siberian captivity. (The Dno station, the *Russia* steamer, Freedom House, the Ipatiev house—was all this history's irony?) Freedom House had two floors; the family lived on the second, and on the first were the dining room and rooms for the servants. There was also a half-cellar, ground floor, where their possessions were taken.

The entire downstairs was stacked with the family's traveling bags, trunks, and suitcases. Special belongings were kept in two small wardrobes, and there was a trunk filled with albums of yellowed photographs. There was also a dark leather suitcase that contained the former tsar's diaries and letters. This was all that remained of their vanished life.

While their people were preparing the house, hanging portieres, arranging the furniture they had brought, and cleaning the furniture bought in town, the family remained on the steamer. They even took rides on it, as they once had on their yacht.

"8 August. Went up the Irtysh and after about 10 versts [6 miles] landed on the right bank and went for a walk. Passed bushes and crossed a stream, then climbed a high bank which had a very beautiful view." Happy days.

On August 13 they moved into Freedom House. Tatiana and the empress rode in a carriage; the rest walked.

"We examined everything in the house from the bottom to the attic. Occupied the second floor. . . . Many rooms . . . have an unattractive view. Then we went into the so-called garden—nasty! Everything has an old, neglected look. Unpacked our things in the study and in the washroom, which is half mine and half Alexei's."

Freedom House reminded them of Noah's ark: the emperor and empress of a nonexistent empire, the aide-de-camp to a nonexistent emperor, the marshal of a nonexistent imperial court, and the ladies-in-waiting of a nonexistent empress gathered in the large dining room in the evening and called each other nonexistent titles: "Your Highness . . . Your Excellency."

The servants were well matched to their masters. These accomplished liveried people passed silently from one generation to the next. The menu was written on cards with the tsar's seal: it did not matter that modest dishes were inscribed. As in the Alexander Palace, the gentlemen of the suite were invited to the tsar's table.

A dance of shadows, a fantastic masquerade, unfolded in this Siberian house. The last outpost of a three-hundred-year-old empire.

"14 August. . . . Spent all day sorting through photographs from the cruises of 1890, 1891."

He was still trying to live in a vanished world—in that round-the-world trip when he saw Tobolsk for the first time. And here he was again in Tobolsk. Full circle.

Life in the Tobolsk house proceeded peacefully.

"9 August. In the morning we sat in the garden for an hour, and in the afternoon for 2 hours. Set up the trapeze there for myself."

This was the same trapeze that would go with him all the way to Ekaterinburg. In the morning he swung on it, in the afternoon he played *gorodki,* a game similar to skittles, or sawed wood.

"After all, is this any worse than the Time of Troubles?" Nicholas said to Valya, chuckling, over his sawing.

"A lot worse, Your Highness. A prince is sawing wood."

Tatishchev and Dolgorukov took turns joining in the tsar's sawing: when one got tired the other took over. Nicholas was indefatigable. How he loved movement and thirsted for his beloved walks.

"22 August. What a marvelous day. One gets frustrated at not being able to take walks along the riverbank or in the woods in weather like this. We read on the balcony."

They had a favorite spot.

"16 August. Now every morning we have tea with all the children. . . . We spend a great part of the day on the balcony, which is warmed by the sun all day."

Freedom Street opened out from the balcony. And from Freedom Street there was a good view of the family seated on the balcony: an average-size man in a military tunic, girls in white dresses, and a majestic lady, also in white, holding a lace parasol.

The appearance of the family on the balcony was a favorite spectacle and the principal theater in quiet Tobolsk.

From a letter I received from Andrei Anuchin in Magnitogorsk after my article about the execution of the tsar's family was printed in *Ogonyok:*

"They would come out on the balcony. Especially, I remember, we were all amazed at the girls. Their hair was shorn like little boys. We thought that was the fashion in Petrograd. True, later people said they had been sick, but I don't know for sure. Still, they were very pretty, very clean. . . . The empress was an imposing lady, but not young—my father kept wondering, What, he said, did Grigory see in that old woman? My father had worked with Rasputin in the rooms in the Tobolsk hotel. And Rasputin had been our guest."

So went this monotonous life, where everything was an event.

"24 August. Vladimir Nikolaevich Derevenko arrived with his family. This made the event of the day."

Dr. Derevenko was Alexei's physician, but at this time the boy was healthy—a rare period in his life when he had been in good health for quite a while. The doctor brought his son Kolya along—he was allowed to come on Sundays to play with Alexei.

A quiet, quiet life, but. . . .

"25 August. Walks in the garden are becoming incredibly tedious, here the sense of sitting locked up is much stronger than at Tsarskoe Selo."

What about her?

Upstairs and down the hall, the first and largest room was Alix's.

She spent the greater part of the day there, or on the balcony. Rarely did she go downstairs, even before dinner. She had her favorite books. She read her Bible—in its brown binding and with its many bookmarks—and her "good books," the multitude of spiritual books she had brought along.

They would later be found in the cesspool of the Ekaterinburg house.

The usual scene: a fire in the fireplace, although it was still warm outside, the little dog resting on its knees. The sounds of the piano: Tatiana playing in the drawing room.

Alix was writing another letter to Anya.

"Often I scarcely sleep. . . . My body pains me, my heart is better since I live so tranquilly. I am terribly thin. . . . My hair is graying quickly too."

(She paid a high price for this "I live so tranquilly." That year her hair turned gray and she wasted away.)

"We have settled far from everyone, we live quietly & read about all the horrors—but let us not talk about that. You are living in all that horror, that is enough."

The "horrors." Anya wrote to her about them in detail. The tension was mounting around the unhappy Romanov family. Misha had been arrested. Savinkov, the former terrorist and one of the organizers of Sergei Alexandrovich's murder, was now running the War Ministry. It was on his demand that both Misha and his wife—"that woman," the smug Countess Brasova (now Alix had forgiven her, now Alix only pitied her)—were arrested. And poor Paul Alexandrovich (she had forgiven him as well for all the nasty things he had written in the papers immediately following this horrible revolution).

History had come full circle: yesterday they were locking these bomb throwers up; today the bomb throwers were locking them up. It was a new world. Although Kerensky did free Misha and Paul soon after, they were both eventually killed by the Bolsheviks, Misha in 1918 and Paul in 1919.

In this time of "horrors," the tsaritsa began to dream of moving to the Ivanov monastery. Their dynasty had begun in a monastery, and it ought to end in one as well.

Late in 1904, while Russia was being defeated in its war with Japan, Nicholas had had an amazing idea. The question had arisen in the Holy Synod about restoring the ancient Orthodox patriarchy in Russia. After long reflection and conversations with the empress, Nicholas decided to abdicate the throne, take monastic vows—and

become patriarch! As once, during the Time of Troubles, his ancestor Filaret had been patriarch. The Synod, however, had taken a dim
view of this idea.

Now in 1918, during the triumph of the new Time of Troubles—
how he wished he could live in a monastery.

The spiritual master in Tobolsk was Archbishop Hermogen.
Once he had been a jealous admirer of Rasputin, but when he became Rasputin's sworn enemy he had been persecuted and sent into
exile. For all those oppressions, the new authorities had appointed
him archbishop of Tobolsk, and he had become the family's hope
and support: the Lord's slave Hermogen had forgotten his oppressions and was prepared to serve God's anointed.

Hermogen greeted their idea with enthusiasm.

Volkov was sent to the mother superior. A new building was under construction at the monastery, and the mother superior joyfully
prepared to receive the family. But this idyllic change of fate was not
destined to be.

RISKY AFFAIRS

In September Vasily Pankratov, a commissar of the Provisional Government, arrived, and the idea was buried then and there.

"1 September. A new commissar arrived from the Provisional
Government, Pankratov. He settled in the suite's house with his
assistant, some disheveled ensign who looks like a worker or a poor
teacher. He will be censor of our correspondence."

The "suite's house"—that was the pretty name he gave to the
merchant Kornilov's home. There, opposite Freedom House, lived
the suite—Tatishchev, Dolgorukov, Dr. Botkin, and Botkin's daughter, who would later describe all that had gone on.

Commissar Pankratov had been sent to Tobolsk in the evolution
of that same striking game that Kerensky had dreamed up: Pankratov
had served fourteen years—the greater part of Nicholas's reign—in
the infamous Schlusselburg Fortress. So Kerensky sent him to guard
Nicholas himself.

In all this Alix saw one and the same thing: the world had been
stood on its head—a convict was guarding God's anointed. She did
not favor the strange man in the big fur cap with so much as a
glance. He saw the contemptuous disdain on her face when he
stopped in to return letters, the letters that she had written to Anya
and that this revolutionary had now read (dared read!).

This correspondence was her life.

In Petrograd Anya, who had been released from the Fortress of Peter and Paul, was feverishly beginning to gather funds to free the family. It is ridiculous, but in this whole enormous empire, Anya was probably the only true conspirator trying to free the tsar's family. Back in August Anya had sent one of the empress's young ladies-in-waiting, Rita Khitrovo—a friend of Nastya Gendrikova and Grand Duchess Olga—to Tobolsk with some letters. Anya was furiously energetic, as ever, but she was an inexperienced conspirator. She explained to Rita the importance of the letters. Young Rita caught fire: the romantic aureole of the conspirator turned her head. Her imagination started working, and soon utterly trusting Rita was telling her friend about a certain organization. They were going to save the family! But then Rita's friend told. . . . And then. . . .

Nicholas's diary:

"18 August. . . . In the morning Rita Khitrovo appeared on the street, having come from Petrograd, and spent some time with Nastenka Gendrikova. This was enough that in the evening they conducted a search of her room. The Devil knows what this is! . . .

"19 August. . . . Nastenka has lost the right to walk in the street for several days, and poor Rita Khitrovo has to go back with the evening steamer."

She did not simply "go back." She was taken to Petrograd for interrogation. The charges were the gravest; they were looking for a "Cossack organization." Naturally, they did not find one, but Rita did not betray Anya.

Anya would manage to quit perilous Petrograd: Vyrubova was deported. She took the train from Petrograd to Finland. Soldiers and sailors surrounded the train at Helsingfors, Finland. Someone had spread a rumor that there were grand dukes on the train.

"Give us the grand dukes!"

"Give us the Romanovs!" the furious crowd raged.

What hatred! Yes, Blok was right: the future of the tsar's family could have been read then, during the period of the Provisional Government.

The Helsingfors Soviet arrested Anya and sent her to the *Polar Star*, which had been seized by revolutionary sailors. She was put into the hold, which was teeming with parasites. She was led along the spat-upon, butt-strewn deck to be questioned in the same drawing room where once she had played four hands on the piano with the tsaritsa. In Petrograd her mother went to see Trotsky, the leader of the powerful Petrograd Soviet, who alone could influence the

Baltic sailors—"the pride and glory of the Russian revolution." Trotsky honored her request, and the "pride and glory" released Anya. Once again she was in Petrograd, and once again she corresponded with the tsaritsa.

Alix's diary:

"Sept. 7th. . . . I heard that Ania was taken with the others on her way to Sweden, seized at Helsingfors and ended up on the *Polar Star.*"

Alix's elegiac letters to Anya:

"My dear. . . . Yes, the past is over, I thank God for all I had & was given—& will live in my memories, which no one can take away. My youth is over. . . . My near and dear are all far far away. . . . & am surrounded by their photographs and possessions . . . a robe, slippers, a saucer, an ikon. . . . I would love to send you something, but fear it would be lost. . . .

"You know I am with you in my heart & soul, I share all your sufferings & pray for you fervently. . . . The weather is changeable: frost & sun, then it melts & dims. . . . Terribly boring for those who like long walks & cant have them. . . . How time flies. . . . Soon will be 9 months since I said goodbye to so many . . . & you are alone in your suffering & loneliness. . . . All are generally healthy excepting for slight colds & my knee & wrist swell, tho' thank God, without any great suffering. My heart has hurt me lately. I read much & live in the past, so full of rich & precious memories. . . . Dont lose heart, I wish I could send you something tasty.

". . . I left all the albums in a trunk & am sad without them, but its better that way because it would be painful to look & remember. . . . I drive things away, they destroy me, all too fresh in my memory. . . .

"I remember Novgorod & the terrible 17th. . . . Russia too suffers for this, all must suffer for this, what they have done, but no one understands."

(The "17th"—the day of Rasputin's murder. She was certain that "no one understands": the country had had a revolution in punishment for the "17th.")

After writing about her murdered spiritual pastor, she told Anya about the country's captive pastor—the tsar, who was devoted: "He is absolutely stunning, such fortitude of spirit, tho' he suffers endlessly for his country. . . . How old I am, but I feel like the country's mother & suffer as if for my own child and love my Homeland despite all the horrors & sins. . . . Despite its black ingratitude to the sovereign which tears at my heart. . . . Lord have mercy on Russia and save her."

Anya's indomitable energy. The lesson of Trotsky's might did not pass unappreciated. She continued to improve her ties with the new world, this time with the famous "stormy petrel of the revolution"—the writer Maxim Gorky.

Poor Alix with her firm principles could not understand Anya's new acquaintances, and she branded Gorky in her letters. But Anya knew: new times, new names. And those new names could come in handy in her risky affairs.

Anya did not for one second abandon the "tsar's family, abandoned by all"; she acted. She waited impatiently for news from a certain Boris Soloviev, whom she had sent to Tobolsk immediately after the family.

THE LITTLE MAN

At Freedom House it was the era of Commissar Pankratov. "The little man," as Nicholas mockingly referred to him.

"You yourself have experienced much. You have the ability to fulfill your mission with dignity and nobility, as befits a revolutionary. You and the guard entrusted to you will be guarding and protecting the former tsar and his family until the Constituent Assembly decides his fate." These were Kerensky's parting words to Pankratov the revolutionary, who had spent fourteen years in solitary confinement, and then had been sent from Siberian prison to another. And here he was—overseeing the tsar!

Unlike the empress, delicate Nicholas was gracious with the commissar, but their conversations gradually came to focus on Nicholas's request (or rather, dream):

"Why won't you let us walk in town? You can't actually be afraid that I shall run away?"

The little man did sense the concealed ridicule, and he responded gravely. "I don't have the slightest doubt of it, Nicholas Alexandrovich. Generally speaking, an attempt to escape would only make matters worse—for you and your family." (Just in case, he warned him.)

"So what is the matter, kind sir? I was in Tobolsk in my youth, I remember it is a very beautiful town, and I would like to see it—along with my family."

But the commissar rejected the notion of a walk.

Nicholas's diary:

"Recently E. S. Botkin received a paper from Kerensky from which we learned that we are allowed walks outside town. . . . Pankratov, the rascal, has replied that there can be no question of that now due to some incomprehensible fear for our safety."

Good-natured Pankratov did not want to disappoint him so he did not explain his "incomprehensible fear": the chancellery had been inundated with letters and telegrams from all ends of Russia full of threats and obscenities. People were sending nasty depictions of the tsaritsa and Rasputin. What particularly alarmed the commissar was that many of the letters came from Tobolsk. Soldiers back from the front were hanging around town, poor and hardened men "who had spilled a little blood because of the tsar." No, he could not let the family out into town.

For this Nicholas did not like him.

Nor did the suite—Dolgorukov and Tatishchev—to Pankratov's astonishment, understand anything either. They never stopped demanding that the tsar be allowed to take walks, citing Kerensky's promise. Meanwhile, their own walks around town had already begun to provoke grumbling. The soldiers on the street warned the commissar with a chuckle: "If the prince [Dolgorukov] doesn't stop roaming around town, we're going to beat him up for starters." Russia was on the rampage.

The good Pankratov put up with Nicholas's dislike. He had long since forgiven him for the fortress and fourteen years of his life. Now he simply saw Nicholas as the father of a large family who had absolutely no understanding of this terrible new life. Pankratov became attached to Nicholas's children and gave the duchesses a book he had written about his sufferings and wanderings through Siberia. The girls read it aloud and liked it. He volunteered to be Alexei's geography teacher. Nonetheless, Nicholas did not like him.

In Dr. Botkin's papers I found a poem that evidently enjoyed great success at that time in Freedom House, a poem written in an elegant hand similar to the empress's:

> Whispering mirrors.
> Mirrors in the sad quiet
> Of the Winter Palace,
> Reflect the brazen glance
> Of a shaven face.
> In every hall, indifferent,
> In every corner,

Someone in a jacket
Gazes upon his greatness.
Once yielding to the dazzle,
The country's hero imagines,
That all must fall before him
In humble worship.
That the road to splendid glory
Lies before him.
Barely audible, though, in reply,
The mirrors whisper:
"What care we for empty speeches,
Impertinent newcomer,
The triumph of centuries past
Guards this palace.
Power glorious, imperial,
Shadows incorporeal.
No momentary guest shall drive away
The guests of ages past. . . .
. . . Stop! Never forget too long
Of the crown of the tsar,
He will rise up soon, rise up terribly,
Yellow dawn,
. . So, witnesses of the past,
Just as the gloom appears—
The mirrors whisper the word.
The coming truth."

TOBOLSK 1917

To Nicholas, Pankratov was also a typical civilian with the audacity to lead soldiers. Like a true Romanov, Nicholas did not look favorably upon men who lacked military bearing.

That was why Pankratov remained the "little man."

The soldiers of the guard too, following Nicholas's lead, despised the good commissar and obeyed only Colonel Kobylinsky, who had been appointed commandant at Tsarskoe Selo by General Kornilov, having recommended himself as a devoted supporter of the February Revolution and the Duma.

But the colonel had changed greatly since then. He did try to do his duty, but . . . Nicholas's strange charm . . . his gentleness and delicacy, and those charming little girls, and the empress, so helpless in her arrogance. That was the colonel's portrait of the family, and more and more he was beginning to feel responsible for their fate.

"I have given you what is most precious, Your Excellency, my honor." He had every right to say that to Nicholas.

The colonel began to feel close to Nicholas and his family. Thus, in that quiet town, where the sole military force were those 330 riflemen guarding the family, their commander was heart and soul on the side of the tsar—a strange puzzle.

The head of the guard was for the tsar. The riflemen received endless gifts from the family. Dr. Botkin's daughter wrote very specifically: "During those months [from August to the October Revolution], the family could have escaped. The guard most definitely would have helped them."

Quiet Tobolsk, the influence of the mighty Archbishop Hermogen—everything ought to have facilitated an escape.

Clearly Kerensky had sent them to Tobolsk with the secret intention of creating the conditions for their liberation (as if their flight would have simplified his life). That was why he chose the quiet and very good-hearted Pankratov to watch over the family.

Nonetheless, they did not flee. Why?

*T*HE TSARIST CACHE

Kobylinsky's deputy in the guard was a certain Captain Aksyuta, who ran the affairs of the entire detachment—quite a noteworthy individual. Two years later, in the heat of the Civil War, in the bloody year 1919, a White officer, Count Mstislav Gudovich, was traveling through the unimportant town of Eisk, where he saw a familiar face, that of Captain Aksyuta, whom the count had known during his service at Tsarskoe Selo.

Aksyuta invited him to spend the night in his home and all night he told the count stories about life with the tsar's family in Tobolsk. Aksyuta described in detail the whole story of the tsar's family's departure from Tobolsk as well, and how before their departure they gave things to Captain Aksyuta: the tsaritsa a pearl necklace and diamonds; the sovereign his saber. Aksyuta hid these things on the outskirts of Tobolsk. Only two people knew about the cache: he himself and General Denikin, whom he had told at the inquiry. (Aksyuta was arrested upon his return from Tobolsk and accused of bolshevism, but he was released when they did not find him guilty of anything.)

By the way, we can verify these nighttime stories of Aksyuta's through the tsar's diary.

Like Prince Dolgorukov and Pierre Gilliard, the tsar, of course, would have taken along the pride of any soldier—his saber. In April 1918, shortly before the tsar's departure from Tobolsk, the house was searched, and the tsar recorded the results of that search in his diary:

"This morning the commandant, a commission of officers, and two riflemen walked around a part of our quarters, the result of this 'search' being the confiscation of sabers from Valya and Gilliard and a dagger from me."

So they did not take his saber away. Evidently someone had warned him of the search beforehand and he had given it to that someone—evidently Captain Aksyuta—for safekeeping.

But the little southern town of Eisk was hopelessly distant from Tobolsk, lost in the expanses of Siberia, and in the bloody jumble of the Civil War neither of the two initiated was likely to have been able to reach the hiding place. So in all likelihood the tsar's saber and the tsaritsa's jewels are still buried there somewhere.

We can trust Aksyuta's testimony. That is why his answer to the very important question Gudovich asked him is so interesting: "Why didn't you give the sovereign a chance to escape?"

Aksyuta answered that he and Colonel Kobylinsky did have a plan to free the sovereign, but the tsar told him that in this difficult time for Russia, no Russian should abandon the country. He had no intention of running away and would await his fate right there, he said. We find a reflection of those thoughts in Pankratov's memoirs, where he relates his conversation with one of the grand duchesses:

" 'Papa was reading in the papers yesterday that they are sending us abroad as soon as they can convene a Constituent Assembly. Is that true?'

" 'There's no telling what they write in our papers!'

" 'No, no. Papa says we ought to stay in Russia. Let them send us deeper into Siberia.' "

*P*ATCHED TROUSERS

Time dragged on and on. Everything was an event: the long-awaited wine brought from Tsarskoe Selo was poured out on the wharf. Gray coats, having heard about the wine, had converged on the wharf like flies on sugar. Fearing their "visit" to Freedom House, Pankratov had ordered the wine destroyed.

Nicholas's diary:

"They decided to pour all the wine out into the Irtysh. . . . The departure of the cart carrying the bottles of wine on which the commissar's assistant sat with an axe in his hands . . . we saw from our windows before tea."

General Lavr Kornilov had unsuccessfully demanded dictatorial powers to deal with the Soviets and the Bolsheviks and bring order to the rear and the front.

Nicholas's diary:

"5 September. . . . Clearly in Petrograd there is great confusion. . . . Evidently nothing ever came of General Kornilov's undertakings."

In his confinement, all events were equal, although his disappointment over the loss of the wine may have been greater.

September 17 (again 17!). Shortly before the October overthrow of the Provisional Government Nicholas finished the fiftieth notebook of his diary, the last he was to complete. He began a new one, which he would fill only halfway.

"51," the tsar numbered it. "Begun in Tobolsk."

"18 September. Monday. 1917. Fall this year is remarkable here. Today 15 degrees in the shade and the air utterly southern and warm. In the afternoon Valya and I played gorodki, which I haven't done for many years. . . . Olga's ill health has passed, and she sat on the balcony for a long time with Alix. . . . Mama wrote a letter through the censor Pankratov."

This entry began his fateful final notebook.

A monotonous life.

A letter from Alix to Anya:

"I cant guess what lies ahead. . . . God knows—& will work in His own way. . . . I put all in His hands. . . . am knitting socks for Little One, he asked for a pair: his are full of holes, but mine are thick & warm. . . . We used to knit in winter, remember? Now I do everything for my people: Papa's trousers are all patched . . . the girls' nightgowns are full of holes, Mama has masses of grey hair, & Anastasia is very fat, like Marie used to be—big, thick-waisted, then tiny feet—I hope she grows more. Olga is thin & so is Tatiana—their hair is growing marvelously, so in winter they can go without shawls." (In February the grand duchesses' hair had been shaved when they had the measles.)

They entertained themselves with amateur shows. Gilliard and the daughters and the tsar himself were the actors. "We rehearsed the play," "we did a small play very amicably . . . much laughter."

Nicholas appeared in the leading role in Chekhov's *The Bear*, playing the "not very old landowner" who comes to collect a debt from the "little widow with the dimples in her cheeks" and falls in love with her.

Nicholas's diary:

"18 February. . . . We performed our play [*The Bear*], in which Olga, Marie again, and I acted. At the beginning of the performance there was a great deal of nervousness, but it seems to have come off well."

He stood on his knees before Olga, who played the widow. "I love you as I have never loved before: I have left twelve women, and nine have left me, but I never loved one of them as I love you."

How they all laughed when Nicholas said this. Even Alix. Rarely did she laugh anymore.

Their voices, there in the darkness, in a vanished house, a vanished time.

"*I*T MAKES ME SICK TO READ WHAT HAPPENED" October had come.

Snow-draped Tobolsk dozed, and no one knew about the events in Petrograd. The newspapers had suddenly stopped arriving. Nicholas was reading *1793*.

He did not read this book aloud, but Alix could not have helped but see it—and remembered: Versailles, the Revolution, the execution of the royal couple.

"11 November. No papers or even telegrams from Petrograd for a long time. In such a trying time this is awful."

On November 17 (again 17!) he learned of the Bolshevik seizure of power.

"17 November. . . . It makes me sick to read in the papers what happened two weeks ago in Petrograd and Moscow! Much worse and more shameful than events in the Time of Troubles."

During that time Commissar Pankratov recorded:

"He was quite depressed, but depressed most of all by the looting of the wine cellars in the Winter Palace! 'Couldn't Mr. Kerensky have put a stop to that license?'

" 'Obviously not. A mob, Nicholas Alexandrovich, is always a mob.'

" 'How can that be?' the tsar asked with sudden bile. 'Alexander

Feodorovich was put in by the people. A real favorite of the soldiers. . . . Regardless of what happened— why tear apart a palace, why allow the plunder and destruction of riches?' "

The old revolutionary and the former tsar did not understand one another. The tsar was not talking about cellars, he was talking about "plunder," about the "senseless and merciless Russian insurrection."

Gilliard recalled how during the first days of captivity the tsar had been strangely pleased. But as soon as he learned of Kornilov's rout, and then the fall of the Provisional Government, Nicholas regretted his abdication more and more. It was a Time of Troubles.

Their last New Year's had come. The cold was so fierce the boy went to bed wrapped up in all his blankets, the grand duchesses' room turned into an icebox, and they all sat in Alix's room—where a small fire burned—until late into the night. "It is boring! Today is like yesterday, and tomorrow will be like today. God help us! God have mercy on us!" Alexei wrote in his diary.

"Today was grey and not too cold. . . . Today our boredom is green!" his father wrote on January 2.

They put the New Year's tree right on the table. A Siberian spruce—but no toys. Their severe tree of 1918. Their last tree. For Christmas they made each other small gifts. Tatiana gave her mother a homemade notebook for a diary: a pathetic quadrille note pad inside a cloth cover she had sewn herself—in her mother's favorite color, lilac (from a scrap of the empress's scarf).

On the cover she embroidered a swastika, her mother's favorite symbol.

I am opening the lilac cover. On the back of the cover Tatiana wrote in English: "To my sweet darling Mama dear with my best wishes for a happy new year. May God's blessings be upon you and guard you for ever. Yr own loving girl Tatiana."

Now Alix began a diary that she too would be fated not to finish.

On New Year's Eve she wrote in this diary: "Thank God we are saved & together & He has protected us & all who are dear to us this year."

If the legends are to be believed, this was supposed to be a fateful year for them.

In the Tobolsk house the tsar was reading a book by Sergei Nilus.

(He wrote about this in his diary on March 27, 1918.) The wife of Nilus was known to the empress. When the Niluses were wed, Alix had given them an icon and a samovar with her own initials in blessing.

All this is to the point because the Niluses had entrée to the imperial court and knew a great deal. In the book Nicholas was reading, *On the Banks of God's River,* Nilus recorded a legend told to him by the empress's lady-in-waiting Mrs. Geringer.

A small chest was kept at Gatchina Palace, locked and sealed. Inside was something put there by the widow of the murdered Emperor Paul I, Maria Feodorovna, who had instructed that the chest be opened by the emperor who ruled Russia one hundred years after her husband's murder. That day came in 1901. The tsar and tsaritsa —at the time still very young people—prepared for their journey to retrieve the chest as if it were an amusing outing. But they returned, according to the lady-in-waiting, "extremely thoughtful and sad. . . . After that, I heard that the sovereign had mentioned 1918 as a fateful year for him and the dynasty."

This may be merely an ingenious legend. Nevertheless: the cold house, the empty tree on the large table. There was something fateful in the gathering of this, their last year—1918.

A GAME FROM THE GRAVE

Indeed, by then it had already begun.

This happened on New Year's Eve:

In the Church of the Protective Veil of the Virgin, where the family went on the first day of Christmas of the first revolutionary year, under convoy, the holiday service was coming to an end in the overfilled church when suddenly some very familiar, not yet forgotten words were heard. The deacon solemnly proclaimed: "Their Excellencies the Sovereign Emperor and the Sovereign Empress," followed by the names of their children and all their old titles. At the end the deacon's bass uttered powerfully: "A long life!" Thus in the Tobolsk church, for the first time since the February Revolution, the ancient "wish for a long life" for the tsar's family was proclaimed.

The church responded with a rumble. The senior officer of the convoy and Commissar Pankratov waited till the end of the service and called for the deacon, who cited the instructions of his superior, Father Alexei. "Drag him out of the church by his braids!" the convoy's rifleman raged.

The next day the Tobolsk Soviet proclaimed by the Bolsheviks

formed a commission of inquiry. They blamed Pankratov and demanded that he harshen the regime, and for the first time the call
was heard: "To prison with the Romanovs!" The Soviet even went
after the priest. But Archbishop Hermogen did not give Father
Alexei up for punishment—he sent him to a remote Tobolsk monastery.

How amazingly interlinked everything is in the Romanov history.
The name Hermogen stands at the source of the Romanov dynasty.
During the Time of Troubles Patriarch Hermogen issued the call to
drive the Poles from Russia, for which he was imprisoned and accepted a martyr's death.

Now, three hundred years later, an archbishop by the same
name, here in Tobolsk, was with the last Romanovs. "Master . . .
you bear the name of Saint Hermogen. That is a sign," the dowager
empress wrote him. She was expecting decisive steps from the decisive archbishop.

The empress mother was right. It was a sign. History had come
full circle.

At this time the Russian church was acting independently of the
tsar. Peter the Great had eliminated the patriarchy in 1703, but in
November 1917 a church council again elected a Patriarch of Moscow and All the Russias. Early in 1918, Patriarch Tikhon anathema-
tized the Bolsheviks and sent the host and his blessing to the deposed tsar through Hermogen. Many pastors, including Hermogen
in Tobolsk, behaved in keeping with the head of the church. The
majority of them would perish during the Red Terror in the aftermath of the revolution.

At that time, on the threshold of 1918, the power of the Tobolsk
pastor was great. When Hermogen refused to recognize Father
Alexei as guilty, he challenged the Soviet: "According to the Holy
Scriptures . . . as well as history—former emperors, kings, and
tsars are not deprived of their office when they are outside the country's administration." He was writing about the office given by God
over which the earthly has no power.

Hermogen wanted to help the family escape and could have done
so. Siberia meant secret trails, distant monasteries more like for-
tresses, rivers with hidden boats, parishioners who had not yet come
unstuck from God.

Now, when the Bolsheviks had seized power in the capital, how could they not have made an attempt to free them now?

Alix! No, she could not entrust the family's fate to the holy man's accursed enemy.

"Every day Hermogen holds a service for Papa and Mama," she wrote Anya. "Papa and Mama"—that was what Rasputin had called them. While giving Hermogen his due, even praising him, she unconsciously recalled the holy man, who hated him. No, she could not.

Thus, beyond the grave, Rasputin would not allow them to join forces with the only person who could have helped them then. Instead, the holy man sent them a different emissary.

All this time Anya was collecting money for the family. People gave willingly: better to give the money than to take part in dangerous plots themselves. Anyway, they needed to give the money: what if everything suddenly reverted to how it had been? Count Benckendorff and Anya accumulated large sums for the family's liberation. Then Boris Soloviev leaped from the maelstrom of Petrograd life.

His past spoke for him.

Borya's father was treasurer of the Holy Synod. His mother had belonged to the circle of the holy man's most devoted female proselytes.

Later, while compiling his biography, Soloviev would tell about his adventures. At first he had studied in Berlin but had wound up in India. A Theosophist, in India he had been a disciple of the famous Madame Blavatsky.

During the war, in 1914, Soloviev managed to remain in Petrograd, having set himself up in a reserve artillery regiment, and was a frequent guest at the apartment of Grigory Rasputin, where he met Rasputin's daughters, Varvara and Matryona. After the February Revolution in 1918 Soloviev turned up in the revolutionary Tauride Palace. The ensign had brought his soldiers to swear an oath to the Duma. Now he was a superior officer in the Duma's War Commission. Rasputin's disciple had become a revolutionary.

Vyrubova must have chuckled when she heard his tale about his soldiers dragging him to the Duma to swear allegiance—she had no need of justifications. That was precisely what one had to do now to survive. She judged Soloviev's action and decided to recruit him.

So Boris Soloviev turned up in Tobolsk and easily made contact with the family. His main agent became Father Alexei, who at that time often held services in Freedom House. Through him Soloviev transmitted letters to the tsaritsa.

And that was where he went wrong. Yes, the tsaritsa respected Father Alexei, but Father Alexei was from Hermogen. From "our Friend's" enemy. So every proposal Soloviev transmitted through the priest was greeted with supreme caution. She reacted to his plans for organizing their escape without the slightest enthusiasm. Nicholas replied for her (or rather, she suggested he reply): we must avoid the risks that would inevitably arise for the children with any attempt to free us.

As he was leaving Tobolsk for Petrograd, Soloviev evidently got an idea: he advised Father Alexei to proclaim his wishes for a long life for the tsar's family. Soloviev convinced the priest that such a proclamation would become his great deed, albeit a safe one. For the power of Hermogen would protect him.

As a result of that wish for a long life, what Soloviev had contemplated did indeed happen: the family's tranquil life ended. The events that inevitably followed pushed them toward escape now and forced them to seek his help.

How many more of them would there be, these clever games with the last tsar! At the base of them all, however, one method would show up with exhausting monotony—provocation.

Soloviev returned to Petrograd and evidently complained to Anya of the tsaritsa's mistrust and the impossibility of organizing their flight. Then Anya (how well she knew her imperial friend) gave Soloviev a brilliant idea: marry Rasputin's daughter Matryona. That would be his passport to Alix's heart. Soloviev did so immediately.

(About Soloviev's feelings toward his new bride he wrote the following in his diary: "Continuing to live with her, I ought to ask of her at least a pretty body, which, unfortunately, my spouse cannot boast of, so she cannot serve me simply for sexual relations, as there are many better and more useful than her.")

Soloviev and Matryona returned to Pokrovskoe in Siberia, where Soloviev merged with the image of the holy man. Only after that did he again make contact with Freedom House.

Now a very different reception awaited him. A beloved shadow loomed behind him: now he was "the husband of *his* daughter, who had come to save them," as Alix wrote. The charger had answered the call. As always, Rasputin's name transported Alix to a familiar and fantastic world: the powerful host from the Holy Scriptures was bringing Grigory to them from beyond the grave.

She believed in Soloviev with all her heart. Thrifty Alix herself generously sent him the tsarist jewels to use for the family's liberation.

In Petrograd Anya sent another officer to assist Soloviev: Sergei Markov. Markov was a "Crimean," that is, an officer of the Crimean Cavalry Regiment, whose colonel-in-chief was the empress.

On March 12 Alix recorded joyfully in her diary: "I was on the balcony & saw my ex-Crimean Markov walk by, also Stein."

Who was this Stein that Alix wrote about? This is easy to figure out from the tsar's diary. Nicholas, as always, recorded *everything* in his diary (including what he should not under any circumstances have written).

"12 (25) March. Vlad[imir] Nik[olaevich] Stein came from Moscow for the second time, bringing along a handsome sum from some good people we know, books, and tea. He was with me in Mogilev as second vice governor. Today we saw him walking down the street."

So Stein was an emissary from Anya and Benckendorff who had brought a "handsome sum" for their expenses and liberation.

But the main thing was "my ex-Crimean Markov." Anya had calculated unerringly. Alix was in raptures: they had joined together—the holy man's emissary and the emissary of valorous Russian officers, loyal to their empress. After the next letter from Soloviev she was already raving to Gilliard about the "Three Hundred Officers" who had gathered in Tyumen and were preparing to free them.

Unlike Soloviev, Sergei Markov was hardly a rogue. He was truly devoted to the "tsar's abandoned family" (as he would later entitle his bitter book).

Soloviev arranged a meeting with Sergei Markov and another officer who had turned up from Vyrubova—Sedov. He told them about the "officer staging groups" that had already been formed all along the route from Tobolsk to Tyumen. They would pass the tsar's family down the line during the escape. He informed them that he controlled the telephones of the Soviet itself. His inspired, shameless bravado ended in a convincing introduction: Soloviev presented to them the skipper who was to take the tsar's family away on his steamer.

Who played the role of skipper remained Soloviev's secret. For now the money brought by Stein and the tsarist jewels continued to make their way from Freedom House to the scoundrel.

Alix was inflamed with her belief. Even calm Gilliard immersed himself in her world and remained "at the ready in the event of any and every opportunity."

When in March 1918 the church bells began to ring and armed men rode down Freedom Street in daring "troikas, jingling, whooping, and whistling" (as Nicholas described them), Alix, looking out the window, whispered ecstatically: "What fine Russian faces!" She could see: they had come! The Mighty Host, the three hundred officers the holy man's emissary had written her so much about.

In fact, that day it was daring Red Guards riding into town from Omsk to establish Bolshevik power in Tobolsk. And on that day the idyllic period of their captivity came to an end. The post-October world invaded quiet Tobolsk, jingling, whooping, and whistling.

After his death Rasputin managed to ruin the family yet again.

"There were no officer groups to liberate the tsar's family! There was only talk," Tatiana Botkina, the daughter of the doctor Evgeny Sergeyevich would exclaim in her memoirs.

Already after the tsar had been forced to leave Tobolsk, she asked one of the Tobolsk "plotters"—monarchists: "Why didn't your organization undertake anything?"

"We organized to rescue Alexei Nikolaevich."

When the time came for Alexei and the grand duchesses to leave Tobolsk, however, once again she posed the same question.

"Have pity, after all, we could be discovered and the Red Army could catch us all."

"There were many organizers like that," Botkin's daughter concluded sadly. She considered Soloviev nothing more than a provocateur—as did many in Freedom House.

But who would have dared come out against Rasputin's son-in-law?

Was Soloviev actually a Bolshevik agent?

Hardly. More likely they simply found each other convenient, the Cheka, the Bolshevik's secret service, and Soloviev: two games played with the participation of the unsuspecting family.

There was the plot game organized by Boris Soloviev, who simply robbed the family. And there was one other performance, which took advantage of Soloviev's idea by declaring his false plot genuine—to prove the necessity of the immediate transfer of the tsar's family from quiet Tobolsk.

This second game had been born in the Red capital of the revolutionary Urals, in the town of Ekaterinburg.

Let us try to picture the cast, the game's chief players.

Chapter 10

COMRADES

✦

COMRADE FILIPP

In late April 1917, a guard of Kronstadt sailors stood outside Mathilde Kschessinska's mansion: Lenin had assembled a conference of Bolsheviks in the palace of Nicholas's former lover. It is telling that the poet Blok sensed their strange and terrible power even then.

Not long before, these men had been rotting in exile, wandering hopelessly in emigration through the cities of Europe. Now they were talking about ruling the largest country in the world. "The party that does not want power is unfit to call itself a party," said Trotsky, the second in command of the Bolsheviks.

This was no utopia. The Bolsheviks had a powerful conspiratorial apparatus left over from their past struggles with the tsar. Russia at that time was the freest country imaginable—so they were able to act.

It was to this old conspiratorial organization that two old friends belonged who met at this conference in the Petrograd mansion—Yakov Sverdlov and Filipp Goloshchekin. Here he is in a photograph, Comrade Filipp. He is already over forty. By the standards of the revolution he is already an old man—a face flaccid from sleepless nights and bad food. And, of course, bearded. They all were—Lenin, Sverdlov, Trotsky, Kamenev. . . . Goloshchekin had been studying to become a dentist, but he became a professional revolutionary instead: conspiratorial apartments, party cells. His most recent nom de guerre, Filipp, became his name. He had been a member of the Bolshevik Central Committee since 1912. In 1913, while Nicholas was celebrating the tricentennial of the dynasty, Goloshchekin was captured by the police and sent to the Turukhansk region, where he met another prominent Bolshevik in exile, Yakov Sverdlov. "Sverdlov and Goloshchekin were linked not only by a commonality of views but also by personal friendship," Sverdlov's wife wrote in her memoirs. Both friends were freed from Turukhansk in February 1917.

After the conference in Kschessinska's palace the head of the Ural Bolsheviks, Sverdlov, was left in Petrograd to become secretary of the Central Committee. Replacing Sverdlov in the Urals was his old friend Comrade Filipp.

As leader of the Ural Bolsheviks, Goloshchekin set out for Ekaterinburg to organize a new revolution.

At that time, in April 1917, Lenin declared they would take power by peaceful means. By July, though, the Bolsheviks were already flexing their muscle: the Kronstadt sailors entered Petrograd. But the July demonstration was put down, and Lenin declared Kerensky's government an organ of the victorious counterrevolution and the Soviets a "fig leaf" concealing the power of the bourgeoisie. Lenin was beginning to prepare for an armed uprising.

The Provisional Government initiated a judicial inquiry: the Bolsheviks were accused of mutiny and of receiving money from Russia's enemy, Germany. But Lenin and his closest comrade-in-arms, Zinoviev, refused to appear at the trial and hid. And although many leading Bolsheviks were arrested, the party was not banned, and three hundred party members participated in the next Bolshevik congress.

Commander-in-chief General Kornilov attempted to avert a seizure of power by the Bolsheviks. He demanded from Kerensky full authority to bring order to the rear and the front. General Krymov's Cavalry Corps had advanced toward Petrograd.

Kerensky removed Kornilov and turned to the Soviets for help.

Lenin decided to enter into an alliance with the government—against Kornilov—and Kerensky accepted this gift. But it was a gift he would soon regret.

"Only developing this war [with Kornilov] can lead us to power," Lenin wrote. *Power!* Lenin exploited the fight against Kornilov and his contact with the government magnificently for the legal arming of his own supporters in Russia's major cities.

Comrade Filipp in Ekaterinburg was indefatigable: workers' detachments were armed and a Red Guard headquarters created. He made the Baltic sailor Pavel Khokhryakov, picture-perfect handsome draped in ammunition belts, chief of staff.

Neighboring Perm, too, was readied for the uprising. There Goloshchekin depended on two Bolsheviks, the Lukoyanov brothers: Mikhail, leader of the Perm Bolsheviks, and Feodor, who led the workers' Red Guard.

By fall of 1917 the Provisional Government had become a fiction. All those brilliant intellectuals had expired in interparty struggle and were incapable of controlling the dark elements they had stirred up. "The government apparatus's collapse was complete. . . . A wave of barbaric pogroms incurred by greedy, hungry muzhiks rolled over Russia. . . . The food situation was no better. In Petrograd we had crossed the line beyond which famine began. . . . All the industrial centers suffered constant strikes. . . . The situation on the railroad was becoming ominous. . . . The entire press . . . howled in the identically same way about imminent economic catastrophe. . . . Wherever bold military-revolutionary committees had appeared, there was no longer any question of legal authority," N. Sukhanov wrote in *Notes on the Revolution*.

In early October Goloshchekin left for Petrograd as a delegate from the Urals to the Congress of Soviets. Soon after, an urgent telegram arrived in Ekaterinburg: on October 25 the Bolsheviks had overthrown the Provisional Government.

At that point the Ekaterinburg Bolsheviks, their "bold military-revolutionary committees," and the Red Guard began taking over the town.

The same happened in neighboring Perm.

As soon as the Bolsheviks had won in the Urals, Red Ekaterinburg's gaze turned on quiet Tobolsk. There, not so far away, were the tsar and his family. The revolutionaries' holy dream—retribution visited upon Nicholas the Bloody! That was from the realm of ideas. Moreover, rumors about the incalculable Romanov treasures brought from Petersburg . . . that was already the prose of life: "Behind all ideas there is always a steak," one of the Bolshevik leaders joked.

In Ekaterinburg, Goloshchekin was working on a plan.

COMRADE MARATOV

After my first article was printed in *Ogonyok,* I received a brief message in the mail: "Honored Comrade Radzinsky! I can tell you certain details on a topic of interest to you." The signature: "Alexander Vasilievich." His first name and patronymic, but no last name, just a phone number. I called.

An old man's voice: "Only talk louder. Bad telephone." (Old people do not complain about their hearing, they complain about the telephone. During my inquiries I would have dealings mostly with very old people—and I would hear this sentence many times.)

I: "I received your letter. . . . I would like to meet with you."

He: "We can do that. . . . I'll come to you myself." (How many times would I hear all this! They had been through a good school—Stalin's school of fear. He did not want me to come to his place and find out who he was. He was afraid.)

He came himself: a frail old man with a cloud of translucent white hair. Slats of medals on his jacket. He began.

"If you decide to use what I'm going to tell you . . . I don't want my name used."

I interrupted. I spoke very loudly. He was hard of hearing.

"Don't worry. After all, I don't know your last name."

He knew that very well, but he wanted to hear it from me one more time. No one anywhere else in the world could understand what he was afraid of now, but for anyone born in this country it was understandable: just in case, he was afraid.

He: "It's just that this story torments me for some reason. In those years . . . you weren't in the world yet . . . in those years people didn't ask too many questions. . . . It wasn't done. . . . So that the man . . . well, the man I'm going to speak of now I know very little about. This happened in the very early twenties. I know the man was from the Urals . . . my older brother was a famous neurologist he went to for treatment. I know this man had a relative who worked in the Central Committee—a 'big fish in a little pond.' Well, they called my brother in to examine him in his apartment, which he did. Privately, so to speak.

"This was how he came to our house.

"That evening at tea my brother told my father about it in my presence. I remember. You do remember everything that happened in your youth. . . . This man, it turned out, had worked in the Ural Cheka and had practically run the tsar's execution. Ever since then his nerves had been bad. Every spring he checked into a neurology clinic. Spring had come and he had an exacerbation. My brother called him the spy."

He stopped, evidently, for me to ask a question.

I did.

" 'Spy' because he'd been sent to their house in the beginning, before Ekaterinburg, when the tsar was in another town."

"Tobolsk."

"Maybe. You know better. But there was a big house there. He went to work as a carpenter there in that house, and he followed the tsar. That's what he told my brother. The tsar and tsaritsa spoke English, and no one understood them, but they needed to. So they sent him and. . . . But someone from the Guard was helping him inside the house."

He fell silent.

"And then?"

"Then nothing. My brother got scared. Or rather, our father said: 'He'd better not show his face in our house.' My father did not exactly welcome the new authority."

"Tell me, when did you write this down? The whole story?"

"What do you mean? Who would write something like that down? All my life I've been afraid to talk about it. He told my brother about the execution. But my brother didn't even want to tell us about it. All he said was: 'The blood gushed out.' Everything was covered in blood."

How many times, working on these documents, have I encountered their mystical quality. It's like that saying "The beast ran into the hunter." I call it "evoking documents." Soon after, while studying Goloshchekin's comrades, I ran across an amazing biography in *Revolutionaries of Prikamie* (Perm, 1966):

"Lukoyanov, Feodor Nikolaevich (b. 1894) studied at the Perm Grammar School and in 1912 was a student at Moscow State University Law School."

His father, an official, "senior comptroller of the treasury, died, leaving a wife and five children. As of 1913 a member of a Bolshevik student circle at Moscow University. His brother Mikhail and sisters Nadezhda and Vera were all Bolsheviks.

". . . Returning to Perm, he joined a Bolshevik group at the newspaper *Perm Life*. . . . After the triumph of Soviet Power he began working in the Cheka and was chairman first of the Perm Provincial Cheka and then, after June 1918, of the Ural Regional Cheka."

So, in July, when the Romanovs were executed, the Ural Cheka in Ekaterinburg was under the direction of Feodor Lukoyanov.

Later in the book: "A severe *neurological* disease acquired in 1918 during his work at the Cheka made itself felt more and more. In 1932 Feodor Lukoyanov was sent to the People's Commissariat of Supply, in 1934–37 he worked on the editorial board of *Izvestia*, then in the People's Registry Commissariat. Died in 1947; buried in Perm."

And here was his face in a photograph—a thin, nervous, and intelligent face.

I began to search.

Soon after, I received a letter from Kira Avdeyeva in Sverdlovsk along with an excerpt from the autobiography of Feodor Lukoyanov kept in the Sverdlovsk KGB Museum, to which I did not have access. He had written the autobiography in 1942.

"Throughout 1918 and early 1919 I worked in the organs of the Cheka, first as chairman of the Perm Cheka, then as chairman of the Ural Regional Cheka, where I took part in directing the execution of the Romanov family. . . . In the middle of 1919 I fell ill and for purposes of recovery transferred to party work. . . . My health did not improve, though, and in early 1922 the Bolshevik Central Committee placed me in a Moscow sanitarium."

A "spy"?! No, we dare not say that. It is much too fantastic; it smacks of literature, not science. But we can conjecture. Especially since the autobiography includes a curious detail: "Throughout 1918 and early 1919 I worked in the organs of the Cheka, first as chairman of the Perm Cheka. . . ." But he was not appointed chairman of the Perm Cheka until March 15. What was he doing for the first part of 1918—and where?

Feodor Lukoyanov's party nom de guerre was Maratov (he had named himself after the most inexorable French revolutionary; the educated youths of Bolshevik circles liked the French Revolution). So we can propose that in late February Comrade Maratov was sent from Ekaterinburg to Freedom House—the "spy."

Thus they began to implement their Ekaterinburg plan to seize the tsar's family.

*N*OR DID PETROGRAD SLUMBER
The tsar's family would indeed have been very useful for the Bolshevik Soviet of People's Commissars (Sovnarkom), Lenin's government beginning in 1917. It could become the trump in their game with the Romanovs' powerful relatives in England and Germany. Moreover, those Romanov jewels they had heard so much about were still. . . . And all this lay somewhere in defenseless Tobolsk.

On November 2 the victorious Petrograd Military-Revolutionary Committee entertained a question about holding the Romanov family. The committee sent a proposal to the Sovnarkom to transfer the Romanovs from Tobolsk to Kronstadt, the bulwark of the revolution—to put them under the control of the bullet-strung Baltic sailors.

From a letter of Viktor A. Blokhin in Moscow:
"The brutal execution of the tsar's family seems implausible and terrible now. I am a very old man and I saw that time. . . . Atrocities, brutality, frenzy—they were very common. The murder of the tsar's family only fills in that picture. That's all. I knew Vladimir Dmitrievich Bonch-Bruevich, a charming bespectacled civilian from a good family (his brother was a tsarist general). Dear sweet Vladimir Dmitrievich himself was responsible for the terrible Room 75 at Smolny, which was the predecessor of the bloody Cheka. Vladimir Dmitrievich loved to go on 'about the terrible part of revolution' and about the affairs of the revolutionary sailors. I have known many who after the revolution, after many many years had passed, reveled in how they sent White officers off to be shot. An entire generation happily went to the grave with this brutality on their souls. Or not so happily (if Comrade Stalin took an interest in them). For the West to understand us and for us to understand ourselves we have to remember that the murder of the tsar's family did not seem strange at the time because it wasn't terrible, it was ordinary.

"Here you have an incident with the sailors described by that same acquaintance of mine, Vladimir Dmitrievich Bonch-Bruevich. It was quite a commonplace and frequent kind of incident during those days in 1918: sailor-anarchists from the ship *Republic* were detaining three officers on the street. The elder Zheleznyakov was in command of the sailors. Half-drunk, his crazed eyes staring off into space, he was sitting on a chair, making the sign of the cross in the air, and muttering from time to time: 'De-e-eath . . . de-e-eath . . . de-e-eath' (as Bonch-Bruevich himself described it).

"So this guy, along with the sailor boys from the *Republic,* put the detained officers into a car and made them an offer: either get a ransom—a few thousand rubles—or get shot. They drove the unfortunate men from one terrified Petrograd apartment to another, and the officers begged their friends to give them the money. They did give a little—they were afraid the bold sailors would think there was more to be had there. The revolutionary sailors grew bored with this fussy tribute collecting. The heroes stopped in to amuse themselves at a bordello, to put it bluntly. So that the detained officers wouldn't get bored while they entertained themselves with the girls, they dislocated the jaw of one of them with the butt of a revolver. True, they did not get to do anything else: the madam would not let them drip blood on her rug. The sailors spent their time with the girls—and got bored again. So they sat the officers in the car, drove to some remote spot, and ordered them to get out. They did. 'Take off your coats'— they surrounded the officers and seized their revolvers, all the while cursing obscenities. The officers took them off. They ordered one of them to take the coats to the automobile. He did. While he was at the automobile he heard shots. Then the sailors returned. 'Ah, son of a bitch! How could we have forgotten about you? Ah, to hell with you. You're still good for something. Tomorrow we'll all drive around again' (that is, from apartment to apartment). They shoved him under their feet between the seats and beat the prostrate man with their heels all the way—they were having a good time. This I am quoting almost word for word from the published memoirs of my friend Vladimir Dmitrievich. When you start getting horrified about the execution of the tsar's family or the execution of Michael Romanov—don't forget that remote spot where they killed those officers like dogs. Don't forget the elder Zheleznyakov, who made the sign of the cross in the air and kept muttering, 'Death . . . death . . . death.' By the way, Zheleznyakov was a very famous name in the history of the October Revolution because the 'bad' elder Zheleznyakov, with his bad sailors from the *Republic,* was the brother of the 'good' younger Zheleznyakov, who dispersed the Constituent Assembly, the first and last free Russian parliament, with good sailors from the same *Republic.* Only History could dream up something like that! 'De-e-eath . . . de-e-eath . . . de-e-eath.'"

The revolutionary Kronstadt sailors wanted to seize the tsar's family, especially with those innocent virgins and the jewels into the bargain. "De-e-eath, de-e-eath, de-e-eath." But the Bolshevik Sovnarkom already had its misgivings about the "pride and glory of the Russian revolution."

The Sovnarkom declared the transfer "untimely."

Bolshevik pragmatists did, however, discuss how best to exploit the tsar's family. The new government had its romantics. Romantics mad about the French Revolution. The romantics were in favor of bringing the family to Moscow immediately—for a great show trial to be arranged featuring the people against the deposed tyrant, and the principal orator of the revolution, Lev Trotsky, was eager to act as plaintiff. Oh, how popular Lev Davydovich was then. . . . A comb of black hair, blue eyes, fervent speeches. "The perpetually excited Lev Davydovich," his enemies said with sarcasm—or rather envy, for that was the peak of Trotsky's popularity. And the face of Lev—the "lion" of the revolution—hung like an icon in the houses of all true revolutionaries.

He would destroy the pathetic, fork-tongued tsar before all progressive humanity. It would be the triumph of the revolution! The idea of trying the tsar in Moscow won out, which was all well and good—but how were they to get the tsar to the capital? "Three hundred thirty armed guards picked from the tsar's former soldiers" were guarding the Tobolsk house. They passed the matter on to the All-Russian Central Executive Committee, the highest organ of power in the Republic.

"HE BORE HIS SERVICE IN EXEMPLARY FASHION"

At that time someone we already know stood at the head of the Central Executive Committee: Sverdlov. In January 1918 Sverdlov received representatives from the detachment guarding the Romanovs. Chief among them was Peter Matveyev (the author of the Notes).

Matveyev was a typical figure from the early years of the revolution: a gray overcoat that sensed power. Chosen chairman of the soldiers' committee, yesterday's tsarist sergeant-major hung a thick tablet on his door: "Lodging of Peter Matveyevich, Comrade Matveyev."

From Matveyev's Notes:

"The first news about the fall of the Provisional Government came to us on about November 20. . . . But Commissar Pankratov . . . tried to prove that the Bolsheviks had been driven out of Petrograd a long time ago. . . . I managed to convince the guard, to prove that . . . we must immediately send a delegation to Petrograd to obtain more accurate information from the Center."

Matveyev returned from Petrograd greatly changed.

"We spent a few days in Peter [Petrograd] and on January 11 went back to Tobolsk, having been given a specific assignment: to get rid of the Provisional Government's commissar, the detachment having submitted, in any case, to Soviet power. We were ordered not to give up Romanov without the specific knowledge of and instruction from the Central Executive Committee and the Sovnarkom. . . . On January 23 a general meeting of the entire detachment was called. After my report . . . the detachment split into two parts: one for Soviet power; the other, the 'right,' for Kerensky."

Now in the evenings Matveyev was disappearing from the house; he was beginning to stop in at the Soviet—to see the Tobolsk Bolsheviks. Matveyev put an enormous globe in his "lodging": "Give us world revolution!"

According to the memoirs of the Bolshevik Koganitsky, at one of the Soviet's evening meetings, Matveyev, "who then represented only twelve or thirteen of the guard," swore an oath to the Soviet: "We would sooner die than let the family escape with their lives. . . . To ensure this, our people were to be interspersed in every shift of the guard."

Soon afterward the committee drove out Commissar Pankratov, but it still did not dare raise a hand against Colonel Kobylinsky.

Later Peter Matveyevich would receive the following document for his activities, written on the stationery of the Tobolsk Bolshevik Soviet:

"The present certificate attests to the fact that Comrade-Citizen Peter Matveyevich Matveyev was in the Special Detachment guarding the former tsar and his family. . . . Moreover, he bore his service in exemplary fashion and honestly, fulfilling unquestioningly the duties placed upon him as a soldier-citizen and fighter for the Revolution, not abandoning the deed entrusted to him during all the difficult moments and stages of the Russian Revolution. . . . Signature—Khokhryakov, May 18 (5), Tobolsk."

"He bore his service in exemplary fashion." Could it have been Comrade-Citizen Peter Matveyevich Matveyev who brought the "spy" into the house?

Let us return to the "spy." I am trying to imagine how he was sent.

He is called up from Perm to the capital of the Red Urals. Heading the Ural Cheka formed in February is Mikhail Efremov—a Bolshevik since 1905 who was sentenced by a tsarist court to hard labor for life. But the true leader of the Ural Cheka has been turning into more of a Bolshevik ever since that same terrible year 1905—the future regicide Yakov Yurovsky.

COMRADE YAKOV

One of many children from a poor Jewish family, his father had been a glazier and his mother a seamstress.

In 1938, exactly twenty years after the Romanovs' murder, Yakov Yurovsky would be dying in the Kremlin Hospital from an excruciatingly painful ulcer. In his dying letter to his children he would talk about himself:

"Dear Zhenya and Shura! On July 3, new style, I will turn sixty. As it turns out, I have told you almost nothing about myself, especially my childhood and youth. . . . Ten children grew up in my father's family, and with them poverty bordering on destitution. We could not break out of it, even though the children began working for masters at the age of ten, and father and mother worked to the point of exhaustion. . . . [He left a tailor to study with a watchmaker.] My watchmaker master got rich off the sufferings of his adolescent workers—I worked for him until I was nineteen and never knew what it meant to eat my fill. But then I was fed my fill after a strike and was thrown out as a ringleader and forbidden to enter the town's watch and jewelry shops."

What rage! A temperament of hatred. But after all, this was being written by an old man racked by terminal illness.

"Beginning in 1905, I never ceased working for the party for a single day." Yes, the whole rest of his life—the jewelry business, in which he prospered, his strange trip abroad, his acceptance there of Catholicism—everything was a cover for his main, secret occupation. A successful watchmaker, a rich jeweler, and a photographer, he in fact maintained conspiratorial apartments for the Bolsheviks. In 1912 he was arrested—but he was a marvelous conspirator. The police came up with only circumstantial evidence, and he was sent to Ekaterinburg, where he opened a photography studio. In 1915, Yakov Yurovsky was drafted, but he got out of the front by completing medic training and taking a job in the surgical department of the local hospital.

Then came the February Revolution. The hospital elected him to the Soviet. With Goloshchekin he began to prepare for the Bolshevik seizure of the town. And then—the October Revolution of 1917: the Soviet became the government of the Urals, and he became deputy justice commissar, a common route for Bolshevik leaders. Beginning in early 1918 he worked in the Cheka as chairman of the terrible commission of inquiry under the Revolutionary Tribunal. This was the man: former medic and photographer, now arbiter of human fates in the cruel Ural Cheka—Comrade Yakov Yurovsky.

The Cheka occupied the luxurious American Rooms hotel. Yurovsky settled in the most luxurious— Room 3: mirrors, rugs, the receding luxury of the richest Ural merchants. Downstairs was a famous restaurant where not long before those merchants had boozed it up.

All this—the merchants and the food—vanished in an instant under the new power. But the ravishing smells of that rich restaurant lingered strangely and upset the Chekists.

It was in Room 3 of the "American hotel" that Yurovsky evidently received Feodor Lukoyanov.

I am trying to listen in on their conversation:

He began the conversation, of course, with an exhortation. Like many not very literate people, Comrade Yakov loved to hold forth.

"When Lenin named Felix Dzerzhinsky leader of the Cheka, he said: 'We need a good proletarian Jacobin for this post.' . . . And an educated Jacobin. . . . That's the kind of man we are looking for to be chairman of the whole Ural Cheka. As you know, Comrade Finn [the party nom de guerre of Efremov, who was then head of the Cheka] did not complete university. . . . And I have no education at all. . . . But in Petrograd professors sit in the government. . . . You studied at the university, my son [that was what he called all the young Chekists], you even studied law. . . . That is just what we need for the head of the Cheka . . . in order to placate our 'public' [Yurovsky's favorite word]. The question about you has been more or less decided. . . . There's nothing for you to do in Perm—you'll become the leader of all the Urals. However, my son, we are going to give you a trial run. . . . Comrade Filipp [Goloshchekin] is in Moscow right now. He is planning to propose there—in view of the presence in Tobolsk of a monarchist plot—moving the Romanovs here, to Ekaterinburg. Actually, we need proof of the plot." He fell silent and added distinctly, "That is what you can get for us. . . . You speak English and German . . . so you can understand what they're talking about. . . . And one more important thing: the jewels. Figure out what and how many they are. Everything must be returned to the working people."

*T*HE NIGHTMARE OF BREST

Let us return to Tobolsk. While the family's fate was being decided elsewhere, in the snow-covered quiet house their old monotonous life went on. Only it had become frightening to read the papers.

Nicholas took the Russian papers and foreign magazines (French —with very frivolous cartoons that so intrigued the guard that they reached the tsar only with great delay).

But he received the papers promptly and followed events closely. As before, he considered himself responsible for Russia's destiny.

The papers told of the Constituent Assembly's brief fate. The Bolshevik government had also called itself "provisional" and was supposed to rule until the people elected a parliament—a Constituent Assembly. The Bolsheviks had declared as much in a decree.

In January 1918 the Constituent Assembly was convened, the "first freely elected Russian parliament," but the Bolsheviks had no intention of ceding power. The Bolshevik government prepared for the opening of the parliament as if for battle. They created a special military headquarters and divided Petrograd into districts; patrols of sailors and soldiers controlled the streets. At the Tauride Palace, where the Constituent Assembly was to convene, the Bolshevik Moisei Uritsky was named commandant. When the Constituent Assembly did convene, sailors from the battleship *Republic* were led into the hall under the command of Zheleznyakov the younger. To them fell the honor of cutting short the history of Russian parliamentarism. At the opening of the first day of sessions, Zheleznyakov the younger approached the chair, banged his fist on the table, and uttered these historic words: "The guard is tired, we cannot protect you anymore. Close down the meeting."

Thus Lenin rid his government of that extra "provisional." The power of Bolshevik rule combined in a surprising way with impotence, though. When Uritsky appeared to disperse the Constituent Assembly, he looked very unhappy and very cold. Out on the street, which the Bolshevik sailors were patrolling, the terrible commandant had his fur coat stolen by bandits! And when Lenin, the head of the Sovnarkom, bitterly quit the Constituent Assembly, having prescribed its closing, he discovered that the pockets of his coat had been cleaned out and his automatic pistol stolen! The fact of which the robbed Lenin indignantly informed the robbed Uritsky. This split between the authorities and the brigandage of the streets did not end in 1917 by any means. In March 1918, when Lenin's government moved from Petrograd to Moscow, it was still going on. In December 1919, in Sokolniki, Lenin's wife was waiting for her husband for the children's New Year's party, but the leader of the country arrived very confused. En route robbers had stopped his automobile. The evildoers had taken away weapons and papers—from him, the guard, and the driver. They also took the automobile. When the leader of the world proletariat announced to his attackers, "I am Lenin. Here are my documents," the reply was unexpected: "We don't care who you are!"

Echoes of these horrors, these lawless anecdotes of this Time of Troubles, reached Nicholas accurately from papers and letters (despite the destruction and chaos, the mails were working). The parliament's disbanding might still elicit a sarcastic chuckle from the man who had fought with the Duma for so many years, but the actions of the new authorities in February and March 1918 truly shook the former commander-in-chief.

In March the Bolsheviks concluded the Treaty of Brest with the Germans. Russia admitted defeat in war.

Nicholas's diary (now he kept his diary with double dates, as putting the new style in parentheses):

"12 (25) February. Monday. Today telegrams arrived informing us that the Bolsheviks, or the Sovnarkom, as they call themselves, must agree to a peace on the German government's humiliating terms in view of the fact that enemy forces are advancing and there is no way to stop them! It is a nightmare!"

This was indeed a nightmare for him, a hallucination. The Baltics, Poland, part of Belorussia, part of the Caucasus—all this was lost to Russia. The empire he had received from his father no longer existed.

Nicholas was a typical Taurus, with all the qualities of that astrological sign. Sluggish, stubborn, and secretive, taciturn, adoring of his children and family. He had been deprived of one Taurean quality, however: *force*—the ability to fall into a frenzy. "Would you please finally get angry, Your Excellency!" one of his ministers pleaded in vain.

Yes, he was a special Taurus, a golden calf, a calf born for sacrifice, Job the Long-Suffering.

That day, though, as he read the report on the Treaty of Brest, he felt the fury of a Taurus.

She would echo him in a letter to Anya: "March 3rd [16th] 1918. . . . God save Russia & help her. . . . one great humiliation &

horror. . . . I cant reconcile myself, cant think about this without a terrible pain in my heart."

Exactly one year after his renunciation, he cursed all his sacrifices, thousands upon thousands of lives—all in vain.

Lenin had been preparing for the Treaty of Brest for a long time. Only by concluding peace with the Germans could he demobilize the army—a dangerous force—and reinforce the power his party had so easily taken. When the Bolsheviks disbanded the first Russian parliament, Lenin saw his dream before him—the Treaty of Brest, which the Constituent Assembly had never ratified.

Many in the party considered the treaty humiliating. The second most powerful Bolshevik leader, Trotsky, was adamantly opposed. But Lenin broke his opponents by convening a special party congress and, in exhausting debates and votes, won. All this time, his shadow was Yakov Sverdlov, his loyal executor. (When Sverdlov died, Lenin would search feverishly for a "new Sverdlov"—and would find him: Stalin. But this time Lenin miscalculated: the shadow would become independent and in the end would vanquish his master.)

Thus peace was concluded. The former tsar now had plenty of time to ponder events.

A religious man, he consoled himself. He knew it was God's will. Only with the passage of time, when they could step back from events, when the revolution and the catastrophe that had overtaken Russia had drifted off into oblivion, would the intention of He who creates history be revealed. That was why he would read so attentively Lev Tolstoy's reflections on history—that "part of *War and Peace* that I had not known before": "Marie and I have been caught up reading *War and Peace*."

But Alix was incredulous: what about their allies? How could they stand for this? No, she felt something had to happen. Might this horrible peace with the Germans somehow change their fate as well? Alix was right. It was at this time in Moscow that their fate was being decided.

𝒜N AGREEMENT AMONG OLD FRIENDS

In February in Moscow, the congress's seventh session, during which the Treaty of Brest was discussed, was attended by the head of the Ural Bolsheviks: Filipp Goloshchekin.

With Lenin, he voted for the Treaty of Brest. Against Trotsky, against those who did not understand the need for a respite. It did not really matter; once they were strong they could repudiate all of it. The Bolsheviks had already established the principle: concluding an agreement, they immediately began to think about how to break it later. "Policy is nothing more than a saving lie—in the name of revolution."

At the same time, immediately after the Leninists' victory, Goloshchekin had a conversation with another supporter of the Treaty of Brest, his old friend the chairman of the Central Executive Committee Sverdlov. This conversation concerned, of course, what most upset the Uralites: the transfer of the tsar's family to Ekaterinburg.

Goloshchekin had the right to a reward for his loyalty to the Leninist line, for his loyalty to the Brest peace. He asked his old friend, the Uralites' old friend, for his support.

What about Sverdlov? Sverdlov probably sketched out the situation for him: as chairman of the Central Executive Committee he must (and would) insist on the transfer of the tsar's family to Moscow. That had been the decision: supremely powerful Trotsky was organizing a trial against Nicholas Romanov.

(Sverdlov knew that the "perpetually excited Lev Davydovich" was eager to turn that trial to his own benefit. But did the chairman of the Central Executive Committee need to do anything more for Lev? Yes. Brawls had already broken out between yesterday's allies, and if previously the formation of factions inside the party had meant a contest of ideas, now it meant a contest of power in the guise of ideas.)

They understood each other virtually without words, Sverdlov and Goloshchekin. Sverdlov would carry out Moscow's line, but . . . but if the Urals were sufficiently energetic, the Central Executive Committee would (could) accede.

Having received Sverdlov's assurance, Goloshchekin reported to the presidium of the Central Executive Committee about the current lack of supervision over the tsar's family and the threat of a monarchist plot in Tobolsk. He proposed moving the tsar and his family to Ekaterinburg under the strict supervision of the capital of the Red Urals.

Upon his return to Ekaterinburg Goloshchekin began his own turbulent activities and evidently made contact with the "spy."

The "spy." I can picture his first meeting with Matveyev in Freedom House. Lukoyanov would find out that the family had already begun to know great need. Soloviev had extracted huge sums "for the plot," and now the tsar's family did not have enough money. The new government of workers and peasants was not about to give them any. Kobylinsky, Tatishchev, and Dolgorukov had gone around to the merchants of Tobolsk borrowing money. At first they gave willingly— they did not expect the new authorities to last—but now they were not giving at all.

The abundant meals in the house continued, however. As before, the empress's only walk was out to the yard, where the ducks and geese roamed and she carried on entertaining conversations with the chef, Kharitonov. In captivity, food is entertainment. They ate and ate, and the smells of the scraps lingered in the back yard.

But now the aroma had faded: there was no more money. To Matveyev's delight, the Moscow government had put the family on soldiers' rations. Nicholas Romanov had been given a soldier's ration card.

The new, meager meals were served as before by servants in livery. But the servants had begun to rebel, too: no wages.

Nicholas's diary:

"14 (27) February. We have had to cut our expenditures for food and servants significantly. These last few days we have been busy figuring out the minimum for us to make ends meet. . . .

"15 (28) February. For this reason we must part with many of our people, since we cannot support everyone who is in Tobolsk; this naturally is very hard, but unavoidable."

Just then the "spy" appeared in the house.

A conversation in Freedom House:

"What can you do?" (This is Matveyev.)

"I'm a carpenter. You can set up a workshop in the building next to the storeroom. Where the Romanov things are kept. That way they'll be safer."

He searched the storeroom for the first time late that night. The house was long since asleep. Matveyev brought a great clutch of keys and began opening the innumerable trunks and suitcases. Just what wasn't there in those trunks! Multitudes of the odd and useless—you could see they had packed clumsily, in haste. There was a suitcase filled with riding crops, a trunk with tiny children's booties—evidently for Alexei when he was little. Many dresses and linens. No jewels, of course. Those were kept upstairs. But there was a large brown leather suitcase stuffed with papers, black notebooks covered in a precise handwriting—the tsar's diary! Lukoyanov immediately sensed how important this brown suitcase would be for him.

Later there was a ball in honor of their departing "people." The drunken servants made a racket all night long. The family locked themselves in their rooms.

"AT TIMES IT SEEMS I HAVEN'T THE STRENGTH TO GO ON"

Nicholas's diary:

"9 (22) March. Today is the anniversary of my arrival at Tsarskoe Selo and my confinement with my family at Alexander Palace. Cannot help but remember this difficult year gone by—and what lies in store for us? All is in God's hands, all our hopes are on Him."

Now he could only recall anniversaries of his confinement.

The guard had been changing before his very eyes. After Matveyev's return, many "good riflemen" were dismissed.

"During my morning walk said goodbye to our best riflemen, who are going home. They are leaving now in the winter unwillingly and would gladly stay on until the opening of navigation."

From Matveyev's Notes:

"The rightist diehards got their 'wolf' passports [indicating their political unreliability] in the teeth and were told to clear the hell out."

With the appearance of the "spy," matters accelerated. Kobylinsky was barely managing with the remaining riflemen and was already begging the tsar to let them go home: "I can no longer be of use to you." Nicholas asked him to stay on: "We are enduring it and you will too." He stayed on.

Soon after, Lukoyanov was able to report to the capital of the Red Urals: "The guard's mood has changed. It's time!"

*C*OMRADE LYUKHANOV AND COMRADE AVDEYEV
At the Urals' Zlokazov Factory (named after the owners, the Zlokazov brothers) there was a machinist, a short man, middle-aged, with an unprepossessing, pimply face: Sergei Lyukhanov. He was a remarkable worker, a jack-of-all-trades. He was married to an "educated woman"—a teacher with the exotic name Avgusta. Before the revolution Avgusta's brother—a certain Alexander Avdeyev—had come to the factory. Lyukhanov made him his assistant and did all his work for him. Avdeyev had not come to the factory to work. He was a professional revolutionary and occupied himself with Bolshevik agitation—at which he was very good. Tall, blond, mustached Avdeyev soon became a favorite with the Zlokazov workers. Immediately after October 1917, the workers seized the factory under his leadership: Sergei Lyukhanov's former assistant became the factory commissar. It was he who took the former boss away on a cart, saying, "I'm taking him to jail." But no one ever saw the boss again. A serious man was Avdeyev. "Smacking" and "liquidating" were favorite words in 1918. At the factory he formed his own armed detachment.

Now at the end of February 1918 Avdeyev was called to meet with the Cheka at the "American hotel," where he was awaited by Pavel Khokhryakov, head of the Red Guard and now a leader of the Cheka: light brown curls, a rosy flush suffusing his face. The Baltic sailor was a handsome man and in possession of the most terrible strength. Strength and revolutionary ardor.

Here at the Cheka they discussed Goloshchekin's plan: Khokhryakov and Avdeyev, along with his Zlokazov workers, must secretly enter Tobolsk, throw over the old rule there, and establish a new Bolshevik rule, after which they would enter into contact with Freedom House and, taking advantage of the guard's mood, move the family to the capital of the Red Urals.

*T*HE BATTLE FOR FREEDOM HOUSE
They entered the town at night in small groups. As Avdeyev himself would later describe, "the first to filter in were the secret agents, Pavel Khokhryakov and the Bolshevik Tanya Naumova." They pretended to be lovers and one can only guess how much happiness the handsome sailor and the young girl accrued from this game, which

later ended in marriage (although they would not be happy in that marriage for long—the frenzied Khokhryakov would perish the same year in the Civil War).

Then Avdeyev's group entered Tobolsk—sixteen men. Cleverly, though, they spread a rumor about a thousand Bolsheviks surrounding the town. Tobolsk's frightened inhabitants seized on the rumor and the thousand turned into thousands. But Avdeyev's men were too late.

Yet another pretender to the title of jailer to the tsar's family had entered the game: Omsk, the revolutionary capital of western Siberia. Its men too had come to Tobolsk—for the tsar's family and their jewels.

Nicholas's diary:

"14 (27) March. . . . The arrival of this Red Guard [from Omsk], as any armed unit is now called, has provoked all sorts of conjectures and fears here. . . . The commandant and our detachment have also been disturbed—the guard has been strengthened and the cannon brought in as of yesterday. It is good that people have come to trust one another at the present time."

The Omsk men attempted to force the guard to let the detachment into the house. The house was surrounded. But Kobylinsky and the detachment had brought out the cannon. Freedom House remained under guard.

Goloshchekin sent through Tyumen for one more detachment from Ekaterinburg. But the Omsk men were stronger.

Nicholas's diary:

"22 March [Nicholas went back to the old style. From now until the end of his diary he would remain true to the old style, the style of his world]. In the morning we heard from outside the Bolshevik brigands from Tyumen leaving Tobolsk. . . . In 15 troikas, jingling, whistling, and whooping away. The Omsk detachment drove them out of here."

The Omsk men had celebrated their victory prematurely, however. Ekaterinburg dealt a new blow. A third armed detachment of Ekaterinburg men under Zaslavsky entered the town. Simultaneously the Ekaterinburg men seized power in the Soviet. Now Khokhryakov became chairman of the Soviet and Avdeyev and Zaslavsky its most influential members. The Soviet of Ekaterinburg men began to run Tobolsk, but their expectations were not borne out. Despite the fact that they were now the municipal authority, despite all Matveyev's efforts, they were not allowed into Freedom House either.

Kobylinsky announced to the Soviet: "We have been sent here by the central authorities, and we will hand over the tsar and his family only to the central authorities."

A battle of telegrams began around the house. The Omsk Soviet telegraphed Moscow to order the "old guard" replaced by an Omsk detachment. The Tobolsk Soviet demanded that Moscow replace the old guard with the Ekaterinburg Red Guard.

Simultaneously Goloshchekin was sending Moscow "accurate information" obtained from Lukoyanov about the monarchist Soloviev's plot and the flight being readied for the family "as soon as the rivers open." He even specified that the escape was supposed to be accomplished on the vessel *Maria*. But Moscow was enigmatically silent.

Meanwhile in Tobolsk, the Red Guard detachments were waiting for someone to approach the house. They were afraid of the guard's excellently armed, tsarist-trained riflemen. They were afraid of each other.

Finally Moscow decided to intervene.

Chapter 11

SECRET MISSION

✦

*T*his puzzling episode began at the very beginning of April 1918, when announcements started appearing in the papers about "the impending trial in Moscow against Nicholas the Bloody."

On April 1 the Central Executive Committee passed a secret resolution: "To form a detachment of 200 men and send it to Tobolsk to reinforce the guard. Should the opportunity arise, to transfer the prisoners to Moscow." The resolution was not intended for publication in the press; however, it immediately became known to the Uralites (Sverdlov? Of course, Sverdlov!), provoking a storm of indignation in Ekaterinburg.

As a result Sverdlov "was forced to back down": the Central Executive Committee passed an "addendum" to the earlier resolution: "1. The tsar and his family shall be moved to the Urals. 2. For this, military reinforcement will be sent to Tobolsk."

Sverdlov sent an official letter covering all this to Ekaterinburg on April 9.

Why did the powerful supporters of a Moscow trial against the tsar agree to this "addendum"? Only because Sverdlov evidently reassured them, and there was only one way he could have done that: by explaining that the "addendum" had been passed only to quiet the energetic Uralites and avert an independent seizure of the tsar's family by Ekaterinburg.

Indeed, the "armed reinforcement" sent to Tobolsk had a *secret mission:* to bring the tsar and his family to Moscow.

Clever Sverdlov did not explain, however, that the "addendum" would now give Ekaterinburg the legal right to demand the tsar's family for itself.

Sverdlov's double game had begun. Oh, how that game would mislead all future investigators.

Placed at the head of the secret mission was Vasily Yakovlev.

Commissar Yakovlev. Here he is in his big fur hat, a sailor's shirt visible underneath his open sheepskin coat. His face is "rather intelligent," as Dr. Botkin's daughter described it.

What biographies! And how infuriatingly bland our own lives!

Vasily Yakovlev—that was his party nom de guerre from one of his many fake passports. His real name was Konstantin Myachin. Born in 1886 in Ufa, he had worked quietly and peaceably as a turner for the railroad until the First Russian Revolution drew him into its many storms. The nineteen-year-old turner Myachin became a member of an armed workers' detachment—in plain words, a terrorist. Lenin had very eloquently defined the tasks of those armed workers' detachments in a letter to the Petersburg Bolshevik Action Committee dated October 3, 1905: "Establish . . . armed workers' detachments anywhere and everywhere—especially among students and workers. . . . Each should arm itself immediately according to its own abilities: one with a revolver, another with a knife, another with a kerosene-soaked rag to set fires, etc. The detachments must start their military training right away in immediate operations. One right now could undertake the murder of a secret agent or the bombing of a police station; another could assault a bank to confiscate funds for the uprising. Let each detachment train itself, if only for assaulting policemen."

This ruthless and sinisterly romantic group in the party took shape on spilled blood: bank robberies, bombings, assassinations of officials. "Starting with my first speech, bullets and a soaped rope dogged my heels," Myachin wrote with pride.

Very quickly the party status of these armed detachments became rather ambiguous. At their 1907 congress, the Bolsheviks discussed terror and prohibited expropriations. As always in Bolshevik history, though, the obvious concealed the hidden. The First Revolution had ended in defeat, and the Bolsheviks feverishly sought funds—both to live in emigration and to create a secret underground in Russia. Having prohibited terrorism for the sake of public opinion, they secretly encouraged it. It was then, in Tiflis in 1907, that Joseph Stalin prepared his attack on a post office and seized funds totaling more than a million dollars. It was then in 1907 that Myachin became leader of the Ufa armed workers' detachment. And soon after, at the Miass station, a mail train was seized: led by Myachin, the workers stole 72 pounds of gold. They were tracked down, and arrests followed. Myachin escaped by shooting his way out.

Ever since his youth, secret activity had shaped this man's character.

He crossed the border illegally—with a passport in the name of Vasily Yakovlev. In Italy—in Bologna and on Capri—he created a Marxist school (that is what the tsarist gold was used for!). Yakovlev and his comrades did not recognize parliamentary struggle against the authorities. In their school they taught underground work—how to hide and murder. During this time he crossed the Russian border illegally more than once. In a conspiratorial apartment in Kiev in 1911, he prepared to seize the treasury, but the police came upon his trail. Yakovlev managed to vanish from the city, fleeing Kiev right as Tsar Nicholas II was making a triumphant entrance into the city. (It was at this time in Kiev that Stolypin was murdered right in front of the tsar.)

Another illegal border crossing: Yakovlev turned up in Belgium. The bomber and expropriator became a modest electrical repairman for the General Electric Company in Brussels.

After the February Revolution he returned posthaste to Russia. In October 1917 he was in Petrograd preparing for the Bolshevik takeover and secretly bringing in weapons. During the Bolshevik overthrow, Vasily Yakovlev, perched on a cannon, and a detachment of sailors traversed all of Petrograd to seize the telephone station and cut off the provisional government, gathered in the Winter Palace, from the world.

After the Bolshevik victory Yakovlev became commissar of all the telegraph and telephone stations in Petrograd. In 1918, Vasily Yakovlev was among five men whom the Bolshevik government instructed to create the sinister Cheka. Throughout 1918 Yakovlev's name popped up in many political events. On the night the Bolsheviks dispersed the Constituent Assembly on Lenin's order, Yakovlev repeated his October trick: he disconnected the telephone system in the Tauride Palace. Later he brought forty train cars of grain to starving Petrograd. In his wake there was a great deal of crossfire and blood. He made one more lucky transshipment: he brought twenty-five million gold rubles out of besieged Petrograd to the Ufa bank—accompanied once again by chases and shooting.

This was the legendary man who was sitting in Sverdlov's office in the early spring of 1918.

It was Sverdlov who proposed sending Yakovlev to Tobolsk to bring out the Romanovs. Trotsky, who knew Yakovlev well, also approved his candidacy: after all, Yakovlev had already made more than one high-risk run.

There was one detail in Yakovlev's biography, though, known only to Sverdlov, who had worked in the Urals for a long time. Back during the time of the underground and expropriations, a "black cat" had run between Ufa's Yakovlev and Ekaterinburg's armed workers, and at the very beginning of 1918, when Moscow appointed Yakovlev military commissar of the entire Urals, Ekaterinburg flatly rejected him. They preferred someone else. So Goloshchekin, the head of the Ural Bolsheviks, became military commissar. Yakovlev's mandate had to be reversed. The mutual ill will between Yakovlev and the Uralites had acquired new fuel.

Was this why the clever leader of the Central Executive Committee appointed Yakovlev to head the secret mission?

Sverdlov handed Commissar Yakovlev the ominous mandate of a Central Executive Committee plenipotentiary, a mandate bearing the signatures of Lenin and Sverdlov that obligated everyone to facilitate the plenipotentiary's mission—or be shot for failure to obey orders. The powerful mandate said not a word, however, about the mission's purpose.

Sverdlov explained Yakovlev's task to him orally: the tsar's family must be brought to Moscow.

Sverdlov asked Yakovlev his plan of action. Yakovlev proposed the typical plan of that insane period: without explaining anything to anyone (citing state secrecy), he would take the tsar's family out of Tobolsk and down the frozen Tobol to Tyumen, where there was a railroad. He would put the family on a train and start out in the direction of Ekaterinburg, so as not to provoke any hostility on the part of the Uralites. But once he was well out of Tyumen he would turn toward Omsk—eastward. He would take the tsar's family to Moscow via Omsk, which was at odds right then with Ekaterinburg. Should circumstances intervene, he would take the tsar's family to his own Ufa, where there were people loyal to him and where it would be quite simple to continue on with the family to Moscow whenever necessary.

Sverdlov suggested keeping a *third* plan in reserve: if all else failed, Yakovlev could take the family to Ekaterinburg. The former terrorist was quite sure of himself, however. In his previous high-risk escapades he had always triumphed, and he would triumph this time as well: the tsar's family would be in Moscow.

Yakovlev had two telegraphists put at his disposal—he must maintain constant contact with Moscow and Sverdlov. The telegrams were to use a code of sorts: "cargo" and "baggage" meant the tsar's family; the "old route" was the Moscow route; the "new route" was the Ufa route; and finally, the "first route" was the Ekaterinburg route.

Having received his assignment, Yakovlev immediately left for Ufa to assemble a detachment. Ufa was his home, he had old friends there. The local Cheka formed a detachment of reliable men, the majority of them former comrades who had taken part in seizing the Miass gold. Yakovlev referred to them affectionately as the Miass robbers.

In Ufa, Yakovlev summoned the leader of the Ekaterinburg Bolsheviks, Military Commissar Filipp Goloshchekin.

Yakovlev presented his mandate and demanded that Goloshchekin write orders subordinating all the Ekaterinburg men in Tobolsk—the head of the Tobolsk Soviet Pavel Khokhryakov, Avdeyev, and so on—to Yakovlev.

Certainly, Goloshchekin was prepared to give him the paper, but first he demanded that Yakovlev disclose the purpose of his mission: after all, the Central Executive Committee had already promised the tsar's family to Ekaterinburg. Yakovlev explained that the tsar's family would be brought to Ekaterinburg, just as the Central Executive Committee had promised, but no one must know that yet. Especially in Tobolsk. Why the secrecy? Yakovlev had a likely explanation: otherwise the Omsk detachment in Tobolsk would make trouble and matters might go as far as open conflict. Moreover, the old guard could mutiny as well. They had a long-standing dislike for the Ekaterinburg Bolsheviks from the Tobolsk Soviet—it was no accident that they refused even to let them into Freedom House. That was why Yakovlev asked Goloshchekin to order the Ekaterinburg men to obey him without question.

Goloshchekin gave him his written order.

All this was a game. Of course, Goloshchekin, Sverdlov's old friend, had had information about the true purpose of Yakovlev's secret mission for a long time, and he had prepared for it.

What was Lukoyanov doing while Yakovlev and his detachment were leaving for Tobolsk?

After the middle of March, after Khokhryakov and Avdeyev and their detachment entered the town, he evidently left for Perm. In any event, on March 15, 1918, Feodor Lukoyanov was named head of the Perm Cheka. At the end of April, however, he left Perm again—"to put down kulak disturbances." In fact, he evidently returned to Freedom House: Goloshchekin had declared that the decisive moment was near.

Meanwhile, in Freedom House, life went on as usual.

Nicholas's diary:

"7 [20] April. Saturday. . . . Vespers at 9. An excellent bass sang."

As always, vespers on Saturday. An electric light burned dimly in the large hall, and the icon of the Savior shone in the half-dark.

Alix entered the empty hall and covered the lectern with her own embroidery. And left. At eight the priest, accompanied by four monks from the monastery, entered the hall with a chasuble. Candles were lit. Dolgorukov, Tatishchev, and Botkin formed a line to the left of the lectern, and then came the ladies-in-waiting of the former court and the various "people."

Finally a tiny door in the wall opened, and in walked the family.

The chorus and the "excellent bass" began to sing: "Glory to God from on high." The family knelt, whereupon everyone else dropped down as well.

Thus they greeted their favorite day, April 8, the twenty-fourth anniversary of their engagement. That night, as always, they reminisced . . . brother Ernie, Wilhelm, Georgie, Ella. Where were they now? Grandmother Queen Victoria was long since in her grave. Nevertheless, all that had happened. There had been a kiss in Coburg Castle. And there had been a young man and a young woman—insanely happy. Or rather, happy and insane, for, "Though thou exalt thyself as the eagle, and though thou set thy nest among the stars. . . ."

But on this special anniversary Nicholas learned he was no longer allowed to wear his epaulets. Nor was "Little One" either. His epaulets were a kind of connecting thread: he wore epaulets with his father's initials, and his son wore his, Nicholas's.

I can imagine how impatiently Matveyev and the "spy" waited for him to go on his walk—to read what he had written in his diary.

Evidently, the usual ritual took place: Matveyev roamed the halls, keeping watch, and Lukoyanov entered the room.

On the desk, as usual, all was compulsively in place: pencils, a few watches—part of his collection—and, finally, the diary.

Lukoyanov read:

"8 [21] April. Sunday. The 24th anniversary of our engagement! . . . Mass at 11.30, after which Kobylinsky showed me a telegram from Moscow that confirmed the detachment committee's decision to take our epaulets away from me and Alexei. My decision: not to wear them for walks but wear them only at home. Shall not forget this beastliness!"

Lukoyanov finally understood: the tsar was stubbornly writing *everything* in the diary. Even assuming (he had to assume!) the possibility of the diary's being read by his enemies. Herein lay Nicholas's contempt for them.

That was when the "spy" got an idea!

He could not carry out his idea in Tobolsk, though, for the next day everything changed.

𝒯HE PLENIPOTENTIARY ARRIVES

On an April morning in 1918, Avdeyev, a member of the Tobolsk Soviet of Ekaterinburg Bolsheviks, was on his way from Tobolsk to his native Ekaterinburg. Avdeyev was pleased because he was carrying the long-awaited documents: information (the tsaritsa's correspondence and so on) about the monarchist plot of Rasputin's son-in-law Soloviev, obtained by the "spy," and a resolution of the Tobolsk Soviet: in view of the threat of escape by Nicholas the Bloody from Tobolsk, begging the Ural Soviet to transfer the tsar's family to Ekaterinburg.

On the platform where Avdeyev was waiting for his train, he saw a military unit disembarking. The sight of unfamiliar armed men greatly disturbed him. He counted fifteen cavalry and twenty infantry. This was a time of furious hostility between Omsk and the Urals, which made him think another Omsk detachment had arrived, so he decided to ferret out information about what kind of soldiers they were.

He walked over to the train, asked for the officer in charge, and was led to a man wearing a sheepskin coat over a sailor's shirt and a big fur hat. Avdeyev presented the man his papers from the Tobolsk Soviet. The man read them, got very excited, announced, "You're just the man I need," and showed the Ekaterinburg man his mandate with the signatures of Lenin and Sverdlov. He also showed him the written instructions signed by Goloshchekin ordering all Ekaterinburg Bolsheviks in the Tobolsk Soviet to obey Central Executive Committee plenipotentiary Yakovlev without question.

Avdeyev had to return to Tobolsk with the detachment.

Avdeyev and Yakovlev were on horseback. Yakovlev was asking Avdeyev about Freedom House. Avdeyev replied listlessly: he did not know the details, the guard would not let them inside the house.

After traveling some 20 versts (13 miles), they noticed chains of soldiers up ahead. At first they thought: White Cossacks! Fortunately, matters did not go so far as firing: through binoculars they saw a red flag and red ribbons on fur hats. The horsemen galloped toward one another.

It turned out to be the detachment sent from Ekaterinburg to Tobolsk . . . for the Romanovs!

This was Ural Military Commissar Goloshchekin's first surprise. Yakovlev was shocked to realize that Ekaterinburg was controlling him.

Now they proceeded together, the two detachments. Yakovlev galloped on his horse flanked by two Ural horsemen—Avdeyev and the detachment commander, the Uralite Busyatsky.

One of the Miass robbers recorded in his memoirs their amazing conversation en route. Busyatsky suggested a plan to Yakovlev: when Yakovlev took the tsar and his family out of Tobolsk, en route, near the village of Ievlevo, Busyatsky's detachment could stage an ambush on Yakovlev's detachment, as if they were trying to free the tsar and his family. In the crossfire they could do away with all the Romanovs. "We should be finishing off the executioner, not wasting our time on him," said the Ekaterinburg man.

In reply Yakovlev silently showed Busyatsky his mandate: that all should obey him, the plenipotentiary of the Central Executive Committee, in everything. Busyatsky only chuckled. He was silent the rest of the way.

Thus, on April 22, 1918, both detachments entered the town of Tobolsk.

In Tobolsk there was one more surprise: another detachment from Ekaterinburg, led by the Bolshevik Zaslavsky, was waiting for Yakovlev.

Thus from the very first day Yakovlev found himself surrounded by two detachments of Uralites. Goloshchekin had prepared for his encounter with the Central Executive Committee's plenipotentiary.

Yakovlev stayed in Kornilov's house, where the Nicholas's "suite" was housed. That very night he went to the Tobolsk Soviet to present his mandates.

The Ekaterinburg Tobolsk men listened to Yakovlev's short speech. He informed them of the goal of his secret mission: to take the tsar and his family out of Tobolsk.

To the natural question, Where? Yakovlev replied that "it was not for them to discuss that, as prescribed in the mandate." In response Yakovlev heard the furious words of Zaslavsky, the Ural detachment's commander: "We shouldn't be wasting our time on the Romanovs, we should be finishing them off!"

From Yakovlev's memoirs:

"I told him just one thing: all your detachments must obey me and fulfill my instructions! I hope you understand?"

Zaslavsky muttered through his teeth: "Yes."

In conclusion Yakovlev announced a change of the guard for tomorrow. Local Red Guards were to take up all the posts in Freedom House. Yakovlev appointed his friend from the platform, Avdeyev, Freedom House's new commandant. This was a nod in the direction of the Uralites.

As soon as Yakovlev left, however, the Uralites passed a resolution—to keep a sharp eye on the plenipotentiary from Moscow!

Goloshchekin had prepared well for Yakovlev's arrival.

Once he realized that the Uralites in the Tobolsk Soviet were his enemies, Yakovlev had to exercise supreme caution with the guard and Kobylinsky. If that did not work out, the mission would fail.

In the morning he called in Kobylinsky.

The Moscow commissar's unusually gracious manner won the colonel over. Yakovlev explained that he had come to take the tsar and his family away. Unfortunately he could not announce the secret route, but the colonel could be assured he would learn everything, and very soon.

Kobylinsky repaid a confidence with a confidence. He informed Yakovlev of all the difficulties in store for his mission. Alexei was very sick, and there was no possibility of moving him.

Lately the boy had been amazingly healthy and had played endless games in the house, including a desperate game: riding a wooden boat down the stairs from the second floor. His boat whooshed down with a crash that made the inhabitants of the house cover their ears. It was as if he were trying to prove something to himself. There was another game, too—swinging on a log swing. "I do not know during which of these games he bruised himself and, as always, was taken to his bed," recalled Dr. Botkin's daughter.

What a bruise meant for Alexei given the conditions of their confinement was described by Dr. Botkin himself:

"Alexei Nikolaevich is subject to a disease of the vessels under the influence of insults utterly unavoidable for boys of his age, attended by . . . the severest pain. In such instances, the boy can suffer so inexpressibly day and night that none of his closest relatives, to say nothing of his mother, who has a chronic heart ailment, not sparing themselves for him, can bear caring for him for very long. My waning powers are also insufficient. N. G. Nagorny, who has remained with the patient through several sleepless and torture-filled nights, is wearing thin and would be in no condition at all to hold out if not for being spelled and assisted by Alexei Nikolaevich's teachers, Mr. Gibbes and especially his tutor Gilliard. . . . Taking turns reading and exchanging impressions, they distract the patient during the day from his sufferings" (from the statement of E. S. Botkin before the Tobolsk Executive Committee).

On April 23, Yakovlev, accompanied by the new commandant, Avdeyev, and Colonel Kobylinsky, went to Freedom House. The night before, however, the family had prepared for this meeting.

Nicholas's diary:

"9 [22] April. We learned about the arrival of the special plenipotentiary, Yakovlev, from Moscow. He is staying in the Kornilov house. The children imagine he will come today to make a search and burn all the papers, and Marie and Anastasia even burned their diaries. . . .

"10 [23] April. At 10.30 in the morning Kobylinsky and Yakovlev appeared with his suite.

"Received him with my daughters. We had expected him at 11, which is why Alix was not ready. He entered, clean-shaven, smiling and embarrassed, asked whether I was content with the guard and the quarters. Then almost ran into Alexei's room, not stopping to inspect the other rooms, and excusing himself for the disturbance, went downstairs. He stopped in at the others on the other floors just as cursorily.

"Half an hour later he appeared again to be introduced to Alix. Again he hurried in to see Alexei and went downstairs. That so far has been the extent of the search of the house."

How sympathetically all this was written in the tsar's diary: "excusing himself for the disturbance," "smiling." The former master of half the world had already forgotten about smiles and excuses.

Chekist Yakovlev knew how to get along with people.

Twice that day the commissar from Moscow viewed the sick boy. He kept trying to imagine whether it was possible, after all, to move him—and realized it was not. His task had become even more complicated.

The Uralite Avdeyev, appointed commandant of the house, was bringing about a change of the guard. Instead of the soldiers from Tsarskoe Selo, Red Guards took up the posts. On one side there was a platoon of handsome mounted soldiers in formation, dressed in uniform. On the other, the Red Guard—the comrades—some in greasy sheepskin coats, some in woolen coats, some in faded overcoats. Instead of riding boots they wore sewn and patched felt boots. Their weapons corresponded. One had an ammunition belt across his shoulder, another a rifle, still another a revolver. Their lineup was unusual, too: the Red Guard formed up according to friendship, not height.

Both detachments regarded each other with astonishment. A fragment of an empire and the army of the revolution—a great photograph of the era.

"WE IMAGINE THAT THIS IS MOSCOW"

The next day Yakovlev did not come to the house.

Nicholas's diary:

"A fine day and rather warm. Sat a lot on my favorite greenhouse porch, the sun warms up marvelously there. Worked by the hill and clearing out a deep ditch."

While the tsar was clearing out the ditch and reflecting on the porch of the hothouse, Yakovlev was faced with his hardest task—his encounter with the tsar's guard. They had meekly allowed themselves to be replaced by Red Guards, but as of yesterday they were already starting to grumble.

Gathering the guard, Yakovlev spent a long time flattering the sharpshooters. Then came the important part: he triumphantly handed them their unpaid salaries for six months of Soviet power and informed them of wonderful news: their service was at an end, and they could go home to their families at last. In the evening he called a meeting of the guard's soldiers' committee, where he announced his purpose: he must take the tsar and his family out of Tobolsk. To the recurring question Where? Yakovlev answered with the same sentence: "This is not a subject for discussion." They began to grumble and he immediately capitulated: he proposed including eight sharpshooters from the former guard in the guard that was going to accompany Nicholas and the family to the designated place, to convince themselves that the tsar and his family would be safe.

Yakovlev had been told back in Moscow that he could rely on the committee chairman, Matveyev.

From Matveyev's Notes:

"Yakovlev calls me in and asks me a question: have I ever had to carry out secret military instructions. Upon receiving an affirmative answer, Yakovlev announces he's been given the task of *transferring the former tsar to Moscow*. He suggests I choose eight men from my detachment to escort Nicholas Romanov en route."

One can only guess whether Matveyev shared this astonishing news with his friend, the "spy."

That evening, at Yakovlev's quarters, the main meeting was held, with Kobylinsky. In his conversation with the colonel, Yakovlev made his move. He informed Kobylinsky that he must take the tsar to Moscow for trial, although naturally there would not be a trial; the tsar and his family would be sent straight to Scandinavia. He extracted a promise from the colonel not to spread this secret, knowing full well he would. He needed it spread. To calm the family and the tsar and the suite so that all would go smoothly.

That same night Kobylinsky secretly informed Botkin, and Botkin his daughter.

His daughter wrote:

"Father has told us important news. . . . Yakovlev has come here on Lenin's order to take Their Excellencies to Moscow for trial, and the issue is whether to let the guard go unimpeded. Despite the terrible word 'trial,' everyone has taken this cheerfully, since they are convinced it does not mean a trial at all but departure abroad. Yakovlev himself must have talked about this, since Kobylinsky was walking around very happy saying, 'What trial? There's not going to be any trial, they're going to take them straight from Moscow to Petrograd—and on to Finland, Sweden, and Norway.' "

Kobylinsky did not manage to inform the tsar of all this, however.

Early on the morning of April 25, Yakovlev showed up again at Freedom House.

He told Nicholas he had to take him away from Tobolsk, but he did not have the right to disclose where.

Nicholas was stunned. He had not expected this; he had been certain that Yakovlev was just the new commissar, replacing the departed Pankratov. Such a "little man in a big fur cap." The situation heated up: Nicholas refused to leave—Alexei was too ill, he must not be touched.

Yakovlev went down to the commandant's room, where Avdeyev and Khokhryakov were sitting. Yakovlev was distraught. (A new game!) He conferred with the Uralites about what to do. In fact, he was still trying to involve the Uralites in his mission.

Once again Yakovlev went up to the tsar's room. He declared: resistance was useless; if Nicholas did not agree to go peacefully, he would be taken by force. Of course, he said all this gently, again endlessly begging his pardon. He suggested to Nicholas that he go alone. "Alone!" Naturally, it occurred to the tsar: a way out! After all, without him, *they* would probably be freed immediately.

Then Nicholas agreed.

Yakovlev left to prepare for the departure. An immediate departure, at dawn. He realized the departure rumor could not be confined to the house now.

Nicholas returned to his family, where something unexpected awaited him: Alix! She had already found out from Kobylinsky that they were taking the tsar to Moscow. She was horrified. Her first thought was the Treaty of Brest. The trial was a ploy, of course. They were taking him there to sign that dishonorable peace. They wanted to sanctify that loathsome paper with his name. The Germans must be demanding it. Only a peace signed by the tsar would have any value. That was why they wanted to take him to Moscow without her! Without her, he had always been forced to make dreadful decisions. No, she would not allow that. There was the duty of a sick child's mother, and there was the duty of a tsaritsa. Her duty before the people and God.

He went out for a walk, and she, who could not stand for even five minutes because of her weak legs, paced restlessly around his office for an entire hour. Her thoughts were leaping about, she was going mad.

Alix's diary:

"This is the first time in my life I have no idea how to act. Until now God has shown me the way. Right now tho' I cannot hear His instructions."

When the tsar got back from his walk she said determinedly: "I am going with you."

Then she went to see her son. She took herself in hand and explained to the boy very calmly that she and the sovereign must leave. When he was better, he and his sisters would join them.

"*T*HAT NIGHT, NATURALLY, NO ONE SLEPT"
In the evening the boy cried out in pain, calling to her, but she would not go to him in his room again. She was afraid she would not have the strength to say goodbye to him one more time. She wept, repeating: "No, this is impossible, something has to happen. . . . No, I am certain something will have happened by morning. . . . God will send an ice floe—and this trip will not take place."

Gradually she calmed down; she had made her final decision. But the boy kept crying and calling out to her.

She decided to split up the family; she could not travel alone. But which of her daughters to take? Tatiana—the most reliable—had to take care of Alexei and run the household. Olga's health was too fragile—it was 300 kilometers to Tyumen in an open cart. Anastasia was too small, and Alexei loved her so much. "I will go," said Marie.

Thus witnesses (Gilliard and others) recounted this scene.

But Alix and Nicky too described the whole drama in their diaries.

He: "12 [25] April. Thursday. After breakfast Yakovlev came with Kobylinsky and announced he had received an order to take me away, not saying where. Alix decided to go with me and take Marie: no point protesting. Leaving behind the other children, with Alexei sick, and given the present circumstances, was more than difficult. We have already begun packing the essentials. But then Yakovlev said he would come back for O., T., An., and A. . . . We spent a sad evening, that night, naturally, no one slept."

She: "I had to decide to stay with ill Baby or accompany him. Settled to accompany him as can be of more need & too risky not knowing where or for what (we imagine Moscow). Horrible suffering. . . . Took leave of all our people after evening tea with all. Sat all night with the children. Baby slept & at 3 went to him till we left. Started at 4 1/4 in the morning."

Thus the entire family sat in the sleeping boy's room.

Yakovlev did not sleep that night either. While Avdeyev was rushing around town scavenging horses and carts, Yakovlev was preparing for the trip. As if for battle. He called in the commander of the second Ural detachment, Busyatsky.

From Yakovlev's memoirs:

" 'I charge you with the task of guarding the road out of Tobolsk. . . . It is your responsibility to guard my passage. You and your detachment will answer with your heads for our safety. . . . If anything happens, you will be the first shot.' Busyatsky was standing in front of me as white as a sheet."

Busyatsky was broken for the time being.

Yakovlev had ordered one of his most desperate Miass robbers to guard the exit from Tobolsk. He and his men must occupy the Tobol crossing and try to keep the other, very dangerous Ural detachment —Zaslavsky's—from leaving town for as long as possible.

Dawn. The readied "carriages" stood in the yard. They were Siberian carts, called *koshevy*—woven baskets set on long poles—no seats; one sat or lay directly on the bottom.

There was only one covered cart, which Commandant Avdeyev had managed to find in the town, in which the tsaritsa was to ride. A mattress was put in there and hay thrown on top.

At five in the morning they started carrying out their things.

From Yakovlev's memoirs:

"Sobs were heard from every corner of the house. The Romanov daughters and their entire staff had gone out on the porch. Nicholas was going from one to another, making the sign of the cross over his daughters with convulsive movements. His proud wife bore up to her daughters' tears. Each of her gestures said: you must not display weakness before the 'Red enemy.' "

A long, hard journey lay ahead of them: to traverse the 300 kilometers to Tyumen in these carts with the roads so bad, switching back and forth from sleighs to wagons (in many places the sun had already melted the snow) and back again to sleighs. Farther on by train—into the unknown where Commissar Yakovlev was supposed to take them.

They seated themselves in the carts. Alix wanted to ride with Nicholas, but Yakovlev explained gruffly that he himself must sit with the former tsar. She got in silently with Marie. She would "maintain this persistent silence" nearly the entire terrible way.

Three servants were sent along with them: the tsar's valet Chemodurov, the parlormaid Demidova, and the lackey Sednev. Also taking their seats in the carts were Dolgorukov, from the suite, and Botkin, as the physician. This was all Yakovlev would allow.

The tsaritsa had begged Gilliard not to see them off, so he was sitting in the darkness by the sleeping boy.

"Is it really possible that no one has made the slightest attempt to save the tsar's family? Where, finally, are those who remained loyal to their sovereign?" Thus this strange Swiss, loyal to the Russian tsar to the very end, exclaimed in his diary. Now he realized there was no one.

From a neighboring house, yet another witness looked on: Dr. Botkin's daughter.

She was seeing her father for the last time. He had blessed his daughter in parting and kissed her, but she kept watching as he crossed the street in his civilian coat and felt hat. Previously her father had worn a general's greatcoat. But after the order to remove the epaulets, he had not wanted to remove Nicholas's initials, so he exchanged his greatcoat for a civilian coat (and immediately changed once he put his civilian's coat on, as Baron Tuzenbakh had in Chekhov's *Three Sisters*).

The night before, they had come for his suitcases and his fur-lined fur coat. And here was the dawn and she saw the carts in Freedom House yard and her father wearing Prince Dolgorukov's rabbit fur coat. They had wrapped the empress and Marie in her father's fur. Yes, they turned out not to have an adequate fur coat for the savage morning frosts, for this penetrating wind in the cart racing over the ice.

Six in the morning. For the last time she saw her father's face, Marie's sweet face, the empress's mournful face. And Nicholas's calm face.

The carts got under way. Gilliard's three pupils ran down the halls of Freedom House—three sobbing girls.

*T*HE FINAL JOURNEY

Avdeyev galloped alongside the cart where the tsar and the Central Executive Committee's plenipotentiary were sitting. Up ahead were carts carrying Red Guards and three cannon. Cavalry detachments rode in the lead and at the rear of the sleigh train. Way up ahead galloped the scouting party.

Thus, accompanied by dashing horsemen (his whole life was "accompanied by," at first to protect him, now to guard him—what did it matter!) on their hot Siberian horses, his final journey began.

He had missed this freedom, this air of freedom. How little one needs: to breathe and be free. The road was difficult, and he suffered for her.

What about her? She was darkly silent. She was thinking about Alexei, still hearing his cry. A fracture had rent her soul. The luxurious yachts, the carriages on soft springs with rustling tires—all was coming to an end in these pathetic, filthy carts.

Carts, carts. Soon, in this same kind of cart, very soon, their bodies would be taken away.

Nicky talked to Yakovlev without letup the entire way. They found they had something to talk about—the former terrorist and the former emperor. The coachman driving them later told how all the way they argued about politics. Yakovlev would attack—"skewer the tsar" —but the tsar would not give in.

While responding to the former autocrat and joking with him, however, Yakovlev was thinking about something completely different.

Patrols left by Yakovlev stood all along the route from Tobolsk to Tyumen, and fresh horses awaited them. But his patrols were so few. How would Busyatsky, who was in the van, behave? Would he stay scared for long? The people he had left along the way were scarcely going to be able to restrain Zaslavsky's numerous detachment.

Yakovlev realized that he was traveling between two detachments of Uralites, one in back and one in front, squeezing him like pincers. That was the reality! He kept wondering whether they would dare attack.

Nicholas's diary:

"13 [25] April. Friday. . . . At 4 in the morning said goodbye to our dear children and got in the tarantasses. Yakovlev, Alix and Marie, Valya [Dolgorukov] and Botkin, and I. The people who went with us: Nyuta Demidova, Chemodurov, and Sednev. Eight sharpshooters and a 10-man mounted Red Guard convoy. It was cold, the road very difficult and terribly bumpy from the slightly frozen ruts. Crossed the Irtysh through quite deep water, had four changes of horses, arrived at the village of Ievlevo to spend the night. We were quartered in a large, clean house and slept soundly on our cots."

The tsaritsa wrote in her diary as well: "Journey by carriage. . . . dead tired & aches all over."

At dawn the journey continued. At Ievlevo cold water was already running over the ice. The wind lashed at their faces. They went into the water in their carts. Alix refused to ride on water. Planks were brought from the village, they fashioned a bridge, and the empress and Marie, leaning on the arms of gallant Valya (as once at balls in the Winter Palace) and the good doctor, crossed the water over the boards. That day they reached Pokrovskoe.

She saw Rasputin's house and was happy: a sign, a promise of future luck.

She wrote in her diary: "14 (27) April. Saturday. Journey by carriage. . . . About 12, got to *Pokrovskoe* . . . stood long before our friend's house, saw his family & friends looking out of the window at us."

Thus the Holy Devil blessed them for death.

Now the last stage remained to Tyumen. Should the Uralites decide to attack, it would happen here. Yakovlev's detachment had become more numerous as the patrols attached themselves. The plenipotentiary had prepared for a battle. To his amazement, though, it was again avoided.

Nicholas's diary:

"14 [27] April. . . . The last stage was made slowly taking all military precautions. Arrived in Tyumen at 9.15 under a beautiful moon with the entire squadron surrounding our carts as we entered the town. It was nice to get on a train, tho' not a very clean one. We ourselves and our things had a desperately filthy look. Went to bed at 10 without undressing. I on a cot and Alix, Marie, and Nyuta [Demidova] in a section nearby."

In Tyumen Yakovlev waited for his detachment of 250 men. For the first time in the whole journey he breathed a sigh of relief. He did not know that both Ural detachments had a very different mission. They were supposed to follow only as far as the train: the worst awaited him ahead—on the railway.

The train stood ready for departure.

TRAIN CHASE

The family occupied a separate train car.

In the central compartment were Yakovlev and Avdeyev. The compartment to the right of them had Nicholas and Alix, the one to the left Marie and Anna Demidova.

As soon as the family were settled in their compartments, Yakovlev and his telegraphist went to the telegraph post and his direct line.

Avdeyev tried to leave the car right after him, but Yakovlev's sharpshooters would not let him out.

Yakovlev made contact with Moscow.

His message to Sverdlov: "The route remains the old one or have you changed it? Inform Tyumen immediately."

A short while later the ribbon spewed out an answer from Moscow: "The old route. Report whether taking Cargo or not? Sverdlov."

Yakovlev reported: "Taking Cargo."

Yakovlev returned to the train, which got under way. Having ridden as far as the nearest fork, Yakovlev gave an order to couple on a new engine and change direction. Very quickly Avdeyev realized the train was not going to Ekaterinburg. Its lights extinguished, the train moved off to the east—toward Omsk.

"Where is the train going?" the Uralite demanded.

Yakovlev explained that he had learned that a Ural detachment was preparing to attack them en route for the purpose of destroying the family. He was afraid to take the family to Ekaterinburg via the old route and had decided to take a roundabout route to Ekaterinburg—through Omsk.

Avdeyev did not believe him, of course. He realized they were not taking the family to Ekaterinburg. But where then?

The morning of April 28. The family was waking up.

Nicholas's diary:

"Everyone got a sound sleep. We have guessed by the names of the stations that we are going in the direction of Omsk. We have begun trying to guess where they will take us after Omsk. Moscow or Vladivostok? The commissars, of course, have not been saying anything. Marie often went to see the riflemen—their compartment is at the end of the car. . . . At the stations we covered the windows, since due to the holiday there were a lot of people. After a cold bite to eat and tea we went to bed early."

But Marie did not find anything out from the sharpshooters, and Yakovlev was not explaining anything.

That night, while they lay sleeping, the main events flared up.

Yakovlev was rushing to Omsk but without knowing the most important thing: informed by Sverdlov as to the true purpose of the secret mission, Goloshchekin had made peace with the Omsk Bolsheviks. As always, a province was reconciled by its dislike for the capital. While Yakovlev, triumphant, was on his way to Omsk, telegrams were already flying from Ekaterinburg.

To Moscow: "28 April. Ekaterinburg. Your Commissar Yakovlev has taken Romanov to Tyumen stop Put him on a train comma Set out toward Ekat[erinburg] stop Went one stage comma changed direction comma went back stop Now the train with Nicholas is near Omsk stop Why this was done we do not know stop We consider this action treasonous stop *According to your letter of 9 April* Nicholas should be in Ekaterinburg stop What does this mean? In keeping with the decision passed by the Party's Regional Soviet and Regional Committee instructions have been given to detain Yakovlev and the train no matter what, to arrest him and take him and Nicholas to Ekaterinburg."

Simultaneously, telegrams were going to Omsk and other points declaring Yakovlev outside the law.

"Moscow. Sverdlov. . . . Having discussed the conduct of Commissar Yakovlev, by unanimous decision we deem it a direct betrayal of the revolution. The desire to take the former tsar beyond the limits of the revolutionary Urals for some unknown purpose in contradiction to the precise instruction of the Chairman of the Central

Executive Committee is an act placing Commissar Yakovlev outside the ranks of revolutionaries. The Ural Regional Soviet proposes that all Soviet revolutionary organizations, especially the Omsk Soviet of Deputies, take the most extreme measures, including the use of force, to stop the train."

Soon after, Yakovlev was brought one of these Ural telegrams. He found out that his train was supposed to be stopped in Omsk and he himself arrested.

Yakovlev lost his self-possession. He burst into Avdeyev's compartment and screamed at the smiling Uralite: "What, have all of you there gone out of your minds?" But it was too late.

The train was approaching Omsk, where a detachment of Red Guards was waiting.

Yakovlev went "for the bank." Not far from Omsk, he stopped the train, uncoupled the engine, and set out in the night with his telegraphist into the inferno—to Omsk.

From Yakovlev's memoirs:

"As soon as the train stopped [in Omsk] and we got out on the platform, we were surrounded by a dense mass of people."

He stood alone amid the furious armed crowd, which was electrified by rumors of the traitor to the revolution. He was on the brink of death, but that had already happened many times in his life.

From Yakovlev's memoirs:

"I announced, shouting over the crowd: 'I am Special Commissar Yakovlev of the Central Executive Committee! I need to see the Chairman of the Omsk Soviet!' "

And now, for the first time on this trip, he was lucky.

From Yakovlev's memoirs:

"The chairman of the Omsk Soviet turned out to be my friend Kosarev. . . . I recognized my old comrade, whom I had once been together with in the party school in Italy. I sketched out the events to him in general terms and asked him to go with me to the telegraph post: there we would contact Sverdlov. From whom I would first of all receive further instructions and secondly, Kosarev would understand that I was acting on instruction from the center. . . . As we raced to the telegraph post, we saw armed detachments everywhere."

So he managed to convince his old friend, but. . . . At the telegraph office Yakovlev learned he had risked his life for nothing. By that time the long telegraph conversation between Ekaterinburg and Moscow had ended.

Goloshchekin had to be energetic.

And he was. Till the end. A threatening telegram followed from the Uralites: "In his letter of 9 April, Comrade Sverdlov said that Romanov would be transferred to Ekaterinburg and put under the responsibility of the Regional Soviet. Seeing that today the train is slipping away from the Urals for reasons unknown to us . . . we have informed Sverdlov. His reply greatly amazed us. It turns out Yakovlev is driving the train to the East in accordance with his instruction, and he asks that no obstacles be put in Yakovlev's way. . . .

"Our only solution to the current predicament is to send instructions to Yakovlev in Omsk to turn the train back to Ekaterinburg, otherwise the conflict could take on acute forms, for we feel that Nicholas does not need to wander the roads of Siberia but should be in Ekaterinburg under strict watch."

Yes, they had stuck it out. Now Sverdlov could give in.

Moscow agreed, of course, "on condition that everything is done for the safety of the Romanovs," that the "appropriate guarantees" are given. The guarantees were given immediately.

So when Yakovlev sat his telegraphist down, Sverdlov's instructions arrived from Moscow: "Return to Tyumen immediately. Have come to an agreement with the Uralites. They have taken measures and given guarantees."

Yakovlev was dumbfounded: so it had all been in vain. He began a long telegraph conversation with Moscow. He reported information that gave Sverdlov sufficient grounds for refusing Ekaterinburg: "Without question I shall obey all orders from the Center. I will take the Baggage wherever you say. But I consider it my duty to warn the Sovnarkom once more that the danger is quite justified. . . . There is one more consideration: if you send the baggage to Simsky District [in Ufa Province, Yakovlev's home], then you are always free to take him to Moscow or wherever you like. If the Baggage is taken according to the first route [Ekaterinburg], then I doubt you will ever be able to drag it out of there. . . . Just as I doubt the Baggage will always be completely safe. So, we warn you for the last time and unburden ourselves of any moral responsibility for future consequences."

To Yakovlev's astonishment Sverdlov was deaf: Moscow's decision stood. Yakovlev must take the family to Ekaterinburg.

Yakovlev returned to the train on the same engine. The train started back.

Nicholas's diary:

"16 [29] April. This morning we noticed we were going back. It turned out they wouldn't let us enter Omsk, so we were a little freer, we even took two walks: first alongside the train, and then rather far into a field, with Yakovlev himself. Everyone was in a cheerful mood."

Nicholas was in a cheerful mood because he still did not know the true reason for the train's turning around.

From Matveyev's Notes.

"We said the turning around was due to damage to one of the bridges."

Nicholas continued to believe they were going to Moscow. Their wild journey continued, but this meant he would have his beloved walk. "With Yakovlev himself," he recorded in his diary, not without a grin.

They walked alongside the train. And they talked. About what? Power? The mob? Revolution? Or Nicholas's favorite theme—people quarrel, they irritate one another, when all around is the marvelous, wise life of the trees, green spaces, the sky and its timeless clouds?

Thus ended the last tsar's last walk in freedom.

When Nicholas awoke in the morning he understood everything. He could tell by the names of the stations that they were approaching Ekaterinburg.

Yakovlev ordered the curtains lowered: he had no doubt how they would be met by the capital of the Red Urals. Nor did the tsar. An amazing scene took place in the train on their approach to the town. Matveyev saw Nicholas go into Matveyev's compartment and walk out soon after, chewing on some black bread. When he saw Matveyev, Nicholas was flustered.

From Matveyev's Notes:

" 'Pardon me, Peter Matveyevich, I broke off a piece of your black bread without your permission.' I offered Romanov a white roll the men had bought at one of the stations since I knew that the crust of bread lying on the table was incredibly dry, I had been planning to throw it to the dogs at the station."

The Emperor of All the Russias was gnawing on a crust of black bread intended for the dogs?

No, there is another altogether unsentimental interpretation to that scene.

From Matveyev's Notes:

"I looked at Romanov and saw he was very agitated and chewing the dry crust more out of agitation than anything else."

Yes, the closer they got to Ekaterinburg, the more agitated he became. He did not want to frighten Alix and was probably reassuring her. But he told Matveyev the truth.

From Matveyev's Notes:

"Nicholas said, 'I would go anywhere at all but the Urals. . . . Judging from the papers, the Urals are harshly against me.'"

He was still hoping that the "good riflemen" from the old guard would undertake something.

At 8:40 in the morning, the train stopped among the countless tracks of the Ekaterinburg's main station. The train was standing a few tracks from the nearest platform. From behind the lowered curtains the tsar saw that, despite the early hour, the platform was filled with a restless crowd.

Early on the morning of April 30, a driver from the Ural Soviet's garage was ordered to take a car to the house belonging to the engineer Ipatiev, at the corner of Ascension Avenue and Ascension Lane. Very recently, at the order of the Ural Soviet, Ipatiev had been told to vacate the premises within forty-eight hours. The house was surrounded by a high fence. A guard was posted. Soon after, an astonishing rumor spread through the town: the tsar's family would be living in that guarded house.

An immense crowd was standing by it.

Ural Commissar Goloshchekin himself walked out through the gates of the Ipatiev house as the automobile drove up. He ordered the driver, Feodor Samokhvalov, to take him to Ekaterinburg's main train station, where Goloshchekin ordered him to wait while he ran off somewhere, then returned and ordered Samokhvalov to drive to Ekaterinburg's freight station.

All this was Goloshchekin's sly maneuver to get the crowd by the house to disperse.

From the memoirs of Housing Commissar Zhilinsky (kept in the Sverdlovsk Party Archive):

"We decided to trick the people and send cars to the main station and from there continue to the freight station, where we were to pick up the Romanovs. That was what we did. Everyone followed the cars to the main station."

*T*HE FINAL STRUGGLE

The crowd was indignant.

From Yakovlev's memoirs:

"The air was filled with an unimaginable din, threatening shouts were heard time and again. . . . The disorderly crowd had begun to advance on our men. . . . The guard standing on the platform was not making much of an effort to hold back the press of people.

" 'Bring the Romanovs out, and let me spit in his face. . . .'

" 'Get out the machine guns. . . .'

"That had an effect. The crowd recoiled. Threatening shouts flew in my direction."

At the same time the train sent by the stationmaster advanced on the crowd. The crowd rushed back—and a long line of comrades walled off the raging crowd from the train.

From Yakovlev's memoirs:

"Curses and shouts were heard . . . and while the crowd was making its way through the buffer of a freight train . . . we got under way and disappeared among the countless tracks of the Ekaterinburg station. Fifteen minutes later we were in complete safety at the freight station."

From Nicholas's diary:

"17 [30] April. Tuesday. Another marvelous warm day. At 8.40 we arrived in Ekaterinburg. Stopped for about 3 hours at one station, where there was powerful ferment between the local commissars and ours."

And not a word about the raging crowd! The tsar did not want to describe his crazed former subjects.

A meeting had been arranged at the freight station.

Forty Red Guards immediately uncoupled the train.

On the platform stood three leaders of the Ural Soviet:

Twenty-seven years old, blue-eyed, wearing a large white fur cap —Comrade Alexander Beloborodov. A former electrical repairman, now chairman of the Soviet, or, as he liked to refer to himself, head of the revolutionary government of the Red Urals;

Comrade Filipp (Isai) Goloshchekin—leader of the Ural Bolsheviks;

And yet another influential member of the Soviet—Comrade Boris Ditkovsky, son of a tsarist officer, educated in Petersburg, student at the Military School, graduate of the University of Geneva, brilliant mining engineer.

All were very decisive men.

At that moment the sharpshooters of the old guard rebelled. They had realized what lay in store for the Romanovs. The sharpshooters stood in the doors of the train car and would not let anyone in. Yakovlev attempted to use this last opportunity to his advantage. The commissar was not one to give up until he had reached the end of his rope. Yakovlev demanded to be put in contact with Moscow.

All this went on for an hour and a half. The troika was tired. The three decisive men were sick of waiting.

They announced that if they were not allowed into the car immediately, the Red Guard would open fire on the train. Only then did Yakovlev placate the sharpshooters.

All eight sharpshooters were disarmed, and by evening they were sitting in the Ekaterinburg jail, whence Yakovlev freed them with great difficulty.

Beloborodov entered the train car. After exchanging dry greetings with the plenipotentiary, he sat down and wrote a receipt (see Appendix). Yakovlev led the family out of the car.

Ten years later the artist V. Pchelin drew a picture for the Sverdlovsk Museum of the Revolution, *The Delivery of the Romanovs to the Ural Soviet*. That was what it was, a delivery. It was not just chance that "cargo" and "baggage" had been the designations for the powerless family in Yakovlev's telegrams. The Bolsheviks did receive them like baggage—at a freight station—and signed for them. This was the Ural revolutionaries' savage humor.

What a picturesque group of the slain it was that day at the Ekaterinburg freight station: Nicholas, his wife and daughter—all would be shot in a little more than two months. But those who were receiving them—Goloshchekin, Beloborodov, Ditkovsky—would also be shot, albeit twenty years later.

They were put into automobiles. In one were Nicholas, the Uralite Avdeyev, now appointed commandant of the Ipatiev house, or the "house of special designation," as it would be called in all the official papers, and next to Nicholas Comrade Beloborodov. The former tsar next to the present ruler of the Urals. In the other car were Comrades Ditkovsky and Goloshchekin, the former Grand Duchess Marie, and the former empress.

Behind them in a truck were the Red Guards. Nicholas, I think, appreciated this ironic smile of fate. It was all just like in the good old days: the leaders of the province met him at the station and an escort of soldiers accompanied him to the house.

Nicholas's diary:

"The train went to the other, freight station. After an hour and a half wait we left the train. Yakovlev handed us over to the district commissar and the three of us got in an auto and drove down the deserted streets to the Ipatiev house, which had been made ready for us."

Alix's diary:

"At 3 were told to get out of the train. Yakovlev had to give us over to the Ural Soviet. Their Chief took us 3 in an open motor, and a truck with soldiers . . . followed."

Thus they parted. Comrade Yakovlev and the former tsar. But the Uralites were serious people. They obviously continued to have the most serious intentions with respect to the cunning commissar. Sverdlov was forced to intervene. A telegram arrived addressed to Beloborodov and Goloshchekin: "Everything Yakovlev does *is a direct execution of my order.* . . . Give Yakovlev your complete confidence. Sverdlov."

Goloshchekin understood the signal—and momentarily placated the zealous Uralites. On the evening of April 30, the Ural Soviet heard Yakovlev's report. The Soviet passed a resolution "rehabilitating" the plenipotentiary.

WHO WAS HE?

Yakovlev's life took an astonishing turn after this.

Late in May on the Volga, in the southern Urals, and in Siberia, an uprising of the Czech Legion ignited against the Bolsheviks. To fight them, an eastern front was created, led by former tsarist officer and Socialist Revolutionary M. Muraviev. Ordered to command one of those armies in the area of Ufa and Orenburg was Yakovlev.

But on July 10 Muraviev mutinied against the Bolsheviks and was murdered while under arrest in Kazan.

Then Yakovlev quit the front and returned secretly to his native

Ufa, now freed of Bolsheviks, where he declared that he had "overcome the idea of bolshevism" and went over to the White Army.

He directed an appeal to the soldiers of the Red Army:

"With this letter I appeal to you, the rank-and-file soldiers, not
your irresponsible leaders who through their tyranny are deciding
the fates of our poor, lacerated homeland. . . . The people are
grumbling, protesting, thrashing about in their death throes. Here
and there rebellions are flaring up. . . . A terrible civil slaughter is
in progress—and there is not one free citizen in Russia left who can
be certain of tomorrow. . . . As in the final days of autocracy . . .
when ominous specters of the end of popular patience were in the
air, now too everything is flaring up against Soviet power, and it will
collapse, crushing all of you with its weight. . . . Former Commander-in-Chief of the Bolshevik Ural-Orenburg Front V. Yakovlev."

Further followed an altogether astonishing finale: having gone
over to the Whites, Yakovlev was hastily shot in a White Guard
counterintelligence cellar. Such was the well-known version of the
death of the Central Executive Committee plenipotentiary cited in
so many works.

We have to get used to it, though: the people in our story have a
tendency to get resurrected. "Yakovlev shot by the Whites" turned
out to have survived! A certain investigator into particularly important matters, Major N. Leshkin, who had access to secret documents
(a new type of historian for us Russians) published extracts from the
secret "Yakovlev case."

It turns out that Yakovlev survived happily in China in the 1920s
under the name Stoyanovich. There had been no execution. In 1919
Yakovlev had simply fled Russia for Harbin. In 1927, though, he decided to return to the Soviet Union. Naturally, he would fall in the
hands of the same organization he himself had once helped found.
After a prolonged investigation, he was convicted. Only his revolutionary services saved him from a firing squad. He was sent to the
terrible Solovetsky camp and the White Sea–Baltic Canal.

In his article, however, Leshkin cites some surprising statements
from an old Chekist who in 1929, "while Myachin was being tried as
Stoyanovich, was at the Higher Courses in Moscow and heard the
following story from Artur Artuzov, the head of Soviet intelligence:

" 'In the Civil War there were victims who for the good of the
cause soiled their name with treason. . . . For instance, Kostya
Myachin went over to Kolchak with the approval of the Cheka. He
retreated to China, where he accomplished a great deal as Stoya-

novich. This is not the time to speak of this, as it would shed un-
wanted light on our agents. He was a model resident. They began to
wise up to him. Stoyanovich was forced to return. Now he has been
convicted, but that was necessary. Soon we will vindicate and reward
him."

Indeed, in two years Yakovlev received early release for "selfless
labor on the White Sea–Baltic Canal."

So, was there no treason? Was there no crime? Was he a true
Bolshevik and loyal Chekist, Kostya Myachin? But in the terrible
year 1937, at the height of Stalinist repressions, when Yakovlev was
driven out of every job he got, he would write a desperate letter to
Stalin that included this sentence:

"How can I be allowed to be punished again for the same crime?"

So, there was a *crime!* And for that he was punished?

More confusion—this mysterious man with three names. Who
was he really? A loyal Bolshevik, a model Chekist . . . or . . . ?

A gambler who played complicated double games all his life, who
willingly entered into the most incredible adventures, who after his
secret mission became thoroughly disenchanted with the Bolsheviks.
He realized that high ideals had been replaced by a shameless struggle for power. When he went over to the Whites, though, he soon
saw that they did not believe the former Red commissar and hated
him. His wife tells in her memoirs how often he did not sleep at
night, how he was constantly exclaiming, tormented: "What have I
done?"

Then this fantastic man devised a new twist in his fate: he fled
the Whites for China, where he became an adviser to the Chinese
revolutionary Sun Yat-sen and, evidently, made contact with Soviet
intelligence.

Thus he attempted to earn the right to return to his homeland.
He was wrong, though: he had been too prominent a figure, and too
many of his enemies remained in the homeland. They had not forgiven his betrayal. When he found himself in the camps, he wrote
endless requests to the government for his release, mentioning his
services to the revolution. That was when he created his memoirs,
The Romanovs' Last Trip. Written in the camps, they were nothing
more than another attempt to cite his services. By then Trotsky had
been sent out of the country and Trotskyism had been routed, however, and Yakovlev, of course, was afraid to write that the chief purpose of his mission had been to bring the tsar's family to Moscow to
the trial Lev Trotsky had dreamed of. Instead he repeated the lie that
had once confused the Uralites: from the very outset he had been
taking the tsar to Ekaterinburg. Oh well, Sverdlov was long since in

his grave, and there was no one to refute him, and he did not know that in the Urals his former companion Matveyev would write the following in his Notes: "Yakovlev . . . called me in and asked me a question: Had I ever had to execute secret military instructions. Once he received my affirmative answer, Yakovlev told me that he had been assigned the task of *transferring the former tsar to Moscow.*"

Of course, Yakovlev's memoirs contain no reply to the most important question: When did he "overcome the idea of bolshevism"? If that happened *after* he went to get the tsar, then everything is clear.

But what if it was *before*?

Then his entire journey appears in an entirely new light. His softness, his heartfelt conversations, and, finally, the puzzling telegram the former grand duchesses received in Tobolsk with his signature: "We are traveling well. Christ be with you. How is Little One's health. Yakovlev." What an unlikely vocabulary for a Bolshevik! Of course, this was the tsar's telegram. The last telegram of Nicholas II. Which Yakovlev sent over his own signature. A Bolshevik commissar sending the telegram of Nicholas the Bloody over his own signature?

Revolution is a time of little Napoleons. Perhaps this man with three names was playing his own, third game. There was Sverdlov's game, there was Goloshchekin's game, but there was also Yakovlev's desperate game. Perhaps he never intended to take his train to Moscow after Omsk at all. An interesting note slipped into the tsaritsa's diary:

"April 16 (29). In train. . . . The Omsk Soviet of Deputies does not let us go through Omsk since they are afraid they want to take us to Japan."

Might there be some truth in this half-hint? Might the mysterious plenipotentiary have hinted only to her, the true head of the family, of his goal? Hence his behavior with the tsarist couple?

But the inevitable end awaited those who made the revolution. On September 16, 1938, the last companion of the last tsar, Yakovlev-Myachin-Stoyanovich, was arrested and disappeared forever into Stalin's camps, taking his secret with him.

Chapter 12

THE LAST HOUSE

✛

Above the town, on the highest hill, rose the Church of the Ascension. Next to the church a few houses formed Ascension Square.

One of these houses stood directly opposite the church—low-slung, white, with thick walls and a stone carving all the way across the facade, which was turned toward the boulevard and the church. One of the house's thick sides dropped down a slope along blind Ascension Lane. Here the windows of the first half-cellar barely peeked out from below ground level.

One of these half-cellar windows was between two trees. This was the window of that very room to which we will find ourselves returning.

Driving up to the house, however, they saw none of this. The house was masked nearly to the roof by a very high fence. Only a bit of the uppermost part of the second-floor windows looked out.

Around the house stood the guard.

This house belonged to the engineer Ipatiev, an unlucky man. An influential member of the Soviet and also a graduate of the University of Geneva, Peter Voikov was the son of a mining engineer. He knew Ipatiev and had been in this house with the thick walls that was so conveniently situated (from the standpoint of guarding it).

That is why at the very end of April the engineer was called in to the Soviet of Deputies and ordered to clear out of his house in twenty-four hours. They promised "to return the house soon" (engineer Ipatiev did not understand the portent in this statement). He was ordered to leave all his furniture where it was and put his personal possessions into storage.

The cement storeroom was located on the first floor, next to a half-cellar room—the execution room.

Both cars drove along the fence to the plank gates.

The gates opened and the cars were allowed in. Neither Nicholas nor Alix nor their daughter would ever leave those gates alive.

They were led across the paved courtyard to the house. In the entry, a carved wooden staircase ascended to the second floor.

Standing by the stairs, Beloborodov made a formal announcement: "By decision of the Central Executive Committee, the former tsar Nicholas Romanov and his family are transferred to the conduct of the Ural Soviet and shall henceforth be located in Ekaterinburg with the status of prisoners. Until their trial. Comrade Avdeyev has been appointed house commandant, and all requests and complaints shall be made to the Ural Executive Committee through the commandant."

After which both Ural leaders, Goloshchekin and Beloborodov, went off in a car and the family was invited to tour their new quarters in the company of the commandant and Ditkovsky.

Nicholas's diary:

"Little by little our people arrived, as well as our things, but they would not let Valya in."

Yes, their things arrived, and along with them Botkin and their people.

But not Dolgorukov. Poor Valya was taken away somewhere directly from the station. Somewhere. . . .

Subsequently a rumor spread that two guns and many thousands in cash had been found on Prince Dolgorukov. This was reported in Tobolsk by the returning riflemen of the old guard. Why would Dolgorukov have had two guns? One way or another, Nicholas would not see Valya again; the prince had disappeared for good.

M. Medvedev (the son of a Chekist who participated in the execution of the tsar's family) told the story to me:

"Dolgorukov was shot by the young Chekist Grigory Nikulin.

Nikulin said so himself. I don't remember the details anymore, I remember he took Dolgorukov out with his suitcases into a field."

"You mean this was immediately after the train? If there were suitcases?"

"I just don't remember. I only remember there was snow, and after the execution Nikulin himself had to carry Dolgorukov's suitcases across a snowy field. The snow was deep and he cursed all the way."

Thus perished this charmer, the gallant cavalier at the brilliant Winter Palace balls.

Nicholas's diary:

"The house is fine, clean. We have been assigned 4 rooms: a corner bedroom, a lavatory, next door a dining room with windows onto a little garden and a view of a low-lying part of town, and finally, a spacious hall with arches in place of doors.

"We arranged ourselves in the following manner: Alix, Marie, and I together in the bedroom. A shared lavatory. Demidova in the dining room, and in the hall—Botkin, Chemodurov, and Sednev. In order to get to the washroom and water closet one must go past the sentry. A very high wooden fence has been built around the house 2 sazhens [14 feet] from the windows: a chain of sentries has been posted there and in the little garden too."

Here the drama's last act would unfold. The dynasty's finale.

*T*HE FINALE SET

The tsar and tsaritsa would be staying in the spacious corner room with four windows. Two windows looked out on Ascension Avenue, but the high fence two sazhens from the windows closed off the view. Only the cross over the bell tower was visible from the rooms. The two other windows looked out onto Ascension Lane, which was a dead end. The room was very light, with pale yellow wallpaper covered by a tree-form frieze of faded flowers.

A rug on the floor, a baize-covered table, a bronze lamp with a handmade lamp shade, a small card table, a bookcase between the windows where she would put her books. Two beds (Alexei would sleep on one of them when he was brought from Tobolsk), and a couch.

Her vanity and mirror with two electric lamps on the sides, on the table a jar of cold cream with the inscription "Court Pharmacy to His Excellency."

How strange that inscription sounded already.

A washbasin on a cracked marble counter and an armoire, which now held all the clothing of the former tsar and tsaritsa.

Next to their room, with windows on Ascension Lane, was a large empty room. In it were a table, chairs, and a large pier glass. The four daughters would live in this room. They would come, in May, and until their camp beds were brought they would sleep on mattresses right on the floor.

Both these rooms were directly above that half-cellar room.

Next to the daughters' room, in the dining room "with the view on the garden," slept Anna Demidova. In the large hall (the drawing room) slept Botkin, Chemodurov, and Sednev.

There was one more as yet sealed room—designated for Alexei.

Catercorner from the former grand duchesses was the commandant's room—date palm wallpaper, gold baguette molding, and the head of a dead deer. And one more—next to the commandant's—set aside for the watch.

Completing the suite was the lavatory. The porcelain vessel left over from engineer Ipatiev would be fouled by the commandant and the guards, and amid the shameless drawings on the lavatory walls depicting the tsaritsa and Rasputin, amid the obscene utterances of the guard and reflections such as "I don't know why I wrote either, but you strangers read it," was a note nailed to the wall: "You are implored to leave the seat as clean as you found it."

This was the joint creation of the former tsar and his personal physician Botkin.

Entering the bedroom, Alix walked over to the right-hand window and on the jamb penciled her favorite symbol, the swastika, and the date of their arrival: 17 (30).

She drew another swastika as an incantation directly on the wallpaper over the bed where Alexei was to sleep.

17 (30). Thus she innocently signaled the start of the last game with the last tsar.

It began right away.

*T*HE LAST GAME

When their belongings arrived they were taken out into the hall and, in the presence of the former military academy student and present member of the Ural Executive Committee Ditkovsky and the former turner and present commandant Avdeyev, the inspection began.

The captors opened the suitcases and looked through them carefully. They examined Alix's hand luggage. They confiscated the camera she had brought from Tsarskoe Selo and also, as Commandant Avdeyev would write in his memoirs, "a detailed map of Ekaterinburg." How could that have turned up in her bag if they had assumed they were going to Moscow? Even if it couldn't have, though, it did. Like the two guns allegedly found on Dolgorukov.

They even opened the medicine bottles—they dug through her entire traveling pharmacy.

Nicholas's diary:

"17 [30] April [continued]. . . . The search of our things was like at customs: just as strict, right up to the last vial in Alix's pharmacy. That exasperated me and I expressed my opinion sharply to the commissar."

Alix did not understand the reason for the search. She was nervous and indignant: "This is an insult!" Her accent made the searchers smile; the impotent anger of the former empress was funny. But she continued her irate monologue; she even mentioned "Mr. Kerensky." She cited the example of the revolutionary who was nevertheless a gentleman. The word *gentleman* amused the former turner Avdeyev. Finally, Nicholas blew up. He declared: "Up until now we have dealt with decent people!" This was the ultimate manifestation of anger for this most well-bred of monarchs.

Why did they make this search?

To demonstrate the conditions of their new life in the capital of the Red Urals? In part. But only in part.

They were looking for the jewels. The legendary tsarist jewels. The "spy" had not been napping. Evidently in Tobolsk he found out that Alix used the word "medicine" when talking in the presence of outsiders about the jewels (that was how she would refer to them in her letters to her daughters from Ekaterinburg). That was why they examined the vials of medicine so thoroughly and vainly, though they did not find anything.

They realized the jewels had been left in Tobolsk.

There was a third reason for the harsh examination. Since the day of the family's arrival in Ekaterinburg they had begun to gather evidence of a "monarchist plot." That was why they took the camera away—as evidence. That was apparently why they discovered the map of Ekaterinburg—more evidence (plus the rumor about the two guns confiscated from unlucky Valya—another link in the evidence).

This terrible game with the tsar began at the Ekaterinburg station. We shall call it the monarchist plot game. The plot that would serve as grounds for their execution. The "just punishment" had been decided upon from the very start.

Nicholas's diary:

"21 April [4 May]. . . . All morning wrote letters to the girls from Alix and Marie. And drew a plan of this house."

He wanted those in Tobolsk to be able to picture their new quarters. He was preparing them for their encounter with the crowded house. But—

"24 April [7 May]. . . . Avdeyev, the commandant, removed the plan of the house I had done for the children on a letter the day before yesterday and took it away, saying I could not send it."

In his memoirs Avdeyev would describe this incident quite differently:

"Once while reviewing the letters my attention was drawn to one letter addressed to Nicholas Nikolaevich [!]. Upon examination of the envelope lining, I discovered a thin sheet of paper on which was drawn a plan of the house."

Avdeyev further described how he called Nicholas into the commandant's room and how the tsar lied, refused to admit it, and begged for the commandant's forgiveness. This was not simply a fabrication. The plan of the house, allegedly concealed under the envelope lining, was one more "irrefutable proof." As was the "frightened and exposed Nicholas." They were making their case. And waiting.

Waiting for the children to arrive from Tobolsk. And the jewels.

"*J* BREATHED THE AIR THROUGH AN OPEN PANE"
"17 [30] April. . . . The sentry has been put in the two rooms by the dining room, so that to go to the washroom and water closet one must pass by the guard and sentry by the doors," Nicholas wrote in his diary.

On May 3, however, the sentry was moved to quarters downstairs, where that half-cellar room was, and they who had so recently owned the most magnificent palaces in Europe were happy at this new convenience and opened up space.

On the first day of their stay in the Ipatiev house, their "false titles were rescinded" by resolution of the Ural Soviet. Avdeyev made certain the servant did not address Nicholas as "Your Excellency." He was now to be called Nicholas Alexandrovich Romanov.

"18 April [1 May]. On the occasion of the first of May we heard music from some parade. We were not allowed to go out in the garden today. Felt like washing in an excellent bath, but the water was not running. This is tiresome, since my sense of hygiene has suffered. Marvelous weather, the sun shone brightly, I breathed the air through an open pane."

A year before, at Tsarskoe Selo, the arrested former emperor had written the following angry words on this day:

"18 April, 1917. Abroad today is May 1, so our blockheads have decided to celebrate this day with parades through the streets with choruses, music, and red flags."

By now he had learned not to get annoyed. He realized that "breathing the air through an open pane" was itself happiness, and "washing in an excellent bath" could be an unrealized dream.

Gradually things improved. Their captors started letting them out for a walk. For two whole hours. He still believed that Dolgorukov would return and kept worrying about his loyal friend.

"20 April [3 May]. From the vague hints of those around us we are given to understand that poor Valya is not at liberty, and that an inquiry will be carried out against him after which he will be freed: there is no possibility of entering into any contact with him, no matter how Botkin has tried."

Their daily life at that time was recounted by a certain V. Vorobiev, editor of the *Ural Worker*. He described it, naturally retaining the revolutionary's "class" point of view:

"Besides the commandant, for the first while in the Ipatiev mansion members of the Regional Executive Committee took turns standing guard. Among others, it fell on me as well to perform this type of sentry duty. . . . The prisoners had only just gotten up and greeted us, as they say, unwashed. Nicholas looked at me dully and nodded silently. . . . Maria Nikolaevna on the contrary looked at me with curiosity, wanted to ask me something, but evidently embarrassed by her morning toilette, became flustered and turned away toward the window. . . .

"Alexandra Feodorovna, spiteful, constantly suffering from migraine and indigestion, did not deign to look at me. She reclined on the couch, her head bound with a compress.

"I spent all day in the commandant's room. I was supposed to check on the sentry. During their walk Nicholas paced the road with a soldier's steps.

"Alexandra Feodorovna refused to go for a walk."

At the end of Vorobiev's guard duty, the former tsar asked him to subscribe to the *Ural Worker* for him. "He had not had any newspapers for more than a week and was suffering greatly as a result." Vorobiev promised to do so and asked the tsar to send the money.

The *Ural Worker* would print the first report of his execution.

"1 [14] May. Tuesday. Was gladdened by the receipt of letters from Tobolsk. Got one from Tatiana. We read them to each other all morning. . . . Today we were told through Botkin that we are allowed to walk only one hour a day. To the question, Why? . . . 'So it looks more like a prison routine.' . . .

"2 [15] May. . . . The application of the 'prison routine' has continued and expressed itself in the fact that in the morning an old housepainter painted over all the windows in all our rooms with lime. It was like a fog you see out the window. . . .

"5 [18] May. . . . The light in the rooms is dim. And the tedium is incredible."

Thus he wrote in his diary on the eve of his fiftieth birthday.

"THAT SPRING CHRIST WAS NOT RISEN"

Inside the house, "Latvians" from the Cheka and the young workers Avdeyev had selected from his old Zlokazov factory were rushing around with revolvers and bombs. "Latvians" was the name given to the Austro-Hungarian prisoners who had joined up with the Russian revolution and the Latvian sharpshooters. The "Latvians" were slow to speak, and when they did talk among themselves the workers could not understand them.

This internal guard lived in the house in the first-floor rooms. Next to that half-cellar room. Part of the guard lived across the way, in the Popov house (named after the former owner).

The outside guard around the house was borne by the Zlokazov workers.

The house had its own automobile. As driver, Avdeyev appointed his sister's husband—Sergei Lyukhanov. The elder Lyukhanov son had also been taken into the guard. Avdeyev did not forget his Lyukhanov relatives. It was an enviable position to guard the tsar—they paid cash and fed you and you were alive—not like dying in the Civil War.

Avdeyev himself did not stay in the house. In the evening he went back to the Lyukhanov house, where he spent the night. His assistant remained in the house—another Zlokazov worker, Moshnik.

Moshnik was a genial drunkard. As soon as the commandant was across the threshold, Moshnik started to get smashed. From the sentry room the family heard the piano, songs to a harmonica. The merrymaking went on half the night: the sharpshooters were on a binge.

In the morning—once again—Avdeyev appeared at 9. Avdeyev liked his position. The former turner did not forget whom he was now in charge of. This was his hour to shine. When he was given the family's requests, he answered, "Oh, to hell with them!" and watched triumphantly to see what impression he made on the sharp-shooters. Back in the commandant's room, he specified at length what he had been asked about in the family's room and what he had refused them.

Commandant Avdeyev, the guard Ukraintsev, a certain "pop-eyed" someone—these were the new names in the tsar's diary. They replaced Count Witte, Stolypin, and the countless European monarchs.

"This evening chatted at length with Ukraintsev and Botkin" (April 22) [May 5]. Whereas before he had chatted . . . just whom had he not chatted with!

"My 'pop-eyed' enemy was sitting there instead of Ukraintsev" (whereas before his enemy had been Emperor Wilhelm).

As we come to the end of the next to last, fiftieth notebook of his diary, we can draw some conclusions. Everything that truly touched him, truly upset him, all his internal storms—only slip by in individual phrases. No, he wrote beautifully. Suffice it to recall his letters to his mother, or his Manifesto of Abdication.

That was simply the style of his diary.

He was secretive and reticent. He wrote about conversations with Avdeyev and Ukraintsev, about the painted-over windows. And just as briefly, in passing, mentioned: "this morning and evening, as on all days here, read the proper in the Holy Gospels aloud."

That was the main thing.

———

Their forced arrival in Ekaterinburg coincided with Holy Week.

The bloody Easter of 1918 was approaching. The country was drenched in blood—"Russia washed in blood."

During these great days of the Lord's Passion, as the hour of His Crucifixion was approaching—they entered the Ipatiev house. For the mystical Nicholas, the family's arrival in the Ipatiev house at that particular time was replete with meaning. He had to have felt a flutter of foreboding.

On the third day of Easter, Alix's sister Ella was sent out of Moscow. At first the new authorities had not touched Ella or her Cloister of Martha and Mary. She wrote in one of her last letters: "Obviously we are not yet worthy of the martyr's crown." Her favorite thought: "Humiliation and suffering, drawing us closer to God."

So her path to that crown had begun. At Eastertime, the arrested Ella was brought to Ekaterinburg, where she stayed in the same Novotikhvinsky monastery that would soon be bringing food to the tsar's family. But by the end of May Ella would be sent even farther, 140 versts (93 miles) away, to the small town of Alapaevsk, where the Romanovs sent from Petrograd were gathered: Sergei Mikhailovich, the companion of Nicky's childhood games; Grand Duke Konstantin's three sons; and Grand Duke Paul's son by his second marriage, the seventeen-year-old poet Prince Oleg Paley.

On Easter the tsar and his family received gifts from Ella.

The martyr's crown was Ella's main theme. During those days she must have written to them about this. Ioann of Kronstadt, whom Nicholas respected, as had his father, had said in his sermons: "The Christian enduring misfortunes or sufferings must not doubt in God's goodness and wisdom and must guess how much of God's will is manifested in them. . . . May every man bring his own Isaac to God's sacrifice."

"Guess how much of God's will is manifested in their sufferings" —that is what he had to be contemplating during those days.

A notable event linked with these thoughts then:

"6 [19] May. . . . I have lived to 50; even to me it is strange."

Romanovs did not live to fifty very often. The tsars of this dynasty had lived little, and here the Lord had given him this age. Why had He given it to someone whom his own country had rejected?

A martyr's crown? A reward of suffering?

The land was burning, towns were in flames, brother had gone against brother, and the people God had entrusted to him were creating evil. He himself had been at the beginning of the evil. He had assisted at its birth.

A redeeming sacrifice? Perhaps his whole life had been for this? "Guess how much of God's will. . . ."

The days dragged on slowly, identically, as did the "bull's" slow, persistent contemplation . . . or was he a lamb?

Alix spent her days in the pale yellow bedroom between her four lime-washed windows—in that white fog—in her wheelchair, her head bandaged (a migraine). The former tsaritsa went out for walks only rarely. She daydreamed, read her holy books, embroidered, or drew. Her small watercolors were scattered around the house. How she disdained those little men who dared guard them, God's anointed. But the guards respected her, feared her even. "The tsar, he was a simple man . . . not much like a tsar. But Alexandra Feodorovna was a severe lady and an absolutely pure tsaritsa!" (as their guards would later say).

As before she awaited her liberation. The holy man would protect them; it was no accident that his village had appeared on their journey. Indeed, legions of deliverers were already approaching. She knew that all Russia was in flames. In the north, the south, the east, and the west there was civil war. And in her correspondence with her daughters, in her semi-encoded letters to the Tobolsk house, she wrote about the "medicines . . . that are extremely important for you to bring along to Ekaterinburg." Although her Tobolsk friends implored them to leave the jewels in reliable hands in Tobolsk rather than take them to the terrible capital of the Red Urals, she was implacable. She believed her liberation was drawing nigh, and they must have their jewels with them.

In Tobolsk, under the guidance of Tatiana (the "governor"), the nurse Sasha Tegleva and her helper Liza Ersberg began to prepare the jewels for the trip. They concealed them by sewing them into the girls' bodices: two bodices were placed on top of one another and the stones sewn in between.

They hid the diamonds and pearls in buttons and sewed them into the fur linings of hats.

*T*HE EXODUS FROM TOBOLSK

What about Feodor Lukoyanov, the "spy"? He, of course, was in Tobolsk, for that was where the jewels were. Now he was their sentry. So that they would be returned "to the working people of the Red Urals, whose sweat and blood had won those jewels."

Leaving Tobolsk, Nicholas had embraced Alexander Volkov and instructed him: "Protect the children." It was not easy for the devoted old servant to fulfill his tsar's instruction. Now the remaining family was in the charge of the Soviet and its chairman, the former stoker from the steamer *Alexander III* who was now master of Tobolsk, Pavel Khokhryakov. He was readying the departure of the tsar's children, the remaining suite, and the people from Freedom House. They were going to the capital of the Red Urals. For many, this would be their last journey.

Inside the house Commissar Rodionov and his detachment were in charge. Subsequently Sasha Tegleva would tell White Guard investigator Sokolov: "I have nothing bad to say about Khokhryakov, but Rodionov—there was a malicious snake."

Baroness Buxhoeveden identified Rodionov. Sofia Karlovna asserted that she had once seen him at Verzhbolovo, a station on the German border. A policeman, who was as like Rodionov as two drops of water, had checked their passports.

Kobylinsky spoke about Rodionov: "You immediately felt the policeman in him. . . . A bloodthirsty, cruel police detective."

It turned out, though, that they were both partially wrong.

From a letter of Yakov Verigin in Tver:

"At one time, in my youth, in the fifties, I lived in Riga in the apartment of a university professor, the old Latvian Bolshevik Yan Svikke. . . . He had an amazing biography. He had been a professional revolutionary and carried out important party orders; he even managed to infiltrate the tsarist secret police. . . . In 1918, Commissar Yan Svikke, under the name of Rodionov, was sent to Tobolsk, where he led the detachment transferring the tsar's children. . . . He died in 1976, in Riga, at the age of ninety-one—in complete senility and isolation. He walked around town wearing all sorts of pins—he thought they were medals."

In 1918 the revolutionary-policeman was young and zealous.

During services, Rodionov-Svikke placed a Latvian rifleman near the altar, explaining: "He's watching the priest." He searched the priest, and the nuns as well. He was suspiciously fond of undressing them during the search. He also introduced a strange innovation: the girls were not allowed to lock their doors at night. The tsar's daughters did not even have the right to close their doors.

"So that I can walk in at any moment and see what is going on."

Volkov tried to object: "How can you . . . they are young girls, after all."

They had grown up before his very eyes, and he had always looked forward to seeing them marry. He had always tried to guess which king they would wed. And here—the former grand duchesses were now to sleep with their doors open at night.

"If my order is not carried out, I have the authority to shoot them on the spot." The policeman-revolutionary was enjoying himself.

His time would come. The spirit of the timeless Russian institution would triumph.

Meanwhile the rivers opened up and Alexei began to recuperate.

Olga reported in one of her last letters from Tobolsk:

"Little One is better. But still in bed. As soon as he is better we shall join our people. You, dear heart, understand how hard It is It's grown lighter. But there is no green yet at all. The Irtysh is running as far as Strastnoi. Summer weather. . . . God be with you, my dear."

At Easter the Tobolsk Soviet learned that during the procession Archbishop Hermogen, having pronounced anathema on the Bolsheviks, intended to take his parishioners to the governor's house and free Alexei.

(Was this another ruse of the Soviet, to obtain grounds for handing the family over sooner to Ekaterinburg? Or had the pastor indeed decided to do as the dowager empress had written? Just as three hundred years before his namesake had dreamed of driving out the Poles, had he conceived a wish to drive the Bolsheviks out of town?)

The Cheka took steps: during the procession, Chekists intermingled with the parishioners. A heat wave had descended on Tobolsk, much in advance of any expected date. The sun beat down mercilessly, and the parishioners—none of them young—gradually abandoned the procession. As the believers drifted off, the Chekists pressed closer and closer to the archbishop.

Finally they surrounded—and arrested—him.

"Then I took him out to the middle of the river and we tied on iron gratings [from stoves] I pushed him into the river. I myself saw him go to the bottom." Thus, according to the Chekist Mikhail Medvedev, Pavel Khokhryakov told him what happened.

Finally the day of departure arrived.

They took the endless Romanov suitcases on the steamer *Russia* —the same one that had carried them to Tobolsk. Now it was carrying them back—to Tyumen, to the train.

A motley crowd boarded the steamer—the suite, the people, and the guard. They were assigned cabins.

Rodionov's strange whims continued on the *Russia*. He shut Alexei and his companion Nagorny into his own cabin for the night.

The doors of the former grand duchesses were opened, however. They were strictly, most strictly, forbidden to lock their doors at night. Guards were posted at their doors. Merry sharpshooters by the girls' open cabin doors.

Tegleva (from her statement to Inspector Sokolov):

"On the steamer Rodionov forbade the duchesses to lock their cabin at night, but Alexei and Nagorny were locked in from the outside. Nagorny even made a scene: 'What effrontery! A sick boy! He can't even go out to the washroom.' All in all he was valiant with Rodionov and predicted his own fate."

The *Russia* sailed merrily on, although the revolutionary soldiers' behavior rather shocked the old soldier Volkov. The Red Guards fired their rifles at passing birds. They also fired machine guns.

Seagulls fell, machine guns chattered: the lads were having a fine time—freedom! Thus, in the second year after the birth of the revolution, to chaotic firing, past quieted banks, sailed this insane, this crazy steamer called the *Russia*.

From a letter of Alexei Saltykov in Kiev:

"I read your story about Ekaterinburg [one of my articles in *Ogonyok*]. I read it in two sittings—my heart was so weary from all those horrors. . . . I want to inform you, true, I do not know whether all this is so, but you can verify it. In our house there lived an old man, a soldier from the Red Guards, Uncle Lyosha Chuvyrin, or Chuvyrev. . . . He died in 1962, at the latest. He used to say that as a young man he was on the steamer from Tobolsk with the tsar's children. He was a sentry when they were moved. He said something that I don't even know whether it's worth writing. The grand duchesses had to spend the night in open cabins and at night the sharpshooters got the idea of going in to them. He always told the end to this story differently: either someone forbade them, or they passed out drunk first. . . . Whether he wasn't telling everything or was simply bragging, I don't know."

Oh well, the young sharpshooters liked to brag. The young Red sharpshooters.

Might this be our "spy"?

I keep thinking about him.

———

Four charming girls in captivity. And this man. Quite young. After all the filth, all the reprisals against the peasants, the cellars of the Cheka, these pure, enchanting young girls. The coquettish Anastasia. She must certainly have liked him. And Lukoyanov? Just as the iron revolutionary-comrade Maratov would be expected—Tatiana, of course, who hated the revolution. The proudest and most beautiful. He tried to run into her in the hall. And her majestic, contemptuous look.

The story developed. They were good, ordinary young girls living in an ordinary girlish world. The strange young carpenter with his student coat and intellectual face, of course he could not have been missed among the jolly, fat-faced sharpshooters Anastasia, "good, marvelous Tiutka," teased her older sister for being sympathetic to the "horrible revolutionary."

He made a board for Alexei (planing it neatly), which was put on the sick boy's bed. Alexei ate, read, and wrote at this board, using it as a table.

They would take this board to Ekaterinburg, and it would remain standing in the room when the boy was gone.

The "spy." No, no, he had carried out his mission. He had not let himself go. For him they remained "the tyrant's daughters." He conquered himself!

They sailed away from Tobolsk on this insane steamer with the Red Guards firing at birds, with the bleeding heir. With the suite, which was already awaited at the Ekaterinburg Cheka. Oh, our bitter, bitter revolution. On the ship Lukoyanov overheard the sharpshooters from the detachment agreeing to make mischief with the tsar's daughters. What did he care about a tyrant's daughters when thousands of soldiers, torn away once from hearth and home, were being drained of their male strength and daily committing terrible excesses? Nonetheless, at the last moment he could not resist: he ordered Rodionov to forbid the sharpshooters. He closed the cabin door for the night.

*T*HE END OF THE TSAR'S SUITE

In Tyumen a special train awaited them. The girls, Alexei, his companion Nagorny, former Adjutant General Tatishchev, the old court reader Schneider, and the lady-in-waiting Countess Gendrikova, were put in a second-class car.

All the rest—the tutors Gilliard and Gibbes; the tsar's lackey Trupp; the parlormaid Tutelberg; Countess Buxhoeveden; the nurse

Tegleva and her helper Ersberg; the cook Kharitonov; the kitchen boy Leonid Sednev, Alexei's friend; and others—in a fourth-class car. The train arrived in Ekaterinburg on the night of May 21–22.

The train immediately moved onto a siding. It was drizzling, and the lamps barely shone.

Nicholas's diary:

"9 [22] May. We still do not know where the children are or when they shall arrive? Tiresome uncertainty. . . .

"10 [23] May. This morning for an hour they announced first that the children were a few hours from town, then that they had arrived at the station, and finally, that they had arrived at the house, although their train had been here since 2 in the morning."

In the morning droshkies were brought up to the train. Those sitting in fourth class were forbidden to get out. Gilliard and Volkov watched out the window.

The grand duchesses themselves dragged their suitcases through the drizzling rain, their feet swallowed up by the mud. Tatiana brought up the rear, making sure no one dropped behind. She truly felt like the eldest, dragging her two suitcases and her little dog.

Then Nagorny quickly bore the heir past the train car to the droshky. He wanted to go help the duchesses carry their suitcases, but he was pushed back: they must carry them themselves! Nagorny could not restrain himself and said something. Another mistake for the former sailor: the new authority did not brook insult. The authority was nervous. And touchy. The only payment recognized now was a life, which is what people paid for an incautious word, too. It may have been Upper Isetsk Commissar Peter Ermakov himself whom he replied to. In any event, within a few days poor Nagorny would be taken away.

In the 1930s, by a Pioneer campfire, the former commissar, Comrade Peter Ermakov, would tell the young Pioneers how in the Cheka he had shot "a tsarist lackey—the former heir's companion."

Nicholas's diary:

"10 [23] May [continued]. . . . Great joy to see them again and embrace them after four weeks of separation and uncertainty. No end to the mutual questions and answers, the poor things endured much moral suffering in Tobolsk and during their three-day journey."

While Nicholas was greeting his children, his people and suite were led out of the train cars—Tatishchev, Countess Gendrikova, Volkov, Sednev, Kharitonov, the lady-in-waiting, the nurses, and so on—and put into droshkies.

Volkov later recounted:

"Rodionov walked up to the car: 'Get out. We're going now.'

"I got out, grabbing a large tin of jam, but they told me to leave the tin behind. I never did get that tin." He survived so much—and forgot it all! But he did not forget that tin of jam.

The droshkies set out In the first sat the head of the Red Urals himself, Alexander Beloborodov.

The droshkies drove through Ekaterinburg.

But what about Volkov?

The old servant outlived his masters: shortly afterward he was moved from one prison to another. When the Whites took Ekaterinburg, he was already in a prison in Perm.

One day he was called into the prison office with his things. There he saw his old acquaintances from Tsarskoe Selo—the young Countess Gendrikova and the old lady Schneider. They made up a group of eleven people—all "formers"—and they were led away from that prison and told they were being taken to a transfer prison and then to Moscow.

Oh that "to Moscow." We shall see more than once what that meant.

They walked for a long time, and old Schneider could barely move her feet. She was carrying a handbasket, which Volkov took from her. In it were two wooden spoons and some bits of bread—the entire worldly goods of the teacher of two empresses.

They passed through the town and came out onto a highway. Their escorts became very polite and offered to help carry suitcases. It was already nighttime, and obviously they had already been thinking ahead—they did not want to be splitting up the loot in the darkness. That was when Volkov understood. He made a leap into the darkness and ran. Lazy shots rang out in pursuit, but he ran and ran . . . and got away, the old soldier Volkov.

His acquaintances from Tsarskoe Selo—young Countess Gendrikova and the old court reader Ekaterina Schneider—were destroyed. The Whites later found their corpses. The enchanting Nastenka had a crushed skull—she had been struck with a rifle butt. They had not wanted to waste a bullet.

Nicholas's diary:
"10 [23] May [continued]. . . . Of all those who arrived they only let the cook Kharitonov and Sednev go. We waited until night for them to bring the beds and necessary things from the station. . . . The girls had to sleep on the floor. Alexei spent the night on Marie's cot, in the evening he had bruised his knee, as if on purpose, and suffered terribly all night."

Thus on his first day in the Ipatiev house the boy was taken to his bed. He would not get up until his very last.

Meanwhile, Gilliard, Gibbes, Baroness Buxhoeveden, and Liza Ersberg spent the night in the train car on a siding. Thousands of homeless gathered here in heated cargo vans. Why were they spared? Some were saved by their German surnames. After all, there was the Treaty of Brest with the Germans. Others—Gilliard and Gibbes—were also foreign born.

But why did they spare Tegleva?

She was on fond terms with the Swiss Gilliard, and evidently whoever spared her knew that. Yes, I think this is again our "spy." Naturally, knowing French, he must have made friends in Tobolsk with the talkative Swiss. So he decided not to break up the couple. But enough of conjectures.

In a heated cargo van, amid thousands of sacks, in a mass of humanity, were these remnants of the court.

The strange Gilliard, loyal to the Russian tsar, kept trying to obtain permission to return to the family. But they repeated: "Your services are no longer needed." Gilliard appealed to the English consul, who explained that for the good of all those arrested it was better not to attempt anything. The favorite explanation of foreigners when they are afraid to intervene in Russian affairs.

At night a locomotive was coupled to their van, and the car with the court remnants was pulled out of Ekaterinburg to Tyumen. The Ekaterinburg Cheka was toying with them. After the Whites freed him, Gilliard would return to Switzerland, where he would marry Tegleva.

*T*HE DARK GENTLEMAN
Nicholas's diary:

"12 [25] May. . . . The children sorted out some of their things after an incredibly lengthy inspection in the commandant's room."

So the family had arrived. As had the "medicines."

The jewels were in cases. They were also on the hands, ears, and necks of the Romanov women. Jewels "created by the people's labor, sweat, and blood." Now they had only to be taken away and put back into the hands of the people. From that moment events began to speed up.

Nicholas's diary:

"13 [26] May. We slept well, except Alexei, whose pains continued. . . . Like every day of late. V. Derevenko came to examine Alexei. Today he was accompanied by a dark gentleman, whom we identified as a doctor."

The "dark gentleman" who appeared that day in the family's room and whom they "identified as a doctor" was the Chekist Comrade Yakov Yurovsky.

"Let us drive mankind to happiness with an iron hand"—this was a slogan at the Solovetsky labor camp.

Subsequently, in attempting to explain the inhuman event in the half-cellar of the Ipatiev house, some would brand Yurovsky and his comrades murderers and sadists. Others would see in the execution of the family the Jews' blood revenge against the Orthodox tsar (to the revenge of Goloshchekin and Yurovsky they would add that of other purely Russian names). Indeed, it was easier to explain what went on that way. Revenge for the brutal pogroms and daily humiliation!

Had it had been like that then, as horrible as it is to write, there would at least have been something in it that the human mind could understand.

But it was not.

"Our family suffered less from the constant hunger than from my father's religious fanaticism.

". . . On holidays and regular days the children were forced to pray, and it is not surprising that my first active protest was against religious and nationalistic traditions. I came to hate God and prayer as I hated poverty and the bosses." This is what Yurovsky would write in his last letter, as he lay dying in the Kremlin hospital.

Yes, he came to hate the religion of his fathers and their God.

Yurovsky and Goloshchekin rejected their Jewishness at an early age, and they served a completely different people. This people also lived all over the world. They were called the worldwide proletariat. The people of Yurovsky, Nikulin, Goloshchekin, Beloborodov, the Latvian Berzin. . . . "The world must live without a Russia, without a Latvia, as one human community," their poet Vladimir Mayakovsky proudly wrote.

The party to which they belonged promised to confirm the mastery of this people all over the land. Then mankind's long-awaited happiness would come to pass.

This could happen, however, only through harsh struggle. They called blood and violence the "midwife of history."

Once the nineteenth-century revolutionaries Nechaev and Tkachev had discussed how many people from the old society would have to be destroyed to create a happy future. They came to the conclusion that they should be thinking about how many to "leave."

"The method of sorting out Communist humanity from the material of the capitalist era" (Bolshevik leader Bukharin). So they took up this work of sorting. Out of human material.

Trotsky: "We must put an end once and for all to the Papish-Quaker babble about the sanctity of human life."

They did. Inexorable class hatred took possession of their souls.

"In your investigation do not look for material or proof that the accused acted in word and deed against Soviet power. The first question is . . . *Which class does he belong to?* . . . Herein lie the idea and essence of Red terror" (M. Latsis, Cheka board member, in the November 1, 1918, issue of *Red Terror*).

The murder of the Romanovs, who symbolized the overthrown classes, was to become a private declaration of the Red terror. Of worldwide class war.

"At least a hundred Romanovs must have their heads chopped off in order to unlearn their descendants of crimes" (Lenin). That is why the tsar and his family were doomed the moment they arrived at the Ekaterinburg station.

Yakov Yurovsky in 1918: a high-cheekboned face on a short neck; important, unhurried speech; a black leather jacket, black beard, black hair—he really was the "dark gentleman." He evidently had already learned from the "spy" that Nicholas was keeping a diary in the old style. That was why he came to the door on the thirteenth "old style." He knew that the mystic tsar noted omens. He appeared before him, the "dark gentleman" did, on that unlucky day like an ominous augury. Like advancing vengeance. He went to see him in the guise of a physician. As a medic, it was easy for him to play that role. Even Derevenko, a doctor, believed it and would later say how professionally he had examined the heir's leg. In fact, this was more of the same revolutionary symbolism. They were healing this world with revolvers. Carrying out the great mission bequeathed to them in the name of the future by their teacher Marx: "Hasten the agony of the outlived classes." In the name of this bright future, the tsar's family had to die.

They began to prepare the Romanovs for the end.

"14 [27] May. . . . The guard under our window shot at our house when he thought someone was moving by the window after 10 at night. In my opinion he was just fooling around with his rifle the way guards always do."

I am leafing through a big black notebook in the archive. This is the watch journal: "June 5 at post no. 9 guard Dobrynin fired accidentally, having left off the safety. The bullet went through the ceiling and stuck without causing any damage.

"8 June. Due to the incaution of the guard on duty a bomb exploded. No victims or injuries."

The comrades handled their weapons artlessly and freely. So the tsar was correct in his entry.

But the guard's "fooling around" immediately turned into a story about the tsar's daughters giving someone signals from the windows and a vigilant rifleman immediately shooting at the window. That was how Avdeyev described the incident in his memoirs.

They were making their case.

The valiant Nagorny and the servant Sednev were taken from the house.

"14 [27] May [continued]. After tea Sednev and Nagorny were called in for questioning to the District Soviet."

At that time, hanging around the Ipatiev house, Gilliard saw Red Army soldiers putting the arrested Nagorny and Sednev into droshkies. They silently exchanged looks but did nothing to betray the Swiss's presence.

They never came back.

"16 [29] May. Supper at 8 in daylight. Alix went to bed earlier because of migraine. No word about Sednev or Nagorny."

The Cheka was already at work, combing and weeding out, cutting back the doomed company around the family. To minimize confusion on the decisive night. It was approaching—*that* night!

They lived their usual life. And kept their diaries.

He: "20 May [2 June]. At 11 o'clock we had vespers. Alexei attended, lying in bed. The weather was magnificent, hot. . . . It was unbearable to sit that way, locked up, and not be in a position to go out into the garden when you wanted and spend a fine evening outside. The prison regime!"

She: "May 23 (June 5). Wednesday. Get up at 6.30, now at 8.30 by the watch. [That day they changed the clock to the new time.] Glorious morning. Baby did not sleep well. Leg ached probably more because Vlad[imir] Nik[olaevich, Dr. Derevenko] carried him out before the house and put him in my wheeling chair. I sat out with him in the sun . . . he went to bed as leg ached much for dressing and carrying about. Lunch only brought at 3 o'clock, are putting yet higher planks before all our windows so that not even the top of trees can be seen."

So, they were "putting yet higher planks before all our windows." The house was already being readied for something, but what?

At that point Nicholas took to his bed. From the constant sitting in the rooms. He loved his walks, not only because he liked walking. He had hereditary hemorrhoids. They got worse.

He: "24 May [6 June]. All day suffered from the pain of hem[orrhoids], therefore went to bed, since it is more convenient to apply compresses. Alix and Alexei spent half an hour in the fresh air, and we spent an hour after them. The weather was marvelous."

She: "May 25 [June 7]. Friday. Beautiful weather. N[icholas] stayed in bed all day since he slept poorly last night due to the pains. *P - - - a* [these two Latin letters conceal the Russian word for "bottom," which she modestly shortened to insert in her English text] is better when he lies quietly. . . .

". . . Vladimir Nikolaevich did not come today either."

Dr. Derevenko was no longer allowed to see Alexei.

He: "27 May [9 June]. Finally got up and quit my bed, it was a summer's day, walked twice. The green is very fine and lush, a pleasant smell."

Again Nicholas felt something was going on. Something was about to happen.

"28 May [10 June]. . . . Outward relations . . . have changed lately. Our jailers are trying not to talk to us, as if they did not feel right, and one senses alarm and worry in them! Incomprehensible!"

But beyond the limits of the Ipatiev house, everything was quite comprehensible. In the middle of May there was an uprising against the Bolsheviks by former tsarist war prisoners—the Czech Legion, who were joined by Cossack units. Chelyabinsk fell. Now they were advancing on the capital of the Red Urals.

The town was expecting them. On June 10 there were sinister riots. The night before, June 8–9, a certain Ensign Ardatov and his detachment had gone over to the Whites. Now the chief support of the Ural Soviet in the town was the detachment of Upper Isetsk workers led by Commissar Peter Ermakov. A huge, shouting crowd gathered on Ascension Square. Ermakov and his Isetsk detachment, Yurovsky and his Chekists, and Commissar Goloshchekin had a hard time dispersing the mutinous crowd. They just did not have enough loyal soldiers. Meanwhile, how many Red Guards were guarding the "tyrant and his family."

He: "31 May [13 June]. This afternoon we were let out into the garden for some reason. Avdeyev came and talked for a long time with E. S. [Botkin]. According to him, he and the Regional Soviet are worried about anarchist acts and therefore we may be facing a hasty departure, probably to Moscow. He asked us to prepare for departure. We immediately began to pack, but quietly, so as not to attract attention from the sentry officers, at Avdeyev's special request. At about 11 at night he returned and said that we would remain another few days. Therefore on the 1st [14th] of June we stayed bivouacked, not unpacking anything. Finally after dinner Avdeyev, slightly tipsy, told Botkin that the anarchists had been captured, the danger had passed, and our departure had been postponed. After all the preparations it was rather tiresome."

The former tsaritsa wrote obscurely that day:

"May 31 [June 13]. Pray morning. Sunshine.

"12.30 Avd[eyev]no walk. . . . said to pack up as any moment. . . .

"At night Av[deyev] again . . . said not before several days."

What a strange story. Not long before, the Ural Soviet had done battle with Moscow, explaining how dangerous it was to transport the Romanovs by rail. Now, frightened by anarchists, the Urals themselves wanted to take the tsar and his family to Moscow. Now— when the Czechs were advancing on the town. When there was an uprising in the town itself, when the land around Ekaterinburg was burning! And all this out of concern for the bloody tyrant?

No, something is not right here. It is hard to believe in this sudden concern on the part of the Uralites. This was a very strange trip for Moscow being planned.

Let us recall a conversation between Commissar Yakovlev and the commander of the Ekaterinburg detachment—Busyatsky—en route to Tobolsk, when the latter suggested to Yakovlev: "During the Romanovs' trip, en route, stage an attack and kill them."

Kill them on a trip?

$\mathcal{M}$ISHA'S LAST JOURNEY

If only Nicholas had known, when he heard the "concerned" Uralites' proposal to travel to Moscow, what had happened the previous night. If only he had known the "trip" that had already been taken. He never would, though, not even on the day he died.

On the night of June 12–13, three strangers appeared at a Perm hotel owned by a merchant named Korolev and presented an order from the Cheka to take away Nicholas's brother Michael and his secretary, Brian Johnson.

When he was sent away from Gatchina, Michael had gone to live in a hotel in Perm, where, as Moscow confirmed several times in letters to the Perm Soviet, he enjoyed "all the rights of a citizen of the republic."

With him in the hotel were his secretary, the Englishman Brian Johnson, his valet, and his driver (the grand duke was a passionate motorist—witness his daring trip through the Alps with his bride-to-be). But that day he had a very different trip ahead of him. The three strangers went up to the grand duke's room and when they went back down beside them walked the tall grand duke and his short, fat secretary, who looked like Mr. Pickwick.

The grand duke, the secretary, and their three escorts got into two droshkies and drove away.

All that transpired in the hotel room was recounted to Alexander Volkov by the grand duke's valet, Chelyshev, when the two were in prison together.

The visitors woke Michael, who did not want to go with them and demanded an important Bolshevik: "I know him, not you." The one in charge swore and grabbed the former grand duke by the shoulder.

"Oh, you Romanovs! We're sick and tired of it all!"

After which Michael dressed silently. His valet said: "Your Highness, do not forget to take your medicine." The visitors swore again and took them away without the medicine.

In the morning the Cheka announced that they had issued no orders and that Michael had been abducted. A telegram went to Petrograd. "Tonight, unidentified men dressed as soldiers abducted Michael Romanov and his secretary Johnson. Searches have yet to yield results. The most energetic measures are being taken."

Soon after, however, rumors spread that the role of the "unidentified men" had been filled by some very well known people: Myasnikov, who was chairman of the Motovilikha Soviet, and his comrades. They took Michael and his secretary away—and shot them. Their action was proclaimed an act of proletarian vengeance. The rumors were confirmed. The Perm Cheka and local authorities called it "an anarchistic lynching" and firmly distanced themselves from it.

*T*HE WHOLE TRUTH ABOUT THE GRAND DUKE'S MURDER
In 1965, in Moscow, in his declining years, a deserving man died, a holder of the Red Banner of Labor: Andrei Vasilievich Markov.

A year before his death, he met with the head of the Perm Party Archives, N. Alikina, who had compiled the biographies of the Perm Bolsheviks, to make known the most glorious deed of his life. Before telling his story the old man showed her an unusually shaped silver watch, resembling a segment of a cut hard-boiled egg. Markov said that the watch had run without repair for nearly fifty years, and then he told her the whole story. Until recently these statements of Markov were kept in classified storage in the Perm Party Archives.

Markov told how the principal organizer of Michael's murder, Myasnikov, had chosen for his assistants Chief of Police Ivanchenko and him, Markov. But three armed men seemed too few, so they brought in two more, Zhuzhgov and Kolpashchikov, both workers.

"At about seven in the evening, in two closed phaetons," recalled Markov, "we set out for Perm. The horses had been furnished us in the Cheka courtyard, so we initiated the chairman of the provincial Cheka, P. Malkov, into the affair. That was where the plan for abducting Michael Romanov was worked out in full. . . . Malkov stayed at the Cheka, Myasnikov left on foot for the Royal Rooms hotel, and we four—Ivanchenko and Zhuzhgov on the first horse and Kolpashchikov and I on the second—approached the front door of the Royal Rooms at about eleven. Zhuzhgov and Kolpashchikov went into the hotel, and Ivanchenko and I stayed outside in reserve."

Everything went just as the grand duke's valet had told Volkov: Michael refused to go with the men, demanding that Cheka Chairman Malkov (the "important Bolshevik") be telephoned and citing "the decree on my free choice of residence."

While Michael was defending his rights, the men waiting outside were growing exasperated.

"Armed with a revolver and a bomb, I entered the room, having first cut the telephone line in the hall," Markov continued. "Michael Romanov was still being stubborn, citing illness, and demanding a doctor and Malkov. Then I ordered him taken as he was. They threw whatever came to hand on him and started to take him away, after which he began to get ready and asked whether he needed to take any things with him. I told him someone else would collect his things. Then he asked to take along at least his personal secretary, Brian Johnson. Since that was in our plans, we consented. Michael Romanov threw on a raincoat. N. V. Zhuzhgov grabbed him by the collar and told him to go outside, which he did. Johnson followed voluntarily. Michael Romanov was put in a phaeton. N. V. Zhuzhgov sat behind the coachman, and V. A. Ivanchenko next to Michael Romanov."

They bravely grabbed the grand duke by the collar (not the shoulder as the valet had testified, concealing the gentleman's humiliation)—five armed against three unarmed men. To his death—by the collar!

"We rode as far as the kerosene storehouses," Markov recounted, "which is 5 versts [3.5 miles] from the village of Motovilikha. We went another verst from the storehouses and turned right into the forest. . . . We met no one on the road [it was night]. When we had gone 100–120 sazhens [750 feet], Zhuzhgov shouted: 'Get out.' I jumped out quickly and demanded that my rider Johnson get out, too. As soon as he got up to get out of the phaeton I shot him in the temple; he swayed and fell. Kolpashchikov fired at Johnson, too, but his bullet stuck in his pistol. Zhuzhgov was doing the same thing, but he only wounded Michael Romanov. Romanov ran toward me with his arms spread open begging to say goodbye to his secretary. Zhuzhgov's drum got stuck in his revolver [his bullets were home-made]. I had to make the second shot at a rather close distance (about a sazhen) from Michael Romanov's head and felled him on the spot.

". . . We couldn't bury the corpses since it was growing light quickly and it was so close to the road. We just dragged them to-gether to one side, heaped them with twigs, and returned to Motovilikha. Zhuzhgov and a very reliable policeman went back that night to do the burying."

Tall, thin Michael, after taking a bullet, his arms spread wide, runs, begging to say goodbye, and in reply—another bullet!

After the murder Markov took the watch off the murdered Johnson, "a souvenir," as he explained to Alikina. We will have cause to recall this tradition of murderers: taking watches off the slain.

Alikina recorded a most interesting detail at the end of the conversation. "Andrei Vasilievich Markov said at the end that after the execution of Michael Romanov he went to Moscow. With the help of Sverdlov he was received by Lenin, whom he told about the event."

Such was the "lynching" in which the leaders of the local Cheka, the police, and the head of one of the Soviets participated. And about which they went with pride to tell the head of state.

WHAT WAS SUPPOSED TO HAVE HAPPENED? As they put an end to Michael, the unsuspecting family was fever-ishly preparing for the trip to Moscow.

We now know how Michael's individual trip went. We can also imagine how the group trip of Nicholas and his family proceeded.

———

A month later, according to the scenario worked out in Ekaterinburg, a group trip for some other Romanovs would be carried out. Alix's sister Ella, Grand Duke Sergei Mikhailovich, the sons of Grand Duke Konstantin—Ioann, Igor, and Konstantin—young Prince Oleg Paley, and their servants had all been held since May on the outskirts of Alapaevsk.

On July 18 a local cook would see them all get into wagons *very calmly* with the Red Guards: they too had been told they were going on a trip—to a place of safety.

The wagons would stop by a nameless mine shaft not far from Alapaevsk, and the Red Guards would start beating the captives with their rifle butts. The old grand duchess, too. Nicky's childhood playmate and Kschessinska's admirer, Sergei Mikhailovich, naturally would resist. For which he would get a bullet, the old dandy. He alone would be thrown into the mine dead; the others would still be alive. Grenades would be tossed in, brush and fallen branches heaped on, and all of it set afire. For a long time local residents—this is not a pretty legend—would hear the singing of prayers from underground. Ella would be dying in agony but would have strength for more than prayer. In the dark of the mine, gasping from the smoke, the crippled grand duchess crawled to the dying Ioann and bandaged his smashed head. To the end she fulfilled the vows of the Convent of Martha and Mary.

When the Whites would take Alapaevsk later that summer, they would find these bodies in the strewn mine. An examination of the corpses would reveal the trip's denouement. As in Michael's case, the Cheka in Alapaevsk staged the slain Romanovs' escape.

A telegram dated July 19, 1918, to the Sovnarkom, Moscow, from Alapaevsk: "Reporting that in Alapaevsk I have learned of an assault on the quarters where the former Romanov princes were being kept and the removal of such. My brief inquiry and examination at the scene has shown that . . . the attackers broke into the building, freed all the Romanovs and servants, and took them away. . . . Examination of the building has shown the Romanovs' things had been packed and stowed. . . . I assume that the attack and flight had been previously planned. Political Representative Kobelyanko."

This is what awaited the family on their trip.

The same scenario lay at the base of all the Romanov murders, and all of them contained an element of provocation.

Yes, Russia's revolutionaries had grown up with the secret police's provocations, and when they conquered they adopted the familiar methods. The immortal, all-Russian institution—the secret
police—was resurrected then and there, like a phoenix from the
ashes. Now it was called the Cheka. It would become more powerful
than its creators. And it would kill them. In 1917 the revolutionaries
destroyed the secret police, and in 1937, at the height of the Great
Terror, the secret police would destroy the revolutionaries.

So, the general action was planned for June 13–14: the night of the
long knives, the destruction of both tsarist brothers and the annihila-
tion of the tsar's entire family at one fell swoop.

But only Michael's murder was accomplished.

In the heat of preparations, Avdeyev suddenly arrived and the
family's trip was postponed.

What had happened?

Most likely carrying out the executions had been a local decision
made by the ferocious Ural Bolsheviks. When they conceived of
destroying the Romanovs, they were on their own. To them Moscow
was a distant myth.

The decision, naturally, had been made by the head of the Ural
government—Beloborodov. Subsequently Chekists captured by
White Guards would corroborate this fact, stating that the Romanovs in Alapaevsk had been destroyed in response to a telegram from
Ekaterinburg over the signatures of Beloborodov and his assistant
Safarov. But there was one more person without whom Beloborodov
could not have acted: the head of the Ural Bolsheviks, the military
commissar of the Urals, Comrade Filipp Goloshchekin.

Beloborodov was hot-headed, young, and fierce. Goloshchekin
was much older and more circumspect. As military commissar he
was directly involved in fighting the White Army. When the Bolsheviks had conceived of their proletarian vengeance—the annihila-
tion of the Romanovs—the military situation did not yet threaten
irrevocable catastrophe. Now Commissar Goloshchekin knew for
certain that Ekaterinburg would fall to the White forces. Soon they
would have to flee, and the only place for them to go was Moscow. If
yesterday they had treated the capital with mocking disdain, today it
was their only island of salvation. No, without Moscow, without the
permission of Lenin and his old friend Sverdlov, nothing important

could be contemplated. The elimination of the tsar's family—it was too dangerous to undertake something like that now.

At the last moment, Goloshchekin evidently rescinded his decision to proceed with the murders. He decided first to obtain Moscow's consent.

Meanwhile he let go a trial balloon: to see how Moscow would react to Michael's destruction.

The organizer of Michael's murder, Myasnikov, did not want to be a guinea pig. That was why he disappeared the moment they brought Michael out of the hotel. According to Markov's statements, Myasnikov was not involved in the actual murder at all. A shrewd man, Myasnikov. During the first postrevolutionary years he took part in the workers' opposition and did battle with Lenin himself. When the persecutions of the workers' opposition began in 1921–22, he managed to flee abroad and lived happily in Paris, where he forgot all about our bitter revolution. In vain. Just as he had once taken Michael away by force, so he too would be abducted by Stalin's bold Chekists, who brought the poor forgetful man back to his homeland. And just as Michael had once been shot without trial, like a dog, so too would Myasnikov.

Or else it had all been conceived in Moscow—how to destroy both pretenders to the Russian throne—and now, when the days of Bolshevik power seemed numbered, the Central Committee panicked and decided to limit themselves to Michael and see how the world would react. They could leave the family for now, a trump card in possible negotiations with the Allied powers.

One way or another, the plan to kill the family was postponed. For now the Ural leaders decided to take the tried and true path.

Once again the days dragged on.

Nicholas's diary:

"3 [16] June. . . . All week have been reading and today finished *The History of Emperor Paul the First* by Schiller [Schilder]—very interesting."

What was he thinking about as he read the history of his unlucky ancestor? About his mother's prophecy back in 1916, when he became commander-in-chief, that he would repeat Paul I's story? Or was he simply reading a book about a past life that had vanished so very quickly? As if there had always been this pitiful house and these long, boring, maddeningly hot days.

"5 [18] June. Dear Anastasia has turned 17. The heat outside and inside was terrific. . . . The girls are learning how to cook from Kharitonov and in the evenings they knead flour and in the morning bake the bread. Not bad!"

Chapter 13

FLIGHT

✤

THE LETTER

It happened—in June.

That morning. . . . They had just gotten up. Getting up early was torture for her. She had to, though: every morning Commandant Avdeyev came "to verify the presence of the prisoners."

Nicholas was standing by the window, examining a tiny piece of paper.

With the commandant's permission they were now being brought food from the Novotikhvinsky monastery: out of the generosity of the father superior they were brought cream, eggs, and bottles of milk. In one of the monastery bottles he had found this letter.

Dull light through the lime-smeared window. It was still morning and not yet hot. Later would come the furnace—and in the rooms it would become unbearable. They were not allowed to open the windows, though. Once he had done battle with emperors—of Japan, Germany, Austria-Hungary. Now he was doing battle for permission to open the windows in a room.

"9 [22] June. Saturday. . . . Today at tea 6 men walked in, probably from the Regional Soviet—to see which windows to open. The resolution of this issue has gone on for nearly 2 weeks! Often various men have come and silently in our presence examined the windows.

"The fragrance from all the town's gardens is amazing."

But he has forgotten all about the windows and the gardens' fragrance. He is torturously trying to read the letter—this scrap of paper cleverly slipped into the milk stopper.

He is pacing around the room with a marching step—his unbreakable guardsman's habit. He is thinking about the letter.

In the translucent light of morning, through the smeared window, we are trying to see him.

The same strong muscular body. But he has filled out slightly from the enforced immobility. He is not very tall (the guards were very disappointed in his height. In their simple imaginations a tsar was supposed to be great, that is to say, tall). Compared with his father, his giant uncles, and his brother Misha, he has always seemed small. (Long ago his great-great-grandmother the Princess Württemburg-Stuttgart, the wife of the unlucky Paul I, brought her family's beauty and build into the Romanov family. Ever since, tall men had been born—Alexander I, Nicholas I, Alexander III.) He is of ordinary height. His body is not perfectly proportioned: his muscular torso is rather massive and his strong legs relatively short. His neck is unusually powerful for his small, neat head. A pleasant face and a small nose, reddish mustache, tobacco-yellow beard. Not long ago he had grown a beard, but thanks to Alix. . . .

Her diary: "June 7 (20) . . . I cut N.'s hair."

She managed to cut it *before*.

Right now, in the light of day, scattered gray hairs can already be seen in his mustache and beard. His head, cut by the empress's firm hand, is already graying evenly. His eyes are changeable—first bluish-gray, then sky blue . . . and sometimes steely green. A "charmer." The enigma of his gaze. He always felt a little like a child. Was it because of the powerful size of his father, uncles, and brother? Was it because of the strength of the women by his side? This childlike quality of his combined with the constant foreboding of future suffering—all this is in his gaze. And it is upsetting. The gaze of a helpless and gentle sacrificial lamb. Those who saw him remembered that gaze.

Many years later his lover Kschessinska, already very old, would meet a mysterious woman who declared herself to be his daughter—the miraculously saved Anastasia. In answer to a journalist's questions she would say:

"This woman has *his* gaze. . . . No one who looked into his eyes . . . could ever forget. . . ."

"And you knew those eyes?"

"Very well. . . . Very well," the ninety-year-old Little K. whispered with frightening tenderness.

Now his face is darker, coarsened from the sun. His neck is red, and there are bags under his light eyes.

Finally, he hands the letter to her. But Alix never gets the chance to read it.

In walks Commandant Avdeyev, "to verify the presence of the prisoners." Nicholas walks from behind the table toward the commandant, as he always used to greet petitioners during audiences—standing, in front of his desk. Thus he now meets the former Zlokazov worker.

As always in the mornings, Avdeyev is gloomy, having overindulged the night before. He reeks of wine—in a room with closed windows.

Nicholas cannot bear drunkards.

In an even, quiet voice (none of his ministers had ever heard him raise his voice) Nicholas greets the commandant.

Finally, Avdeyev leaves.

"W̲AIT FOR A WHISTLE TOWARD MIDNIGHT" Alix reads the mysterious letter, which is written in French. With suspicious mistakes. But immediately she believes in it. It is just not written by aristocrats. Where are they—those aristocrats?! They have betrayed them. Common people are writing. "Good Russian people." She feverishly absorbs the long-awaited text: "We are a group of Russian army officers. . . ."

This is how the letter promising them escape appeared. It was signed: "Prepared to die for you, an officer of the Russian army." Oh, how Alix likes this signature. Her migraines are but a memory. She is once again the old *spitzbube*. Yes, it has come to pass. They have come. They have not abandoned their tsar! Good Russian people! They are prepared to liberate their emperor. The holy man has sent the family a "legion of angels."

She begs Nicky to reply. As always, he calmly agrees. Yes, he will write an answer.

He does, and so this secret correspondence is established.

"Your friends do not rest," it says in the next note, sent in another bottle from the monastery. "The hour we have waited for so long has come. With God's help and your presence of mind we hope to achieve our goal without risking anything."

Another letter that same day:

". . . One of your windows has to be unsealed so that you can open it. I beg you to indicate to me precisely which window. In the event that the young tsarevich cannot go, matters shall be greatly complicated. . . . Would it not be possible, an hour or two before the time, to give the tsarevich some kind of narcotic? Let the doctor decide. Rest assured, we will not undertake anything unless we are assured of success."

It was an escape conceived in the style of a Dumas novel.

But how to open the window? Suddenly, as if at the holy man's behest, the window was opened.

Nicholas's diary:

"10 [23] June. Whitsunday. . . . Marked by various events: one of our windows was opened this morning. . . . The air in the room became clean, and by evening even cool."

The former commander-in-chief sent another message in a milk bottle, as if it were a disposition of battle.

"Second window from the corner on the square has been open for two days and even at night. Windows 7 and 8 by the main entrance are also always open. The room is occupied by the commandant and the assistants who make up the inner guard at any given moment. There are 13 men armed with rifles, revolvers, and bombs. . . . The commandant and his assistant come in to see us whenever they like. The guard on duty makes the rounds of the house at night twice an hour. . . . There is one machine gun on the balcony and another under the balcony—in the event of a disturbance. Opposite our windows on the other side of the street the guard is staying in a little house. There are 50 men. From each guard post there is a bell to the commandant's room and a wire to the guard quarters and other points."

These bells . . . they would ring that night, their last night.

"Inform us," concluded Nicholas, "as to whether we shall be able to take our people with us."

As always, he carefully recorded everything, revealing the secret of this plot.

Nicholas's diary:

"14 [27] June. Our dear Marie turned 19. . . . The weather was the same, tropical. 26 degrees [79°F] in the shade, and 24 [75°F] in the rooms. It is even hard to bear! . . . Spent an uneasy night and kept vigil fully dressed. All this because a few days ago we received two letters, one after the other, telling us to prepare to be abducted by some loyal people! The days have passed, though, and nothing has happened, and the waiting and uncertainty have been very trying."

Now in his diary he testified before the entire world "about a monarchist plot for the purposes of the family's escape and liberation."

Alix was more cautious: her entry for June 27 does not say a word about the letters or a plot. But she was waiting. Oh, how she was waiting—for the next night. She listened to the nighttime silence.

As if someone were mocking them, instead of the rustle of plotters stealing up, through the open window:

"June 15 (28). Friday. At night we heard under our windows the guard strictly ordered to watch every movement in our window."

*W*HO WROTE IT?
Seventy years later I am sitting in the Central State Archive of the October Revolution.

The archive file on my desk: "The Family of the (Former) Tsar Nicholas the Second 1918–1920."

For a very long time—seventy years—this thin little file has not been released. I am one of the first (the very first perhaps) to see it upon its declassification. We shall return to its astonishing contents more than once. I will spend many hours alone with this bloody file!

In the middle of it I find the same letters signed "An officer" and once sent to the Ipatiev house in a milk bottle. They would become one of the grounds for the execution of the Romanov family.

Here is the last letter. Written neatly, in a student's hand, in French:

"We are a group of Russian army officers who have not lost our conscience, our duty before our tsar and fatherland. We are not informing you about us in detail for reasons you can well understand, but your friends D. and T. [Dolgorukov and Tatishchev], who are already saved, know us."

The hour of liberation was approaching and the usurpers' days were numbered. In any event, the Czechs were getting closer and closer to Ekaterinburg. They were but a few versts from town. "Do not forget that at the last moment the Bolsheviks will be ready to commit any crime. The moment has come, we must act. Wait for a whistle toward midnight—that will be the signal. An officer."

Dolgorukov and Tatishchev, however, "who are already saved," had long been lying in unmarked graves.

How strangely mendacious this well-wisher was. Moreover, how well informed he was that the Romanovs knew nothing about the fate of "D. and T."

Now, just as I became weary of the constant suspicion, I receive a letter from the historian M. M. Medvedev, the son of the Chekist M. A. Medvedev, one of the executioners of the tsar's family. (This letter became the starting point for our many conversations.) Here is what he told me in his letter:

"In 1964, two old men arrived at Moscow Radio.

"These two were felt to be the last people living of those present at the family's execution.

"One of these old men was Grigory Nikulin, the murderer of Prince Dolgorukov and one of the main participants in the execution of the tsar's family. The other was I. Rodzinsky, who did not participate in the execution of the Romanovs but who was a member of the Ural Cheka in 1918."

This conversation and the invitation to the radio station had been devised and organized by this very historian, Mikhail Medvedev. With great difficulty he managed to talk the two into recording their statements for posterity. With equal difficulty he managed to talk the authorities into it: only after he went to Nikita Khrushchev himself was this taping at Moscow Radio permitted. Medvedev asked the questions, but a "representative of the Central Committee" also took part in the conversation.

This taping took a long time, and we will return to it again. Now we are interested in the statements of the Chekist Rodzinsky:

"The letter with the signature 'An officer,' which Nicholas Romanov believed, was composed at the Cheka. Its author was one of the Bolshevik leaders of Ekaterinburg, Peter Voikov."

(Peter Voikov, 1888–1927, party name "Intellectual." Expelled for revolutionary activity first from grammar school and later from the St. Petersburg Mining Institute. Participated in terrorist acts. Emigrated, lived in Switzerland, graduated from the University of Geneva, in August 1917 returned to Russia and joined the Bolsheviks. In 1918, people's commissar for government supply in the Red Urals. As of 1924, Soviet ambassador to Poland. He was lucky—he didn't live until 1938; in 1927 he was killed by a monarchist in Poland for his participation in the execution of the Romanov family.)

According to Rodzinsky's statements, this University of Geneva graduate composed all the letters in the bottles.

But Voikov had terrible handwriting (or he may not have wanted to leave evidence of his role as a provocateur), and he suggested that Rodzinsky copy out the letters. The Chekist had good handwriting, so he did. To ensure that there could be no doubt of the truthfulness of his words, Rodzinsky left a sample of his handwriting at the radio station.

The old Chekist had evidently come not only to reminisce but to repent.

INTRIGUE

How astonishingly well thought out everything in this story is. Beginning with the food from the monastery, which the conscientious Uralites suddenly allowed to be brought to the Romanovs.

It was all done very cleverly. In early June a certain Ivan Sidorov (an obvious pseudonym) arrived in Ekaterinburg with a large sum of money from Vyrubova and other loyal friends of the tsar's family. Through Dr. Derevenko, Sidorov made contact with the Novotikhvinsky monastery and, simultaneously, with Commandant Avdeyev. Soon after, the suddenly soft-hearted commandant allowed food to be brought from the monastery (to establish his "concern" for the family and to fatten his own pocket—with the money Dr. Derevenko offered him for the food. Thus the tsar's family began to connect the monastery with their good, loyal friends. That was why they believed in the letters.

And how well thought out the story with the window!

A closed window meant a torturous stuffiness. It had to engender bad nerves. Even more—anger. It must have hastened the family's consent to escape.

Then the simple-hearted Avdeyev suddenly proved surprisingly vigilant: he carefully checked all the food brought from the monastery—and "discovered" the correspondence. Finally, the finale anticipated all along: Nicholas's entry about the plan for escape in his diary. Now the monarchist plot was in hand.

Whoever thought all this up knew Nicholas's habit of recording *everything* in his diary.

Without this entry the game would not have been over. The entry provided irrefutable proof.

No, the cruel, straightforward Yurovsky does not fit here. Here a more intelligent person was acting; a psychologist had thought all this through. Someone who had studied Nicholas well.

Yes, more than likely, this was Lukoyanov, our "spy."

After his arrival from Tobolsk, he had lived in Perm and headed the Perm Cheka, but in June he was in Ekaterinburg. At the end of June he was appointed to a new high position.

From a letter of Xenia Sorokina:

"My father, an old Bolshevik and student of local history, studied documents about Feodor Lukoyanov. A note from the KGB Museum in Sverdlovsk was left in his papers: 'Lukoyanov, F. N., as of March 15, 1918, chairman of the Perm Province Cheka. As of June 21, 1918, chairman of the Ural Cheka. Directed the Central Executive Committee's special mission relating to the tsar's family.'"

He did an excellent job on the "Central Executive Committee's special mission relating to the tsar's family."

I can imagine his triumph: the family went out for a walk, and he read Nicholas's entry in the diary. Yes, he had calculated it all. He felt like an astronomer who has calculated the presence of a star and sees it through his telescope in the sky. Only later, when our "spy," as usual, carefully put the diary back in its place so that the tsar would not notice anything—only then did he realize that he had sentenced them to death. Him, her, Tatiana, all those sweet girls. And the sick boy. This happens with gamblers. The game overshadows the goal.

Nicholas believed. Naively. Almost stupidly. And he made the fateful entry in his own diary.

But did he really believe?

WHO WAS PLAYING?

The Czech Legion was already outside Ekaterinburg. Subsequently much would be written about how furiously they and the Whites burst into Ekaterinburg.

But, they were going about their "bursting" in rather an odd fashion. Tyumen had fallen, all the major towns around had been taken—and Ekaterinburg was still standing.

Moreover, they skirted Ekaterinburg to the south: Kyshtym, Miass, Zlatoust, and Shadrinsk had already been captured. There was no "furious bursting"; they wanted to encircle it slowly and slowly choke it. It seemed as if they were in no hurry at all.

At that time in Ekaterinburg there were only a few hundred armed Red Guards, but there were many tsarist officers; the Academy of the General Headquarters, which had been evacuated from Petrograd, was there. Still, there was not a single honest attempt to free the Ipatiev prisoners!

After overthrowing the Bolsheviks, the Czechs and the anti-Bolshevik Siberian army were not about to restore tsarist rule. They would restore the rule of the Constituent Assembly.

In this strange year the former autocrat had understood a great deal. Most important: no one needed him alive. Indeed, anyone capturing him alive would doubtless have a serious problem on his hands.

But dead?

A sacrifice. . . . "There is no sacrifice I would not make" (his words before his abdication). Sacrifices to redeem all that had happened.

He also thought that once they had killed him they would let his family go free. His death was the only way to free them all.

His death was a good in itself.

Of course, sensible Nicholas immediately realized who the "officer" was with his primitive French.

All his life they had been playing these games with him: the Department of Police, his mother, Kschessinska, Alix, the Duma, Vyrubova, Rasputin. This time it was his game. He played it himself —and won. By sending letters to the "officer," by leaving that entry in his diary, he knew that he was sentencing himself to death. They threw the bait, but they themselves landed on his hook.

*M*OSCOW, JULY 1918

So, at the end of June, the Ural Soviet received proof of a monarchist plot!

Goloshchekin left for Moscow.

Moscow waited in trepidation for news from the Urals. How long could Ekaterinburg hold out, and what would happen next? "Move the maximum of workers from Peter [Petrograd], otherwise we will fall, for the situation with the Czechoslovaks is quite bad," Lenin, wrote.

Yes, the Bolsheviks were about to fall. It seemed a matter of days. Ruin surrounded them, from the Pacific and all across Siberia and the Urals, their power had collapsed.

The Germans were in charge in the Ukraine, where a voluntary army was forming against the Bolsheviks, and the English were landing in the north. As was famine.

Arriving in Moscow, Goloshchekin would fall into a boiling caldron. There were ominous events daily.

The Fifth Congress of Soviets convened on July 4. Once this congress had intended to decide whether to put the tsar on trial. Now a trial was out of the question. The revolutionary parties were skirmishing. The Left Socialist Revolutionaries, who had quit the government after the "treachery of the Treaty of Brest," were giving Lenin a thrashing. The holy virgin of the Russian revolution, the famous terrorist Maria Spiridonova, had given a fanatical speech against the Bolsheviks.

On July 6 a bomb exploded in the German embassy. Two people leaped the embassy fence and rushed into a waiting automobile. The Left Socialist Revolutionaries had murdered the German ambassador, Count Wilhelm Mirbach.

"The Socialist Revolutionaries have attempted to sunder the shameful Treaty of Brest"—that was the government's official version. The unofficial version was that it was all a provocation arranged by the Bolsheviks to deal with the very dangerous opposition. It was no accident that one of Mirbach's assassins, the Socialist Revolutionary Blyumkin, would later become an agent for Trotsky. Right after Mirbach's assassination, the Bolsheviks arrested the entire Left Socialist Revolutionary faction at the congress. In retaliation, the Socialist Revolutionaries seized the telegraph, the telephone, and the Cheka building. Then Lenin brought out his Latvian sharpshooters—the Bolsheviks' striking force—and the uprising was put down.

This is the Moscow—torn apart and bloodied by furious internecine war—in which Goloshchekin arrived in early July 1918.

In the future all the tsar's Ural assassins would unanimously state that Goloshchekin discussed only the defense of Ekaterinburg in Moscow, not the fate of the tsar's family; the Ural Soviet, they would insist, decided to execute the Romanovs on its own initiative.

This was a patent lie. How could Goloshchekin have discussed the possible fall of Ekaterinburg and not have mentioned the fate of the tsar and his family? How could he not have tried to decide what to do with them should the town be overtaken?

*T*ROTSKY'S TESTIMONY
In his diary, Trotsky, back from the front, described his conversation with Sverdlov:

" 'The tsar is where?'

" 'Shot, of course.' [Imagine Sverdlov's cool triumph when he told Lev to his face that they had torn his favorite bone right out of his mouth: there would be no trial.]

" 'And the family is where?'

" 'The family as well.'

" 'All of them?'

" 'Yes. What about it?' [Again Sverdlov's invisible grin between the lines: "Does the fiery revolutionary Trotsky pity them?"]

" 'Who decided this?' [Fury: he wants to know who dared not consult with him, and so on.]

" 'We all did. Ilich [Lenin] felt we could not leave them a living banner, especially given our trying conditions.' "

Yet when his anger had passed, Trotsky, who during the terrible days of the revolution had said, "We will leave, but we will slam the door so hard the world will shudder," could not have helped but admire this superrevolutionary decision:

"In essence this decision was inevitable. The execution of the tsar and his family was necessary not simply to scare, horrify, and deprive the enemy of hope, but also to shake up our own ranks, show them that there was no going back. Ahead lay total victory or utter ruin. . . . The masses of workers and soldiers would not have understood or accepted any other decision. Lenin had a good sense of this," Trotsky wrote.

So, according to Trotsky, it was all decided in Moscow. That was what Goloshchekin negotiated in Moscow!

This is only Trotsky's testimony, however. History recognizes documents—and I found one. First a clue, from a letter of O. N. Kolotov in Leningrad:

"I can tell you an interesting detail about the topic of interest to you: my grandfather often told me that Zinoviev took part in the decision to execute the tsar and that the tsar was executed on the basis of a telegram sent to Ekaterinburg from the center. My grandfather can be trusted; by virtue of his work he knew a great deal. He said that he himself took part in the shootings. He called the execution a 'kick in the ass,' asserting that this was in the literal sense: they turned the condemned to the wall, then brought a pistol up to the back of their head, and when they pulled the trigger they simultaneously gave them a kick in the ass to keep the blood from spattering their uniforms."

$\mathcal{T}$HERE WAS A TELEGRAM!
I found it! Even though they were supposed to destroy it. The blood cries out!

Here it is lying before me. One stifling July afternoon I was sitting in the Archives of the October Revolution and looking at this telegram, sent seventy-two years before. I had run across it in an archive file with the boring label "Telegrams About the Organization and Activities of the Judicial Organs and the Cheka," begun on January 21, 1918, and ended on October 31 of the same 1918. Behind this label and these dates lie the Red Terror. Among the terrifying telegrams—semiliterate texts on dirty paper—my attention was struck by a two-headed eagle. The tsarist seal!

This was *it*. On a blank left over from the tsarist telegraph service and decorated with the two-headed eagle was this telegram: a report on the impending execution of the tsar's family. The irony of history.

At the very top of this telegram, on a piece of telegraph ribbon, is the address "To Moscow Lenin."

Below, a note in pencil: "Received July 16, 1918, 21:22." From Petrograd. And the number of the telegram: 14228.

So, on July 16, at 21:22, that is, *before* the Romanovs' execution, this telegram arrived in Moscow.

The telegram was a long time in getting there, having been sent from Ekaterinburg to "Sverdlov, copy to Lenin." But it was sent through Zinoviev, the master of the second capital, Petrograd—Lenin's closest comrade-in-arms at the time. Zinoviev had sent the telegram on from Petrograd to Lenin.

The individuals who sent this telegram from Ekaterinburg were Goloshchekin and Safarov, another leader of the Ural Soviet.

Here is its text:

"To Moscow, the Kremlin, Sverdlov, copy to Lenin. From Ekaterinburg transmit the following directly: inform Moscow that the trial agreed upon with Filipp due to military circumstances cannot bear delay, we cannot wait. If your opinion is contrary inform immediately. Goloshchekin, Safarov. On this subject contact Ekaterinburg yourself.

And the signature: Zinoviev.

Knowing that Comrade Filipp is Goloshchekin's party nom de guerre, it is easy to understand the code of this telegram sent hours before the execution of the tsar and his family. "The trial agreed upon with Filipp" is rather sly code for "the execution of the Romanovs agreed upon with Goloshchekin." (They had been getting ready to try Nicholas, but now that the Bolsheviks had to abandon Ekaterinburg, a truly revolutionary trial against the tyrant was his execution.)

"Military circumstances"—this was Ekaterinburg's hopeless situation; any day the town had to fall.

So the content of the telegram: through Zinoviev, the Ekaterinburg Ural Soviet informed Sverdlov and Lenin in Moscow that the execution of the tsar's family agreed upon with Goloshchekin could not bear any further delay in view of Ekaterinburg's deteriorating military situation and the town's imminent surrender. If Moscow had any objections, they must inform Goloshchekin and Safarov of such immediately.

After this telegram one can speak of Goloshchekin's mission in Moscow definitively: he discussed the fate of Ekaterinburg and *agreed upon* the family's execution.

*T*wo "educated" marxists

The telegram mentioned two others who evidently played a significant role in the fate of the tsar and his family. A photograph of the presidium of the Ural Soviet: beside Goloshchekin and Beloborodov stands a typical bespectacled intellectual with weak eyes that somehow do not mesh with his bold fur cap. This is Safarov, a member of the presidium and the chairman's comrade. The signature of this intellectual was on the Ural Soviet's bloodiest telegrams.

Georgy Ivanovich Safarov, son of an engineer, born 1891. The typical biography of an "educated Marxist": exile, emigration to Switzerland. . . . It was during this exile that a most powerful name arose alongside Safarov—Grigory Zinoviev, a figure right behind Lenin and Trotsky in the Bolshevik hierarchy. The close tie between Zinoviev and Safarov persisted over the entire course of their lives.

They became close in Switzerland. Zinoviev introduced Safarov to Lenin. Immediately after the February Revolution, thanks to Zinoviev, Safarov arrived in Petrograd in the sealed car that Germany, Russia's military adversary, allowed to pass through to Russia. The revolution conquered, and after September 1917 Safarov was "Comrade Chairman of the Ural Soviet." Safarov's actions in Ekaterinburg were highly reminiscent of those of his idol Zinoviev in Petrograd.

In Petrograd, surrounded by the Whites, Zinoviev introduced the institution of hostages. In response to a White attack he and Stalin, who had come to Petrograd, arranged a bloody bacchanalia: nighttime executions of hostages—White officers, priests, and other "formers." In 1919 Zinoviev would carry out another bloody retaliation for the murder in Berlin of the German Communists Karl Leibnecht and Rosa Luxemburg. Hostages were executed in the Fortress of Peter and Paul: four grand dukes—Nicholas Mikhailovich and George Mikhailovich, Paul Alexandrovich, and Dmitry Konstantinovich Romanov. (Soon after this display of international solidarity Lenin would recommend Zinoviev to run the Comintern.)

Naturally, from the beginning Zinoviev supported the Uralites' idea of executing the Romanovs. According to his logic, that was the proper response to the Whites' advance on Ekaterinburg. Also, he did not want a trial: he hated Trotsky. "The party has wanted to smash Trotsky's face in for a long time," this educated Marxist wrote sweetly of his rival in the struggle for power.

All this time the old friends remained in close contact, as they would till the very end. When in 1919 Zinoviev headed the Comintern, he took with him the head of the eastern division, his friend Safarov. After Lenin's death, Zinoviev, the leader of Petrograd, strengthened his rear. He made the loyal Safarov director of the party newspaper, *Leningrad Pravda*, and when Stalin rewarded Zinoviev with a bloody "kick in the ass," it fell upon Safarov to get even.

From a letter of Sergei Pozharsky in Rostov-on-the-Don:

"*Ogonyok* printed your 'Execution in Ekaterinburg' and there in the photo is Safarov. Since you are involved with the material, perhaps you can tell me what ever happened to him. I can explain. In 1941, in Saratov, I shared a prison cell with Safarov. A most remarkable individual. According to him he was with Lenin, either as a secretary or librarian in emigration. . . . He was a delegate at some party congress. And a newspaper editor. Then for many years he was a witness at almost all the 'cases' of 1937, etc. Tell me briefly: was he all this or not, my cellmate?"

"AGREED UPON WITH MOSCOW"

Sverdlov and Zinoviev—those two in Moscow were the mighty support of the Ural Bolsheviks, who dreamed of reprisal against the

Romanovs. That was the purpose of Goloshchekin's main meeting in Moscow, his meeting with Lenin.

Might this meeting not have taken place? Might Goloshchekin— a member of the Central Committee, the leader of the dying Urals, where according to Lenin the destiny of all Bolshevik power, the matter of the tsar and his family, was being decided—not have been received by Lenin? The fact that Lenin's journal does not indicate such a meeting may only prove his understandable disinclination to have it known.

Goloshchekin had to resolve two issues concerning the tsar and his family at this meeting, the first being to agree upon what to do with the tsar should Ekaterinburg fall. Here there was no hesitation, especially since they could show the world indisputable evidence of a monarchist plot, which Goloshchekin had brought. The other issue was to agree upon the family.

From a letter of Leopold Shmidt in Vladivostok:

"Bonch-Bruevich once recalled the words of the young Lenin, who was reveling in the successful reply of the revolutionary Nechaev, the hero of Dostoevsky's *Devils*. To the question Who of the ruling house must be destroyed? Nechaev gave a precise answer: 'The whole litany.' 'Yes, the entire house of Romanovs, after all, it's so simple, it's ingenious!' Lenin was thrilled."

A murdered emperor might cast a shadow of martyrdom on his children. Alexei and his sisters could also become a "living banner."

This must have occurred to the man who had once appreciated Nechaev's answer.

By sentencing himself to death, Nicholas sentenced his entire family to death as well.

Evidently the fate of Ella and all the Alapaevsk prisoners was decided *at one and the same time*.

Naturally they agreed upon the ticklish question of how to announce the execution. Evidently they decided then that the official announcement must refer only to Nicholas. Thus this horrible formula was born: "the family has been evacuated to a safe place." The caustic Zinoviev may well have been its author.

Yes, the family's death had to remain a secret for the time being, but an open secret. Trotsky was right: Lenin knew that the danger of reprisals for the bloody deed must close the ranks in these terrible times for the revolution.

Also, anticipating a possible collapse, the government naturally wished to keep its distance from the execution. The decision to execute had to come from the Ekaterinburg Soviet. This was very handy: the Uralites who executed the tsar were left with only two options—victory over the Whites or death. This must have served to close the ranks of the doomed town's defenders.

Unlike the bloody romantics Trotsky and Zinoviev, Lenin was a pragmatist. The execution of the tsar and his family was to be carried out in one instance only: if Ekaterinburg fell. Otherwise they must remain as before—a card in the future game with the great powers.

It was at the fateful meeting in Moscow that the mechanism must have been devised: the signal to initiate the family's execution could not come from the savage Ural revolutionaries. It had to come from outside Ekaterinburg. But who on the outside? That we shall learn later.

Such was to be the outcome of the meeting between Lenin and Goloshchekin. Lenin could not have helped but feel how extraordinary it was.

July is a bad month for revolutionaries. In France, Robespierre was executed in July; in Russia, five eminent Decembrists, who had revolted against Nicholas I, were hanged in July. And now in July the hour of vengeance had come. Vengeance against the son and grandson of the man who had once killed Lenin's brother. The revolutionaries' age-old hunt for Russian tsars was drawing to a close.

The discussion of the tsar's fate must have evoked some associations. During that period, when all around him was collapsing, Lenin suddenly developed an interest in implementing the decree "on the removal of monuments honoring the tsars and their servants." (On July 9 he posed this question insistently at the Soviet of People's Commissars.)

Lenin fought with surprising enthusiasm against the stone images of the Romanovs.

From the memoirs of Kremlin Commandant P. Malkov:

" 'They still haven't removed this monstrosity'—Lenin pointed to a monument erected on the spot of the murder of Grand Duke Sergei Alexandrovich. . . . Ilich [Lenin] deftly fashioned a noose and hurled it over the monument. We got down to business and very soon after, the monument was ensnared in ropes from all sides. Lenin, Sverdlov, Avanesov . . . and other members of the government . . . harnessed themselves to the ropes, bore down, pulled, and the monument crashed to the cobblestones."

After Lenin's death the tradition continued. While destroying one of the Kremlin's cathedrals, the Bolsheviks would open the sarcophagi and strip them of the remains of the shrouded Muscovite tsaritsas, which they would dump onto a cart. And a horse would drag them across the Kremlin's ancient St. John's Square. On one cart were the mother and wife of Ivan the Terrible, the wives of the first Romanovs, the mother of Peter the Great—which would be dropped into the cellar of the Palace of Justice through a hole in the boards.

Seventy years later people in Russia would be tumbling monuments to Lenin from their pedestals—history the joker!

But let us return to 1918. In Moscow an agonizing July week was drawing to a close. Goloshchekin was on his way to Ekaterinburg; Lenin to Kuntsevo in the country, where he spent his free days with his wife and sister. And relaxed.

Chapter 14

PREPARATIONS FOR MURDER

HE LAST TWO WEEKS
In Ekaterinburg, in anticipation of Goloshchekin's return, preparations for the end were already under way.

On July 4, Commandant Alexander Avdeyev was replaced by Chekist Yakov Yurovsky. Simultaneously the entire guard inside the house was replaced; the outer guard, however, made up of the Zlokazov workers brought in by Avdeyev, remained.

Also remaining was the husband of Avdeyev's sister—the driver of the house automobile—Sergei Lyukhanov.

Inside the house, unfamiliar, taciturn young blond men appeared: the Cheka's new Latvians, who occupied the entire downstairs.

Nicholas felt it immediately: the "dark man" had come. Now it would be soon.

Yurovsky had entered the Ipatiev house in the guise of a deliverer. First he had been a doctor. Now he was a battler against dishonest thievery.

He informed Nicholas of the many robberies by the former

guard. Silver spoons, which had been found buried in the garden, were returned to the family triumphantly.

At the same time, however, all the family's property was recorded —for purposes of learning the extent of the robberies, naturally. This record began with the jewels.

The Romanovs were under arrest, and of course they were not allowed to wear jewels, such being the lot of all prisoners, explained Yurovsky. For now they must not. The experienced Chekist cleverly weighed this "for now" in his conversation. *For now.* Until the denouement. Until their fate was decided.

That was what Nicholas understood, although he did not believe him, of course.

This secretive and at the same time very trusting man. He did not know the slogan of the great revolutions: Rob the robbed. It seemed to him that for the first time an understanding had arisen between him and this altogether incomprehensible power. The town would fall, and they had decided to take his life, but in doing so, naturally, they must surrender to the family that which belonged to it, intact and preserved. The jewels—that was all they had. It was unclear where they would have to live afterward. Or how. He was the father of the family, and he was obliged to consider their future. He was happy with this unspoken gentlemen's agreement.

Nicholas's diary:

"21 June [4 July]. Today there was a change of commandant. During dinner Beloborodov and others came and announced that instead of Avdeyev they were appointing the man we took for a doctor, Yurovsky. In the afternoon before tea he and his assistant compiled a list of gold things: ours and the children's. The greater part [rings, bracelets] they took with them. They explained that there had been an unpleasant story in our house. . . . Am sorry for Avdeyev, but he is to blame for not keeping his own people from robbing from the trunks in the shed."

Yurovsky appreciated Nicholas's trust. He did not even begin to conduct a search, so as not to undermine this faith. Although, why did he need to search them now, when he could do it after?

Alix did not trust the new commandant. She did not trust a single word he said. She was happy that she had prudently concealed everything most valuable.

Alix's diary:

"June 21 (July 4). Thursday. Avdeiev is being changed a[nd] we get new commandant (who came once to look at Baby's leg . . .) with a young help who seems decent where as the others vulgar a[nd] unpleasant. All our guards inside left. . . . Then made us show all our jewels and the young one [the assistant] wrote them all down in detail and then they were taken from us (where to, for how long? why? don't know) Only left me two bracelets I can't take off."

The commandant's "young help," who "seems decent" to Alix was indeed a most pleasant young man. Clear-eyed, with a clean side-buttoned shirt and a name soothing to the tsaritsa's ears—Grigory. This was Nikulin, who in just a few days would shoot her son.

From Nikulin's autobiography (kept in the Museum of the Revolution in Moscow):

"My father was a bricklayer, a stove-fitter, and my mother was a housewife. His education was the lowest, he completed two grades.

"Starting in 1909 I worked as a bricklayer and then at a dynamite factory (this was during the war, to get excused from military service). Ever since the factory closed in March 1918, I have worked in the Ural Regional Cheka."

Yurovsky noticed him immediately. Nikulin did not drink, a rarity among former workers who joined the Cheka. Most important, he knew how to inspire confidence immediately. Yurovsky appreciated all this and tenderly called him "my son." When Yurovsky became commandant, he took Grigory Nikulin for his assistant.

Alix's diary:

"June 22 (July 5). The command[ant] came with our jewels before us. . . . Left them on our table a[nd] will come every day to see we have not opened the packet."

As before, Nicholas believed in the new commandant.

Nicholas's diary:

"23 June [6 July]. Saturday. Yesterday Commandant Yu[rovsky] brought a small box with all our stolen jewels, asked us to verify the contents, and sealed it in our presence, leaving it with us for safe-keeping. . . . Yu. and his helper are starting to understand what type of people surrounded and guarded us, robbing us. . . .

"25 June [8 July]. Monday. Our life has not changed a bit under Yu. He comes into the bedroom to check that the seal on the box is intact and looks out the open window. . . . Inside the house new Latvians are standing guard, outside it is the same—some soldiers, some workers. Rumor has it that several of Avdeyev's men are already under arrest. The door to the shed with our baggage has been sealed—if only they had done that a month ago. Last night a storm and now even cooler."

———

A stormy summer. He noted the storms in his diary. Lightning in the sky—and water on the land. A lot of water.

For that reason the forest roads had largely washed out and it would be hard for the truck to drive down those roads with its corpses.

Meanwhile, the house was already being readied for the final event. He paid no attention, but she took note.

"June 25 (July 8). Lunch only at 1.30 because they were repairing the electricity in our rooms."

The jewelry had been listed and the electricity fixed.

The next day, July 9, Dr. Botkin began writing his final letter. . . .

"*J* AM DEAD, BUT NOT YET BURIED"

After the execution, Yurovsky collected in Dr. Botkin's room the papers of the last Russian court physician.

I am looking them over: "1913 Calendar for Doctors," "notice from main headquarters on the death of [his son Dmitry] in battle, December 1914."

And here is his letter, which he wrote to a classmate who had graduated with him long before, in 1889. He began writing it on July 3 and evidently continued to work on it throughout the following days. Then he copied out this very long letter in his minuscule handwriting. He was copying it out on the last day when someone interrupted him in the middle of a word:

"My dear, good friend Sasha. I am making a last attempt at writing a real letter—at least *from here*—although that qualification, I believe, is utterly superfluous. I do not think that I was fated at any time to write anyone from anywhere. My voluntary confinement here is restricted less by time than by my earthly existence. In essence I am dead—dead for my children, for my work. . . . I am dead but not yet buried, or buried alive—whichever: the consequences are nearly identical. . . . My children may hold out hope that we will see each other again in this life. . . . but I personally do not indulge in that hope. . . . and I look the unadulterated reality right in the eye. . . . I will clarify for you with small episodes illustrating my condition. The day before yesterday, as I was calmly reading Saltykov-Shchedrin, whom I was greatly enjoying, I suddenly saw a reduced vision of my son Yury's face, but dead, in a horizontal position, his eyes closed. Yesterday, at the same reading, I suddenly heard a word that sounded like *papulya* [papa dear]. I nearly burst into sobs. Again—this is not a hallucination because the word was pronounced, the voice was similar, and I did not doubt for an instant that my daughter, who was supposed to be in Tobolsk, was talking to me. . . . I will probably never hear that voice so dear or feel that touch so dear with which my little children so spoiled me. . . .

". . . If 'faith is dead without deed,' then deeds can live without faith. If any of us does combine faith and deeds, then it is only out of God's special kindness. One such happy man— through grave suffering, the loss of my firstborn, my half-year-old little boy Seryozha— was I. Ever since then my code has significantly expanded and defined itself, and in every case I have also been concerned about the patient's soul. This vindicates my last decision, too, when I unhesitatingly orphaned my own children in order to carry out my physician's duty to the end, as Abraham did not hesitate at God's demand to sacrifice his only son."

Nicholas's diary:

"28 June [11 July]. Thursday. In the morning, at about 10.30, three workers came up to the open window, hoisted a heavy railing, and attached it to the outside of the frame without any warning from Yu. We like this man less and less! Began to read the eighth volume of Saltykov-Shchedrin."

This was the last straw. It was awful to enter the room and see that dark railing. He suffered both for her and for the boy.

And she . . . she was living the hard existence of captivity. She explained in her diary Nicholas's obscure entry: "We like this man less and less."

"June 28 (July 11). Thursday. . . Command[ant] insisted to see us all at 10, but kept us waiting 20 m. as was breakfasting & eating cheese wont permit us to have any more any cream. Workmen turned up outside and put up iron railings before our only open window. Always fright of our climbing out no doubt or getting into contact with the sentry. Strong pains continue. . . . Remained in bed all day."

Yes, the dark man wielded them two blows that day. In the final analysis, the cream, cheese, and eggs brought from the monastery had been a distraction to Alexei's perpetual boredom.

("It's boring! What boredom!" These exclamations filled the boy's diary.) And now on top of that—the railings.

But Yurovsky was only doing his job.

Their days were numbered, and he had already begun to isolate them from the world. He feared the monastery. Yes, the Cheka had conceived of transmitting the deceitful letters, but what if suddenly someone else. . . . He had to consider that "suddenly." There was anarchy in Ekaterinburg. The gold reserves had been evacuated, the archives had already left town. Only the small detachment—that was all he had.

That was all right, though, for a few days.

*T*HE DECREE OF EXECUTION

It happened on July 12—the day after the railings were put up.

Upon his return from Moscow, Goloshchekin called a meeting of the Ural Soviet Executive Committee.

The loyal Goloshchekin did not say a word about his agreements with Moscow: only the most restricted circle knew about them—the Ural Soviet presidium. The Soviet's rank-and-file members were certain that today they themselves would decide the Romanovs' fate. The Whites were advancing. All of them realized what this decision might mean in their lives.

Nevertheless, they passed the decree unanimously. The Ural Soviet's decree of execution.

From a letter of Alexander Kruglov in Perm:

"My father kept a copy of the text of the decree on shooting the tsar, which was posted around town after the execution:

" 'Decree of the Ural Executive Committee of the Soviet of Worker, Peasant, and Red Army Deputies. Possessing information that Czechoslovak bands are threatening the Red capital of the Urals, Ekaterinburg, and bearing in mind that the crowned hangman could hide and escape the people's tribunal, the Executive Committee, carrying out the will of the people, has decreed to execute the former tsar Nicholas Romanov, guilty of countless bloody crimes.' "

Implementation of the decree was entrusted to Yakov Yurovsky, commandant of the "House of Special Designation."

"WE HAVE NO NEWS FROM THE OUTSIDE"
Nicholas's diary:

"30 June [13 July]. Saturday. Alexei took his first bath since Tobolsk. His knee is improving, but he cannot bend it completely.
Weather is warm and pleasant. We have no news from the outside."

With this hopeless sentence, the day after the execution decree,
as if he had sensed something, Nicholas closed his diary (see Appendix).

What follows are empty pages carefully numbered by him to the
end. There is something awful in those blank pages.

All these days she had been waiting. Waiting for more news from the
suddenly silent "Russian army officer."

She listened and listened to the sounds outside the window.
Alix's diary:

"June 29 (July 12). . . . Constantly hear artillery passing, infantry & twice cavalry, during the course of two week. Also troops
marching with music—twice. It seems to have been the Austrian
prisoners who are marching against the Czechs (also our former
prisoners), who are with the troops coming through Siberia & not far
from here now. Wounded daily arrive to the town. . . .

"June 30 (July 13). At 6½ Baby had his first bath since *Tobolsk*.
He managed to get in and out alone, climbs also alone in & out of
bed, but can only stand on foot as yet. . . . Rained in the night.
Heard three revolver shots in the night."

THE FINAL THREE DAYS
Three days before their end, Nicholas broke off his diary. She continued hers. She took their story to its end.

"July 1 (14). Sunday. Beautiful summer's morning. Scarcely slept
because of back & legs. 10½. Had the joy of a *vespers*—the young
Priest for the 2nd time."

It was Sunday. And while the new leader of the country, the
atheist Ulyanov, was relaxing at his dacha in Kuntsevo, the former
leader of the country, prisoner Romanov, received permission for a
service.

Father Storozhev was invited to serve the vespers the family had ordered. Father Storozhev had already held services once in the Ipa-tiev house, and Yurovsky agreed to call him a second time.

The commandant's room was slovenly and filthy; grenades and bombs littered the piano. Grigory Nikulin was sleeping on the bed fully clothed after his shift. Yurovsky was slowly drinking his tea and eating his bread and butter. While the priest and deacon arrayed themselves, they began to talk.

"What's wrong with you?" asked Yurovsky, noticing that Father Storozhev kept wringing his hands.

"I have pleurisy."

"I had active tuberculosis, too."

Yurovsky began giving him advice. He was a medic, and he loved dispensing medical advice. In addition, only he understood the im-portance of the moment: he, a tailor's pupil from a poor Jewish family, was allowing the last tsar his last service. His last—that he knew for certain.

When Father Storozhev walked into the family's quarters, the family had already gathered. Alexei was sitting in the wheelchair; he was quite grown up, but his face was pale after his long illness spent in stuffy rooms. Alexandra Feodorovna was in the same lilac dress she had worn when Father Storozhev had seen her during the first service. She was sitting in a chair beside the heir. Nicholas was standing, dressed as he had been the last time—in a field shirt, khaki trousers, and boots. The daughters were standing, dressed in white tops and dark skirts. Their hair had grown out and reached to their shoulders. In the back, behind the arch, stood Dr. Botkin, the ser-vants, and the little cook Sednev.

According to the vespers ceremony, they had to read the prayer "Rest with the Saints."

Naturally he was the first to drop to his knees. He was the tsar, who always knew that the tsar's lot "is in the hands of God."

He also knew: Soon! Very soon.

On the way back the deacon told Father Storozhev, "Something has happened to them. They are *different.*"

THE SOLICITOUS COMMANDANT
During that period Yurovsky was often away from the house. He was taking trips with Upper Isetsk Commissar Ermakov to the Koptyaki

countryside, 18 versts (12 miles) from Ekaterinburg. There, not far from the village, in the deep woods, were abandoned mines.

Yurovsky knew that the execution of the Romanovs was only the beginning of his job. Then came the hardest part: burying them so that they could not be found.

"The family has been evacuated to a safe place." Yurovsky and Ermakov were searching for that safe place.

Alix's diary: "July 2 (15). Monday. Greyish morning. Later sunshine. Lunched on the couch in the big room, as women came to clean the floors, then lay on my bed again & read with *Maria* . . . Ezra 26–31. They went out twice as usual. In the morning T[atiana] read to me the *Spiritual Reading*. At 6½ Baby had his second bath. Bezique [a card game]. Went to bed 10¼. . . . Heard the report of an artillery shot in the night & several revolver shots."

The women who washed the floor on the next to last day later told how they were ordered to wash all the floors –in the family's rooms and downstairs, on the first floor, where the guard lived. They also washed the floor in the half-cellar room.

They had repaired the electricity, put in railings, and washed the floors. Yurovsky had thought of everything.

During that period he was finishing up the entries in the sentry journal:

"July 10. Notification of Nicholas Romanov about opening the windows to air out the rooms, which he had been refused.

"July 11. The family had its usual walk: Tatiana and Marie asked for their camera, which the commandant naturally refused them."

Yes, there was a camera in the house. The one that had been confiscated from the tsaritsa when she first entered the Ipatiev house. The camera was lying in the room of the commandant— commandant and former photographer Yakov Yurovsky.

The Chekist's son Mikhail Medvedev:

"My father said that during that time Yakov Yurovsky held a meeting in the American hotel. Participation in the execution was voluntary, and the volunteers gathered in his room, no. 3. They agreed to aim for their hearts, so that they wouldn't suffer. And then and there they figured out who would shoot whom. Peter Ermakov took the tsar for himself. By rank he was the Upper Isetsk military commissar. He had people who were supposed to help bury the bodies.

"Most important, Ermakov was the only one among the executioners who had done hard labor as a political prisoner. This was one of the most honored pasts for a revolutionary. Anyone who did hard labor was for the revolution!

"Yurovsky took the tsaritsa, Nikulin Alexei, my father got Marie."

(Mikhail Medvedev could have felt insulted. The next most honored past for a revolutionary was political prisoner, which Mikhail Medvedev had been—a professional revolutionary, a former sailor, who had served in a tsarist prison, although he had not done hard labor. His real name was Kudrin. Medvedev was his party pseudonym, from one of the countless false passports he had used during his underground work in Baku. In 1918 he began working for the Cheka. This was not all that common among "old" revolutionaries. As a rule they refused to work in the Cheka because they did not like to arrest Socialist Revolutionaries, their old comrades in the struggle against the tsar.)

The remaining daughters and retainers were left to another Medvedev, Pavel Medvedev, the head of the guard in the Ipatiev house, another Chekist, Alexei Kabanov, and six Latvians from the Cheka.

Yurovsky agreed: at exactly midnight a truck was to drive into the courtyard. Peter Ermakov was to come with the truck, which they planned to take from the Soviet's garage. And replace the driver.

The truck was to be driven by Sergei Lyukhanov—the Ipatiev house driver. This truck would take away the bodies.

The town was restless, which was why Yurovsky designated a password. The password on the day of the execution was "chimney sweep."

They adored revolutionary rhetoric. They chose "chimney sweep" because they were planning to clean out the dirty chimneys of history.

Now it remained to decide where to carry out the execution. The commandant did not hesitate. Next to the storeroom was a room—he had noticed it right away. The room let out onto Ascension Lane, which was a dead end. There was a grating on the window, and the window jutted out into a slope, so that the room was a half-cellar, and if they turned on a lamp—a bare bulb at the ceiling—the light would not be visible at all from the street because of the high fence.

It was a hungry time. They had to work all night. Yurovsky allowed the nuns from the monastery to bring milk and a basket of eggs for Alexei. And he asked them to pack the eggs better so they wouldn't break. He took pains with everything.

*T*HE LAST DAY

On that last day, July 16, they got up at nine. As always, they gathered in the room of the father and mother and prayed together.

Before they had often sung religious songs together. But this last day for some reason they did not sing.

At nine in the morning, as always, Commandant Yurovsky arrived at the house. At ten they had tea and the commandant walked around the room, verifying the prisoners' presence.

He also brought the eggs and milk.

Yurovsky informed Alix of this; he was pleased with this idea of his—in any event they would be in a good mood. And the eggs would come in handy. Later.

He allowed them to walk for an hour that day, as always. They walked half an hour in the morning and half an hour before dinner.

On their walk they saw the guard Yakimov, who said that only the tsar and his daughters walked; he did not see Alexei or the tsaritsa.

She did not go out but spent the entire day in her room.

From Yurovsky's Note:

"July 16, 1918. The telegram arrived from Perm in the code language containing the decree to exterminate the Romanovs. At six o'clock in the evening Filipp Goloshchekin ordered the decree executed."

What was this telegram? And where did this word *decree* come from? Who could issue a decree to Goloshchekin, the military commissar of the entire Ural district?

Even earlier, in late June, when a false rumor had spread in Moscow about the execution of Nicholas II, the Sovnarkom had sent an inquiry to the Urals. The reply—"All information about the murder of Nicholas Romanov is a provocation—arrived over the signature "Commander-in-Chief of the Northern Ural-Siberian Front R. Berzin."

After Muraviev's betrayal, power in the Urals had been given to the Latvian revolutionary commanding the front against the advancing Czechs—Reinhold Berzin, whom Moscow had evidently instructed to set the family's execution in motion. This was logical; he could be a guarantee that the Ural Soviet did not do this before

Ekaterinburg's fate at the hands of the Czechs had been decided. Only he, the commander of the army, could know this fateful hour precisely. Only he, the commander-in-chief, could issue an order to a military commissar. On July 16, realizing that the town's situation was hopeless, Berzin clearly gave his order, sentencing eleven people to death—including a minor.

In 1939, Reinhold Berzin would be shot in Stalin's camps.

BEFORE THE APOCALYPSE

It was seven o'clock in the evening.

The Romanov family was having tea. Their last tea. That morning the guards had come and taken away the little cook Sednev. Alix was very concerned and sent Botkin to ask what was going on. They explained that the boy had gone to see his uncle. He would return soon.

Having received Berzin's order, the cautious Filipp Goloshchekin decided in any event to telegraph Moscow, so he sent that telegram —to the effect that the family's execution agreed upon with Moscow could not be delayed because of the town's imminent surrender.

"If your opinion is contrary, inform us immediately."

He wanted to secure a direct decision from Moscow. He sent the telegram through Zinoviev—the execution's ardent supporter. He understood that Zinoviev would not allow the execution decision rescinded. Zinoviev sent the telegram on to Lenin in Moscow. At 21:22 it was in Moscow, as the telegram itself attests.

Did Ekaterinburg receive an answer? Or, as always, was Moscow silent, implying agreement?

WAS THERE AN ANSWER FROM LENIN?

On August 11, 1957, an article was printed in *Construction Newspaper* entitled "On Lenin's Advice." An article with a title like that scarcely had many readers, which was too bad—the essay was as curious as could be.

Its hero was a certain Alexei Feodorovich Akimov, a senior lecturer at the Moscow Architecture Institute. Akimov had a meritorious revolutionary past, about which the essay's author wrote. From

April 1918 to July 1919, Alexei Akimov served in the Kremlin guard—first guarding Yakov Sverdlov and then Vladimir Lenin.

The newspaper recounted an event that involved Akimov in the summer of 1918:

"Most often he stood at his post by Lenin's reception room or on the staircase to Lenin's office. But sometimes he had to carry out other orders as well. Run down to the radio station or the telegraph office, for example, and transmit especially important telegrams from Lenin. In those instances he brought back not only the original of the telegram but also the telegraph ribbon. After transmitting one such telegram of Lenin's the telegraph operator told Akimov that he would not give him the ribbon but would keep it. 'I had to take out my pistol and insist,' recalled Akimov. But when he returned to the Kremlin half an hour later with the original of the telegram and the telegraph ribbon, Lenin's secretary said pointedly: 'Go in to Vladimir Ilich, he wants to see you.'

"Akimov entered the office with a bold military step, but Lenin stopped him cold: 'What were you up to there, comrade? Why did you threaten the telegraph operator?

" '. . . Go to the telegraph office and publicly apologize to the operator.' "

This essay contained one very strange detail: not a word was said about the *subject* of that "especially important telegram" that Alexei Akimov took away from the telegraph operator while waving a revolver.

From a letter of Nikolai Lapik, director of the Progress Factory's museum in the town of Kuibyshev:

"We have in our museum a typed record of a conversation between A. F. Akimov and A. G. Smyshlyaev, a veteran of our factory whose hobby was searching for materials on its history.

"In the stenographic record of this conversation, which took place on November 19, 1968, the following was written down from the words of A. F. Akimov:

" 'When the Ural Regional Party Committee decided to shoot Nicholas's family, the Sovnarkom and Central Executive Committee wrote a telegram confirming this decision. Sverdlov sent me to take this telegram to the telegraph office, which was located then on Myasnitskaya Street. He said to send it as cautiously as possible. This meant that I was to bring back not only a copy of the telegram but the ribbon as well.

" 'When the telegraph operator sent the telegram, I asked for the copy and the ribbon. He would not give me the ribbon. Then I pulled out my revolver and began to threaten the operator. When I got the ribbon from him I left. While I was on my way to the Kremlin, Lenin found out about what I had done. When I arrived, Lenin's secretary told me, "Ilich is asking for you, go, he's going to give you a dressing down right now." ' "

So, the Sovnarkom and Central Executive Committee (that is, Lenin and Sverdlov) sent that telegram to Ekaterinburg "with confirmation of this decision" about the execution of the tsar's family.

In Ekaterinburg at that moment it was already getting on toward midnight. They were still waiting for a reply.

When he received the reply after midnight, Goloshchekin sent the truck. That was why the truck and Ermakov arrived only at 1:30 in the morning, two hours late. Yurovsky would write about this delay with annoyance in his Note.

While they were awaiting the telegram in Ekaterinburg, the family was getting ready for bed. That night Alexei slept in his parents' room. Before bed she wrote at length in her diary—the whole day— the last day (see Appendix).

"July 3 (16). Tuesday. . . . Grey morning, later lovely sunshine. Baby has a slight cold. All went out 1/2 hour in the morning, Olga & I arranged our medicines. T[atiana] read the spiritual reading. They went out, T. stayed with me & we read: the book of the prophet Obadiah and Amos."

From the book of the prophet Amos:

"And their king shall go into captivity, and he and his princes together, saith the Lord: (1:15).

"The Lord God hath sworn by his holiness, that, lo, the days shall come upon you, that he will take you away with hooks, and your posterity with fishhooks" (4:2).

"Therefore the prudent shall keep silence in that time; for it is an evil time" (5:13).

"Behold, the days come, saith the Lord God, that I will send a famine in the land; not a famine of bread, nor a thirst for water, but of hearing the words of the Lord:

"And they shall wander from sea to sea, and from the north even to the east; they shall run to and fro to see the word of the Lord, and shall not find it" (8:11–12).

From the prophet Obadiah:

"Though thou exalt thyself as the eagle, and though thou set thy next among the stars, thence will I bring thee down, saith the Lord" (1:4).

Hearing these ominous sacred words, Tatiana suddenly fell silent and got to thinking.

"Every morning the commissar comes to our rooms, at last after a week brought eggs again for Baby.

"8. Supper. Suddenly Leshka Sednev was fetched to go see his uncle & flew off—wonder whether it's true & we shall see the boy back again."

Alix still did not believe him: she remembered how everyone who had been taken away had vanished without a trace: Sednev, Nagorny. . . .

"Played bezique with N[icholas].

"10½. to bed."

At that moment two rather drunk guards, the sharpshooters Proskuryakov and Stolov, walked up to the Popov house across the way, where the guards lived.

The day before had been payday (we shall also remember this). They had been drinking at a policeman friend's house, and they reached the Popov house in a jolly mood. They were met by the head of the guard, Pavel Medvedev, who was for some reason very nasty. Cursing, he drove them both into the bathhouse in the Popov house yard. The night was warm. They lay down and fell asleep immediately.

Meanwhile the guard Yakimov was posting the watch.

Sharpshooter Deryabin to post 7.

Sharpshooter Kleshchev to post 8 in the garden by the window to the entry.

Yakimov posted the watch and went to bed.

Alix finished writing in her diary.

It was cool. She recorded the temperature in her diary. These became her last words: "15 degrees."

She said her prayers before going to bed. The girls were already asleep.

At eleven o'clock the light in their room went out.

Part III

THE SECRET
OF THE
IPATIEV
NIGHT

Chapter 15

THE INVESTIGATION BEGINS

$\mathscr{T}$HE DAYS FOLLOWING THE MURDER (A CHRONICLE) July 17, 1918: early morning. Opposite the Ipatiev house, in the Popov house, where the guard was quartered on the second floor, ordinary inhabitants of the town lived on the first. Late on the night of July 16–17, two of them woke up. Muffled shots . . . many shots—there, outside, from somewhere beyond the fence of that terrible house. The Ipatiev house.

They whispered quietly to each other.

"Hear?"

"Yes."

"Understand?"

"Yes."

Oh, life was dangerous in those years, and people were wary, they learned well: only the wary survived. So they said no more to each other and hid in their rooms until morning.

Later they told their White Guard investigator about this night-time conversation—on that warm, "garden fragrant" night of July 16 -17.

July 17: dawn.

From a letter of Peter Lyurtsov in Kuibyshev:

"In 1918 my grandfather Peter Nikolaevich Lyurtsov was working in a Soviet institution in Ekaterinburg. On July 15 they were paid, and he went out with his friends. Toward morning they decided to go home. It was a warm night. He was walking not far from the race-track. Dawn was already breaking. A truck was driving down the empty street, and in it were armed men. Calculating the look of the Red Guards in the cab, my grandfather decided to make himself scarce just in case. When the Whites came, everyone starting talking about the execution. My grandfather immediately realized what that truck had been. Later he told us, 'Well, what's so savage and horrible about that—a truck, but for some reason I can't forget it, and whenever I want to think about that terrible thing—I think about that dark truck in the dawn.'"

July 17: morning in the Ipatiev house. The morning was overcast. But again the gardens had blossomed—"the fragrance of the gardens," as he had written.

As always, sentries were posted around the Ipatiev house. A novice came from the monastery that morning again and, like the day before, brought eggs and cream. They did not let the novice into the house; she was met on the porch by the commandant's young assistant Nikulin. He did not take the food but said: "Go back and don't bring anything else."

The head of the guard, Yakimov, arrived at the Ipatiev house early in the morning. The Latvians were not inside the house anymore. The sentries were only outside. Yakimov was told the Latvians had gone back to the Cheka that morning and only two remained. But after what had happened last night they hadn't wanted to sleep downstairs, so they were sleeping in the commandant's room on the second floor. Yakimov walked to the commandant's room and saw the Latvians sitting on the grand duchesses' camp beds (which had been brought from their rooms). Yurovsky was not there, and Nikulin and Pavel Medvedev were sitting at the table, which was strewn with jewels, some of which were in open boxes and some simply dumped on the cloth. Medvedev and Nikulin seemed rather tired, depressed even. They were silently putting the jewels away in the boxes. The door to the family's room was closed.

The spaniel Joy stood quietly, poking its nose at the closed door. And waiting. Not a sound came from the family's room, although usually you could hear voices and steps.

That is what Guard Commander Yakimov later told the White Guard investigator.

On July 17, Beloborodov acted out his amusing play entitled "Informing Unsuspecting Moscow about the Execution" for the uninitiated members of the Ural Soviet Executive Committee.

One of those uninitiated—the editor of the *Ural Worker,* V. Vorobiev—conscientiously described this scene in his memoirs:

"In the morning I was given the text of the official announcement of the Romanovs' execution for the newspaper at the district soviet presidium. 'Don't show it to anyone yet,' they told me. 'The execution announcement text has to be coordinated with the center [Moscow].' I was discouraged, anyone who has ever been a newspaper worker will understand how much I wanted to scoop such unusual and sensational news in my newspaper: it's not every day we have events like the execution of a tsar!

". . . Every other minute I kept calling to find out whether they had gotten Moscow's consent to publish. My patience was seriously undermined by this ordeal. Only the next day, that is, on July 18, was I able to get a direct line through to Sverdlov. Beloborodov and some other member of the presidium went to the telegraph office to talk with him. I couldn't stand it and went too. The telegraph commissar himself sat down at the apparatus. Beloborodov started telling him what he was supposed to tell Moscow." [He was *supposed* to tell Moscow that as a result of the advance of the Whites and the monarchist plot, by decision of the Urals Nicholas Romanov had been shot and his family evacuated to a "safe place."]

He did.

"In view of the advance of the enemy on Ekaterinburg and the Cheka's discovery of a significant White Guard plot having as its purpose the abduction of the former tsar and his family stop the documents are in our hands, by resolution of the Reg[ional] Soviet Presidium Nicholas Romanov has been shot stop his family has been evacuated to a safe place. Because of this we have issued the following announcement: 'In view of the advance of counterrevolutionary bands on the Red capital of the Urals and the possibility of the crowned hangman eluding the people's justice (a plot has been uncovered involving White Guards attempting to abduct him and his family and compromising documents have been found) . . . the Regional Soviet Presidium, by the will of the revolution, has resolved to execute the former tsar Nicholas Romanov, guilty of innumerable bloody crimes.'

"After which we started to wait for an answer from Moscow. Steadying our breathing, we all leaned toward the emerging ribbon of Sverdlov's reply: 'Today I will report of your decision to the Presidium of the Central Executive Committee. There is no doubt that it will be approved. Notice about the execution must follow from the central authorities, refrain from publication until its receipt.'

"We breathed more freely, the issue of taking the law into our own hands could be considered exhausted."

The day before, on July 17, at nine o'clock at night, the initiated members of the Ural Regional Soviet had sent the initiated in Moscow the following encoded telegram:

"Moscow, Kremlin, to Sovnarkom Secretary Gorbunov with return confirmation. Tell Sverdlov that the same fate has befallen the entire family as has its head. Officially the family will perish in the evacuation."

This telegram was later seized by the White Guard at the Ekaterinburg telegraph office and decoded by the White Guard investigator, Sokolov.

July 18: Moscow, the Sovnarkom. In the evening Sverdlov appeared at a meeting of the Soviet of People's Commissars, the Sovnarkom, which was under the chairmanship of Lenin. They heard the report of the people's health commissar. Sverdlov sat down behind Lenin and whispered something in his ear. Lenin announced: "Comrade Sverdlov asks for the floor for an announcement out of turn."

Sverdlov informed the Sovnarkom of all that had been officially transmitted from Ekaterinburg and of the fact that the tsar had been preparing to escape, that Nicholas had been shot and the family evacuated to a safe place, and so on.

An excerpt from Proceedings No. 1 of the Central Executive Committee meeting:

"Heard: Announcement about the execution of Nicholas Romanov (telegram from Ekaterinburg).

"Resolved: Upon discussion the following resolution was passed: The Central Executive Committee in the person of its Presidium approves the decision of the Ural Regional Soviet. Instructs Comrades Sverdlov, Sosnovsky, and Avanesov to compose an appropriate announcement for the press. Instructs the documents in the possession of the Central Executive Committee (diary, letters) be published. Instructs Comrade Sverdlov to form a special commission of inquiry."

During the discussion Lenin was silent; then the meeting continued.

Attempts have been made to find in his silence Lenin's condemnation of what had happened. Lenin could be accused of many things, but not of being able to keep silent when he disagreed with something.

On July 18 the sentries were posted around the Ipatiev house as before, and on that day two men were seen in town who then mysteriously disappeared—Commandant Yurovsky and Commissar Goloshchekin.

July 19: Ekaterinburg. In the morning Yurovsky finally returned to town. The fall of Ekaterinburg was expected from hour to hour, and Yurovsky was in a hurry.

A coachman drove up to the Ipatiev house. Yurovsky came out and began loading his things. The coachman helped. In his statements to the White Guard investigator, the coachman noted that Yurovsky had seven pieces of luggage and one large dark suitcase sealed with wax. This was the Romanov archive.

Yurovsky was departing for Moscow. He was in such a hurry that he forgot his wallet with all his money on the table in the Ipatiev house. (En route he sent a telegram about it—the Whites would find the telegram at the telegraph office.)

But the money was nothing; he was also unable to get his own mother, Esther, out of the town. The Whites would arrest her, but fortunately they did not have sufficient class consciousness to shoot the unlucky old woman, and Esther Yurovskaya would live to see her son's triumphant return to Ekaterinburg.

On that day, July 19, Moscow officially announced the execution of Nicholas Romanov.

July 20: Ekaterinburg. The other chief participant in the events was also leaving town—the commandant's assistant Nikulin.

In the Museum of the Revolution I found a sinister certificate written on the letterhead of the Ural government and issued that day to Nikulin: ". . . issued to Comrade Nikulin, G. P., to the effect that he is under orders from the Ural Soviet to safeguard the specially designated cargo located in the two train cars proceeding to

Perm. All railway organizations and municipal and military authorities must render Comrade Nikulin the utmost assistance.

"The procedure and location of the unloading are known to Comrade Nikulin from the instructions in his possession. Ural Soviet Chairman A. Beloborodov."

Those cars were transporting the packed-up property from the Ipatiev house.

Separately, in a dirty sack, Nikulin was also carrying something else.

Travel was terrifying. Merry bands roamed the countryside, plundering trains and passengers mercilessly. That was why Nikulin was proceeding to Perm in the poor clothing of a clumsy peasant.

The contents of his dirty sack were dangerous. That sack could cost him a painful death.

In 1964, during that radio recording session, old Nikulin would tell how he carried the Romanov jewels out of Ekaterinburg in a dirty sack. The same jewels that had been kept in their cases in the Ipatiev house.

Engineer Ipatiev's house was empty. The sentries had been removed and the guard sent directly to the front. They would have to fight to their last drop of blood, for under no circumstances could they fall into White captivity. White captivity would be fatal for them after the Ipatiev house.

On July 20, at the last meeting in the municipal theater, Commissar Goloshchekin formally announced the execution of Nicholas Romanov. Official announcements of the execution of the tsar and the evacuation of the family to a safe place were pasted on poster columns all over town.

Only after this was Editor Vorobiev permitted to print his long-awaited report in the *Ural Worker* along with Safarov's article:

". . . Many formal aspects of bourgeois justice may have been violated in this process, nor was traditional-historical ceremony observed in the execution of the crowned persons. However, worker-peasant power was manifested in the process, making no exception for the All-Russian murderer, shooting as if he were an ordinary brigand. [Oh well, once the Savior hung on a cross "as if he were an ordinary brigand."]

". . . Nicholas the Bloody is no more. . . . And the workers and peasants have every right to tell their enemies: 'You placed your bet on the imperial crown? It's broken, take one empty crowned head in change!' " (Evidently this picturesque phrasing of Safarov's gave rise to the legend about Yurovsky taking the tsar's severed head with him to Moscow.)

July 21. The Soviet called in Ipatiev the engineer and gave him back the keys to his own house.

How did he feel walking into that trash-filled, terrible house of his, now stained with the incredible horror of the night of July 16–17?

*T*HAT ROOM

On July 25 the Bolsheviks surrendered Ekaterinburg to the Czech Legion and Siberian White Army units entering the town. White officers rushed to the Ipatiev house immediately.

The house was a spectacle of hasty departure. All the quarters were trashed. Pins, toothbrushes, combs, hairbrushes, empty vials, and broken photograph frames had been dropped on the floors. Empty hangers hung in the wardrobe, all the stoves in the rooms were stuffed with ashes from burned papers and possessions.

An empty wheelchair stood by the fireplace in the dining room. The old, worn-out wheelchair with three little wheels where she had spent almost all her days, her feet aching, incapacitated from constant headache. Empress Alexandra Feodorovna's last throne.

The girls' room was empty. A box with one fruit drop, the sick boy's bedpan—that was all. A woolen blanket hung across the window. The grand duchesses' camp beds were found downstairs in the guard's rooms. No jewelry and no clothing at all. Grigory Nikulin and his friends had done a good job.

Scattered throughout the rooms and the rubbish dump of the Popov house, where the guard had lived, they found what had been most precious to the family—the icons. There were books as well. Her brown Bible with its bookmarks, a prayer book, *On Suffering Grief*, and of course *The Life of Saint Serafim of Sarov*, Chekhov, Saltykov-Shchedrin, Averchenko, volumes of *War and Peace*—all this had been dropped in the rooms or dumped on the rubbish heap.

In the bedroom they found a well-planed board—this was the board on which the sick boy played and ate. There were also numerous vials of holy water and medicine. In the entry lay a box of the grand duchesses' hair, which had been cut off in February when they had had the measles.

In the corner of the dining room lay the slipcover of one of the daughters' headboards. The cover bore the bloody trace of wiped hands.

In the rubbish heap in the Popov house they found the St. George's ribbon that the tsar had worn on his greatcoat until the last days. By that time the house's former inhabitant, the servant Chemodurov, and the tutor Gilliard had already gone to the Ipatiev house.

Chemodurov was an old lackey, the archetype of the loyal Russian servant, a kind of devoted Chekhovian Firs who all his life walked behind his master like a child.

The tsar had brought Chemodurov to Tobolsk, but when another lackey came to the Ipatiev house with the children, young Trupp, the tsar decided to let the old man go get some rest and treatment. In those days, though, tsarist lackeys did not go for treatment—old Chemodurov was sent to prison. He grieved in prison and did not know that prison would save his life. He would wait it out there happily until the arrival of the Whites. Now he had been brought to the Ipatiev house. When Chemodurov saw the icon of the St. Feodor's Mother of God among the holy icons scattered about the house, the old servant paled. He knew his mistress would never part with that icon as long as she lived! They also found her other favorite image—of Saint Serafim of Sarov—in the rubbish. Looking at the terrible devastation, the loyal lackey kept trying to find "his master's personal belongings." How many times did he enumerate for the investigator everything he had brought from Tsarskoe Selo: "one coat of officer's cloth, another of plain soldier's. One short fur coat from Romanov sheep, four khaki shirts, three high-collared jackets, five pairs of wide trousers and seven box calf boots, and six service caps"—the old servant remembered everything. But there were no shirts, no jackets, and no coats. . . .

Books and icons amid "abomination and desolation"—this was the picture of what had happened.

Among the books they found one belonging to the Grand Duchess Olga—Rostand's *L'Aiglon* in French. She had taken with her this story of the son of the deposed emperor Napoleon. The eldest daughter of another deposed emperor was rereading the story of a boy who remained faithful to his deposed father to the very end.

Like that boy, she idolized her father. On her chest she wore an image of Saint Nicholas. A poem copied out in Olga's hand and inserted into her book reflected her father's thoughts in their long days together in Ekaterinburg. It remained there like a legacy, hers and his, to those who would come to the looted house:

PRAYER

Send us, Lord, the patience
In this year of stormy, gloom-filled days,
To suffer popular oppression
And the tortures of our hangmen.
Give us strength, oh Lord of Justice,
Our neighbor's evil to forgive
And the Cross so heavy and bloody
With Your humility to meet.
And in upheaval restless,
In days when enemies rob us,
To bear the shame and humiliation,
Christ our Savior, help us.
Ruler of the world, God of the universe,
Bless us with prayer
And give our humble soul rest
In this unbearable, dreadful hour.
At the threshold of the grave
Breathe into the lips of Your slaves
Inhuman strength—
To pray meekly for our enemies.

They descended from the second floor of the house to the first—the guard's rooms. Here the same garbage predominated.

But one room. . . . To get to that half-cellar room from the second floor where the family's rooms were, they first had to go downstairs, then outside, then through the garden, in by another door, and through the whole suite of first-floor rooms where the guard lived, to reach the small entry.

This entry had a window onto the garden. Out the window they saw trees and the joy of the July summer's day.

The door from the entry led to that room. It was a small room, 100–115 square feet, hung in checkered wallpaper. The room was dark, its window jutted out into the slope, and the shadow of the high fence lay on the floor. A heavy railing had been installed over its sole window.

This room was in perfect order: everything had been washed.

It adjoined the storeroom and was separated from it by a partition; the storeroom door was nailed shut. This entire partition and the nailed door were sown with bullet holes. It was obvious: this was where they had been shot.

Along the baseboards were traces of washed blood. Bullet holes fanned across the other two walls: evidently the people doing the shooting had rushed about the room.

The floor had dents from bayonet blows (where some of the family were stabbed), and two bullet holes gaped in the brown floor, where they had fired at someone lying down.

Most of the bullets in the room had been shot from a revolver, but there were also bullets from a Colt and a Mauser.

On one wall someone had scratched a line from Heine in German: "This night Belshazzar was murdered by his fellows."

By this time the Whites had dug up the garden near the house, searched the pond, and dug up the communal graves in the cemetery, where a special contractor had brought bodies from the Cheka, but no traces of the eleven people who had lived in the house could be found. They had vanished.

Mr. SOKOLOV

The investigation began.

The ideas of the February Revolution were strong in the Ural government. In instituting an investigation the government worried that it might be providing "the givens for reactionary principles . . . fuel for monarchist plots."

The first two investigators, Nametkin and Sergeyev, were quite cautious. But Kolchak, the supreme ruler of that part of Russia under White control, replaced the Ural government, and a third investigator was named—thirty-six-year-old Nikolai Sokolov.

Before the revolution he had been a special investigator. After the October Revolution he had attempted to dissolve into the peasantry and had left for the countryside. When Soviet power collapsed in Siberia, he made his way to the Urals in his peasant clothes. Appointed by Kolchak as the new investigator in the case of the tsar and his family, he brought to the investigation passion and fanaticism. After Kolchak was shot in 1920 and Soviet rule returned to the Urals and Siberia, he continued his work. In emigration in Paris he took down countless statements from surviving witnesses. He died from a heart attack, in France, while continuing his endless investigation.

From a letter of Peter Aminev in Kuibyshev:

"In 1918 I was living in Irbit. Irbit had been occupied by the Whites and life followed its prerevolutionary course. *The Irbit District News* came out with a report that upset our town. I am sending you a cutting from that newspaper (1918, no. 18):

" 'To the Fate of Nicholas II

" '*New York Times* correspondent Ackerman reported in his paper the following news, written by the abdicated tsar's personal servant.

" ' "Late on the night of July 16–17, the guard commissar walked into the tsar's room and announced: 'Citizen Nicholas Alexandrovich Romanov, you are to come with me to a meeting of the Ural Soviet.' . . . Nicholas Alexandrovich did not return for nearly two and a half hours. He was very pale and his chin was trembling.

" ' " 'Give me some water, old man.'

" ' "I did and he gulped down a large glass.

" ' " 'What happened?' I asked.

" ' " 'They informed me that in three hours they would come to shoot me,' the tsar told me.

" ' "After Nicholas' return from that meeting Alexandra Feodorovna and the tsarevich went in to him and both were crying. The tsaritsa fainted and the doctor was called in. When she came to, she fell on her knees before the soldiers and begged for mercy, but the soldiers responded that this was not in their power.

" ' " 'For the love of Christ, Alice, calm yourself,' said Nicholas several times in a quiet voice. He made the sign of the cross over his wife and son, called me over, and said, kissing me: 'Old man, do not abandon Alexandra Feodorovna and Alexei.'

" ' ". . . They took the tsar away, but no one knew where. That same night he was shot by twenty Red Guards." ' "

That was how people imagined what had happened when they still believed: "The family has been evacuated to a safe place."

*T*HE FIRST STATEMENTS

Soon after Ekaterinburg was liberated, Lieutenant Sheremetievsky appeared before the military commandant.

Before the Whites' arrival, the lieutenant had hidden in the village of Koptyaki—18 versts (12 miles) from Ekaterinburg on the shores of Lake Isetsk. Not far from this little village, surrounded by ancient forest, there were old abandoned mines. The lieutenant recounted:

"On July 17 a few peasants from this village were detained while walking through the forest by a picket of Red Guards. And were turned back. They had been detained near an obscure area of the forest known as the Four Brothers. They were told that the forest had been cordoned off and maneuvers were going on—there would be shooting. Indeed, as they were walking home, they heard muffled hand grenade explosions.

"After the fall of Ekaterinburg, when the Bolshevik detachments were retreating from the town toward Perm, the Koptyaki peasants immediately went to the Four Brothers to see what had happened there.

"Four Brothers"—the name had been given to the spot because of four tall pines that had once stood within the ancient woods. The pines had long since fallen down and died; only two half-ruined stumps remained. And the old name, Four Brothers. Not far from those pathetic stumps, 4 versts [2.5 miles] from the village itself, were some old mines concealed by trees. At one time prospectors had dug for gold here, but all the gold had been taken away long before, and the old mines had filled with rain. A small pond had formed in one of them, which had been given the name "Ganya's Pit." About 50 sazhens [350 feet] from Ganya's Pit there was another mine, but without a name. This nameless mine was filled with water also. This is where the peasants went, to the deep forest, to the abandoned mines.

Fresh branches and burned wood were floating on the surface of the nameless mine. The mine edge showed evidence of grenade explosions. The entire clearing by the mine had been trampled by horses' hooves—and carts had left deep ruts in the wet earth.

They found traces of two bonfires, one by the nameless mine and the other right on the forest road under a birch. These were strange fires. In one of them the Koptyaki peasants glimpsed charred human bones. When touched, the bones immediately disintegrated. Digging in the forest, the peasants found a charred emerald cross, topaz beads, a child's military buckle, an eyeglass lens, buttons, hooks, and so on. They also found a large diamond.

The investigation compared the items with those in the Ipatiev house—the same buttons, hooks, and shoe buckles. It was obvious that they had burned the clothes here. Did that mean the bodies had been thrown in the mine?

They decided to pump the water out of this nameless mine and the mine next to it, Ganya's Pit. They found nothing in Ganya's Pit, but in the nameless mine they reached bottom, panned, and found an amputated manicured finger with a long nail, false teeth that were soon recognized as belonging to Dr. Botkin, his tie clasp, and a pearl earring from a pair the empress wore. In the mine they found the body of a tiny dog and the frame of the photograph of Alix that Nicholas always carried and the dented icons his daughters wore for the journey—as well as Olga's icon of Nicholas the Miracleworker. The gilded silver military badge discovered in the silt—the insignia of the regiment of which the empress was colonel-in-chief—had been given to her by the regiment's commander, her mystical friend Adjutant General Orlov.

It was strange to say the words "Her Highness's Regiment" and "adjutant general" while standing on the edge of that dirty hole digging in the stinking silt. All that was left of her life was a large piece of a blood-spotted tarpaulin hauled up from the mine pit.

But they found no bodies.

Afterward they trampled over and dug up that entire remote area —but there were no bodies.

At that point a mining technician came forward and said that in mid-July he had come across the commandant of the Ipatiev house in this remote area. Yurovsky had asked him whether a very heavy truck could use the Koptyaki road.

Details about the truck became clear as well. On the evening of July 16, a truck was taken from the Soviet's garage on orders from the Cheka. The truck's driver was replaced, and the truck was driven out of the garage by a short, hook-nosed middle-aged man. One of the drivers in the garage recognized him as Sergei Lyukhanov, the driver for the Ipatiev house. The truck was not returned until the nineteenth, and it was utterly filthy. The back had been wiped but there were clearly visible traces of blood.

Now it was obvious to the investigation which truck this was and what it had taken to the mine.

The tracks of this truck were still evident on the storm-washed road to Koptyaki.

They also found witnesses to the truck's journey down the Koptyaki road.

The guard in railway booth number 184, where the road crossed the mining factory railway line, said that at dawn on July 17 she was wakened by the sound of an approaching truck. She heard the truck skid in the marshy place not far from her booth. Then there was a knock at the door, and she opened it and saw the driver and the truck's shadowy silhouette in the dawning sky.

The driver said that the motor had overheated and asked for some water. The guard started to grumble in her usual way when the driver suddenly turned nasty for some reason. "You here are sleeping like lords . . . and we've been breaking our backs all night long."

The watchwoman was going to say that she saw the figures of Red Guards around the truck—but instantly fell silent. "We'll forgive you the first time. But don't do it again," the driver threatened in parting. She saw them placing poles on the marshy ground—they had taken them from around her booth—and then the truck continued on.

Other statements were forthcoming. At dawn on July 17, men had set out for town from Koptyaki.

Coming out on the road, they had seen a strange procession. Someone by the name of Vaganov, dressed in a sailor's striped shirt, had been galloping in the lead. He was a Kronstadt sailor who worked for the Cheka. Some of the residents recognized him immediately. Behind the mounted Chekist came some carts covered with a tarpaulin. Seeing the peasants, the sailor shouted furiously, "Get back there! Turn around. And don't look back." He cursed and cursed at them and drove the shocked and terrified peasants back toward the village, chasing them for a third of a mile.

Searches and arrests were being made all over town.

Pavel Medvedev, who had commanded the entire guard at the Ipatiev house, had not been able to leave with the Reds. He had been ordered to blow up the bridge, but he did not blow up the bridge and he did not get out of town. Shortly afterward Medvedev was being questioned by the investigator. They also arrested the guard Proskuryakov. The head of the guard, Yakimov, who had posted the sentries on the night of July 16–17, was also arrested. As was the guard Letyomin. Alexei's dog, the rust-colored spaniel Joy, had given him away. He had taken the dog home—"So that he wouldn't die of hunger," as he later explained to the investigator. But the dog proved dangerous. Photographs of the heir with the spaniel were well known all over Russia. So they arrested Letyomin. Other things besides the dog were also uncovered at his house: Alexei's diary begun at Tsarskoe Selo in March 1917—immediately after their arrest—and completed in Tobolsk in November 1917.

Letyomin had also taken the holy relics from Alexei's bed and the icon he carried.

By that time many tsarist objects had been found in various Ekaterinburg quarters. The guards had given them to their wives and lovers. Goloshchekin and Beloborodov too had given some to their friends and retinue—savage souvenirs of the world they had so thoroughly eradicated. They found the empress's black silk parasol and a white linen one, her lilac dress, even the pencil with her initials that she always used to write in her diary, and the grand duchesses' little silver rings. The valet Chemodurov went from apartment to apartment like a bloodhound. Tsarist possessions became dangerous. Many people were packed off to the investigator.

𝒫RISONERS' STATEMENTS

Filipp Proskuryakov the guard. The same man who had come home drunk on the night of July 16–17 and fallen asleep in the bathhouse with his fellow guard Stolov. He and Stolov had been scheduled to go on duty at five in the morning.

At three in the morning Pavel Medvedev woke them.

He brought them into the half-cellar room. What greeted them there sobered them up immediately.

Smoke— gunsmoke—still filled the room. On the walls were distinct bullet holes. And blood. Everywhere. Spots and splashes on the walls and small puddles on the floor, as well as many traces of blood in the other rooms. It must have dripped as the slain were carried out. The people carrying them out tracked blood too from their boots.

Medvedev ordered the two guards to clean the room. They began by cleaning the floor with sawdust and water and then wiped it off with wet rags. With them worked two Latvians from the Cheka, three other guards, and Medvedev himself.

When they had cleaned up the room, Medvedev and the guard Strekotin told them everything that had happened. (Strekotin had been posted at the machine gun in the downstairs rooms and had seen everything.)

From Proskuryakov's testimony:

"Both of them [Medvedev and Strekotin] said the same thing:

"At twelve o'clock Yurovsky began waking the tsar's family. . . . According to Medvedev, Yurovsky gave them some kind of explanation about the night being dangerous . . . it would be dangerous to be upstairs if there were shooting on the streets so he demanded they all go downstairs. The family complied.

"Downstairs Yurovsky began reading a paper. The sovereign

didn't quite hear and asked, 'What?' Yurovsky, according to Medvedev, raised his hand and revolver and answered the sovereign, 'This is what!'

"Medvedev said he himself took two or three shots at the sovereign and the other people they were shooting at.

"When they had all been shot, Andrei Strekotin, as he himself told it, stripped off the jewels, which Yurovsky immediately took away, however, and brought upstairs. After that the slain were dumped onto a truck and taken away somewhere. Lyukhanov was the driver."

The guard Letyomin did not see the execution himself either, but he gave the investigator statements based on what Strekotin had told him:

"On July 17 he went on duty at eight in the morning. He stopped in at the barracks and saw a boy who was in the service of the tsar's family [the little cook Leonid Sednev]. And he asked him why he was there. Strekotin just waved his hand and, taking him to one side, told him that the night before the tsar and tsaritsa, their whole family, the doctor, the cook, and lackey, and the woman in attendance with them had been killed. According to Strekotin, that night he had stood by the machine gun post downstairs.

"During his shift [from twelve midnight to four in the morning] the tsar and tsaritsa, all the tsar's children, and the servant were brought downstairs . . . and taken to that room next to the storeroom. Strekotin explained that he saw Commandant Yurovsky read a piece of paper and say, 'Your life is over.'

"The tsar didn't quite hear and asked him to repeat it, and the tsaritsa and one of their daughters crossed themselves. At that moment Yurovsky shot the tsar, killing him on the spot, then the Latvians and the guard commander began firing."

In the barracks on July 18, Letyomin saw the driver Lyukhanov, who told him that he had taken the slain away in the truck and added that they had almost not made it: "It was dark and there were lots of little stumps." But where he took the corpses, Lyukhanov did not say.

The investigator interviewed Yakimov, the head of the guard:

"At dawn, at four o'clock, Yakimov was awakened by the guards Kleshchev and Deryabin and told the following:

"Medvedev and Dobrynin had come to them at their posts and warned them the tsar would be shot that night. At this news, they both went over to the windows.

"Kleshchev went to the window of the downstairs entry, next to his post. Through that window, looking toward the garden, he could see the door to the room where they were going to be shooting. The door was open, and Kleshchev could see everything going on in the room.

"Deryabin's post was next to the other window, the only barred window of the execution room. He saw what happened, too.

"Through their windows they saw men going into the room from the courtyard. In front were Yurovsky and Nikulin, behind them the sovereign, his wife and daughters, as well as Botkin, Demidova, the lackey Trupp, and the cook Kharitonov. Nicholas was carrying the heir. In the rear walked Medvedev and the Latvians, whom Yurovsky had signed out from the Cheka. They arranged themselves like this: to the right of the entrance was Yurovsky, to the left of him stood Nikulin, the Latvians stood right in the doorway, and behind them was Medvedev [Pavel]. Through the window Deryabin could see part of Yurovsky's body but primarily his arm. He saw Yurovsky saying something and waving his arm. What exactly he said Deryabin could not tell. He said he could not hear the words. Kleshchev, though, stated positively that he did hear Yurovsky's words: 'Nicholas Alexandrovich, your relatives have tried to save you, but they have not succeeded, and we are forced to shoot you ourselves.' Immediately after Yurovsky spoke several shots rang out, followed by a woman's wail, shouts, and several female voices. Those being shot began to fall one after the other: first the tsar, after him the heir. Demidova was rushing about. Both of them told Yakimov that she shielded herself with a pillow. According to them she was stabbed with bayonets.

"When all had fallen, they began to examine them and finish off a few of them with a shot or a stab. But of those with the name Romanov, they cited only Anastasia as being stabbed with bayonets. When they all had fallen, someone brought a few sheets from the family's rooms. They began winding the slain in the sheets and carrying them out to the truck, where they put the corpses on a cloth from the storeroom and covered them all with that same cloth."

But again, these are not eyewitness statements. This is still a story at second hand.

At long last, though, the investigation took the first and only statement from someone who himself had been in that half-cellar room.

From the investigator's interview with Pavel Medvedev, guard commander:

"He went on duty on the evening of July 16, and at eight o'clock Commandant Yurovsky ordered him to take away all the detachment's revolvers and bring them to him. . . . Yurovsky said, 'Today we are going to shoot the entire family and the doctor and servant, too—warn the detachment not to worry if they hear shots.'

"The little boy cook was moved to the Popov house—to the sentry detachment's quarters—at six in the morning, on Yurovsky's instruction. At about ten I warned the detachment not to be alarmed if they heard shots. At about twelve at night (old style)—two o'clock new [daylight saving time]—Yurovsky woke the tsar's family. He told them why he was disturbing them and where they must go. Medvedev did not know. . . .

"About an hour later the tsar's entire family, the doctor, the maid, and two servants got up, washed, and dressed. Even before Yurovsky went to wake the family, two members of the Cheka had arrived at the Ipatiev house: Peter Ermakov [from the Upper Isetsk factory] and someone else he did not know. . . . The tsar, the tsaritsa, the tsar's four daughters, the doctor, the cook, and the lackey came out of their rooms. The tsar was carrying the heir in his arms. The sovereign and the heir were wearing field shirts and forage caps. The empress and her daughters wore dresses but not wraps. The sovereign walked ahead with the heir. In my presence there were no tears, no sobs, and no questions. They went downstairs, out into the courtyard, and from there through the second door into the downstairs quarters. They were led into the corner room adjacent to the sealed storeroom. Yurovsky ordered chairs brought in.

"The empress sat down by the wall where the window was, closer to the rear column of the arch. Behind her stood three of her daughters. The emperor was in the middle, next to the heir, and behind him stood Dr. Botkin. The maid, a tall woman, stood by the left jamb of the storeroom door. With her stood one of the daughters. The maid had a pillow in her arms. The tsar's daughters had brought small pillows; they put one on the seat of the heir's chair, the other on their mother's. Simultaneously, eleven men walked into the room: Yurovsky, his assistant, the two from the Cheka, and seven Latvians. According to Medvedev, Yurovsky told him: 'Go out to the street and see whether anyone's there and the shots will be heard.'

"He walked out and heard the shots. By the time he returned to the house, two or three minutes had passed. Walking into the room he saw all the members of the tsar's family lying on the floor with numerous wounds to their bodies.

"The blood was gushing . . . the heir was still alive—and moaning. Yurovsky walked over to him and shot him two or three times at point blank range. The heir fell still. The scene made me want to vomit.

". . . The corpses were brought out to the truck on stretchers made of a sheet stretched on shafts taken from the sleigh standing in the yard. The driver was Sergei Lyukhanov. The blood in the room and yard was washed off. By three o'clock it was all over."

The investigator asked him about Strekotin.

"I do remember—he really was at the machine gun. The door from the room where the machine gun was into the entry was open, and so was the door from the entry into the room where the execution was carried out," stated Medvedev.

From this the investigation concluded that Strekotin and Kleshchev really could have seen what happened—witnesses of the Apocalypse.

Medvedev denied that he himself had done any shooting, but his wife established his guilt:

"According to Pavel, all those awakened got up, washed, dressed, and were led downstairs, where they were put into a room where a paper was read to them that said: 'The revolution is dying, and so shall you.' After that they started firing, and they killed them, one and all. My husband fired, too."

Proskuryakov, to whom he had also recklessly recounted how he fired at the tsar and "emptied two or three bullets into him," also established Medvedev's guilt. He must have told his wife as well that he had fired *at the tsar*. But she did not want to establish her husband's guilt in such a heinous crime.

Actually, for her that crime was a matter of pride, of course, as it was for Pavel Medvedev. The Ipatiev house guard commander must have been a reliable man, that is, fanatical, otherwise Yurovsky and Goloshchekin would not have taken him for such a post. He was making statements about the execution because he knew that others would tell the story anyway. It made no sense to refuse to talk.

The investigation continued. It was established that two more trucks went to the Koptyaki forest on July 18, bringing three barrels, which they moved onto carts and took into the forest. One of those barrels was filled with gasoline.

The investigators learned that there had been other barrels as well. They found a note from the supply commissar, "Intellectual,"

P. Voikov, in the Ekaterinburg pharmacy about supplying a large quantity of sulfuric acid.

After the witnesses' corroborating statements, the investigation came to its conclusion: on the night of July 16–17, the tsar, his family, retainers, and servants—eleven people—were shot in the half-cellar of the Ipatiev house.

Then, according to the investigation's hypothesis, the corpses were stowed in a truck and taken to an unnamed mine near the village of Koptyaki. On July 18, a large quantity of gasoline and sulfuric acid was brought to the site. The bodies of the slain were chopped up with axes (the investigation found one of the axes), doused with gasoline and sulfuric acid, and burned in bonfires whose remnants were discovered not far from the mines.

*T*HE RESURRECTION OF THE SLAIN

But . . . But Sokolov never did find the bodies of the tsar's family. There was someone's separated finger, someone's false teeth . . . and a bonfire next to an unnamed mine that he declared to be the grave and ashes of the tsar and his family.

Yes, the statements of witnesses to the execution coincided, but. . . .

But Sokolov was a monarchist. He brought a political obsession to his work, and that made the statements he obtained highly suspect. Both sides in the Civil War learned cruelty from each other, and the cellars of White counterintelligence rivaled those of the Cheka. The interrogations may not have been altogether idyllic. May that have been why the statements coincided? Skeptics have argued that it was a biased investigation and that the conclusion—that it is indeed possible to burn eleven bodies without a trace—was debatable. For the fact was indisputable—there were no bodies.

A year and a half after the "family was executed in the Ipatiev house" (as Sokolov asserted) or "the Romanov family disappeared from the Ipatiev house" (as his opponents formulated it), "Anastasia" would appear, a mysterious woman whose fate has continued to disturb the world for seventy years.

A brief account of the well-known story:

In Berlin an unknown young woman decided to commit suicide by jumping into a canal one night in 1920, but she was saved and placed in a clinic, depressed and almost mute. In the clinic she came across a photograph of the tsar's family, which produced a remarkable agitation in her and from which she could not be parted. Soon a rumor arose: the miraculously saved daughter of the Russian tsar, Tatiana, was there, in a Berlin hospital.

Tatiana—that was what she called herself at first. But soon after she changed her name to Anastasia.

No, there was nothing conclusive in this fact. A powerful shock may simply have burned out her memory. She did not remember who she was. She dug deep in her memory—and found herself: she was Anastasia.

She told a fantastic story about her rescue: a shot, she fell, her sister behind her, shielding her from the bullets with her body. Then, senselessness, a gap in her memory . . . then stars . . . she was being taken away on a wagon of some kind. Then the journey to Romania with the soldier who, it turned out, had saved her. The birth of a child fathered by the soldier. Her escape. And all this in incoherent waves.

Moreover, she did not speak Russian. There could be an explanation for this: the Russian spoken during the monstrous murder, as she lay there heaped with the bodies of her family, may have created a kind of permanent taboo in her consciousness. She could not pronounce her native sounds; they brought the horror back to her consciousness. But this circumstance was very heartening to her opponents. (In our opinion, a woman who does not speak Russian and has decided to declare herself a Russian grand duchess either has to be crazy or must truly believe herself to be Anastasia.)

There was also, however, her amazing likeness to the photograph of the Russian tsar's daughter. She even had the trace of a birthmark right where a birthmark had been removed from the young Anastasia, and the shape of her ears, and a similar handwriting. And, finally, the mysterious woman spoke freely about the details of the family's life.

She attempted to defend her right to the name of the tsar's daughter in court and suffered defeat.

But when the mysterious "Anastasia" died, she was buried in a crypt with her Romanov relatives the princes of Leuchtenberg.

Who was she?

To me she was a woman who for terrible reasons had suffered a shock and forgotten who she was and then spent her whole life trying to remember it. She truly believed she was the tsar's daughter, but evidently she did not know precisely which one of the four. She declared herself to be Anastasia because, of the four sisters, she looked most like her, but to the end of her life she continued to dig painfully in her memory. So that for all her certainty, she was to some extent uncertain. That burning torment: trying to remember, going back and forth, into the monstrous past—in an attempt to meet up there, in that horror, with herself . . . and never to do so.

"Anastasia" declared she had been "rescued after the execution." Subsequently books would begin appearing proving that the tsar's daughters had not been shot at all. Only the tsar and the heir had been executed, these books asserted. The retainers and the unlucky Botkin had perished to create the appearance of the entire family's destruction. In fact, at the demand of the Germans, on the basis of secret articles of the Treaty of Brest, the daughters and the tsaritsa were taken out of Russia. True, it is hard to believe that the second most important man in the government, Trotsky, who participated in the conclusion of the Treaty of Brest and in exile asserted that the tsar's entire family had been shot, did not know about that. (What he would have given for it not to have been so!)

That these fantastic versions popped up was inevitable. After all, in the seventy years since the execution *not one voluntary* statement by participants in the execution in the Ipatiev house was published. The terrible night of July 16–17, 1918, remained the object of mysterious rumors and legends.

In the 1970s, at the start of my investigations, I did not believe anyone—not Sokolov and not his opponents. I set myself one goal—to find *voluntary* statements of witnesses to that terrible night. I was sure that they existed in the bowels of the Soviet secret storehouses. Only they could give the answer as to what did happen in the Ipatiev house. About one such document, the legendary "Yurovsky Note," rumors abounded.

I began questioning my former classmates at the Historical Archival Institute, who worked in various archives. Everyone I talked to had heard of it, but no one had read it.

"SUBSTANTIVE EVIDENCE: THE EXECUTION WEAPONS"
In the late 1970s, an old and once close friend called me. We had studied together at the Historical Archival Institute and now, after many years, we met, frightening each other with our changed faces. She got into my car and without saying a word placed a paper on my knees.

I began to read:

"To the Museum of the Revolution, Museum Director Comrade Mitskevich.

"Bearing in mind the upcoming tenth anniversary of the October Revolution and the younger generation's likely interest in seeing substantive evidence (the weapon that executed the former tsar Nicholas II, his family, and those retainers who remained loyal to him to the grave), I feel I must transfer to the museum for safekeeping two revolvers that have been in my possession: Colt no. 71905 with a cartridge clip and seven bullets, and Mauser no. 167177 with a wooden gunstock and a cartridge clip with ten bullets. The reasons for the two revolvers are as follows: I killed Nicholas on the spot with my Colt; the remaining bullets in the one loaded clip for the Colt, as well as the loaded Mauser, went to finish off Nicholas's daughters, who were armored with corsets made of a solid mass of large diamonds, and the strange vitality of the heir, on which my assistant also spent an entire clip of bullets (the strange vitality of the heir must probably be put down to my assistant's poor mastery of his weapon and his inevitable nerves, evoked by his long ordeal with the armored daughters).

"The former commandant of the special house in Ekaterinburg, where the former tsar Nicholas II and his family were held in 1918 (up until his execution in the same year on July 16), Yakov Mikhailovich Yurovsky, and the commandant's assistant Grigory Petrovich Nikulin attest to the above.

"Ya. M. Yurovsky has been a member of the party since 1905, Party ticket no. 1500, Krasnopresnenskaya Organization.

"G. P. Nikulin has been a member of the Bolshevik Party since 1917, no. 128185, Krasnopresnenskaya Organization."

So it did all happen!

She said, "This is a copy of a restricted document held by the Museum of the Revolution. I was told you want to find out how *it* happened? I'm glad I can give you the chance. But this document was copied out at my request, and I don't want to put anyone on the spot. So you have to keep mum about it. Not that you're very likely to be able to talk about all this any time in the next hundred years. So enjoy the abstract knowledge, that's enough."

"This is the Yurovsky Note?"

"What do you mean! This is just an ordinary notice Yurovsky wrote."

(In 1989 I was finally able to look at this "ordinary notice" with my own two eyes. It was indeed written in the commandant-assassin's characteristic hand.)

"No, no." She chuckled. "The Yurovsky Note is something completely different. It's a long document. By the way, in the 1920s he gave it to Pokrovsky."

(Mikhail Pokrovsky was the director of the Communist Academy in the 1920s, the leader of Soviet historical science.)

"You saw it? It's in the Museum of the Revolution?"

"I don't know," she said dryly. "I only know that the NKVD [as the Cheka's successor was called in the 1940s] removed those revolvers of Yurovsky's from the museum before the war, along with all his papers. There's a record of that there. What else could they have done? After all, his daughter was arrested."

"Yurovsky's daughter? Arrested?"

"Her name was Rimma. She was a Komsomol [Young Communist League] leader, apparently a secretary on the Komsomol Central Committee. She spent more than a quarter of a century in the camps. Even if the Yurovsky Note were in the museum, though, you would never get your hands on it, as you must understand. Documents about the execution of the tsar's family are especially secret."

She went, and I was left with his notice. The first voluntary participant statement I had obtained!

So it was all true. There was an execution. And ten years later, Yurovsky was still living that execution. He was incapable of writing an "ordinary notice." The Ipatiev house pursued him—the armored girls, the boy they finished off. If this was an "ordinary notice," imagine his note! I realized she was right—I would get nowhere at the museum.

Yurovsky's biography, in the style of Soviet hagiography, published in a limited edition in Sverdlovsk as *I Am the Chekist*, by Yakov Reznik, contains the commandant's last will and testament, in which he again turned to his loyal "son"—his assistant in the execution, G. Nikulin. As he lay dying from an excruciatingly painful ulcer, he again evoked the specter of the terrible Ipatiev house:

"To G. P. Nikulin.

"My friend, my life is at an ebb. I must dispose of what remains. You will be given a list of the basic documents and a list of my property. The documents give to the Museum of the Revolution. . . .

". . . You have been like a son to me, and I embrace you, as my son. Yours, Yakov Yurovsky."

So, "The documents give to the Museum of the Revolution." The circle was closed. Realizing the futility of it all, I still made a trip to the Museum of the Revolution archives. To my question there was a clear reply: We have no Yurovsky papers! We've never even heard of any "note."

So I decided to compile a list of the institutions where he had worked. I began to run down the events of his life.

After the execution and his departure for Moscow, the commandant went back to the Urals. First he was instructed to take the "gold train"—the treasures of the Ural banks—from Perm to the capital.

In the nights of August 1918, his wife, his daughter the Ekaterinburg Komsomol leader Rimma, his thirteen-year-old son, Alexander, and one more "son" who had returned with him from Moscow, Nikulin, loaded endless canvas sacks of gold, silver, and platinum onto the train. Once again Yurovsky, the commandant, was commandant of the train, and once again his assistant was Nikulin.

Upon his arrival in Moscow, Yurovsky was given familiar work—in the Cheka. After the attempt on Lenin's life by Fanya Kaplan, Yurovsky was assigned to a group ordered to ferret out Socialist Revolutionaries suspected of ties to Kaplan. He was one of the most meticulous of the investigators. To the end, though, Kaplan declared she was acting alone. Kaplan was shot.

After the Whites surrendered, Yurovsky went back to Ekaterinburg, where he was chairman of the Social Security Department and simultaneously one of the leaders of the Cheka. He was involved with all aspects of citizens' social security. The *Ural Worker* regularly published articles under the heading "The Punishing Activity of the Provincial Cheka."

In May 1921 he was transferred to Moscow to work in the Russian Republic's State Depository of Valuables, where the treasures "confiscated from the enslavers" were also kept. He guarded them loyally. "A reliable Communist"—that was how Lenin referred to him in a letter to the people's commissar of finance. At the end of his life our hero was already employed in prosaic jobs, directing the Red Warrior factory and the Polytechnic Museum.

I conscientiously inquired about his documents at every institution where the "reliable Communist" had worked. Either there was no answer or there were "no documents listed."

*T*HE YUROVSKY NOTE

This happened when the archives were only just starting to be declassified.

In a small room in the Central Archive of the October Revolution, I sorted through the formerly secret files of the All-Russian Executive Committee, once the highest organ of power in revolutionary Russia, headed by Sverdlov. One file immediately caught my attention: "File on the Family of Former Tsar Nicholas the Second, 1918–1919."

1919? *File on the Family?* But the family had already been shot by 1919!

This meant that this file contained some document concerning the family but created in 1919—after their execution!

I leafed through the file impatiently.

It began with the telegram about the former tsar removing his shoulder straps. Then came the Ural Soviet's famous telegram to the Central Executive Committee regarding the tsar's execution . . . and the documents of the "monarchist plot"—all those letters signed "Officer."

And at the very end of the file there were two poorly typed copies of a document that had no title or signature.

I began reading. It was a shock: the whole horrible night of July 16–17—the execution, the two days dealing with the corpses—it was all laid out thoroughly and dispassionately. The Apocalypse as recorded by a *witness!* The document was not signed, but one of its typed copies was corrected in the author's hand. At the end of the document, also in the author's handwriting, the terrible address had been added—the location of the grave where the corpses of the tsar and his family had been secretly buried.

By that time I had already seen several samples of Yurovsky's handwriting. Yes, he was the author! Before me lay the legendary "Note of Yakov Yurovsky."

That which had been hidden all these seventy years, that which I had sought all these years.

The Note's style of exposition was surprising. The new ruling power offered yesterday's semiliterate workers, soldiers, and sailors a tempting position as makers of history. In describing the execution, Yurovsky proudly referred to himself in the third person as "commandant" (abbreviated "com." in the Note). For on that night there was no Yakov Yurovsky, there was a terrible commandant—the weapon of proletarian vengeance. The weapon of history.

I decided to publish this document. It was already 1989, the triumph of glasnost. However, the issue of *Ogonyok* in which the statement of the "reliable Communist" which had been held secret for seventy years was to appear was detained by the censor. Times had changed, though, and the magazine eventually did come out. Thanks to the censor's delay, the issue appeared on May 19 (May 6, old style). On the emperor's birthday, this terrible account of his death and his family's saw the light of day for the first time.

"*THE* BIRNAM WOOD"

Letters started coming in, thousands of readers' letters. Millions of my fellow citizens had learned for the first time of the bloodshed in which the dynasty that had ruled the country for three hundred years had come to its end.

The invaluable mails were very busy: I began receiving both letters and telephone calls with more new information and documents. Once lost or concealed forever, they rose up out of nonbeing, and, as in *Macbeth*, the Birnam Wood set out after the murderers.

What I had hoped for had come to pass: at the Museum of the Revolution one more copy of the Note I had already published suddenly was *found*. But it had a title and even a signature:

"Copy of a document given by my father Yakov Mikhailovich Yurovsky to the historian M. N. Pokrovsky in 1920."

Yurovsky's son, Alexander, had sent this copy and certified it with his own hand in 1964, when he himself, Alexander Yakovlevich Yurovsky, was already turning gray.

This document, however, did not include the location of the grave.

So in 1920 Yurovsky had given his Note to a historian! But it had been written earlier, as a report for the authorities. That was why I had found this document in the Central Executive Committee archives.

The historian Pokrovsky was a member of the Central Executive Committee presidium. The leader of official historical science was addressing the "initiated." In giving Pokrovsky his Note, Yurovsky never dreamed it would be published. He had written it for posterity, for history. His contemporaries still lacked the consciousness to know the whole truth about the execution.

"What I will recount here shall see the light only after many years," wrote Yakov Yurovsky subsequently.

WITNESSES AND PARTICIPANTS IN THE APOCALYPSE The letters kept coming; this popular inquiry continued. I was told that in a small district archive, in a little Ural town, in a secret depository, there were the statements of Alexander Strekotin. Yes, the machine gunner Alexander Strekotin on whose account the guards Letyomin and Proskuryakov had based the story they told Investigator Sokolov about the execution.

It turned out that Strekotin himself wrote his memoirs (sent to me by two readers). I now had in my hands the *most important voluntary* statements—most important because Yurovsky was the chief actor and Strekotin's oral tale lay at the base of Sokolov's entire investigation.

Strekotin served in the Ipatiev house guard along with his brother. The guard frequently included relatives: Lyukhanov father and son, the Strekotin brothers, and so on.

"The personal reminiscences of Alexander Andreyevich Strekotin, former Red Guard in the sentry detachment guarding the tsarist Romanov family, and witness to their execution." The guileless title immediately sets the tone and hints at how his story came to be written down: the poorly educated Strekotin reminisced, and someone (evidently a worker in the local museum) wrote. The memoirs were compiled for the anniversary of the execution in 1928. Not until sixty-two years later did I publish in *Ogonyok* an excerpt from them for the first time.

Strekotin begins with some history:

"Volunteers were being signed up in Sysert for the detachment to guard the former tsar Nicholas II and his wife, who had arrived by then in Ekaterinburg. Mostly they recruited workers. A great number were interested, and those joining the detachment included me and my older brother Andrei. Our detachment was quartered in the house opposite, the Popov house.

". . . Appointed head of our detachment was our Sysert comrade Pavel Spiridonovich Medvedev—a worker and a noncommissioned officer in the tsarist army."

He begins by describing Nicholas:

"The tsar—in my opinion he wasn't much like a tsar. The ex-emperor was always dressed in the same outfit, his khaki uniform. He was a little above average height. A solidly built blond with gray eyes. Agile and impetuous. He liked to twirl his reddish mustache."

Finally, Strekotin describes that night.

Another witness was found through whose eyes we will also look on that night: Alexei Kabanov, whom I learned about from the son of the Chekist Medvedev-Kudrin, at whose request, in 1964, Kabanov described that night in detail in a letter.

Finally, there was Upper Isetsk Commissar Peter Ermakov, one of the cruelest participants in the Ipatiev night. His memoirs were kept in a secret file at the Sverdlovsk Party Archives. Thanks to a reader, they found their way into my hands, given to me by a strange assistant (about whose surprising visit I will speak later in detail).

And one more witness: Chekist Mikhail Medvedev-Kudrin.

I chatted at length with his son, the historian M. M. Medvedev, who had grown up around the Ekaterinburg regicides. He had detailed memories of his father, and in his house he kept the black leather Chekist jacket his father had worn that night.

From readers I received excerpts from the "Stenogram of Reminiscences of Participants in the Execution," compiled in Sverdlovsk in 1924, as well as an excerpt from an amazing lecture given to the town's party activists, who had gathered in the Ipatiev house, by the assassin Yurovsky.

In this way I collected the voluntary statements of five men who had been in the room and put them together with the statements of a sixth witness, Pavel Medvedev, the guard commander, whose statements were included in Sokolov's investigation.

Six men who had been in the room described that night.

And something incredible happened. What was supposed to have remained a secret forever was laid out in all its details. That entire impossible, inhuman night.

Now we shall let them speak.

CHRONICLE OF THE IPATIEV NIGHT IN THE STATEMENTS OF WITNESSES

Yurovsky: "In about the middle of July, Filipp [Goloshchekin] told me we had to make preparations for the liquidation in case the front got any closer.

"On the evening of the fifteenth, I think, or the morning of the fifteenth, he came and said that we had to get going on liquidating them that day.

"On July 16 a telegram was received from Perm in code containing the order to exterminate the Romanovs.

"On the sixteenth, at six o'clock in the evening, Filipp G. ordered the decree carried out. At twelve o'clock a truck was supposed to come to take away the corpses."

, Thus, on July 15, having received a signal from Berzin—it's time! —Goloshchekin set the execution mechanism in motion. On July 16 he telegraphed Moscow regarding the impending execution—and waited for a reply from Moscow through Zinoviev. In the meantime, at the Ipatiev house, preparations were in full swing.

Pavel Medvedev: "At eight in the evening, Yurovsky ordered all revolvers taken away from the detachment and brought to him. I took the revolvers away and brought them to the commandant's office. Then Yurovsky said, 'Today we are going to be killing the entire family and the doctor and servants living with them. Warn the detachment not to be alarmed if they hear shots.' I didn't ask who had decided this or how."

Yurovsky: "The boy [Sednev] was taken away . . . which upset the Romanovs and their people badly."

From the tsaritsa's diary:

"8. Supper. Suddenly Leshka Sednev was fetched to go see his uncle & flew off—wonder whether it's true & we shall see the boy back again."

Yes, Yurovsky was right, she did not trust him, and of course it was she who sent the doctor to see the commandant.

Yurovsky: "Dr. Botkin came and asked the reason for this. It was stated that the boy's uncle, who had been arrested and fled, had now come back and wanted to see his nephew. The next day the boy was sent home (apparently to Tula Province)."

Pavel Medvedev: "The little boy cook . . . at Yurovsky's instruction was transferred to the Popov house—to the quarters of the sentry detachment. At about ten I warned the detachment not to be alarmed if they heard shots."

For that night shift Alexander Strekotin was assigned to be machine gunner downstairs. The machine gun stood on the window, and Strekotin took his place by its side. This post was right next to the entry and the half-cellar room.

Strekotin was standing by his machine gun in the darkness when suddenly he heard footsteps on the stairs.

Strekotin: "Someone [Medvedev] came downstairs quickly, walked up to me silently, and also silently handed me a revolver. 'Why do I need this?' I asked Medvedev.

" 'There's going to be shooting soon,' he told me, and he quickly moved away."

Medvedev disappeared in the darkness, and Strekotin remained standing by his machine gun.

From the tsaritsa's diary:

"Played bezique with N[icholas]. 10½ to bed."

At that moment in the courtyard the guard Deryabin was taking up post 7 (across from the railed window of the execution room). Post 8—in the garden near the window to the entry—was taken by the sharpshooter Kleshchev. From the entry the door led right to the room. The door was open to the illuminated room so he could see it clearly.

As soon as Kleshchev and Deryabin found out from Pavel Medvedev what was going to happen, they contrived to stand where they could see everything.

Two tipsy guards walked up to the Popov house—Proskuryakov and Stolov. The guard commander, Medvedev, drove both into the bathhouse in the Popov yard, where they fell asleep.

Midnight was approaching. In the commandant's room Yurovsky was nervously waiting for Ermakov and the truck. But the truck had been detained. "Uninitiated," Yurovsky did not know that Goloshchekin was waiting for an answer from Moscow.

Strekotin: "Soon Medvedev and Akulov or someone else, I don't remember, went downstairs."

(Akulov was one of Grigory Nikulin's Cheka pseudonyms.)

"At that moment a group of six or seven men I didn't know appeared, and 'Akulov' brought them into the room. . . . Now it was absolutely clear to me that this was the execution."

So the detachment of Latvian sharpshooters, all six or seven of them, was already waiting in the room. Next to the other room, *that* room. But that room stood ready and empty, everything cleared out of it.

What were they waiting for? The same thing as Yurovsky. For the truck to come. The last participants had joined them. But Goloshchekin and Beloborodov were also waiting—for an answer from Moscow—so the truck and Ermakov were still being detained. At 21:22, the Ekaterinburg telegram, which Zinoviev sent on to Lenin, was in Moscow.

In Ekaterinburg it was 11:22. But by that time Moscow had already decided.

Akimov: "The Sovnarkom and Central Executive Committee wrote a telegram *confirming* the decision. Sverdlov had me take the telegram to the telegraph office, which was located then on Myasnitskaya Street."

In Ekaterinburg, on the second floor of the Ipatiev house, the family was sleeping. Or rather, he was . . . but what about her? She was probably listening to the sounds outside the window, as she had every night of late . . . to the distant cannonade promising their speedy liberation. And waiting for sleep. Naturally, she must have heard the noise of the truck as it drove into the courtyard.

Yurovsky: "At twelve o'clock the truck had not come; it did not come until one-thirty."

(The answer from Moscow was received in the night, and only at one-thirty did the truck drive up to the Ipatiev house for the bodies.)

At the password "chimney sweep" the gates opened and the truck was let into the courtyard.

Yurovsky: "This delayed the decree's implementation. Meanwhile, all the preparations had been made, twelve men (including six Latvians) with revolvers had been selected to carry out the sentence. Two of the Latvians refused to shoot the girls. . . .

"At the last moment they refused to fire. I had to take them out and replace them with others. . . .

". . . When the automobile arrived everyone was sleeping."

Pavel Medvedev: "Even before Yurovsky went to wake the tsar's family, two members arrived from the Cheka. One was Peter

*N*icholas and Pierre Gilliard, Swiss tutor of Alexei, sawing firewood in Tobolsk, Siberia, 1917.

*R*evolutionary procession passing the Governor's House, where the imperial family was being held in Tobolsk. The largest of the banners states in part, "The Tobolsk Council of Workers', Soldiers', and People's Deputies," 1917.

*M*embers of the Ural Soviet who issued the order to the execution squad: Nikolai Tolmachev, Alexander Beloborodov, Georgy Safarov, and Filipp Goloshchekin, 1918.

Члены Президиума Уралсовета: Толмачев, Белобородов, Сафаров, Голощекин.

Дом Ипатьевых в Екатеринбурге, в котором
помещено было семейство Романовых.

*T*he Ipatiev house, Ekaterinburg, the last residence of the
imperial family, 1918.

*A*lexei in bed in the Ipatiev house during his last illness
before his execution.

The last letter written by Alexei before his death.

Joy, Alexei's spaniel, Ekaterinburg.

The dining room of the Ipatiev house, Ekaterinburg, where the imperial family took their last meal.

The half-cellar room in the Ipatiev house, the scene of the assassination.

The grand duchesses' bedroom in the Ipatiev house after their deaths.

Participants in the murder of Grand Duke Michael Alexandrovich: Markov, Zhuzhgov, Myasnikov, Ivanchenko, and Kolpashchikov, in the Urals. The assassins had this photograph taken as a keepsake of their "exploit."

Yakov Yurovsky, commander of the execution squad.

Chekist Grigory Nikulin, Yurovsky's deputy, taken at the time of the murder of the tsar and his family, Ekaterinburg.

*S*ergei Lyukhanov (seated, center), who drove the truck bearing the lifeless bodies of the tsar's family from the Ipatiev House to the burial site. Photo taken in Osa, 1918.

*S*ergei Lyukhanov, just before his death in 1952.

*W*hite Russians returning to the burial site near Koptyaki to retrieve the bodies of the imperial family.

*A*t the burial site.

*T*he box containing remains of the imperial family after they were retrieved from the mine.

*T*he alleged skull of Nicholas II (found in Ekaterinburg) in the laboratory of a medical expert, 1991.

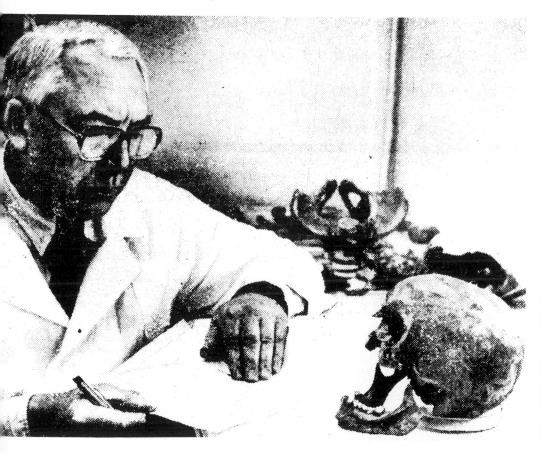

Ermakov (from the Upper Isetsk factory), and the other I didn't know."

The name of the man Medvedev didn't know was revealed by Ermakov himself.

Ermakov: "Received an execution decree on July 16 at eight in the evening. . . . myself arrived with two of my comrades, Medvedev and another Latvian whose last name I don't recall."

Medvedev, who came with Ermakov, was actually Mikhail Medvedev-Kudrin, a former sailor and board member of the Ural Cheka.

(Once in Baku, Medvedev-Kudrin had been in the same underground organization of the Russian Social Democratic Workers Party as Myasnikov. On the day of the Romanov tricentennial, they put out a broadside sentencing Nicholas to death. A month before, Myasnikov had carried out this sentence partially—he had organized the murder of Nicholas's brother. Now it was Medvedev-Kudrin's turn to keep his promise.)

THE DETACHMENT

The detachment was assembled.

Six Latvians from the Cheka—two had refused to join it. One who did not refuse, according to legend, was Imre Nagy, the future leader of the 1956 Hungarian revolution. Nagy's eventual death (executed without trial by Soviet troops invading Budapest) fits our story quite well. Joining the Latvians were Yurovsky, Nikulin, Ermakov, the two Medvedevs—Pavel, the guard commander, and the Chekist Medvedev-Kudrin.

There would be one more. A most curious person. Before the shooting began he would come down from upstairs, from the attic, where he was at that moment standing by a machine gun: Alexei Kabanov, a former soldier in the tsar's Life Guards.

The tsar had an amazing visual memory, the guard Yakimov told Investigator Sokolov: "Once Kabanov was on duty at the inner courtyard post. Walking past Kabanov, the tsar took a good look at him and stopped. 'You served in my cavalry regiment?' Kabanov replied in the affirmative."

Now former Life Guard Alexei Kabanov was serving in the Cheka and had been put in charge of the Ipatiev house machine gun platoon.

This "recognition" by the tsar may have decided everything.

Alexei Kabanov had a brother in an important position—head of the Ekaterinburg prison—and Alexei had thought that the way to prove his loyalty to the new authority was to participate in the execution.

Pavel Medvedev: "At about twelve o'clock (old style), two new style, Yurovsky woke the tsar's family.

"Whether he told them why he was disturbing them and where they were supposed to go, I don't know."

Strekotin: "At that moment electric bells were heard. This was them waking the tsar's family."

Yurovsky: "That was when I came and woke them. Dr. Botkin, who slept closer to the door of the room, came out." (No, the doctor was not sleeping, he was writing his last letter and had broken it off in the middle of a word.)

"The following explanation was given: 'In view of the unrest in the town, it has become necessary to move the Romanov family downstairs.'

"I suggested everyone dress right away. Botkin woke the rest. They took quite a long time getting dressed, probably at least forty minutes. . . . When they were dressed I myself led them down the inner staircase to the cellar room."

Yurovsky: "Downstairs a room had been chosen with a plastered wooden partition (to avoid ricochets), from which all the furniture had been moved. The detachment was at the ready in the next room. The R[omanov]s had no inkling."

Pavel Medvedev: "The tsar was carrying the heir in his arms. The sovereign and the heir were wearing field shirts and forage caps. The empress and her daughters wore dresses but not wraps. The sovereign walked ahead with the heir. In my presence there were no tears, no sobs, and no questions. They went downstairs, out into the courtyard, and from there through the second door into the downstairs quarters. They were led into the corner room adjacent to the sealed storeroom. Yurovsky ordered chairs brought in."

Yurovsky: "Nich[olas] was carrying Alexei in his arms, the rest were carrying small pillows and various little items. Entering the empty room, A[lexandra] F[eodorovna] asked: 'What, no chairs? May we not sit?'

"The com[mandant] ordered two chairs brought in. Nich[olas] put A[lexei] in one and A. F. sat in the other. The rest the commandant ordered stand in a row."

Strekotin: "They were all led into the room. . . . Next to my post. Soon Akulov [Nikulin] came out and walking past me said, 'The heir needs a chair. . . . Evidently he wants to die in a chair. . . . Oh well—let's bring them.'"

Nikulin brought the two chairs Yurovsky wrote about. One for the tsaritsa, the other for Alexei.

The chairs were no whim of Alexandra Feodorovna's. She could not stand for long because her legs ached constantly. That was why she had brought the wheelchair. The boy, who had just had an attack, could not stand either. That was why they "wanted to die in a chair."

Medvedev: "The empress sat by the wall where the window was, closer to the back column of the arch. Behind her stood three of her daughters. The sovereign was . . . in the middle, next to the heir, and behind him stood Dr. Botkin. The maid, a tall woman, stood by the left jamb of the storeroom door. With her stood one of the daughters. The maid had a pillow in her arms. The tsar's daughters had brought small pillows: they put one on the seat of the heir's chair, the other on their mother's."

At this time Deryabin was watching the same scene, but from the other perspective—through the window of the half cellar room. He saw the executioners:

"They arranged themselves like this: to the right of the entrance was Yurovsky, to the left of him stood Nikulin, the Latvians stood right in the doorway, and behind them was Medvedev [Pavel]."

Through the window Deryabin could see part of Yurovsky's body, but primarily his arm. He saw Yurovsky saying something and waving his arm. What exactly he said, Deryabin could not tell. He said he could not hear the words.

Strekotin: "With quick gestures Yurovsky directed who went where. In a calm, quiet voice: 'Please, you stand here, and you here . . . that's it, in a row.' The prisoners stood in two rows: in the first, the tsar's family; in the second, their people. The heir was sitting on a chair. The tsar was standing in the first row with one of his lackeys directly behind him."

Yes, Nicholas was *standing*. It was all just the way it had been at that last service, when they had heard "Rest with the Saints."

Everything in this scene is clear—except for one thing: Why were they arrayed so picturesquely? Earlier, when they had listened to the prayers, they had lined up before Father Storozhev and the deacon, but now—when they were *waiting for it to end?*

They were waiting out some new danger, so why were they so inappropriately, so picturesquely arrayed? And why did they ask for only two chairs; after all they could be waiting for it to end indefinitely.

THE PHOTO-EXECUTION

A man called me after the publication of my first article. He started right in:

"I will tell you what the second generation of Soviet agents was told in agent school. What is the second generation? If the famous Soviet agent Rikhard Zorge was the first generation, then this is 1927–1929. They are all long since in their graves, and you are unlikely to hear this from anyone but me. . . . So, at agent classes we were told the following . . . : they had to arrange the family as conveniently as possible for the execution. The room was narrow, and they were worried the family would crowd together. Then Yurovsky had an idea. He told them they had to go down to the cellar because there was danger of firing on the house. While they were at it, they had to be photographed because people in Moscow were worried and various rumors were going around—to the effect that they had fled. [Indeed, in late June there had been a disturbing telegram to that effect from Moscow.]

"So they went downstairs and stood—for a photograph along the wall. And when they had lined up. . . ."

How simple it all proved to be. Of course, he thought of saying he was going to photograph them. He may even have joked about how he had once been a photographer. Hence his orders, about which Strekotin wrote: "Stand on the left, . . . and you on the right." Hence also the calm obedience of all the characters in this scene. Then, when they were standing, waiting for the camera to be brought in. . . .

Yurovsky: "When they were all standing, the detachment was called in."

Strekotin: "A group of people went to the room where the prisoners had just been led. I followed them, leaving my post. We all stopped at the door to the room."

So the firing squad was already crowding in the wide double doors to the room, and Strekotin was right beside them.

Ermakov: "Then I came out and told the driver: 'Get going.' He knew what to do, the car roared to life, and exhaust appeared. All this was necessary in order to muffle the shots, so that no sound would be heard at liberty."

The driver, Sergei Lyukhanov, in the courtyard, was sitting in the cab of the truck, listening to the motor running—and waiting.

Yurovsky: "When the detachment com[mandant] walked in, he told the R[omanov]s: 'In view of the fact that your relatives are continuing their attack on Sov[iet] Russia, the Ural Executive Committee has decided to execute you.' Nicholas turned his back to the detachment, his face to the family, then sort of came to and turned around to face the com[mandant] and asked: 'What? What?' "

Strekotin: "Yurovsky was standing in front of the tsar, his right hand in his pants pocket and a small piece of paper in his left. Then he began to read the sentence. But he had not finished the last word when the tsar asked very loudly for him to repeat it. . . . So Yurovsky read it a second time."

Yurovsky: "The com[mandant] quickly repeated it and ordered the detachment to get ready. . . . Nicholas did not say anything more, having turned back toward the family; the others uttered a few incoherent exclamations. It all lasted just a few seconds."

*T*HE TSAR'S LAST WORDS

He "asked him to repeat it" and "did not say anything more"! Such were Nicholas's last words, wrote Yurovsky and Strekotin.

But the tsar did say a few more words. Yurovsky and Strekotin did not understand them. Or rather, they did not choose to write them down.

Ermakov did not write them down either, but he did remember them. He did not remember much, but this he did not forget. He even talked about it sometimes.

From a letter of Alexei Karelin in Magnitogorsk:

"I remember Ermakov was asked, 'What did the tsar say before the execution?' 'The tsar,' he replied, 'said, "You know not what you do." ' "

No, Ermakov could not have invented that sentence; he did not know those words, this assassin and atheist. Nor was there any way he could have known that those words of the Lord were written on the cross of Nicholas's slain uncle Sergei Alexandrovich. The tsar repeated them, as Ella must have repeated them at the bottom of the mine: "Forgive them, for they know not what they do."

A few months later in the Fortress of Peter and Paul, another Romanov, Grand Duke Dmitry Konstantinovich, would be led before a firing squad:

"The prison guard said that while Dmitry Konstantinovich was on his way to his execution, he kept repeating Christ's words: 'Forgive them, Lord, for they know not what they do' " (From the memoirs of Grand Duke Gavriil Konstantinovich, *In a Marble Palace*).

His last words. At that moment it came to pass—the story of the sacrifice. And forgiveness.

After reading the piece of paper, Yurovsky jerked out his Colt.

Yurovsky: "The detachment had been told beforehand who was to shoot whom, and they had been ordered to aim straight for the heart, to avoid excessive quantities of blood and get it over with quicker."

Strekotin: "At his last word he instantly pulled a revolver out of his pocket and shot the tsar. The tsaritsa and her daughter Olga tried to make the sign of the cross, but did not have enough time."

Yurovsky: "Nich[olas] was killed by the commandant, point blank. Then A[lexandra] F[eodorovna] died immediately."

Yurovsky wrote that it was he who killed the tsar. Strekotin too saw Yurovsky finish reading the paper and immediately pull out his hand with the gun and shoot the tsar.

Actually, that day Yurovsky had two guns with him.

Yurovsky: "Colt no. 71905 with a cartridge clip and seven bullets, and Mauser no. 167177 with a wooden gunstock and a clip with ten bullets. . . . I killed Nicholas point blank with the Colt."

But Strekotin was only watching Yurovsky reading, and the guard only saw Yurovsky's hand aimed at the former Autocrat of All the Russias.

Two others would later assert that they had shot the tsar.

The son of Chekist Medvedev: "The tsar was killed by my father. . . . As I already said, they had agreed who was to shoot whom. Ermakov the tsar, Yurovsky the tsaritsa, and my father Marie. But when they stood in the doorway, my father found himself directly opposite the tsar. While Yurovsky was reading the paper, my father stood there watching the tsar. He had never seen him so close up. As soon as Yurovsky repeated the last words, my father was ready and waiting and fired immediately. And he killed the tsar. He fired his shot faster than anyone. . . . Only he had a Browning. On a Mauser, a revolver, or a Colt you have to cock it, and that takes time. On a Browning you don't have to."

But Ermakov, to whom the tsar "belonged" by agreement. . . .
Ermakov: "I shot him point blank, and he fell instantly."

I am certain, though, that everyone crowding in the doorway of that
terrible room, all twelve revolutionaries, had come to kill the tsar,
and all twelve sent their first bullet into him. The triumphant inscription left on the wall—"On this night Belshazzar was killed by
his lackeys"—was literally true. That was why Nicholas toppled over
backward with such force. Only then did they turn to the others, and
the chaotic shooting ensued.

Kabanov: "I remember it well: when all of us participating in the
execution walked up to the opened door of the room, there turned
out to be three rows of us firing revolvers, and the second and third
rows were firing over the shoulders of the ones in front. There were
so many arms with revolvers pointed toward those being executed,
and they were so close to each other, that whoever was standing in
front got a burn on the inside of his wrist from the shots of his
neighbor behind."

They gave up the entire space of the tiny room of execution to
the eleven unfortunates, who raced around in that cell while the
twelve sharpshooters, sorting out their victims, fired continuously
from the mouth of the double doors, giving those in front gunpowder
burns.

Hands holding revolvers poked through the doorway.

The son of Chekist Medvedev: "My father had a gunpowder burn
on his neck, and Yurovsky burned his finger." (Yes, they were both in
the first row!)

Yurovsky: "A[lexe]i, three of his sisters, the lady-in-waiting [as he
referred to Demidova], and Botkin were still alive. They had to be
finished off. This amazed the com[mandant] since we had aimed
straight for the heart. It was also surprising that the bullets from the
revolvers bounced off for some reason and ricocheted, jumping
around the room like hail."

So the tsar was down, felled by the first shots, felled by them all.
The tsaritsa was down, too, killed in her chair, and the swarthy
servant Trupp, who collapsed right after his master. And Botkin and
the cook Kharitonov. But the girls were still alive. It was bizarre how
the bullets bounced off them. Bullets flew around the room.
Demidova was dashing about the tiny room wailing. . . . She
shielded herself with a pillow, into which they emptied bullet after
bullet.

The detachment kept firing, almost hysterically. Through the gun smoke the light was barely visible. The prostrate figures lay in pools of blood, and on the floor the boy stretched his arm out through the smoke, shielding himself from the bullets. Nikulin, in horror, not understanding what was going on, fired at him, and fired, and fired.

Yurovsky: "My assistant spent an entire clip of bullets." (The strange vitality of the heir must probably be put down to my assistant's poor mastery of his weapon and his inevitable nerves evoked by his long ordeal with the armored daughters.)

Then the commandant stepped into the fierce, acrid smoke.

Yurovsky: "The remaining bullets of the one loaded clip for the Colt, as well as the loaded Mauser, went to finish off Nicholas's daughters and the strange vitality of the heir."

He put an end to that "vitality" with two shots. So he believed. And the boy fell quiet.

Kabanov: "The tsar's two youngest daughters, pressed up against the wall, were squatting, covering their heads with their arms, and then two men fired at their heads. . . . Alexei was lying on the floor, and they fired at him, too. The lady-in-waiting [Demidova] was lying on the floor still alive. Then I ran into the execution room and shouted to stop the firing and finish off those still alive with bayonets. One of the comrades began plunging the bayonet of his American Winchester into her chest. The bayonet was like a dagger, but it was dull and would not penetrate. She grabbed the bayonet with both hands and began screaming. Later they got her with their rifle butts."

Now all eleven were on the floor—barely visible through the smoke.

Pavel Medvedev: "The blood was gushing out . . . the heir was still alive—and moaning. Yurovsky walked over to him and shot him two or three times at point-blank range. The heir fell still. The scene made me want to vomit."

Strekotin: "The smoke was blocking out the electric lamp. The shooting was halted. The doors of the room were opened for the smoke to disperse. They started picking up the bodies."

They had to get them out as quickly as possible. This truck had to be on its way while the July night still hung over the town. Quickly, hastily, they turned the bodies over, checking pulses. They were in a hurry. The light barely shone through all the gun smoke.

Yurovsky: "The whole procedure, including the checking [feeling pulses and so on] took about twenty minutes."

The bodies had to be carried through all the downstairs rooms to the front entrance, where the truck was waiting with the driver Lyukhanov.

Pavel Medvedev got the idea of carrying them out on sheets, so as not to drip blood in the rooms. He went upstairs, to the family's rooms. After he collected the sheets in the grand duchesses' room he grabbed a cover and wiped his hands, which were spattered with the tsar's blood—and threw it into the corner. That was the cover they later found—from his, Medvedev's, bloody fingers.

Pavel Medvedev: "We took the bodies out on stretchers made from sheets stretched between shafts taken off the cart in the courtyard."

Strekotin: "The tsar's body was carried out first. The bodies were carried out to the truck."

On the bottom of the truck they laid a cloth, which had been in the storeroom covering the family's belongings. Now it was protecting the floor of the truck from the tsar's blood.

The tsar was carried out first in the wide marital sheet. They carried out the head of the family. Then they brought his daughters.

Strekotin: "When they laid one of the daughters on the stretcher, she cried out and covered her face with her arm. The others [the daughters] also turned out to be alive. We couldn't shoot anymore—with the open doors the shots could have been heard on the street. According to the comrades in the detachment, the shots had been heard at all the posts."

When the slain grand duchess rose up with a shout on the sheet—and her sisters rustled on the floor—horror gripped the detachment.

At that point they still did not know the reason for their "strange vitality," as Yurovsky put it. It seemed to them that heaven itself was against them. Again the Chekists did not err. Ermakov set the example. He had no fear of heaven.

Strekotin: "Ermakov took my bayonet from me and started stabbing everyone dead who had turned out to be alive."

Yurovsky: "When they tried to stab one of the girls with a bayonet, the point just would not go through her corset."

The Livadia Palace, the children's balls, the luxury of the Winter Palace, the anticipation of love—it all came to an end on a dirty floor, to the panting of a former convict. In impossible pain from a dull bayonet—it all came to an end.

Remember: When they were carrying her out to the truck, the shot young woman turned out to be alive, as did the other daughters—even though they had checked their pulses!

It is easy enough to write that they "checked," but how could they really have checked—in that smoke, in that horror, in that fever amid the pools of blood?

Again they were carrying bodies to the truck. Before carrying them out, they collected the jewels and precious objects. As it says in Sokolov's inquiry, Strekotin immediately began searching those lying there and removing jewels.

Naturally enough, though, Strekotin did not write about his own efforts.

Strekotin: "While the bodies were being removed, several of our comrades began removing various items from the bodies, like watches, rings, bracelets, cigarette cases, other things. When Comrade Yurovsky was informed of this he hurried back downstairs. We were already carrying out the last body. Comrade Yurovsky stopped us and suggested we voluntarily give back the various items we had taken from the bodies. Some gave it all back, some just part, and some nothing at all."

Yurovsky: "Then they started carrying the bodies out and loading them into the truck, which was spread with a cloth (so the blood would not flow). At this point the stealing began: I had to have three reliable comrades guard the bodies while the carrying was going on. Under threat of execution, everything stolen was returned (a gold watch, a cigarette case with diamonds, etc.)."

The son of Chekist Medvedev: "When they were removing the jewels from the dead Romanovs in the Ipatiev house, a watch disappeared instantly. They also managed to remove the watch from the dead Botkin. Yurovsky said: 'We are going out now, and in three minutes we'll be back. The watch had better be here.' And he went out of the room with my father. Three minutes later he was back. And the watch was there. Yurovsky took great pains to see that nothing was stolen. When the tsar fell, his forage cap rolled into a corner. One of the guards carrying out the bodies took the tsar's cap. . . . Yurovsky immediately pointed it out to my father with a nod of his head. The cap fit my father. It turned out to be a perfectly ordinary cap, no initials. My father took the cockade off but left the cap. We had the cockade in our house for a long time. As a child I used to play with it. Then something happened to it in all our moves. I was already in school when we had a play and I played a policeman with that cockade."

Now the tsar's family was lying in the truck covered with a tarpaulin. Someone found the tiny dead dog—one of the grand duchesses was hugging it . . . she had been lying on the floor with the dog. The dog's body was tossed into the truck—it could guard the tsar's family.

Yurovsky: "The com[mandant] had been instructed only to carry out the sentence. Getting rid of the bodies and moving them was the job of Comrade Ermakov (a worker from the Upper Isetsk plant, a former political prisoner). He was supposed to come with the truck and was let in at the password 'chimney sweep.' The truck's lateness made the com[mandant] doubt Ermakov's thoroughness, so the com[mandant] decided to watch over the entire operation himself. At about three o'clock they left for the site Ermakov was supposed to have prepared, past the Upper Isetsk factory. First they were supposed to go by truck and after a certain point on horses (since the truck could go no farther; the site chosen was an abandoned mine)."

Yurovsky and Ermakov would end up spending two full days together with the bodies.

Yurovsky recorded the burial of the tsar's family in great detail, perhaps concealing an almost fantastic story. But let us break off here. We will return yet again to the terrible truck.

The gates of the house opened and in the advancing dawn the truck drove out onto Ascension Avenue.

Strekotin: "When the bodies had been carried out and the car had left, only then was our shift taken off duty."

Chapter 16

MY GUEST

✠

He called me himself and asked to meet with me. I heard his trembling old man's voice and naturally said: "I can come see you myself." But he immediately replied—as did many of those people of his age and generation who called me—"But why? I will come to you myself." Then he laughed. "You mustn't think that. No, I'm not afraid of anyone. It's others who were afraid of me. It's just I'm an old soldier, and I like to walk."

Here he is sitting in my room.

He slaps his knee and laughs, pointing to his odd trousers: once green wide trousers with piping that have lost all their color and shape.

"These trousers belonged to Nicholas. I got them in 1945—in Czechoslovakia. At that time they belonged to a former legionary. . . . In 1918 he bought them in Ekaterinburg. He had a lot of things that were supposedly from the tsar's family." He chuckles. "No, naturally, I don't believe altogether that these are the trousers of the last emperor, but it's still something from the era. I like the trousers and allow myself this masquerade sometimes. . . . Right now about the matter that interests you. . . . I worked in a certain 'serious institution' [as the organs of state security have long been called in Russia] for many years. . . . I was living in Sverdlovsk then. . . .

For quite a while . . . no, not through my work . . . just for myself . . . I was obsessed with your theme. . . . Or rather, I was interested in *one question*, which came up a long time ago, before you were ever born—and I've been searching for the answer to it all my life. It began with an acquaintanceship—I was rather well acquainted with Peter Zakharovich Ermakov. He was a complicated man. Or rather, simple. His hands itched to kill. For his revolutionary ardor he was called Comrade Mauser. In tsarist times he killed a provocateur in a most original manner—you'll never guess. He sawed off his head. According to an Ekaterinburg legend, when they decided to deform *their* bodies, he went to the pharmacy for a supply of sulfuric acid. The chemist was rather doubtful: Ermakov was asking for quite a lot. Peter Zakharovich was about to try to convince him, but he never did—his reflexes went into action and he fired. By the way, do you know that Ermakov told all and sundry that it was he who had killed the last tsar? And how Yurovsky reacted to that?"

That was something I knew very well.

Beginning in 1921, Yurovsky lived in Moscow, where he worked in the State Depository.

The son of Chekist Medvedev: "They often met in our apartment —all the former regicides who had now moved to Moscow."

Yes, soon after the execution they went to Moscow for their promotions. Beloborodov would become Dzerzhinsky's deputy in the Cheka, Goloshchekin would occupy very important posts. The masters of Ekaterinburg became the boyars of the Kremlin. Here Chekist Mikhail Medvedev proved more modest. He did not go for the brass ring but ended his life a humble colonel, a teacher in a police academy. That was why he survived. The Kremlin boyars would all perish.

But then, in the 1920s, they were all alive—and young. They loved the hospitality at Medvedev's welcoming home. Goloshchekin, Nikulin, and of course Yurovsky came.

The son of Chekist Medvedev: "My father often made fun of his arrogance: of course he killed Nicholas. By the way, my father once proposed an experiment to me. My father had a whole collection of weapons—a Mauser, a Colt, and a Browning. So he proposed we experiment to see which of us could fire faster. From which gun. My father and I did this experiment. Naturally, the Browning fired first. *First*—just as it had then. Yurovsky never disputed that with my father. Moreover, he once told my father: 'Hey, you didn't let me finish reading—you started shooting! But when I was reading Nicholas the resolution the second time, I wanted to add that this was revenge for executing revolutionaries.' "

So they chatted and reminisced peacefully over a cup of tea about how lucky they were to have carried out a historic mission.

But if Medvedev talked at home about the shooting, then very soon another, much more dangerous rival appeared before Yurovsky: Peter Ermakov. The former Upper Isetsk commissar would proclaim far and wide from 1918 on that he had killed the tsar.

So Yurovsky began his fight for "the honor of having executed the last tsar." That is one reason why he gave his Note to the historian Pokrovsky. The chief Soviet historian was supposed to leave the name of Yakov Yurovsky, the tsar's assassin, in official Soviet history for good.

Meanwhile, 1927 came around. The tenth anniversary of the revolution. Yurovsky was already living in anticipation of 1928—the great anniversary—ten years since the execution of the tsar's family.

It was then that he gave both his revolvers to the Museum of the Revolution in Moscow, where the history of their new world was kept.

But a reply followed immediately: in 1927 Peter Ermakov also gave his Mauser to the local Museum of the Revolution.

"From an act of the Sverdlovsk Museum of the Revolution:

"On December 10, 1927, we received from Comrade P. Z. Ermakov a Mauser revolver no. 16174 *with which, according to P. Z. Ermakov's testimony, the tsar was shot.*"

Now it was Yurovsky's move.

The son of Chekist Medvedev: "In 1927, Yurovsky gave the Bolshevik Party's Central Committee the idea of publishing a collection of documents and reminiscences from the participants in the execution (reminiscences of the participants he needed, such as Nikulin and Strekotin, those who would want to confirm his historic mission of shooting the tsar) for the tenth anniversary of the Romanovs' execution. But through a member of the OGPU [the name for the state security organs in the 1930s] board, F. Goloshchekin, Stalin passed on a spoken decree: 'Don't print anything and keep quiet generally.' "

Already then, in 1927, Stalin was beginning his battle against human memory. The death of the tsar's family resurrected several names that were supposed to have been forgotten forever: the chief accuser in the proposed trial against the Romanovs, Trotsky; the chairman of the Ural Soviet, the Trotskyite Beloborodov (even if he had retracted), and so on.

As always, though, there were two models: "for them" and "for us." For them, that is, for the "progressive world public," everything remained as before: the execution of the bloody despot, the holy vengeance of the people's revolution. That was why when the journalist Richard Halliburton turned up in Sverdlovsk in the 1930s, Peter Ermakov willingly told him about the execution of the Romanovs and about how he personally had shot the tsar. But we know that without the permission of the "serious institution" a meeting with a foreign journalist would have been impossible. The sly Chekist explained this by his throat cancer—he was giving his dying testament, so to speak. Ermakov laughed when he lived to thrive another twenty years after that. He had borrowed the "throat cancer" from one of his friends in the Ural Soviet, a friend whom we will talk about again.

To his dying days, the Upper Isetsk "Comrade Mauser" fought relentlessly for primacy. At innumerable Pioneer campfires, on July summer nights at yet another anniversary of the Ipatiev night, he would tell his story with enthusiasm.

From a letter of Alexei Karelin in Magnitogorsk:

"I had the opportunity to see and hear one of the 'heroes' who participated in the execution of the tsar's family, P. Ermakov. This was in 1934 or 1935 at the ChTZ [Chelyabinsk Tractor Plant] Pioneer camp on a lake near Chelyabinsk. I was twelve or thirteen at the time; my youthful memory preserved perfectly everything I heard and saw at this encounter with Ermakov by a Pioneer campfire. He was presented to us as a hero. . . . He was given flowers. My God, how they cultivated patriotism in us! I was looking straight at Ermakov with such envy! . . . Ermakov ended his 'lecture' with especially solemn words: 'I personally shot the tsar.' Then he listed everyone in the tsar's family by name and patronymic as well as some old man from the court. Ermakov said that the execution had been based on Lenin's personal instruction."

That night by the Pioneer campfire Ermakov told them Nicholas's last words.

Ermakov also wrote his own memoirs and on the thirtieth anniversary of the execution gave them to the Sverdlovsk Party Archive.

I heard a great deal about Ermakov's memoirs. Naturally, I could not read them since they were kept in a secret depository in the Sverdlovsk Party Archive. Although from my readers' letters I already knew certain excerpts from them.

All this I conscientiously told my guest. He just chuckled: he knew I did not know how to listen. He continued:

"Oh well, I too got caught up in this struggle for the right to be the tsar's assassin. And you are right, in 1947 Ermakov did write his memoirs. But even before that, while Yurovsky was still alive, he wrote about it many times."

At that point he opened his briefcase and placed some papers before me.

"Don't get excited, and don't try to turn the tape recorder on without my noticing, especially since you can't. I will leave all these documents with you. I brought them for you. Read the first to start with."

I began to read:

"From a brief autobiography of P. Z. Ermakov:

"In late June 1918 the Ural Executive Committee put me in charge of the guard for the special house where the former Romanov tsar and his family were being held under arrest. On July 16, 1918, I carried out the Regional Executive Committee's resolution to execute the former Romanov tsar, so the tsar himself as well as his family were executed *by me*. The bodies, too, were burned *by me personally*. When the Whites took Sverdlovsk, they were unable to find the remains of the tsar and his family. August 3, 1932."

He continued:

"As you see, every word in these few lines is boastful invention. Wouldn't it have been easy for Yurovsky to expose the pretenses of his lying rival once and for all?

"But from the very beginning it's as if something were holding the iron commandant back. It's as if he were avoiding a direct confrontation with Ermakov. Instead, on a January night in 1934 he arranged a public lecture for party activists in the Ipatiev house."

I could picture it. The party activists sitting on the chairs of the Ipatiev house, and among them—those two chairs on which Alexei and the tsaritsa had been sitting at the moment of the murder. Mayakovsky was right; "nails should be made from those people—they'd be the strongest in the world."

"In short, in his lecture Yurovsky defended his Note. But because of Ermakov's pretensions, he somehow reasoned very modestly: 'I have to say that certain comrades, I have heard, are trying to say that they killed Nicholas. Perhaps they did fire, that is correct. . . .'

"In short, Ermakov calmly expounded his fantastic ravings right up until Yurovsky's death. As if he knew for certain that Yurovsky would not dare expose him. As if between them stood some circumstance that precluded their confrontation.

"So after the war, in the late 1940s, this began to interest me greatly.

"By the way, apart from his memoirs about the execution, Ermakov would give the Sverdlovsk Party Archives his long autobiography. It's all kept in a secret depository, although now, I've heard, there has been a proposal to publish them." Chuckling, he added, "But until that's decided. . . . In short, I have brought them to you as well . . . and I'll leave them here, too."

Imagine what came over me when I saw the memoirs! Finally, finally! I could read what I had been hunting for all these years!

"This part of the memoirs is called 'The Execution of the Former Tsar.' But bear in mind, not everything is here—this only goes up to the moment the truck drove out of the gates with the corpses. I'll give you the conclusion later."

Appended to the memoirs was a portion of Ermakov's autobiography:

"The good fortune befell me to carry out the ultimate proletarian Soviet justice against the human tyrant, the crowned autocrat, who in his reign had tried, hanged, and shot thousands of men, for which he had to bear responsibility before the people. I was honored to fulfill my obligation before my people and country and took part in the execution of the tsar's entire family."

After that came Ermakov's reminiscences about the execution:

"The Ekaterinburg Executive Committee passed a resolution to shoot Nicholas, but for some reason the resolution said nothing about the family and their execution. When I was called in they told me: 'You are a lucky man. You have been chosen to execute and bury them in such a way that no one ever finds their bodies, this is your personal responsibility, which we entrust to you as an old revolutionary.'

"I accepted the assignment and said it would be carried out precisely. I prepared the site where they would be taken and hidden, always bearing in mind the significance of the political moment.

"When I reported to Beloborodov that I was ready to carry it out, he said: 'Do it so that all of them are shot, we have decided that.' I did not enter into any further discussion and began doing what I was supposed to do.

"I received my orders on July 16 at eight o'clock in the evening, and came myself with two comrades—Medvedev and another Latvian (I don't remember his name now) who served under me in my detachment—in the punitive section. I arrived at the special house at ten o'clock exactly; my vehicle came soon after, a small truck. At eleven o'clock the imprisoned Romanovs and their people confined with them were advised to go downstairs. To the suggestion that they go downstairs they asked: 'What for?' I said: 'You are being taken to the center, you can't be kept here any longer, it could get dangerous.' 'What about our things?' they asked. I said: 'We will collect your things and bring them to you.' They agreed. They went downstairs, where chairs had been set up for them along the wall.

"It is well preserved in my memory: in the first flank sat Nicholas, Alexei, Alexandra, their older daughter Tatiana, then Dr. Botkin, and after that the lady-in-waiting and all the rest. When everything had settled down, I went out and told the driver: 'Get going.' He knew what he had to do, the truck roared to life, and exhaust started pouring out. All this was necessary in order to drown out the shots, so that no sound could be heard at liberty. Everyone seated was expecting something to happen. They were all tense and only from time to time exchanged words. But Alexandra said a few words not in Russian. When everything was in order, I handed Yurovsky, the house commandant, the Regional Executive Committee's resolution. He was doubtful: 'Why all of them?' But I told him: 'We have to do all of them, and we can't go on talking here for long, time is short and we have to get going.' I went downstairs with the commandant, and I must say that it had been decided beforehand who was to shoot whom and how. For myself I took Nicholas himself, Alexandra, the daughter, and Alexei, because I had a Mauser, and you could work with that. The rest had revolvers. After we got downstairs we delayed a little. Then the commandant suggested everyone stand, which they did, but Alexei sat in a chair. Then he began reading the sentence-resolution, which said: By resolution of the Executive Committee—execution. Then Nicholas burst out with: 'So you're not taking us anywhere?' We couldn't wait any longer, and I shot him point blank. He fell immediately, as did the others. At that time a wail rose up among them, they threw themselves on each other's necks. Then several shots rang out—and everyone fell. When I began examining their condition—the ones that were still alive I shot again. Nicholas died from a single bullet, his wife got two, and the others also several bullets. Checking their pulses, when they were already dead, I gave the order to drag them all out through the lower entrance to the truck and stow them in it, which was done, and covered them all with a tarpaulin" (archive 221, list 2, file 774).

"I noted the archive reference especially for you to preclude any doubts," he said when I had finished reading.

Nevertheless, I did check. By then I had received a letter from a reader in Sverdlovsk with excerpts from Ermakov's memoirs, which her husband, an army political worker who had access to the secret archive, had made at one time. The excerpts coincided exactly, down to nonessential punctuation.

Yes, before me were the genuine memoirs of one of the principal actors on that monstrous night.

"The memoirs are odd, aren't they?" my guest continued. "Nearly every detail is wrong."

Indeed, if Yurovsky's Note and the statements of the other witnesses coincided, Ermakov's story differed surprisingly in many inaccurate details.

"In the first place, he combines himself with Yurovsky, ascribing to himself everything the commandant did. But if we toss out that boastful invention, then the memoirs represent a garbled compilation of well-known facts. As soon as he gets to the details the mistakes begin. The car did not arrive at ten but at midnight old style— that is, about two in the morning new style. Ermakov wasn't the only one with a Mauser, Yurovsky had one as well; Yurovsky read the resolution, there were only two chairs, and so on. The only truthful detail, evidently, is the story about turning on the truck's engine. As for Nicholas's last sentence, that is evidently another invention, Ermakov himself changed that last sentence of the tsar's many times."

At this point I related to my strange guest Ermakov's story told around a Pioneer campfire about the tsar's last sentence.

"Yes, sure, 'They know not what they do'—those are words Peter Zakharovich could scarcely have thought up, indeed. For all his wild imagination! He was after all very far removed from those kinds of words. So that it is quite likely those were Nicholas's last words, which suddenly *surfaced* in Ermakov's memory. We'll be coming back to that 'surfaced.' It's hard to believe that a man who took an active part in the execution could not remember a single truthful detail. And was only capable of garbling well-known facts. You get the feeling he simply wasn't there, as if he were telling it from others' words. Or as if it were all very hazy for him, surfacing in spates. No, I understand he was there but"—he chuckled—"he was *drunk!*"

Of course—he was drunk! Why hadn't I realized that before! To inflame himself, to inspire revolutionary fury? Or was it nerves—that he could not stand the anticipation, the wait for an answer from Moscow and for the truck? Or, what is more likely, was he drunk simply because that was payday, and many sharpshooters in the guard (like Proskuryakov and Stolov) had gotten drunk? The blatant, wild bestiality of Ermakov, who finished off the unfortunate girls with his bayonet in the gun smoke, was a continuation of that loutish, bestial "he was drunk."

I told my guest about one other letter.

From a letter of Mstislav K. Afanasiev in Moscow:

"In the 1920s my father worked as an inspector for the Sapozhek Fire Department in Ryazan Province. The local priest told him a few details he had heard from one of the assassins of the Romanov family. Who this dying assassin was, he did not tell my father, but the dying man's sins were forgiven. The dying man said that the leader of the murder had suggested they rape the grand duchesses. They were all drunk, and that day they had got their wages. They did not want to kill the women, however. 'We're not shooting womenfolk! Just the men!' The chief assassin himself suffered from chronic alcoholism, and he was drunk that day. They shouted at him: 'That's not how you make a revolution!' "

Again my guest choked with laughter: "You mean my old friend Peter Zakharovich promised the girls? No, not to the riflemen, the priest simply misunderstood—to his own dashing lads. He promised them to his Upper Isetsk companions. Naturally, the man dying in the Ryazan town of Sapozhek was not one of the regicides, he was from Ermakov's detachment. Ermakov's men were present at the burial of the bodies, which is why they proudly counted themselves among the assassins. I've come across this before. As for the idea itself: promising rape before execution—that kind of thing happened in those days. Melgunov writes about it in *The Red Terror*. By the way, the Whites practiced it, too—that was nothing new. As far as Ermakov being drunk, I never doubted that. That was why Yurovsky had to go along to 'watch over' the interment of the bodies. Otherwise the commandant would never have dared to shadow Upper Isetsk Commissar Ermakov himself. That is why Yurovsky got into the truck—to transport the bodies. Ermakov probably drunkenly insisted on helping load the bodies too—after all, this was his job. I understood as much from my conversations with Peter Zakharovich, that he even climbed up onto the truck to direct the loading. Evidently he couldn't get down, though, so he stayed in the back with the bodies.

"So that at a crucial moment in revolutionary history Peter Zakharovich was, to be blunt, drunk. Why then, though, in fighting with him for the honor of the execution, did Yurovsky never once take advantage of that circumstance? Or even so much as hint at it? Why did he spare the political prisoner's honor? Or did *something* prevent him?

"I tried to feel out Ermakov himself many times, once I had begun guessing. But I never could find out anything precisely. I'm talking about the *ride*."

Again I asked what he meant. I simply could not adapt to his mode of conversation.

"For a while I tried to calculate at what point that *something* might have happened to them both: the road, the truck with the bodies. That was when I began to question him carefully about the ride. To the simplest questions—well, let's say I asked him, 'Did the sharpshooters in the truck guard ride in the truck or on horseback?' Even that question, though, he answered differently every time: he made out as if he couldn't remember; the madman, he'd drunk away his memory. . . . Yes, he did like to drink. He kept everyone at the town beer stands entertained with stories about how he had killed the tsar. But at the beer stand, drunk as a skunk, not a word about the ride. Still, since he was very drunk. . . . Then I began my conversation again, and he, as always, contributed his part: how he killed them all. On his way out, he suddenly asked, 'I can see you don't believe they were *all* . . . ?' And he chuckled. Then he added: 'They all perished, all of them!' and suddenly gave me a bone-chilling look, like a wild animal.

"Before he died I paid him a visit. In my day, there was a revolutionary idea in the air that a Chekist should visit a dying man instead of a priest. In the end, even atheists need to unburden their souls, and who better to tell than the institution where one was supposed to speak only the truth? So that a special corps could have been created in the Cheka of Chekist priests. They could have been called something like Truthgatherers. It was in this capacity of 'truthgatherer' that I chatted with Peter Zakharovich. But again nothing! By the way, have you ever tried to reconstruct that ride and the truck's route?"

I had studied that route well. Investigator Sokolov had once attempted to reconstruct it from the tracks left by the terrible truck in the rain-wet earth and from the statements of witnesses.

The route the tsarist bodies took to their first grave turned out to have been described in detail in Commandant Yurovsky's secret note.

Finally, two amateurs from Sverdlovsk studying the history of the execution sent me a map of the truck's route.

In the summer of 1989 I went to Sverdlovsk and traversed on foot the entire path to that first grave of the family.

And all the statements coalesced.

THE TRUCK WITH THE BODIES

The Ipatiev house gates open, and the driver Sergei Lyukhanov steers the truck out into the street. It is three in the morning. The truck sets out down Ascension Avenue, then turns down Main Street, drives past the city limits by the racetrack, and then down the road toward the village of Koptyaki.

Passing by the Upper Isetsk factory, the truck then crosses the railroad tracks to Perm and enters a dense, mixed forest that stretches all the way to Koptyaki. About 3 versts (2 miles) to the north of the Perm railway line, the truck crosses a second set of tracks—the mine-factory line—near station number 120.

These are wild places where the only structures are railway booths. Here the road forks: the truck turns toward the railroad crossing, toward booth 184, where there is a marshy, swampy place, and about 100 meters from the booth it gets stuck in a quagmire. Lyukhanov tries to get it out, but the motor overheats. Now he needs water for the engine and planks to lay over the swampy area in order to cross the marsh. Fortunately, nearby is the railroad crossing by booth 184. Lyukhanov gets out of the truck.

At this time the noise of the truck skidding in the swamp awakens the watchwoman in booth 184. There is a knock at the door; she opens it and sees Lyukhanov and the truck's silhouette dark in the dawning sky.

The driver says his motor has overheated and asks her for some water. The watchwoman grumbles, at which Lyukhanov lashes out: "You're sleeping here like god almighty, while we've been breaking our backs all night long."

Through the open door, the watchwoman sees Red Guards

around the truck and immediately begins pumping water readily for the engine. Then the Red Guards take some planks dumped around her booth and lay them over the swampy area, and the truck drives over the planks. Passing the booth, it enters the forest and drives 3 versts along the forest road to the Four Brothers, a landmark in the desolate terrain.

At this time near Koptyaki a picket of Red Guards is standing on a knoll, turning all inhabitants back to the village. Another picket is standing not far from booth 184. They let no one onto the road. They evidently meet the truck and lead it through the Four Brothers.

Yurovsky: "Having gone about 5 versts [3.3 miles] from the Upper Isetsk factory, we ran into an entire camp of about twenty-five men, some on horseback, some in droshkies, and so on. They were the workers (members of the Executive Committee Soviet) whom Ermakov had prepared. The first thing they shouted was: 'Why didn't you bring them to us alive?' They thought the Romanovs' execution would be left to them."

The bloodthirsty, carousing, drunken crowd has been expecting the grand duchesses Ermakov had promised them, and now they are not being allowed to participate in the good deed of finishing off the girls, the boy, and the papa tsar. So they complain: "Why didn't you bring them to us alive?"

Yurovsky: "Meanwhile, they started transferring the bodies to the droshkies, since we had to use carts. It was very awkward. They immediately started cleaning out their pockets—I had to threaten them with a firing squad then and there."

So here too they try to rob the corpses as they move the bodies onto the carts.

Yurovsky: "Here we discovered that Tatiana, Olga, and Anastasia were wearing some kind of special corset. It was decided to strip the bodies naked, not there, but at the burial site."

Not all the bodies fit on the droshkies, however. There are not enough good carts. The carts are falling apart. That is why the truck continues on toward the mine with some of the bodies.

Yurovsky: "It turned out, though, that no one knew where the mine shaft selected for this was. It was getting light. The com[mandant] sent riders to find the place, but no one could. It became clear that nothing had been prepared at all, there weren't any shovels, etc."

No one knows where to take them. Suddenly they have lost their destination. True, it is very hard to believe that Ermakov's Upper Isetsk companions have lost what only the day before they knew so well. But Yurovsky penetrates this crude cunning: they are hoping he will get tired and leave. They want to be left alone with the bodies; they are dying to get a look at the "special corsets."

Yurovsky waits patiently. They have to find the mine. And once again the awful procession sets out.

Riding ahead is Ermakov's loyal assistant, one of the commanders of the Ermakov boys, the Kronstadt sailor Vaganov. The entire area is utterly remote and hidden from the Koptyaki road by tall forest. Here the procession of bodies encounters some Koptyaki peasants, whom Vaganov drives back. The sun is already rising when they ride up to the first turn off the road to the nameless mine Ermakov and Yurovsky have chosen. Here the truck breaks down.

Yurovsky: "Since the vehicle got stuck between two trees, it was abandoned and the procession continued on in the droshkies, the bodies covered with a cloth. They had gone sixteen and a half versts [11 miles] from Ekaterinburg and stopped one and a half versts [1 mile] from Koptyaki. This was at six or seven in the morning."

The truck breaks down at a pit that was once used for sorting ore and that forces the road very close to some large trees; Lyukhanov miscalculates and wrecks the truck.

They are two hundred paces from the mine. While some Red Army soldiers are dragging the truck out, others begin fashioning stretchers from young pines and pieces of the tarpaulin that covers the bodies. (The White Guard inquiry discovered planed, broken off branches along the road.)

Now the bodies move toward the mine—on carts and on stretchers.

Yurovsky: "In the forest we found an abandoned prospector's mine (once mined for gold) three and a half arshins [8 feet] deep. There was an arshin of water in the mine shaft."

Near the mine the bodies are laid out on the clayey ground, a level area right by the mine.

Yurovsky: "The commandant ordered the bodies undressed and a fire built so that everything could be burned. Riders were posted all around in order to drive away anyone who might come by. When they began undressing one of the girls, they saw a corset torn in place by bullets—and through the opening they saw diamonds. The spectators had obviously had their hearts set on. . . . The com[mandant] immediately decided to dismiss the entire group, keeping only a few sentries from the guard and five from the detachment. The rest dispersed."

Next to the mine, on the clayey, rain-drenched ground, lies the tsar's family as well as their servants and Dr. Botkin. The sun is already up when the bodies are undressed and the corsets with the sewn-in diamonds that had saved the unlucky girls for so long are removed from the grand duchesses. And the pearl belt, which had not saved the empress.

Yurovsky: "The detachment started undressing and burning them. A. F. turned out to be wearing an entire pearl belt made from several necklaces sewn into linen. The diamonds were immediately recorded, about half a pood [18 pounds] were collected."

The clothing is burned right there on the fire. The naked corpses lie on the naked earth by the mine. The girls' corset laces have made running knots along their bare bodies.

Yurovsky: "Each of the girls turned out to be wearing a picture of Rasputin around her neck with the text of his prayer sewn into an amulet. The 'holy man' was with them even after death."

From the report of Kolchak's Ministry of Justice:
"November 27, 1919, from N. Mirolyubov, Procurator of the Kazan Palace of Justice, regarding December 12, 1918, Omsk:
" 'According to Kukhtenkov's testimony, after his military discharge he took a position as deputy leader of a workers' club. On July 18–19, at about four in the morning, the chairman of the Upper Isetsk Executive Committee Soviet, Sergei Malyshkin, Military Commissar Ermakov, and prominent members of the party, Bolsheviks Alexander Kostousov, Vasily Levatnykh, Nikolai Partin, and Sergei Krivtsov, arrived at the club.
" 'At the club the abovementioned individuals met secretly. . . . Krivtsov asked the questions, and Levatnykh and Partin gave the answers. Levatnykh said: 'When we arrived they were still warm. I felt the tsaritsa myself and she was warm. . . . Now it was no sin to die because I had felt the tsaritsa.' [In the document the last sentence was crossed out in ink.] Then came the questions: How were the slain dressed, and were they pretty? . . . About their clothing Partin said that they were in civilian dress, that various jewels had been sewn into their clothing, and that none of them were beautiful: 'There was no beauty to see in the dead.' ' "

Finally the bodies are covered with the tarpaulin. After much discussion it is decided to burn the clothing and throw the bodies to the bottom of the nameless mine.

Yurovsky: "Once we had gathered together everything of value into sacks, everything else we found on the bodies was burned and the bodies themselves lowered into the mine shaft. In the process some of the valuables (someone's brooch, Botkin's false teeth) were dropped."

A great many diamonds and pearls are gathered, so they do not worry about the small change. They are tired.

Yurovsky: "It was all buried at Alapaevsk in the cellar of one of the little buildings. In 1919 it was dug up and taken to Moscow."

The historic moment has passed. Life begins anew.

He has a breakfast of eggs on a tree stump. Alexei's eggs. After Yurovsky eats, it occurs to him to toss in a few grenades.

Yurovsky: "In my attempt to collapse the mine shaft with the help of hand grenades, evidently the bodies were damaged and a few parts torn off—that is how the commandant explains the Whites (who later discovered the mine) finding there a detached finger, etc."

After which Ermakov and his comrades go to Upper Isetsk and Yurovsky makes sure the jewels get off to Alapaevsk, where that night Ella and her companions in captivity are to be "liquidated."

There, in a hiding place, in the cellar of an anonymous Alapaevsk house, all the jewels taken from the "Ural Romanovs" are collected.

Yurovsky: "After completing the operation and leaving a guard there, at about ten or eleven in the morning (of July 17 now), the commandant took his report to the Ural Executive Committee, where he found Safarov and Beloborodov. The commandant told them what had been found and expressed regret that he had not been allowed to conduct a search of the Romanovs sooner."

In fact, at the Soviet Yurovsky was dealt a cruel blow, which he concealed in his Note.

The son of Chekist Medvedev:

"In the morning my father went to the bazaar and heard from the local merchants a detailed account of where and how the bodies of the tsar's family had been hidden. That is the real reason why the bodies were buried a second time."

Ermakov's lads could not hold their tongues. Now they had to start all over. Find a new place, think of where to hide the bodies. They had run out of time—the Whites were on the threshold.

Yurovsky: "The commandant found out from Chutskaev (the chairman of the Municipal Executive Committee) that there were some very deep mines suitable for burying the Romanovs located at verst 9 along the Moscow highway. . . . The commandant started out but had only gotten partway when his car broke down. He reached the mines on foot. He did indeed find three very deep mines filled with water, where he decided to drown the bodies, having first attached stones to them. Since there were watchmen around who made awkward witnesses, it was decided that along with the truck carrying the bodies a car would come with Chekists, who on the pretext of a search would arrest all the spectators. The commandant had to drive back on a pair of horses he happened to appropriate en route. In the event the plan with the mines did not work out, it was decided to burn the bodies and bury them in the clayey, water-filled pits, after first taking the precaution of disfiguring them beyond the point of identification with sulfuric acid.

"When they finally got back to town it was nearly eight in the evening on July 17, and they began getting together everything they needed—kerosene, sulfuric acid. Driverless carts and horses were taken from the prison. . . . They did not set out until 12:30 on the night of July 17–18. To isolate the mines (one a prospector's mine) for the duration of the operation, an announcement was made in Koptyaki that Czechs were hiding in the woods and the forest was going to be searched, so no one should go there for any reason. It was decreed that anyone who broke through the cordoned area would be shot on the spot."

Steal a pair of horses from a peasant they happen to run into, shoot an inhabitant who accidentally sets foot on the protected zone —all in the name of the shining future.

THE HIDDEN GRAVE

At midnight, the commandant returned to the original nameless mine.

The son of Chekist Medvedev:

"They lit the mine shaft with torches. Vaganov the sailor climbed down into the mine shaft and stood below in the darkness in the icy water, which was up to his chest. A rope was lowered. He tied the bodies to it and sent them up."

Once again the commandant saw the tsar's entire family in torchlight. At the same time in Alapaevsk they were killing Ella and the other Ural Romanovs.

Yurovsky: "Meanwhile it was growing light. It occurred to me to bury some of the bodies right there by the mine. We started digging a pit and had almost finished when a peasant Ermakov knew rode up and explained that he could see the hole. We had to abandon that idea and decided to take the bodies to the deep mines."

The bodies set off once again, on carts at first and then in the truck. With them went Yurovsky. For three whole days he had been living alongside these corpses, "evacuating them to a safe place."

Yurovsky: "Since the carts proved unstable and were falling apart, the commandant went to town for some vehicles—one truck and two cars for the Chekists. We managed to get on our way only at eight in the evening; we crossed the railroad tracks about half a verst away and moved the bodies onto the truck. We had a hard time, planking over treacherous spots with boards, and still getting stuck several times. At about four-thirty on the morning of July 19 the vehicle got permanently stuck. Since we weren't going to get as far as the mines, all we could do was either bury them or burn them. . . . One comrade, whose last name the commandant has forgotten, promised to take the latter upon himself, but he left without keeping his promise. We wanted to burn A[lexei] and A[lexandra] F[eodorovna], but by mistake instead of her we burned the lady-in-waiting and Alexei. They buried the remains right there under the fire and then scattered the fires in order to cover up completely any trace of digging. Meanwhile a common grave was dug for the rest. At about seven in the morning a pit two and a half arshins [6 feet] deep and three and a half arshins [8 feet] square was ready. The bodies were put in the hole and the faces and all the bodies generally doused with sulfuric acid, both so they couldn't be recognized and to prevent any stink from them rotting [it was not a deep hole]. We scattered it with dirt and lime, put boards on top, and rode over it several times—no trace of the hole remained. The secret was kept— the Whites did not find this burial site."

At the end of his Note, Yurovsky added a notation indicating the precise location of that secret grave:

"Koptyaki, 18 v[ersts] [12 miles] from Ekaterinburg to the north- west. The railroad tracks pass 9 versts between Koptyaki and the

Upper Isetsk factory. From where the railroad tracks cross they are buried about 100 sazh[ens] [700 feet] in the direction of the Isetsk factory."

$\mathcal{D}$ID THIS GRAVE EXIST?

The guest chuckled. "You tell the burial story the way Yurovsky described it in his Note. But after all, there was one other equally important witness, my friend Peter Zakharovich [Ermakov]. After all, he too described how the burial came about. So *two* descriptions exist. True, in the 1950s yet a third description by a witness appeared in the West."

"You're talking about Iogann Meyer's pamphlet?"

"Absolutely correct. But that's a fake, full of mythical people who never existed. . . . So Peter Zakharovich's manuscript is one of two existing authentic documents attributable to the pen of actual participants. Moreover, not just participants, but the men in charge of that terrible burial, if you can call the horror they undertook a burial."

After this tirade my guest again opened his briefcase and gave me the conclusion to Ermakov's memoirs laboriously copied out by hand:

"When this operation was over, the vehicle with the bodies set out for the forest through Upper Isetsk in the direction of the Koptyaki road, where I had chosen a site for burying the bodies.

"I had considered in advance, however, the fact that we shouldn't dig, for I was not alone, but had comrades with me. Generally speaking, I could scarcely entrust anyone with this matter, especially since I had told everyone beforehand that I had decided to burn them, for which I had gotten together sulfuric acid and kerosene; I had anticipated everything. Without tipping anyone off, I said: 'Let's drop them into the mine shaft,' and that was what we decided. Then I ordered them all undressed, so we could burn the clothes, which was done. When they started taking their dresses off, medallions with a picture of Rasputin inserted were found on 'herself' [Alexandra Feodorovna] and the daughters. Further under their dresses, next to their bodies, were specially altered double corsets inside the padding in which precious stones had been placed and stitched in. This was for 'herself' and her four daughters. All this was handed over piece by piece to Yurovsky, the Ural Soviet member. I really wasn't interested in what was there right then for I had no time. The clothing was burned then and there. The bodies were carried about 50 meters and dropped down a mine shaft. It wasn't deep, about 6 sazhens [14 yards], for I know all those mines well. So we would be able to pull them out for further operations with them. All this I did in order to hide my tracks from any extra comrades of mine present. When all this was over it was already full dawn, about four o'clock in the morning [July 17]. This place was located about 3 versts [2 miles] off the road.

"When everyone was gone, I remained in the forest, which no one knew. On the night of July 17–18, I went to the forest again, brought a rope, and was lowered into the mine. I began tying up each one individually (the bodies, that is), and two men pulled them out (the bodies). When they were all out I ordered them put on a two-wheeled cart, carried them away from the mine, unloaded them onto three stacks of firewood, doused them with kerosene, and then themselves (the bodies, that is) with sulfuric acid. The bodies burned to ash, which was buried. All this took place at twelve o'clock on the night of July 17–18, 1918. After all of which I reported on July 18. Now I am finished with everything. October 29, 1947. Ermakov."

I asked him: "May I publish this?"

My guest shrugged his shoulders. "I don't care, I'm old. Soon, very soon, I'll be meeting up with *them*. So that before I go I leave you all this with pleasure." (Soon after, I published in *Ogonyok* these memoirs of Ermakov, which were being kept in secret storage.) "But you've got a dangerous topic there—it will eat up your life the way it did mine. But I'm disappointed in your question. In your place I would be interested in something completely different. Discounting Peter Zakharovich's ordinary boastfulness and his habit of ascribing to himself everything others did, consider the most important point: according to Ermakov there was no second burial—the bodies were burned not far from Koptyaki. He has a completely different reading from Yurovsky, moreover on an important fact. And here Ermakov repeats what Sokolov arrived at: the graves do not exist; the bodies of the family vanished in the flames of the fire. Much as I regretted it, I thought that maybe because Peter Zakharovich was drunk they simply didn't take him to the second burial. No, Yurovsky, recounting the events of July 18, wrote very clearly in his Note: 'A peasant Ermakov knew rode up to him.' So Ermakov was there, and he saw it through to the end. So what's going on? That is why I kept questioning him and he in reply kept repeating, 'We burned the bodies!'

"That is why I met with a *third man*."

CHARON

"In 1943, when I saw him for the first time, the third man was living in Perm [then Molotov]. That's what I called him, 'Comrade Charon.' But he didn't laugh. Even when I explained to him that Charon ferried the Greeks to the kingdom of death. He *never* laughed and *never* talked on the topic of interest to us. I saw him in 1953, not long before his death. A dried-out old man, short, with a narrow, predatory nose and sparse hair, our Charon went around wearing pathetic ear flaps and a threadbare winter coat. The man who had driven the truck carrying the tsarist bodies lived in a tiny room in a horrible shack. And behind a curtain in the same little room lived his youngest son with his wife. This shack was located on Twenty-fifth Anniversary of October Street. That was where he died. This old Bolshevik died in a dirty barracks on a street named after his own revolution.

"Have you figured out who I'm going to tell you about? Sergei Ivanovich Lyukhanov, the *third witness* to that terrible trip. His biography is most curious. Unlike all the regicides, he never mentioned his participation in the great proletarian mission of regicide and never fought for any privileges. Moreover, his son told me that he never ever mentioned that he had been in Ekaterinburg in 1918. All in all, for all our meetings, he never did say a word about it. Oh, it was very hard to talk with this taciturn man. I remember I invited him to a restaurant. He sat the whole evening in silence, then picked up the check, which I paid, and said, 'Too bad, I could live on this for an entire month.' And he left. Everything I learned about him I learned from his youngest son, whose name was Alexei, like the heir, and who did tell me about his papa. It turns out, having lived to age eighty, he was not even receiving a pension—his son explained that Lyukhanov apparently didn't realize that he was entitled to one. Odd? A Bolshevik since 1906 didn't know that in the country of victorious socialism old men receive pensions? A great deal about his life was odd. For example, those constant moves from town to town. Immediately after the execution he quit Ekaterinburg with the retreating Bolsheviks, but after the return of Soviet power to Ekaterinburg Lyukhanov did not go back there but went to Osa—which he soon quit as well. There followed frequent moves, as if he were dashing about the Urals, forever changing places. No sooner did he get used to a place then look out, he refused a good position and off he went! It was as if he were afraid of something. But the most interesting part was his relationship with his wife, Avgusta.

"The schoolteacher Avgusta was the sister of the first Ipatiev house commandant, Avdeyev. In 1918, she joined the ruling powers. By the way, in the cemetery she lies under a star rather than a cross —one of the first in the Ekaterinburg cemetery. Soon after the execution, this "ideological atheist" left Lyukhanov and returned to Ekaterinburg, where she held a party position administering all the children's homes and died from typhus in 1924. Before her death she forgave her husband, her son Alexei told me.

"So, our Charon did something that made her leave him with four children! And for which she had to forgive him before her death. (We can exclude any other romantic entanglement for him at the time—he did not remarry until two years later.) No, something else was going on here, something the 'ideological' sister of the former Ipatiev house commandant could not brook. Evidently fearing what he had done—Lyukhanov dashed around the country and later hid himself away so well that he was even afraid to apply for a pension. I saw a 1918 photograph of him—a gentleman! And his last —a poor, pathetic old man."

THE SECRET

"Enough omissions!" My guest chuckled. "I will tell you what—in my opinion, I emphasize—in my opinion happened.

"This could have happened only in one place, where the truck drove up to railway booth 184, where the watchwoman was sleeping. It drove up and got stuck. Somewhere not far from this booth (as Yurovsky wrote) they were supposed to be met by a picket of Ermakov's men. By this time Ermakov must have passed out drunk —worn out from the bumpy road. Yurovsky woke him up, and the two men went off to look for Ermakov's detachment. At this point the driver Lyukhanov went to the booth to wake the watchwoman and ask for water for his overheated engine.

"The stranded truck stayed where it was, as did the Red Guards accompanying it. How many were there? Three or four, probably. And the half gloom of dawn. Can you picture the situation? The Whites were about to take the town. Soviet power, it seemed, would be done and gone. The officers would be hanged for the tsar's family. So it was no simple matter for them to have gone in the truck. After all, the tsar's slain family was lying under the tarpaulin. While

Ermakov was passed out, they must have heard . . . those moans from under the tarpaulin. And when the dazed Ermakov went off into the woods with Yurovsky to look for his men and Lyukhanov went to wake the watchwoman—that is when it could have happened.

"Here was a chance for the Red Guards left with the truck. Participation in this terrible affair had condemned them to death, but here—to save some of the family! Had they already agreed on this on the way, when they heard the moans? Or did they understand each other without saying anything? How did they drag the *two* who had not been killed from the truck? How did they carry them off into the forest, for there was dense forest all around? Did Lyukhanov see this from the window of the booth? Or did he not, continuing to quarrel with the watchwoman? All this I can only guess. As I can the rest. Did those Red Guards run away immediately? Probably not. That would be suspicious. More likely they returned to the truck and started laying boards over the swampy spot. Then Ermakov and Yurovsky appeared: they had found Ermakov's men.

"What happened to the Red Guards later? Did they manage to escape on the way to the mines? Or return to the forest to the two they had rescued? Did the rescued pair die immediately—there in the forest? Or did someone indeed manage to survive—and were those stars that the woman who called herself Anastasia saw when she came to in the cart the stars of that impossible night? What did Yurovsky tell Ermakov when, as the bodies were being transferred from the truck to the carts, he discovered he was missing two corpses? And Ermakov sobering up instantly, horrified! There was no time, though, to search for the two vanished corpses. The Whites were about to enter the town. They had to finish what they were doing—and destroy the remaining bodies. And Lyukhanov? He was in the cab; he seemed not to have seen anything. He was beside the point. And Ermakov's men were merrily drunk—so naturally did not notice anything. Almost all of them were dismissed immediately, Yurovsky wrote. Only the most loyal remained. Such was the shared secret of the two pretenders to the 'honor of the execution.' The two men concealed the fact that two bodies were lacking. But because he was missing two bodies Yurovsky could not make use of the camera—after all, he must have dreamed of taking a picture of the 'liquidation'!"

"A picture?!"

"Why not? He was a photographer. How could he not want to record this supreme historic moment? It was the moment he had lived for, you might say. Especially since he had lying in the commandant's room the confiscated camera belonging to Alexandra Feodorovna! The executed tsar's family photographed with the tsaritsa's camera. [Was that really the end of the photo-execution?]"

"Why do you keep talking about *two?*"

"Read carefully the Yurovsky Note you published. Yurovsky wrote that three of the daughters were wearing 'diamond corsets.' But what about the fourth? Why wasn't the fourth?" He laughed. "There weren't enough? Or the story with Alexei? After all, they tried to shoot him at two paces. And couldn't. It's unlikely even a very nervous Chekist like Nikulin could fail to hit him at two paces. That meant Alexei was wearing a 'diamond shield'—and it saved him. He was 'armored' as well. That was the reason for his 'strange vitality.' Yurovsky didn't write anything about this, though. Why? Because Alexei was not undressed! If they had undressed him, they would probably have found Rasputin's amulet on him, too! The tsaritsa could not have left her son without an amulet of his savior. But Yurovsky wrote only about amulets on the tsar's daughters. That means they didn't undress him for sure. Why? Maybe they feared God? Funny, eh? Then why?

"Here's your answer—it's at the end of Yurovsky's Note. They only burned two of them: Alexei and someone of the female sex. Why two? Why not burn the rest? Or: if they didn't burn the rest, then why did they burn the *two?* Why didn't they burn Nicholas? After all, wasn't he much more important?" He laughed. "This is why: they were missing *two* corpses: a boy and a young woman. They were also missing the diamonds on them. That's why Yurovsky thought of writing that they'd burned two of them—the boy and a female. So, who was that female? Demidova, as Yurovsky writes? Couldn't they have gotten them mixed up in the insanity of that night? Perhaps that rescued woman was not Demidova, and the stars that the woman who later called herself Anastasia saw when she woke up in the cart were the stars of that impossible night.

Anastasia? In any event, after Anastasia's appearance in Berlin, Ermakov's friend and drinking companion, the Chekist Grigory Sukhorukov, who also participated in the burial, compiled some extremely noteworthy affidavits, which are now kept in the local Party archive. The affidavits repeat the version about burning *two* bodies, but these actually specify a new female name: Alexei and . . .

Anastasia! Not Demidova, as Yurovsky asserted, but Anastasia. Realizing that some explanation would have to be provided for why they burned only those two, Sukhorukov invented a very clumsy explanation: "So no one would guess from the number of remaining corpses that this was the tsar's family"!

Two may have been saved, then. And Lyukhanov, of course, saw two of them being taken off the truck. And he hung back, bickering with the watchwoman, so there would be time to remove them. After all, he had a younger son named Alexei, too. The son said that Lyukhanov liked to say: 'God can do anything.' Evidently, though, he later told his wife everything. He kept silent for a long time, but he couldn't hold back—he told her. Commandant Avdeyev's sister could not understand him, though! She was a person of ideas. Like Yurovsky, like all of them. The most she could do was not inform on the father of her four children. But live with him—that she couldn't do. So he lost his ideological Avgusta. However, the suffering in her dying hour evidently pried something half-open for her. And she forgave him."

We were silent for a while.

I said: "But in the White Guard investigation, someone told a story from one of Ermakov's men that he saw Alexei's body at the mine."

"Exactly: someone told a story from someone else. . . ."

"By the way, Yurovsky was alarmed too; evidently the rumors about Anastasia moved him to take action as well. In 1920, when this mysterious, 'miraculously saved' woman appeared in Berlin, he gave the historian Pokrovsky his Note, the idea behind which was 'They all died.'"

"Can it really be that despite all your clearly major opportunities, you never attempted to open the grave? After all, you knew where it was, didn't you?"

He chuckled, then said, "Whether I tried to or not—it's a horrible place, believe me. How that grave draws you all! In 1928 Mayakovsky came to Sverdlovsk and immediately wanted to see the grave of the tsar and his family. The chairman of the Ural Soviet at the time was a certain Paramonov. Later, of course, he was repressed, but—a rare case—not executed. After his rehabilitation Paramonov came back alive. He used to tell me how they took Mayakovsky to the place 'where the family's bodies were burned'—which was how Paramonov referred to the 'grave.' This was his favorite story—how he searched at the 'burning place' for 'notches left in a birch.' That day, when he took Mayakovsky, there was a hard frost and the trees were hoary, and he searched for a long time but didn't find any notch.

As for the notches in the birches and Paramonov, all of it was confirmed later in a letter I received.

From a letter of literary scholar Kirill Sherstok in Frunze:

"When I was working on my thesis about Mayakovsky, Paramonov told me how Mayakovsky visited him twice and how they went to the last Russian emperor's final refuge. . . . Paramonov said that in the poem 'The Emperor'—about the tsar's grave—Mayakovsky made a mistake, asserting that the emperor had been buried 'under a cedar.' He was buried between three birches. I asked, 'And where is this place?' He answered that there were two men left who knew it: he, Paramonov, and one more man, whom he did not name. I recalled Paramonov saying, 'No one must know this,' and adding, 'so that there are no pilgrimages.'"

As he was leaving, my guest said: "This whole story is like a polemic with Dostoevsky. Starting with the question to Alyosha Karamazov: 'If to erect the edifice of a happy mankind it were necessary to torture just one small child, would you agree to base this edifice on his tear?' One Alyosha was asked this question and with the help of another slain Alyosha [Alexei] they answered." He fell silent. "One thing, though, is clear: he will come back to us."

I asked him to repeat that.

"I mean the sovereign emperor. It's a banal story, though. Killing the family, those idiots preempted his return. 'In my end is my beginning'—those words were once embroidered by his relative Mary Stuart. By the way, after this relative had her head cut off and her headless body was taken away, her wide dress rustled, and a tiny little dog jumped from it, howling. It was exactly that kind of little dog—the same breed—that a few centuries later turned up hidden—also during a murder—in the sleeve of Mary Stuart's descendant—a grand duchess. Everything comes back, everything."

"In my end is my beginning." A sacrifice. Did the last emperor really understand that?

———

Of course, I tried to believe my guest's story. In Perm I was able to find Sergei Lyukhanov's aged son—that same Alexei, the heir's namesake.

In the cramped, pitiful little room where the driver of the terrible truck had lived and died I wrote down from Alexei's words his father's biography:

"My father, Sergei Ivanovich Lyukhanov, was born in 1875, in Chelyabinsk District, in a peasant family. A fourth-grade education. Beginning in 1894 worked in the Stepanov brothers' mill. In 1900 moved to Chelyabinsk, where he worked until 1916 for the Pokrovsky Brothers Company running an electric telephone station. He worked too as the Pokrovskys' personal driver and would go to Petersburg with them. In 1899 he married Avgusta Dmitrievna Avdeyeva (she was four years younger than he, had finished grammar school, and worked as a teacher).

"In 1900 their oldest son Valentin was born, who served with his father in the Ipatiev house guard. Then came Vladimir, myself (in 1910), and a daughter Antonina. In 1907 he joined the Bolshevik Party. In the summer of 1916 he got a job in the Zlokazov brothers' factory as a machinist. Later Avgusta's brother, Alexander Avdeyev, the future commandant of the Ipatiev house, came there from Chelyabinsk. Lyukhanov set him up at the factory as machinist's assistant and did all his work, since Avdeyev didn't know how to do anything.

"My father never reminisced or talked about the Ekaterinburg period of his life.

"After the surrender of Ekaterinburg in 1918, the Lyukhanovs went to Osa in Perm District, where my father got a job at a lumber mill.

"Soon after that he and my mother separated over something. In 1921 she returned to Ekaterinburg with all the children and worked there as the director of children's homes. On March 23, 1924, she died of typhus. Dying, she asked Serzh (as she called father) to be told that she had been wrong. Her oldest son did not carry out her request and only shortly before his death did my father learn from me about my mother's last words. What I said greatly agitated him, and he was very upset not to find about it until the end of his life.

"Avgusta Dmitrievna is buried in Sverdlovsk in the Mikhailov Cemetery. After her death I was given up to a children's home, and my uncle—Avdeyev—took my sister Antonina to Moscow. From 1918 to 1926 my father worked in Osa, where he was in charge of an electric station. In 1923 he married a second time to a German, a German language teacher, Galina Karlovna (who died in 1928). Between 1926 and 1939 my father moved many times—he had jobs in various towns in the Urals—but wherever he worked he was a mechanic. Finally, in 1939, he reached Perm. After the war and up until 1952 he worked as a lathe operator in an infectious hospital there. He worked hard and long and was always fixing all sorts of household utensils for the hospital workers. (He never took more than a ruble for his work.) He worked until he was eighty, and he never suspected he was entitled to a pension. He was very taciturn, he spoke rarely. Beginning in 1944 he lived with me and my second wife in our room at 30 Twenty-fifth of October Street. He died in 1954 and is buried in an old cemetery in Perm."

All this was nearly a word-for-word repetition of what my guest had already told me. When I asked about my guest, Lyukhanov's son replied vaguely: "I think someone did come and meet with Father. . . . I think he was here again after my father died, too." That was all eighty-year-old Alexei could tell me. In parting, Alexei Lyukhanov gave me all his father's remaining documents. Among them was a "Certificate" issued to Sergei Lyukhanov by the Pokrovsky Brothers Company in 1899, decorated with a tsarist medal and a profile of the man whose body he drove in his truck. And a photograph. One of the last. In which the former truck driver is a pathetic little old man.

I never saw my guest again, but I often think of him. And about what he told me. It was all too entertaining. As a rule, the truth is very boring.

Although . . . although at times I think my guest knew a lot more than he told me. And then I recall Shakespeare: "There are more things in heaven and earth, Horatio, than are dreamt of in your philosophy" (Hamlet).

In any event, I thought of my strange guest again when I received this letter from a psychiatrist, Dr. D. Kaufman of Petrozavodsk:

"This will be about a man who for a time was in treatment in a psychiatric hospital in Petrozavodsk, where I worked on staff from September 1946 to October 1949, after graduating from the Second Leningrad Medical Institute, now a medical hygiene institute.

". . . Our patient load consisted of both civilians and prisoners, whom we were sent during those years for treatment or for legal-psychiatric examination.

". . . In 1947 or 1948 in the wintertime another prisoner came to us as a patient. He was suffering from severe psychosis of the type called hysterical psychogenic reaction. His mind was not clear, he was disoriented, he did not understand where he was. . . . He waved his arms about and tried to run away. . . . Amid incoherent utterances in a mass of other expressive exclamations the name 'Beloborodov' flashed by two or three times. At first we paid no attention to it, since it didn't mean anything to us. From his accompanying documents . . . we found out he had been in the camps for a long time and that his psychosis had developed suddenly, when he had attempted to defend a woman (prisoner) from being beaten by a guard. He was tied up and, naturally, 'worked over.' Although as far as I recall no visible bodily injuries were noted when he entered the hospital. His documents indicated his date of birth as 1904; as for his first and last names, I can't remember them exactly. The variations I recall are the following. Semyon Grigorievich Filippov, or Filipp Grigorievich Semyonov. After one to three days, as usually happens in these cases, the manifestation of severe psychosis had disappeared completely. The patient became calm, in full contact. Clear awareness and proper behavior were maintained from then on for his entire stay at the hospital. His appearance, as far as I can say, was like this: a rather tall man, somewhat stout, sloping shoulders, slightly round-shouldered, and so on. A long, pale face, blue or gray, slightly bulging eyes, a high forehead receding into a balding head, the remaining hair chestnut with gray. . . ."

(After this she talked about how the patient was sincere with her.)

". . . So, it became known to us that he was the heir to the crown, that during the hasty execution in Ekaterinburg his father had hugged and pressed his face to him so that he wouldn't see the rifle barrels aimed at him. In my opinion, he had not even realized that something terrible was going on since the commands to fire were uttered unexpectedly, and he didn't hear the sentence read. All he remembered was the name Beloborodov. . . . Shots rang out, he was wounded in the buttocks, he lost consciousness, and he collapsed on a common heap of bodies. When he woke up, he found he had been saved, someone had dragged him out of the cellar, carried him out, and ministered to him for a long time."

Then followed the story of his further life and the stupidities that led him to the camp. But the most interesting part came at the end of this long letter.

"Gradually we began to look at him with other eyes. The persistent hematuria he suffered from found an explanation. The heir had had hemophilia. On the patient's buttocks was an old cross-shaped scar. . . . Finally we realized who the patient's appearance reminded us of—the famous portraits of Nicholas, not only Nicholas I but Nicholas II . . . Dressed in a quilted jacket and striped pajama trousers over felt boots instead of a hussar's uniform.

". . . At that time consultants used to come to us from Leningrad for two or three months at a time. . . . Professor S. I. Gendelevich was consulting with us then. The best psychiatric practitioner I ever met. Naturally, we showed him our patient. . . . For two or three hours he 'pursued' him with questions we could not have asked, since we were not conversant, but it turned out he was. So, for example, the consultant knew the layout and use of every room in the Winter Palace and the country residences in the early part of the century. He knew the names and titles of all the members of the tsar's family and the branched network of the dynasty, all the court positions, . . . and so on. The consultant also knew the accepted protocol for all the court ceremonies and rituals as well as the dates of the various name days in the tsar's family and other ceremonies marked in the Romanov family circle. To all these questions the patient responded utterly accurately and without the slightest thought. For him it was as elementary as a primer. . . . From a few answers it was clear that he possessed wider knowledge in this sphere. . . . His behavior was as always: calm and dignified. Then the consultant asked the women to leave and he examined the patient below the waist, in front and in back. When we walked in (the patient had been dismissed) the consultant was blatantly dismayed. It turned out that the patient had a cryptorchidism (one testicle had not descended), which the consultant knew had been noted in the dead heir Alexei. We had not known that. . . .

". . . The consultant explained the situation to us: there was a dilemma and we needed to make a joint decision—either put a diagnosis of 'paranoia' in a stage of good remission with the possibility of employing the patient in his former occupations at his place of confinement, or consider the case unresolved and in need of additional observation in the hospital. In that case, however, we would be obliged to motivate our decision carefully for the organs of procuratorial oversight, which would inevitably send a special investigator from Moscow. . . . Having weighed these possibilities, we considered it to the patient's good to give him a definite diagnosis of paranoia, of which we were not entirely certain, and return him to camp. . . . The patient agreed with our decision about returning to camp (naturally he was not told his diagnosis) and we parted friends."

Dr. Kaufman's letter was so eloquent that I wondered whether I wasn't a victim of mystification. I believed her.

Here is a letter from the deputy chief physician of Psychiatric Hospital Number 1 in the Karelian ASSR, V. E. Kiviniemi, who verified this patient's medical history, which is kept in the hospital archives:

"In my hands is medical history no. 64 for F. G. Semyonov, born 1904, admitted to psychiatric hospital January 14, 1949. Noted in red pencil 'prisoner.' . . . Released from the hospital April 22, 1949, to ITK [corrective labor camp] No. 1 (there is the signature of the convoy head, Mikheyev).

"Semyonov was admitted to the hospital from the ITK clinic. The doctor's order . . . describes the patient's acute psychotic condition and indicates that Semyonov kept 'cursing someone named Beloborodov.' Entered the psychiatric hospital in a weakened physical condition, but without acute signs of psychosis. . . . From the moment he entered was polite, sociable, behaved with dignity and modesty, neat. A doctor in the medical history notes that in conversation he did not conceal his origins. 'His manners, tone, and conviction speak to the fact that he was familiar with the life of high society before 1917.' F. G. Semyonov told how he was tutored at home, that he was the son of the former tsar, that he had been rescued during the time when the family perished, was taken to Leningrad, where he lived for a certain period of time, served in the Red Army as a cavalryman, studied at an economics institute (evidently in Baku), after graduating worked as an economist in Central Asia, was married, his wife's name was Asya, and then said that Beloborodov knew his secret and was blackmailing him. . . . In February 1949 was examined by a psychiatrist from Leningrad, Gendelevich, to whom Semyonov declared that he had nothing to gain from appropriating someone else's name, that he was not expecting any privileges, since he understood that various anti-Soviet elements might gather around his name and so as not to cause any trouble he was always prepared to leave this life. In April 1949 Semyonov underwent a forensic psychiatric examination and was declared emotionally ill and in need of placement in an Internal Affairs Ministry psychiatric hospital. This last must be regarded as a humanitarian act toward Semyonov for that time, since there is a difference between a camp and a hospital. Semyonov himself regarded it positively."

Appended to this missive was the strange patient's letter to his wife Asya.

A short while later I received a call from an old man, a former prisoner, who turned out to have been in the camps with the mysterious Semyonov—all the prisoners called him "the tsar's son," and they all believed it absolutely.

At my request, the Central State Archive of the October Revolution made a copy of several pages of Alexei's 1916 diary kept there. I took it, along with the letter the strange patient sent his wife Asya from the hospital in 1949, to the Institute of Criminology. They tried to help, but . . . but the documents proved incomparable. The letter to Asya, written in an elegant, refined hand. And the diary of thirteen-year-old Alexei, with his uneven scribbles. They were unable to say yes or no.

EPILOGUE:
PARTICIPANTS
IN THE
EXECUTION
(FATES)

"Vengeance is mine, I will repay."
ROMANS 12:19

THE "SPY"

On the eve of the execution in the Ipatiev house, the chairman of the Ural Cheka, F. N. Lukoyanov, suddenly and unexpectedly left for Perm—to transfer the Cheka archives. The chief of the entire Ural Cheka, the man in charge of the "special mission," was not present when his mission was carried out! Was he not able to conquer his feelings? Was he not able to be there?

In any event, he remained in Perm during the execution.

Soon after, in 1919, Feodor Lukoyanov suffered a severe nervous breakdown, which afflicted him for the rest of his life.

The former chairman of the Ural Cheka died in 1947—on the eve of the thirtieth anniversary of the Ipatiev night. He did not survive the anniversary. He is buried in his hometown of Perm.

YUROVSKY

In the 1930s, the most prominent party members were sent to the camps, to death, one after another. In 1935 it was their families' turn. Beautiful Rimma Yurovskaya, the Komsomol favorite, was arrested and sent to a camp. Yurovsky rushed to Goloshchekin for help, but Goloshchekin could not help him.

Now Yurovsky had to prove that the party was his family. And if the party needed his daughter. . . .

As before, he continued to meet in Medvedev's apartment and reminisce. About the same old thing. The execution. There was nothing else in their lives. They reminisced prosaically about the Apocalypse over a cup of tea. And they discussed who really did fire first. Yurovsky had precedence. Precedence—for the realization of his dream. He was a Jew. Once the monarchists got the ball rolling, the tsar's murder was declared an act of Jewish revenge.

The son of Chekist Medvedev:

"Once Yurovsky arrived triumphant—he had been brought a book that had come out in the West where it was written in black and white that it was he, Yurovsky, who killed Nicholas. He was happy—he had left his mark in history."

BELOBORODOV

Their old friend Sasha Beloborodov, then the people's commissar for internal affairs, never came to these gatherings. Like Yurovsky's daughter Rimma, Beloborodov had supported Trotsky. He had been excluded from the party, repented, and reformed. And he had been restored.

From a letter of Natalia Bialer:

"In the 1930s our family lived in the embassy in Paris. My father Akim Yakovlevich Bialer was secretary to the military attaché. In 1935 my father brought home a man whom he introduced as Nikolai Alexeyevich Sokolov. Was that his real name? I don't know. People did not always come from the USSR under their own name. Why have I remembered him? After all, I saw quite a few people at the embassy and in our house who were famous in their day. Some came with their suites, like Chkalov [a famous Soviet pilot], Tukhachevsky and Yakir [first marshals of the Soviet army]. . . . He had been sent to Paris personally by Voroshilov [head of the army]. To see an oncologist whose name I think was Professor Roccard. My father knew him. Roccard made a diagnosis—throat cancer—and refused to treat him. When Voroshilov was informed of this, he ordered that the man be given a course of treatment anyway. Ambassador V. P. Potemkin himself went to see Roccard, after which a course of treatment was prescribed, including strained, semiliquid food—five times a day. It was my mother who cooked that food for Sokolov. My mother and I drove Sokolov to his treatments, walked with him all over Paris, and generally spent all day with him. . . . I am writing about this in detail so that you understand why Sokolov was candid with my mother. He knew full well that his end was imminent. He told my mother that he had been in charge of the detachment that had executed the tsar's family. He considered that a sin on his conscience. . . . When we returned to Moscow, my father told us that Sokolov had died in the Kremlin hospital in 1938. . . . My mother told me this story in the late 1960s, after my father's death, since she had given him her word that it would remain between them forever."

Why did Attaché Bialer extract his wife's word never to talk about her acquaintanceship with the mysterious Sokolov? Because he had not told his wife the truth about "Sokolov's" end, for he had decided not to frighten his wife. No, this "commander of the detachment that executed the tsar's family" did come to an end in 1938, but not in a hospital.

"Commander of the detachment" is just as much a confusing pseudonym as Nikolai Alexeyevich Sokolov. The latter was an ironic pseudonym, for it was the name of the famous investigator involved in the inquiry into the murder of the tsar's family.

So who was he?

It's not hard to figure out. This man must have held the same rank as Comrade Voroshilov himself—the first marshal made sure the Soviet ambassador in Paris took pains over this strange patient. Of all the participants in the execution, this could only have been one man—Alexander Beloborodov. The cruel Beloborodov. The jolly but cruel young Beloborodov, who left fifteen Romanovs lying forever in the Ural hills. Now he was people's commissar for internal affairs for the Russian republic and a mortally ill, unhappy man, swallowing with difficulty the runny food fed to him on a spoon by a soft-hearted woman. But that was not yet his end. His end was waiting for him in Moscow. In 1938 they would take the all-powerful Kremlin boyar. And in the Lubyanka, a pathetic, powerless man, his belt removed from his trousers, holding up his falling pants, in that moment, he would know . . . he would know a lot. Later, having passed through all the tortures of hell, the Ural Napoleon would go to that last wall. For that "kick in the ass." Thus Alexander Beloborodov greeted the twentieth anniversary of the tsarist execution with a bullet to his heart.

*G*OLOSHCHEKIN AND CO.
Then came his turn.

The long string of titles for Comrade Filipp: from the Twelfth to the Fifteenth Congress, a candidate for membership in the Party's Central Committee; from the Fifteenth Congress on, a Central Committee member. Also chief state arbitrator in the Sovnarkom. With every step up he took one step closer to death.

In the 1940s, Goloshchekin went through the Kremlin boyars' entire inevitable program: the Gulag, a firing squad, and an unmarked common grave—a pit hastily scattered with earth.

In the pit Joseph Stalin had designed for them, the executed ended their days—Ditkovsky and Safarov and Commander Berzin.

One way or another, the men who signed the Ural Soviet's sentence of execution all died by a bullet.

But what about the indirect executioners?

Everyone whose names we know for certain died in bed.

Oh well, "Forgive them, for they know not what they do," prayed the last tsar in his last moment.

*T*HE DETACHMENT LEAVES
In 1938, the twentieth anniversary of the murder of the tsar's family, also in July, the other main participant died from an excruciating ulcer—Yakov Yurovsky.

The son of Chekist Medvedev:

"My father used to say that at the end Yurovsky had a bad heart and suffered dreadfully over his daughter. But there was nothing he could do. There was no way he could help her."

The theory was a lot easier than the practice, and in practice he had sacrificed his daughter in the name of the Party . . . the iron commandant paid for this with a bad heart and an excruciating ulcer. A fatal ulcer ate up his insides. When he knew he was about to die, on that suffocating July day, he wrote a letter to his children.

Surrounded by countless corpses, his beloved daughter sent to the tortures of a camp, in anticipation of his closest friends dying, in the terrible year 1938, he wrote to his children . . . of the marvelous past, present, and future.

"Dear Zhenya and Shura! On July 3, new style, I will turn sixty. As it turns out, I have told you almost nothing about myself, especially my childhood and youth. . . . This I regret. Rimma may remember individual episodes in the revolution of 1905: my arrest, prison, my work in Ekaterinburg. [An awful sentence! Where was the unlucky Rimma when she recalled her father's years in a tsarist prison? In a Soviet prison, compared to which her father's tsarist prison was an idyll, a resort.]

". . . In the storm of October, fate turned its brightest side toward me. I saw and heard Lenin many times, he received me, chatted with me, and supported me like no one else in the years I worked at the State Depository. I had the good fortune to know well Lenin's most loyal pupils and comrades-in-arms—Sverdlov, Dzerzhinsky. . . . To work under their leadership and be in contact with them in a family way.

". . . fate has not insulted me, a man who has passed through three storms with Lenin and Lenin's men may consider himself the happiest of mortals. . . .

"Although I am dead tired from my illnesses, it still seems to me that I will participate with you in future coming events. I embrace you, I kiss Rimma, your wives, and my grandchildren. Father."

As I read this new man's deathbed letter, I kept remembering another final letter—of a man he and his comrades had killed—Dr. Botkin. These two letters are self-portraits of two worlds.

Yurovsky was dying, having achieved his goal: in the Museum of the Revolution lay his Note, which said that *he* had killed the last tsar. This was confirmed in numerous books that appeared in the West. He could call himself "the happiest of mortals."

In 1952, not quite living to seventy, special pensioner Peter Zakharovich Ermakov died happily. A street was named after him in Sverdlovsk.

In 1964, Mikhail Medvedev died equally happily. Shortly before his death he gave his Browning to the Museum of the Revolution.

That same Browning—no. 389965.

The Browning had a history. At the beginning of the century in Baku they had begun to fight against provocateurs sent into the underground organizations of the Russian Social Democratic Revolutionary Party. For this purpose Medvedev had acquired this gun. At that time in Baku the leader of the Baku revolutionaries had accused Stalin of being a provocateur sent to their organization. Stalin was suddenly arrested by the secret police, though, and disappeared from Baku. So it is quite possible that had Stalin remained in Baku, the Browning's first bullet might have gone into the first revolutionary tsar. But Stalin disappeared in the nick of time—and the Browning had to wait for the last tsar of the Romanov line.

By 1964 only two of those who had been in that terrible room were still among the living. One of these was Grigory Nikulin. After the execution, fate had been kind to Nikulin.

From Nikulin's autobiography, written in 1923:

"In 1919, upon my arrival in Moscow, I remained in the administrative department of the Moscow Soviet, where I held the following jobs: head of jailhouses for the city of Moscow, head of MUR [Moscow Criminal Investigation]."

In 1921 the former executioner was transferred to a somewhat surprising job—head of the State Insurance Office. Those working in the insurance office would have been very surprised to learn of their boss's recent past. Not that he ever talked about it. He did not even mention it in his autobiography. Only Yurovsky's authority could force his "son" to sign that statement in 1927—about the transfer of the commandant's sinister weapon to the Museum of the Revolution.

After Yurovsky's death, Nikulin crossed out the past in his mind for good. He married a second time. His wife was a beautiful, commanding, calm young woman.

From a letter of A. I. Vinogradova in Moscow:

"My parents were friendly with him. He was a smart, lean figure. A very pleasant, fine face. He never talked about the execution. And his wife forbade us from asking him about it. Nikulin is buried at the famous Novodevichy cemetery [the most prestigious cemetery in Moscow, where Khrushchev and all important government figures lie], not far from my parent."

The son of Chekist Medvedev:

"At the end of his life Nikulin was in charge of Moscow's entire water supply, the Stalin Water Supply Station. His wife boasted of their abundant life: they lived in their own private house, they even had a separate room for the dog. They really did have an enormous dog. This whole conversation took place on a visit. Rimma Yurovskaya was in the room during the story. She had just returned to Moscow from twenty years in the camps. She had nowhere to live. She joked, 'Hey, let me live in your dog's room.' "

Yes, the favorite of the Ekaterinburg Komsomol had served twenty years, she had passed through the entire school of Stalin's camps, all the charms of the bright future her father so loved to dream of she had seen with her own eyes. And now, without an apartment, without her health, her life lost—the Ural Komsomol's favorite listened to a story about the life of the new rich, the new bosses.

WHO DID KILL THE LAST TSAR? (THE END OF ONE STRUGGLE)
Let us return to Nikulin.

In 1964, the son of Chekist Mikhail Medvedev, historian M. M. Medvedev, convinced Nikulin to tape a statement for the radio.

This was no simple matter. Nikulin was used to "holding his tongue"—as Stalin had once taught him. And although Stalin had died eleven years before, the fear stuck in those people forever.

Nevertheless, the son of Chekist Medvedev was able to convince "son" Nikulin. He had played a part in the death of Medvedev's father. Nikulin felt he was the last witness who could record this for history, who could finally name the true regicide.

M. Medvedev asked, "Did the execution begin with a general salvo?"

"No, the shooting was chaotic."

"There was a first shot, though. Someone had to have fired it."

"Your father, Mikhail Medvedev. He fired the first shot. He killed the tsar."

Now that Yurovsky was dead, his "son" could tell the truth. He did not have long to live.

The son of Chekist Medvedev:

"I asked him to recount the details of the execution. He said: 'There's no need to savor it. Let it remain with us. Let it depart with us.'"

To a question about the "Anastasia" who was causing such an uproar in the West then, Nikulin replied briefly: "They all perished."

Evidently, Yurovsky's son found out about this dangerous tape.

That is why in the same year 1964, the copy of his father's note in which the commandant again declared from the grave, "I killed the last tsar," appeared in the Museum of the Revolution.

Nikulin turned out not to be the last of the regicides still living in this world, however. In the same year 1964, M. M. Medvedev received a letter from distant Khabarovsk from the former Life Guard and regicide Kabanov. Alive! The old dog was alive! Having read the obituary of his old acquaintance Chekist Medvedev in *Pravda*, he wrote to Medvedev's son. They began to correspond, and the old Chekist machine gunner, one of the last witnesses of the Ipatiev night still alive, answered his main question: "The fact that the tsar died from your father's bullet was something every worker in the Ural Cheka knew at the time."

So continued this amazing struggle "for the honor of the execution."

In the same year 1964, when the last witnesses to the death of the family were being taped for Moscow Radio, an eighty-year-old nun was being buried in a local Orthodox cemetery. She had become a nun, but she had not lived in a convent, and she had taken her vows in secret. The secret nun left behind many amazing photographs—Tsarskoe Selo, the palace at Livadia—the whole antediluvian world that had drowned in eternity. She also left watercolors drawn in the last empress's hand, as well as drawings by the last tsarevich and letters from the tsaritsa and her children. This was Anya. Having lived more than half the twentieth century, Anna Vyrubova departed this life.

With her went an era.

AFTERWORD
(NEW MYSTERIES?)

A mountain of new readers' letters—agonizing letters. I keep trying to put an end to the book, but they keep coming.

The niece of Elizaveta Ersberg, the tsar's family's parlormaid, wrote again: "A few words about my aunt's fate after the execution of the tsar's family. When Kolchak took Tobolsk, Elizaveta was called in for questioning to the commission of the jurist Nikolai Alexeyevich Sokolov (who turned out to have been a schoolmate of my father's at the Third Grammar School). Elizaveta arrived in Ekaterinburg with the advance White troops. She hired a boatman and searched for the bodies in a pond and in some swamp (she had received information) but found nothing. Then through the Red Cross mission she traced —via the Far East, Japan, America, France, and Denmark—the tsar's mother, Empress Marie Feodorovna, who gave her a subsidy, then went to Russia via Switzerland and Czechoslovakia in November 1928. She was allowed back into her homeland at my father's personal request to Molotov. At the border Liza was given a written undertaking to appear at the Cheka in twenty-four hours. When she came, she was given a written undertaking about not disclosing the facts of the life of the tsar's family and the circumstances connected therewith. . . .

"Now about the story of my aunt's friend, Anna Demidova, apparently shot in the Ipatiev house.

"No, Anna Demidova's story did not end on the day of the execution, and here is why I draw this conclusion. My father loved to take photographs, and we had a box of negatives with views of parks in the country and on that background photographs of friends. There were many pictures of Aunt Elizaveta in the company of Demidova and other tsarist servants. Therefore I knew Anna Stefanovna's face very well and can see her now right before my eyes. Average height, plump, with a rather common, round face, her hair sleeked back at the temples and a headdress on the top of her head. . . .

"Even before Aunt Elizaveta's return to Russia, I was taken to visit her sister. To amuse me, they got out an album for me with a beautiful onyx binding—Aunt Elizaveta's album. In it were at least ten photographs of Demidova. I already recognized her. But who this was in the album—a tall, lean, pockmarked woman—they couldn't tell me; Aunt Elizaveta could tell me. Christmas 1929, when Aunt Elizaveta was home, we went to visit our aunts. Once again I asked for the album and began leafing through it—but all the photos of Demidova, even in groups, had vanished or been smeared over. To my question about where the photograph of 'papa's fiancée' was, my aunts began hushing me, and when I inquired about the tall, pockmarked woman, Elizaveta said that she was a very good person but she died. And I cried.

"My aunts died from hunger on the same day, March 12. They had been supposed to be evacuated, and their passports had been taken away at ZhAKT [Housing Office], but they didn't go. And no one would give them bread ration cards without a passport. (Thus the tsaritsa's parlormaid died of hunger.)

"Demidova's story surfaced later. I was working in a plant (54 Lermontov, Leningrad). In 1968 a master compressor technician came to see us in shop number 17—Demidov. I saw him for the first time and was dumbstruck. Where had I seen that face? And suddenly I knew—Anna Demidova. I sort of joked, in conversation with him, that if he put on a bonnet he would look like a lady I knew. I asked if he wasn't related to Anna Stepanovna Demidova. He replied, 'Not Stepanovna, Stefanovna—she was my father's older stepsister.' He said she died in the Patriotic War [World War II]. As Demidov described her to me, she was average height, plump with slick-backed hair, she drank, smoked, and never went out of the house. She was either afraid of her nephew or didn't like him. Whenever she met him in the hall, she ran away. In the night she raved and cried out. So that her brother locked her in her room. I asked Demidov to write about his aunt and he said: 'That's just asking for trouble.' The woman shot by the name of Demidova was by all descriptions *tall*. So who was that tall woman from the album who was shot instead of Demidova?"

I set the letter aside. "Instead of Demidova?" Or maybe not instead? Maybe my guest's version about the two being saved is true, and her father and aunts created all this obfuscation about the photographs of "the wrong Demidova" to confuse the girl and hide from her a very dangerous secret: Demidova was saved?

Soon after this letter I received a long-distance telephone call.

First I heard a cough, and then a familiar voice began to speak. My God, I've already finished the book, I've already written that line, so like a citation from a novel: "I never saw my guest again," and here again—again this mysterious man!

The voice spoke without any introduction:

"Yesterday the remains of nine people were brought to the morgue of one of the hospitals in Sverdlovsk, now renamed Ekaterinburg again, as you well know. I hope you understand who I'm talking about?"

"No," I said, although I did.

"Yes, these are the remains that were in the grave Yurovsky described. They opened up the grave yesterday." And he hung up.

Just a few days after that call, reports appeared in the papers: on July 12, outside the village of Koptyaki, the grave was dug up where the remains of the tsar's family supposedly had been buried.

Now my guest is sitting in my house once again.

He has failed significantly in these months; he is obviously ill. The conversation is constantly interrupted by his coughing, but his permanent sarcastic grin is unchanged.

"There, you see. So much has happened in the short time since we last met: Leningrad is Saint Petersburg again, Sverdlovsk is Ekaterinburg, and the Communist Party has been banned. Look at the coincidence: you finished your book about the last tsar simultaneously with the demise of communism in Russia.

"So, the grave Yurovsky described was dug up. [I realized the introduction was over and the story had begun.] By the way, the first attempt to uncover it was back in 1979."

"I know about that."

He continues, though, as if he had not heard me.

"Three Sverdlovsk geologists and one Moscow writer located the grave Yurovsky described. Subsequently, as we know, they talked about all the difficulties of their searches, but that was more to make the story interesting. In fact, one of them had access to the secret archives, and they knew the location of the grave Yurovsky had recorded. In 1979 they decided to dig it up. Then they removed three skulls from the grave, made casts, and put them back. One of the skulls had a gold dental bridge. They conjectured it had belonged to Nicholas. They did not talk about all this, naturally. Only ten years later did they tell the whole story in the press for the first time.

"So now, that is, twelve years later, these Sverdlovsk geologists have opened the grave a second time. The fact of the matter is that a rumor got started in Ekaterinburg that Moscow had decided to open the grave and take away the remains. And just as Ekaterinburg had not given up the Romanovs to Moscow while they were alive, now they decided not to give them up after their deaths. Generally speaking, it was all identical: secret murders and secret digging. Soldiers put a barrier up around the work site and wouldn't let anyone in. Just as in July 1918, it had been terribly hot . . . but on the day of the grave's unearthing there was a downpour."

"You were there?"

"I didn't have to be. I did have to know, however. They opened it up like barbarians, without a priest. It was around midnight when they came across the planking Yurovsky wrote about. Then came bones and entire skeletons, a skull with bullet holes and traces of rifle butt blows . . . fragments from the containers for the sulfuric acid that was supposed to disfigure the bodies beyond the point of recognition, and pieces from the rope used to raise the bodies out of the first mine shaft. . . . Then they hastily brought out the remains in carbine cases. A hole was left at the grave site, which quickly filled with rain. A muddy pool. Then the soldiers threw dirt and turf over it. In the local hospital, in the morgue, in the so-called soil room, where disfigured corpses go, they placed the tsar's family. Forensic medical experts cleaned the dirt off the bones and skulls, dried them, and assigned inventory numbers. The martyrs were transformed into an archeological find."

"You mean you think this was really the tsar's grave?"

"I think they discovered the grave Yurovsky wrote about. Were the remains of the tsar and his family in it? Or had the remains been burned and was this only a false grave?

"If, however, it is proved that this is the tsar's family, then the

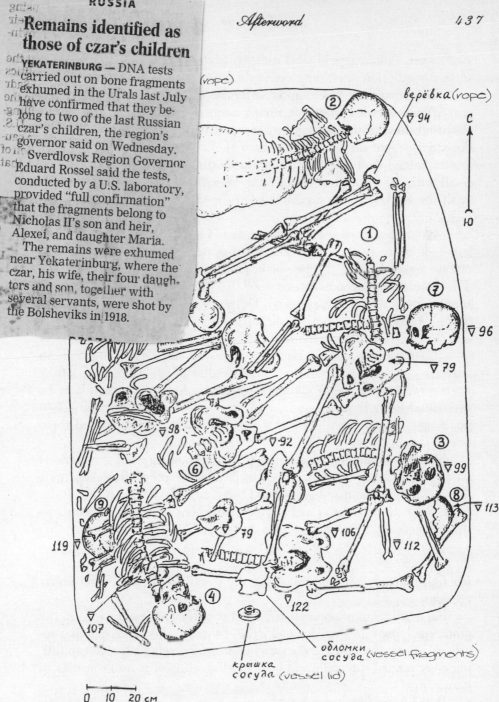

RUSSIA

Remains identified as those of czar's children

YEKATERINBURG — DNA tests carried out on bone fragments exhumed in the Urals last July have confirmed that they belong to two of the last Russian czar's children, the region's governor said on Wednesday.

Sverdlovsk Region Governor Eduard Rossel said the tests, conducted by a U.S. laboratory, provided "full confirmation" that the fragments belong to Nicholas II's son and heir, Alexei, and daughter Maria.

The remains were exhumed near Yekaterinburg, where the czar, his wife, their four daughters and son, together with several servants, were shot by the Bolsheviks in 1918.

верёвка (rope)

крышка сосуда (vessel lid)

обломки сосуда (vessel fragments)

0 10 20 см

*D*iagram of the grave near the village of Koptyaki presumed to contain the remains of the tsar's murdered family. The plan shows the disposition of the corpses, fragments of the jars that contained the sulfuric acid, and segments of the rope that had been wound around the corpses. The diagram was drawn by participants in the 1991 grave opening.

first expert opinions published recently become very interesting: of the eleven people shot, only nine skeletons were found in the grave.

"The remains of Alexei and one female skeleton are *missing*."

After this visit I started receiving astonishing "presents" from him. Although the entire Ekaterinburg investigation was cloaked in strictest secrecy, he sent me a detailed sketch of the corpses' placement in the grave. Later, photographs of their skulls turned up on my desk. This skull with the bullet hole—is this the enchanting Olga? And this one with the gap where the nose had been—is this our hero, the last Russian tsar?

My guest phoned me one last time. "The excavations are still ongoing. They're searching for the missing pair. The experts figure he couldn't have burned the two bodies without leaving any trace at all. That would have taken too much wood, too much gasoline, and too much time, none of which Yurovsky had. Despite all that, they have yet to find them." He laughed. "They're still missing."

"But what if they *are* found?"

"That would mean the rescued pair did not survive for long. We can only assume they died from their wounds after all and then were left by their rescuers in the surrounding woods, only to be discovered later by my friend Peter Ermakov, who had been so unnerved by their disappearance. Then he really may have burned them, or just buried them due to lack of time."

I heard him laugh once again. "Although knowing what this glorious Chekist was like, we have to consider another possibility: When he didn't find them he may have burned two similar bodies, just to be safe. In those years the Cheka had a wide assortment of bodies on hand. So those experts will have to do a painstaking job."

Enough! Enough puzzles, enough of these endless mysteries and resurrections!

But again from nonbeing—the specter of the Ipatiev house, and the grand duchesses on their knees by the wall, and the hands holding revolvers poking through the doorway, and the sovereign's forage cap rolling away toward the wall, and he himself keeling over backward. Lord have mercy!

Will I never finish this book?

*F*inally! After all those years of vain attempts to storm the Central Party Archives without ever being allowed to work there! Still, with help from my readers, I did manage to find out what was in the documents I needed.

Take this intriguingly empty envelope, for instance. . . .

In 1989, after my first article appeared in *Ogonyok,* I received an exceedingly curious letter from an unidentified reader:

"In the days when I was working in the Lenin archive of the Central Party Archives, I saw a strange *empty* envelope stamped 'Directorate of Sovnarkom Affairs.' On the envelope was a note: 'Secret, to Comrade Lenin from Ekaterinburg, July 17, 12 noon.'

"It is not hard to gather from this note that the envelope once held a certain *secret* telegram sent from Ekaterinburg early on the morning of July 17, that is, immediately following the murder.

"Also on the envelope was the signature of Lenin himself: 'Received. Lenin.'

"And there was a note saying a copy of this telegram had been sent to Sverdlov.

"But the telegram itself was not in the envelope: the envelope was empty."

At the time I decided against publishing the letter without first verifying it. But I couldn't. The Central Party Archives categorically refused to admit me.

Times have changed (for long?). I am sitting in the former Central Party Archives of the Communist Party.

Before me lies that same *empty* envelope from the secret telegram with Lenin's signature of receipt.

And although the telegram has been removed as a precaution, I can guess the *subject* of this telegram from Ekaterinburg, which arrived the morning after the execution addressed to the individual who had given the order for that execution.

I can even imagine its content, because of that day, July 17, Ekaterinburg informed yet another initiator of the execution—Yakov Sverdlov—about the "extermination of the Romanovs."

That telegram was preserved, though. It was found and deciphered, as we recall, by Investigator Sokolov. "Moscow, Kremlin. . . . Tell Sverdlov that the same fate has befallen the entire family as has its head. Officially the family will perish in the evacuation."

There is something terrible in this remaining witness to the murder; this empty envelope with its timorously removed telegram and very clear notes.

Yet another very important set of documents turned up in Russia, volumes that had been held for nearly half a century in the secret archives! Eight volumes of documents.

Four volumes had been kept in the Party Archives with a note on the cover: "Do not release to reading room."

The other four volumes were in the archives of the Military Prosecutor of the former USSR.

The title printed on each volume:

"Preliminary investigation carried out by Special Judicial Investigator N. A. Sokolov."

Yes, these were the actual volumes from the famous Sokolov investigation into the murder of the Romanovs!

All the testimony in the case had been signed personally by the witnesses Sokolov had questioned. It was on the basis of this file that he wrote his book, *The Murder of the Tsar's Family*, in which he frequently cited documents from this file.

How did these volumes ever wind up in the archives of the Military Prosecutor and the Communist Party?

More than likely they came out of German archives the Soviet Army captured in Berlin. How did they come to be in Germany? By way of occupied France, of course, where Sokolov lived in emigration, conducting his endless inquiry right up until his death.

An inquiry so enticing to begin but scarcely possible to conclude.

I am leafing through the testimony of the witnesses, and it is like a parade of the characters in our book: N. N. Ipatiev, Evgeny Kobylinsky, Prince Lvov, Alexander Kerensky, Alexander Guchkov, Prince Felix Yusupov, Matryona Rasputin, Gilliard and Gibbes, Tatiana Melnik-Botkina, the tsaritsa's maid Sasha Tegleva, and so on.

And although historians have quoted much of this testimony many times, there is a kind of magic in authentic documents. Certain fine points, certain details, read completely differently in them.

There is the testimony of Prince Georgy Lvov.

How mocking history is: Prince Lvov, prime minister of the Provisional Government, which overthrew and arrested the last tsar, was himself arrested by the Bolsheviks after the October coup!

Moreover, in 1918 Prince Lvov was in prison in Ekaterinburg very near the house that had been a prison for the tsar he had arrested the year previous. The former prime minister describes his encounter there with his Petersburg acquaintance Prince Dolgorukov, who was being held in the very same prison.

It turns out that, upon his arrival in Ekaterinburg, Dolgorukov was imprisoned by the Chekists, not shot. In prison the loyal Valya (Dolgorukov) was in constant distress over the tsarist money the "commissars" had confiscated from him. Actually, he did not remain distressed for very long; soon he was "sent to Moscow"—shot, in fact, in an open field by one of the characters in our book, Chekist Grigory Nikulin.

In prison, too, Prince Lvov saw the prison commissar Kabanov, brother to yet another character—former tsarist Guardsman and later Chekist Alexei Kabanov, who so distinguished himself on the Ipatiev night.

Here is the testimony of that notorious exposer of provocateurs in the revolutionary movement, V. L. Burtsev, who described one very important character in our book:

"Lenin is a 'cynic of the spirit' in the full sense. It is something more than 'Jesuitry.' He has decided once and for all that all means are good and everything is permitted."

Here is another description of a very different character in our story:

"At a depth of seven and a half sazhens [52.5 feet] a woman's corpse was found clothed in a gray rubber cloak, a gray dress, a white cotton bodice, a black shawl on her head, and a cypress and copper cross around her neck. . . .

"Her head and body were covered with many bruises from blows by a blunt instrument, as well as the result of injuries from her fall into the mine shaft."

This was the beautiful Ella, Alix's sister. This was how she looked when they excavated the mine shaft at Alapaevsk.

My guest called again.

As always, he started in without preliminaries. And, of course, about the alleged tsarist grave outside Ekaterinburg:

"I forgot to tell you one awful detail. After the grave was opened, the tsarist remains were kept for a time at the Upper Isetsk police

station, in the building where the policemen took target practice.
. . . So that once again the Romanovs were lying against a wall
strewn with bullets. . . . They showed me a photograph of the
tsarist bones and among them was a black cat that had happened to
wander onto the firing range."

Then he added with his familiar chuckle, "Well, as for the two
missing corpses, those remains have yet to be found." He was silent
for a moment and then changed topics. "I heard you've been out of
the country for a long time. I hope you're up to date on the experts'
latest accomplishments. They really are accomplishments. Com-
puter comparison of skulls and photographs has already established
with 90 percent accuracy that two skulls belong to the tsar and
tsaritsa. Well, for 100 percent certainty, 'fragments of the remains,'
or in plain words, pieces of bone from the skeletons, were sent to the
English. They have a Center for Criminal Investigations there at the
British Ministry for Internal Affairs." A chuckle. "You're a frequent
visitor abroad now, so you'll be interested in the results. They're
going to extract DNA from the bones. They want to compare it with
the genetic code of one of the presently thriving representatives of
the English royal house, who, as you know, are the Romanovs' closest relatives. They've agreed to help out. Well, they didn't help them
when they were alive, so they'll help out now that they're dead. It
looks like the question of just who is in the grave is going to be
decided once and for all very soon." Again he jumped to a different
topic. "By the way, you would be interested in two more finds: some
of Nicholas's hair was found in Moscow; and in Ekaterinburg, in the
archives of the former KGB, they declassified a very interesting file
on the tsarist diamonds. I've always said that the jewels were one of
the reasons the tsar's family was executed. As it turned out, though,
even after the death of their unlucky owners the stones continued to
kill people."

I had known all this. I had known that the remains had been sent
to the country where the family had been so happy at the end of the
last century. I was well informed about the work of the Moscow
team of experts and had even helped them get in touch with the
grandson of Dr. Botkin, Konstantin Melnik, who was living in Paris.

And I had already seen a certain file in the former Archives of the
October Revolution (which has abashedly changed its name to the
Russian State Archives), a file with the terrible title "Envelope with a
crown and the inscription 'Anichkov Palace' " (archive 640, list 2, file
14). Inside the file, indeed, lay a small envelope with "Anichkov Palace" printed on it and an embossed crown. But there was one more

inscription on the envelope, this handwritten, and in English: "Nicky hair when three years old." And a signature: "Alix." Actually, even without the signature it would have been easy to recognize the elegant handwriting of the last tsaritsa.

Evidently, immediately after the wedding, when Alix and Nicky were first living with the dowager empress at Anichkov Palace, his mother had given Alix this little envelope, and punctilious Alix had written it all down on the spot.

The envelope holds little Nicky's golden curls, which you can see in that first photograph of him as a baby.

For this reason I was not listening very closely to that part of my guest's conversation. But when he started talking about the diamonds . . .

He immediately sensed my agitation and said, derisively as always: "I'll try to send you the documents. And I'll call."

He did send me the documents. But he never called.

Soon after I learned from the newspapers that a blood analysis had been done in England on Prince Philip, consort of the English queen. The DNA of the prince—the grandson of Alix's sister—proved identical to the DNA taken from the bones of the alleged skeleton of the murdered tsaritsa. The prince's DNA also matched the genetic code of three other skeletons—the alleged grand duchesses.

Is the story of the tsarist grave over?

I remembered this strange sentence from long ago: "Even opening the grave will not clear up the puzzle for us completely."

Naturally, I waited impatiently for my guest's phone call and usual commentaries.

But he never called me again. Actually, I've written that about him before. So I continue to await his call.

A few extracts from the file he sent me:

"Materials related to the search for the valuables of the family of the former tsar Nicholas Romanov in three volumes.

"Top secret. Report of the OGPU Economics Department for the Urals on the confiscation of the tsarist valuables . . .

"After an extensive search on November 20, 1933, in the town of

Tobolsk, the valuables of the tsar's family were confiscated. While the tsar's family was staying in Tobolsk, the tsarist family's valet Chemodurov had turned these valuables over for safekeeping to Druzhinina, mother superior of the Tobolsk Monastery of St. Ivan."

This was the same monastery where they had so dreamed of living.

"Shortly before her death, Druzhinina gave them to her assistant, the deaconess Marfa Uzhentsova, who hid these valuables in the monastery well, the monastery cemetery, and several other places as well."

Soon, however, after the monastery's closing, the monks were driven out, and Marfa evidently had nowhere to hide the tsarist jewels. She tried to figure out what to do to keep them from falling into the hands of the authorities who had killed the tsar and his family.

"In 1924–25, M. Uzhentsova was planning to throw the valuables into the river. She was dissuaded from this step, however, by former Tobolsk fishing industrialist Kornilov, to whom she entrusted the valuables for temporary safekeeping."

Yes, this was the same Kornilov in whose home the tsar's suite had been housed during their Tobolsk confinement. Evidently, though, either Marfa consulted with someone about the tsarist jewels or she simply let it slip. The former deaconess did not realize that times had changed and that by then it was no longer prudent to seek other people's advice.

"Arrested on October 15 of the same year, Uzhentsova admitted to keeping the tsarist valuables and indicated where they were located. No valuables were found in the indicated place."

She was still trying to save the tsarist diamonds entrusted to her. Evidently, though, they had had her under surveillance for a long time.

"As a result of the secret service's work, V. M. Kornilov was arrested. V. M. Kornilov, who was apprehended in Tobolsk, revealed the actual location of the valuables.

"On Kornilov's instruction, valuables were removed in two large glass jars, which had been placed in small wooden receptacles.

"They were dug up in the cellar of Kornilov's house."

These fantastic jewels, which had glittered at tsarist balls, had been buried under the floor of the Kornilov house.

There is a photograph in the file of the GPU workers "with the confiscated jewels."

"Appraisal of the valuables.

"In all, 154 objects were confiscated, for a total value of 3,270,693 rubles (gold rubles), 50 kopeks.

"Among the confiscated valuables were:

"1. A diamond brooch (100 carats),

"2. Three hat pins (44 and 36 carats),

"3. A diamond crescent (70 carats) [according to reports, this crescent was a gift to the tsar from the Turkish sultan],

"4. 4 diadems of the tsaritsa, and others."

This successful operation inaugurated a real hunt for the tsarist diamonds.

First they went after the relatives of everyone connected with the Romanovs' Tobolsk confinement.

They found and questioned the relatives of the murdered cook Kharitonov, but without success.

They located the widow of Colonel Kobylinsky, who had been shot during the civil war.

They sought her out in the small town of Orekhovo-Zuevo, where the unlucky woman had attempted to hide, living quietly with her fourteen-year-old son Innokenty, and had worked at Karbolit, a local factory.

She told them about the sovereign's cap and the tsarist jewels, which her husband had brought home to show her and which according to rumors had later been hidden on some isolated squatter's holding in the taiga. (Captain Aksyuta had told the truth: the tsaritsa's jewels and the tsar's cap had been buried in the taiga!)

Through the Kobylinsk Secret Police they picked up the trail of Pechekos's sister and brother, whom the Kobylinskys had stayed with in 1918 in Tobolsk and who, according to Kobylinskaya, knew about the cache.

First they arrested Anelia Pechekos. Evidently they interrogated her rather zealously, and Pechekos realized she wouldn't be able to hold out.

"On July 8, 1934, Anelia Vikentievna Pechekos died in prison after swallowing iron objects."

Her arrested brother threw himself out a window, but survived.

Realizing that these people would rather die than reveal the secret, the secret police decided to release Pechekos from prison and put him under permanent surveillance, which went on for decades and was lifted only after Pechekos's death.

The searches kept up. They interrogated people who had known the deceased valet Chemodurov. They determined that the old man had died in the house of the barman Grigory Solodukhin, "who according to rumors had amassed great valuables."

But they couldn't arrest Solodukhin. In 1920 shortsighted Chekists had shot him.

Nonetheless, they did finally pick up a fresh trail.

They determined that the tsaritsa had instructed Father Alexei (the same priest who had once prayed for "A long life!" for the tsar's family in Tobolsk) "to carry out and conceal a case containing diamonds and gold objects of not less than one pood [36 pounds]."

And once again they met with failure: Father Alexei had managed to pass away in 1930.

They interrogated his children. But the children didn't know anything. Father Alexei had safely hidden the tsarist case.

So perhaps even now, buried somewhere in the cellar of an old Tobolsk house, is a brown leather case bearing the tsarist coat of arms and a pood of jewels, and somewhere in the taiga of Siberia still lie the tsar's cap and the Romanov diamonds.

I'm never going to finish this book!

The letters keep arriving, such as this one from St. Petersburg with information on that strange man Filipp Semyonov, who considered himself Alexei's savior. Apparently, during the Khrushchev era the alleged tsarevich went straight from prison camp to Leningrad, where he married and later died in 1979. Before his death, his wife had always called him Alexei. As he was dying, he got his wife's word that she would rebury him alongside the rest of his family. The envelope contained a photograph of him shortly before his death.

Another specter of the Ipatiev house emerging from oblivion.

At the Central Party Archive, I was finally able to read the "Secret statements of Chekist Medvedev-Kudrin on the execution of the tsar's family," which I had heard so much about from his son. One more witness tells the story:

"Yurovsky read the decision to execute. 'You mean they're not taking us anywhere?' Botkin asked. Yurovsky wanted to say something in response, but I was already pulling the trigger. I planted the first bullet in the tsar. . . . Yurovsky and Ermakov shot Nicholas in the chest as well, almost point-blank. . . . On my fifth shot Nicholas II toppled back like a sheaf of grass. . . . There was a woman's scream, and moaning. . . . You couldn't see anything because of the smoke: we were shooting at falling silhouettes we could barely see. . . .

" 'Stop! Cease firing,' Yurovsky commanded.

" 'Thank the Lord! God has saved me!' The surviving maid staggered as she tried to get up. . . . Then the maid was bayonetted. At her dying cry, Alexei, who was lightly wounded, came to and started moaning. He was lying on a chair. Yurovsky walked over and emptied the last bullets from his Mauser into him. The boy became quiet and slowly crawled to his father's feet. . . . Nicholas was completely riddled with bullets. . . . We examined the remaining ones and finished off Tatiana and Anastasia, who were still alive, with the Colt."

Did "lightly wounded" Alexei and Anastasia survive the execution? Only after that, Medvedev-Kudrin asserts, were they finished off—in a room where "you couldn't see anything because of the smoke."

Two tape recordings are also preserved in the Party Archive: those historic 1964 recordings once discussed in such detail by historian Mikhail Medvedev, Medvedev-Kudrin's son. On the tapes are the voices of one of the main regicides, Grigory Nikulin, the assistant to the Ipatiev house commandant, and I. Rodzinsky, who participated in the secret burial of the tsar's family, telling the story of how the tsar and his family died.

Especially interesting are the statements of the man whose name so resembles my own, I. Rodzinsky.

First he tells the tale I have already heard from Medvedev about how the Cheka organized provocations by composing "forged letters over the signature 'An Officer' ":

"We needed proof that preparations were under way to abduct the Family, even though no such preparations were under way. . . . Voikov dictated the letters to me in French, and I wrote . . . so the handwriting was mine."

The Chekist described the execution as well, and here the name of Alexei crops up once again:

"I must say the execution was chaotic. We nearly shot ourselves because of the bullets ricocheting. . . . For example, Alexei II took 11 bullets . . . only after that did he die."

But Rodzinsky himself did not witness the execution. His story is based on what the other executioners told them, and they were clearly amazed at Alexei's "strange vitality."

He did witness the second burial of the tsar's family, however, and even participated in it. He describes all its terrible details. The Chekist remembered everything: how they got to the mine at dawn, "how one man dropped down into the water with ropes and dragged the corpses out of the water . . . we pulled Nicholas out first." He recalled: "The water was so cold that the corpses' faces were red-cheeked, as if they were still alive." He recalled seeing the naked body of the tsar and how amazed he was at "Nicholas's remarkable physical development . . . his muscles, torso, stomach, and arms." He remembered little details, too, such as Yurovsky being sent to town for sulfuric acid and him taking that time to go into the village to drink some milk.

He described in detail how they created this terrible secret grave:

"The truck got stuck in a quagmire, and we barely pulled it out. That was when we got the idea we eventually carried out. We decided we weren't going to find anyplace better. . . . We dug out that quagmire immediately . . . poured sulfuric acid over the corpses . . . disfigured them . . . and dumped them into the quagmire. . . . The railway wasn't far from there." He recalled how they trucked in rotten ties to disguise the grave. But they only buried some of those shot in the grave: "The rest we burned."

As soon as he gets to the burning, the Chekist's memory starts to betray him: "I don't remember how many we burned exactly . . . or exactly who." This is where he starts making strange mistakes: "Nicholas we did burn, I remember. . . . And Botkin, too, and Alexei, I think. . . ."

No, I never am going to finish this book!

APPENDIX

2. Государь Императоръ удалился въ сосѣднее отдѣленіе салонъ-вагона, въ которомъ происходила бесѣда.

Черезъ 20 мин. Онъ вышелъ оттуда съ текстомъ манифеста въ рукахъ и передавая его сказалъ: "Рѣшеніе мое твердо и непреклонно.

Актъ объ отреченіи Государя Императора Николая II отъ престола Государства Россійскаго въ пользу Великаго Князя Михаила Александровича:

Въ дни великой борьбы съ внѣшнимъ врагомъ, стремящимся почти три года поработить нашу Родину, Господу Богу угодно было ниспослать Россіи новое тяжкое испытаніе. Начавшіяся внутреннія народныя волненія грозятъ бѣдственно отразиться на дальнѣйшемъ веденіи упорной войны. Судьбы Россіи, честь геройской нашей арміи, благо народа, все будущее дорогого нашего Отечества требуетъ доведенія войны, во что бы то ни стало, до побѣднаго конца. Жестокій врагъ напрягаетъ послѣднія силы, и уже близокъ часъ, когда доблестная армія наша совмѣстно со славными нашими союзниками сможетъ окончательно сломить врага. Въ эти рѣшительные дни въ жизни Россіи почли Мы долгомъ совѣсти облегчить народу нашему тѣсное единеніе и сплоченіе всѣхъ силъ народныхъ для скорѣйшаго достиженія побѣды и,

Въ согласіи съ Государственною Думою, при
знали Мы за благо отречься отъ престола
Государства Россійскаго и сложить съ себя
Верховную власть. Не желая разстаться
съ любимымъ сыномъ нашимъ, мы передаемъ
наслѣдіе наше Брату нашему Великому
Князю Михаилу Александровичу и благо-
словляемъ его на вступленіе на престолъ Государства Россійскаго. Заповѣдуемъ Брату нашему править дѣлами государственными въ
полномъ и ненарушимомъ единеніи съ предста-
вителями народа въ законодательныхъ
учрежденіяхъ, на тѣхъ началахъ, кои будутъ
ими установлены, принеся въ томъ ненару-
шимую присягу. Во имя горячо любимой
Родины призываемъ всѣхъ вѣрныхъ сыновъ
Отечества къ исполненію своего святого
долга передъ нимъ, повиновеніемъ Царю
въ тяжелую минуту всенародныхъ испы-
таній и помочь ему, вмѣстѣ съ предста-
вителями народа, вывести Государство
Россійское на путь побѣды, благоденствія
и славы. Да поможетъ Господь Богъ Россіи.

На подлинномъ собственною Его Императорскаго Величества рукою написано
"Николай"

Гор. Псковъ.
2 го Марта 15 час. 5 мин. 1917 г.
Скрѣпилъ министръ Императорскаго двора,
Генералъ-Адъютантъ Графъ Фредериксъ

The testimony of A. I. Guchkov on the ceremonial procedure of the signing of the act of abdication.

1918 document signed by the chairman of the Ural Soviet and a Bolshevik party member, Aleksandr Georgievich Beloborodov (1891–1938), concerning the transmittal of the former Tsar Nicholas, the former Tsarina Aleksandra Feodorovna, and their daughter Maria Nikolaevna (1899–1918).

13ᵃ

1.

<u>30го Іюня. Суббота.</u>

Алексѣй принялъ первую ванну послѣ
Тобольска ; колѣно его поправляется,
но совершенно разогнуть его онъ не мо-
жетъ. Погода теплая и пріятная.
Вѣстей путемъ никакихъ не имѣемъ.

*T*he last pages of the diary of Tsarina Aleksandra Feodorovna, 1918.

SELECTED
BIBLIOGRAPHY

ENGLISH-LANGUAGE SOURCES

Alexander, Grand Duke of Russia. *Once a Grandduke*. London, 1932.

Alexandrov, V. *The End of the Romanovs*. Boston, 1967.

Benckendorff, P. *Last Days of Tsarskoe Selo*. London, 1927.

Botkin, G. *The Real Romanovs*. New York, 1931.

Buchanan, G. *My Mission to Moscow*. London, 1923.

Buxhoevden, S. *The Life and Tragedy of Alexandra Feodorovna*. New York and London, 1928.

Chavchavadze, D. *The Grand Dukes*. New York, 1990.

Cyril, Grand Duke. *My Life in Russia's Service*. London, 1939.

Dehn, Lili. *The Real Tsaritsa*. London, 1922.

Kerensky, A. *The Crucifixion of Liberty*. New York, 1934.

Kschessinska, M. *Dancing in Petersburg*. Garden City, 1961.

Kurth, P. *Anastasia: The Riddle of Anna Anderson*. Boston and Toronto, 1983.

Letters of the Tsar to the Tsaritsa, 1914–1917. London, 1976.

Letters of the Tsaritsa to the Tsar, 1914–1916. London, 1923.

Massie, R. *Nicholas and Alexandra*. London, 1969.

Mosolov, A. *At the Court of the Last Tsar*. London, 1935.

Richards, G. *The Hunt for the Czar*. New York, 1970.

Summers, A., and Mangold, T. *The File of the Tsar*. New York and London, 1976.

Trotsky, L. *The History of the Russian Revolution*. New York, 1932.

RUSSIAN-LANGUAGE SOURCES

TsGAOR SSSR here stands for the U.S.S.R. Central State Archive of the October Revolution, located in Moscow.

Alfer'ev, E. E. *Pis'ma tsarskoi sem'i iz zatocheniia.* Jordanville, N.Y., 1984.

Amvrosii, Archbishop. *Svetloi pamiati velikoi kniagini Elizavety Fedorovny.* Jerusalem, 1915.

Autobiography of G. Nikulin. Museum of the Revolution, Moscow.

Autobiography of P. Z. Ermakov. Sverdlovsk Party Archive, f. 41, op. 2, d. 79, ss. 5–6.

Autobiography of Ural Cheka Chairman F. N. Lukoyanov. Copy in author's possession.

Avdeev, A. D. "Nikolai Romanov v Tobol'ske i Ekaterinburge." *Krasnaia nov',* no. 5 (1928).

Berberova, N. *Liudi i lozhi.* New York, 1986.

Biography of Ipatiev house driver S. I. Lyukhanov, compiled by his son Alexei. In author's possession.

Blok, A. A. *Zapisnye knizhki.* Moscow, 1965.

Budberg, A. *Dnevnik belogvardeitsa.* Leningrad, 1929.

Burtsev, V. L. "Istinnye ubiitsy Nikolaia II—Lenin i ego tovarishchi." *Obshchee delo.* Paris, 1921.

Bykov, P. M. *Poslednie dni Romanovykh.* Sverdlovsk, 1926.

Copy of the Yurovsky Note on the execution of the tsar and his family given by him to historian M. N. Pokrovsky and verified by his son A. Yurovsky. Museum of the Revolution, Moscow.

Correspondence of Nicholas and Alice of Hesse (the future empress Alexandra Feodorovna) in 1894. TsGAOR SSSR, f. 601, pp. 1, d. 1147.

Correspondence of Nicholas and his mother Empress Marie Feodorovna. TsGAOR SSSR, f. 642, op. 1, d. 2328.

Diaries of Emperor Nicholas II, 1882–1918. TsGAOR SSSR, f. 601, op. 1, d. 217–266.

Diary of Alexander II. TsGAOR SSSR, f. 678, op. 1, d. 294–295.

Diary of Alexandra Feodorovna, 1918. TsGAOR SSSR, f. 640, op. 1, d. 326.

Diary of Empress Alexandra Feodorovna, 1917. TsGAOR SSSR, f. 640, op. 1, d. 333.

Diary of Grand Duchess Marie. TsGAOR SSSR, f. 685, op. 1, d. 10.

Diary of Grand Duchess Olga. TsGAOR SSSR, f. 673, op. 1, d. 8.

Diary of Grand Duchess Tatiana. TsGAOR SSSR, f. 651, op. 1, d. 26.

Diary of Tsesarevich Alexei. TsGAOR SSSR, f. 682, op. 1, d. 189.

Diterikhs, M. K. *Ubiistvo tsarskoi sem'i i chlenov doma Romanovykh na Urale.* Vols. 1–2. Vladivostok, 1922.

Duty notebook for the special detachment (watch journal). TsGAOR SSSR, f. 601, op. 2, d. 37.

History notes made by Alexander II during his time as heir to the throne. TsGAOR SSSR, f. 678, op. 1, d. 257.

Iakovlev, V. [Miachin]. "Poslednii reis Romanovykh (Vospominaniia)." *Ural,* no. 8 (1988).

Iasenitskii, G. *Za kulisami velikoi katastrofy.* San Francisco, n.d.

Iliodor, Father. "Sviatoi chert." *Golos minuvshego* (March, 1917) pp. 1–187.

Iusupov, F. F. *Konets Rasputina.* Paris, 1927.

Kashits, V. "Poslednii reis poslednego tsaria." *Sovetskii Krym,* no. 212 (1988).

Kasvinov, M. K. *23 stupeni vniz.* Moscow, 1982.

Koganitskii, I. "1917–1918 gg. v Tobol'ske . . ." *Proletarskaia revoliutsiia,* no. 4 (1922).

Kol'tsov, M. E. *Izbrannye proizvedeniia.* Vol. 1. Moscow, 1957.

Lamsdorf, V. N. *Dnevnik.* Moscow, 1934.

Lemke, M. K. *250 dnei v tsarskoi stavke.* Petrograd, 1920.

Lenin, V. I. *Polnoe sobranie sochinenii.* Vol. 34. Moscow, 1958–59.

Leninskaia gvardiia Urala. Sverdlovsk, 1967.

Letter of A. Kabanov on the execution of the tsar and his family. In the possession of M. M. Medvedev, Moscow.

Leshkin, N. "Poslednii reis Romanovykh." *Leninets* (Ufa) (October–November 1976).

"Lichnye vospominaniia A. Strekotina . . ." Copy of one version in the Sysert Party Archives in the author's possession; one version from the Sverdlovsk Party Archives published in *Ural'skii rabochii* (September 23, 1990).

Mal'kov, P. *Zapiski komendanta Kremlia.* Moscow, 1967.

Markov, S. *Pokinutaia tsarskaia sem'ia.* Vienna, 1926.

Meier, I. *Kak pogibla tsarskaia sem 'ia.* Los Angeles, 1956.

Mel'gunov, S. P. *Krasnyi terror v Rossii.* Moscow, 1990.

———. *Na putiakh k dvortsovomu perevorotu.* Paris, 1923.

———. *Nikolai 2, materialy dlia kharakteristiki lichnosti i tsarstvovaniia.* Moscow, 1917.

Mel'nik-Botkina, T. *Vospominaniia o tsarskoi sem'e i ee zhizni do i posle revoliutsii.* Belgrade, 1921.

Memoirs of A. Markov on the execution of Grand Duke Michael. Copy from the Perm Party Archive in the author's possession. Excerpts published in *Vecherniaia Perm'* (January 15, 1990) and *Sovershenno sekretno* (September 1990).

Memoirs of P. Z. Ermakov. Sverdlovsk Party Archive, archive 221, list 2, file 774, pages 7–12.

Miliukov, P. N. *Istoriia vtoroi russkoi revoliutsii.* Sofia, 1921–1924.

Mstislavskii, S. *5 dnei.* Berlin, 1922.

Nemtsov, N. "Poslednii pereezd polkovnika Romanova." *Krasnaia niva,* no. 27 (1928).

Nikon, Bishop. *Den' vseobshchego pokaianiia i posta 4-17 iiulia 1917–1958.* New York, 1958.

Note of Ipatiev house commandant Ya. Yurovsky on the execution of the tsar and his family, documents of the fake monarchist plot, the official telegram of the Ural Soviet on the execution of Nicholas II, etc. TsGAOR SSSR, f. 601, op. 2, d. 35.

Notebook of Alexandra Feodorovna for Russian language study. TsGAOR SSSR, f. 640, op. 1, d. 520.

Notebook of Alexandra Feodorovna with copies of poems and book excerpts (1906–1916). TsGAOR SSSR, f. 640, op. 1, d. 312.

Notebook of Alexandra Feodorovna with quotes from Rasputin. TsGAOR SSSR, f. 640, op. 1, d. 309.

Notice by Ya. Yurovsky on giving the two revolvers used to execute the tsar and his family to the Museum of the Revolution. Museum of the Revolution, Moscow.

Obninskii, Viktor Petrovich. *Poslednii samoderzhets.* Berlin, (1912?).

"Padenie tsarskogo rezhima" (Stenographic record of interrogations and statements made in 1917 by the Special Commission of Inquiry of the Provisional Government). Vols. 1–7, Leningrad, 1924–27.

Paganutstsi, P. *Pravda ob ubiistve tsarskoi sem'i.* Jordanville, N.Y., 1981.

Paleolog, M. *Tsarskaia Rossiia nakanune mirovoi voiny.* Moscow-Petrograd, 1923.

Pankratov, V. S. "S tsarem v Tobol'ske." *Byloe* nos. 25–26 (1924).

Perepiska Nikolaia i Aleksandry Romanovykh, 1914-1917 gg. Vols. 1–5. Moscow-Leningrad, 1923–1927.

"Poezdka v Sarov." *Golos minuvshego,* 4/6 (1918).

Purishkevich, V. M. *Dnevnik.* Moscow, 1990.

"Rasskaz zaveduiushchei Permskim partarkhivom N. Alikinoi o vstrechakh s Markovym i prieme Leninym Markova posle ubiistva Mikhaila." *Vecherniaia Perm'* (February 3, 1990).

Report to the Ministry of Justice, November 27, 1919, by Kazan Palace of Justice Procurator N. Mirolyubov, December 12, 1918. TsGAOR SSSR, f. 601, op. 2, d. 36.

Revoliutsionery Prikam'ia, 150 biografii. Perm, 1956.

Reznik, Ia. L. *Chekist (Povest' o Iurovskom).* Sverdlovsk, 1972.

Romanov, A. V. *Dnevnik velikogo kniazia Andreia Vladimirovicha.* Leningrad, 1925.

Romanov, Gavriil Konstantinovich, Grand Duke, *V Mramornom dvortse.* New York, 1955.

Romanov, N. M. "Dnevniki velikogo kniazia Nikolaia Mikhailovicha." *Krasnyy arkhiv* 49/6 (1931).

Rudnev, V. N. *Pravda o russkoi tsarskoi sem'e i temnykh silakh.* Ekaterinodar, 1919.

———. "Vospominaniia." *Russkaia letopis'* (Paris), no. 2 (1922).

Savchenko, P. *Gosudarynia-imperatritsa Aleksandra Fedorovna.* Jordanville, N.Y., 1983.

———. *Russkaia devushka.* Jordanville, N.Y., 1986.

Savinkov, B. *Vospominaniia terrorista: Izbrannoe.* Moscow, 1990.

Shulenberg, V. E. *Vospominaniia ob imperatritse Aleksandre Fedorovne.* Paris, 1928.

Shul'gin, V. V. *Dni, 1920.* Moscow, 1989.

Simanovich, A. "Vospominaniia byvshego sekretaria Grigoriia Rasputina." *Slovo* (1990).

Sobstvennyi Ego Imperatorskogo Velichestva Konvoi. San Francisco, 1961.

Sokolov, N. A. *Ubiistvo tsarskoi sem'i.* Berlin, 1925.

Struve, P. B. *Razmyshleniia o russkoi revoliutsii.* Sofia, 1931.

Sukhanov, N. *Zapiski o revoliutsii.* Berlin-Petrograd-Moscow, 1922.

Sukhomlinov, V. A. *Vospominaniia.* Berlin, 1924.

Svetlyy otrok: Sbornik statei o tsareviche-muchenike Aleksee. . . . Jordanville, N.Y., 1984.

Telegram from Ekaterinburg to Moscow on the planned execution of the tsar and his family, July 16, 1918. TsGAOR SSSR, f. 130, op. 2, d. 653, s. 12.

Telegrams of V. Yakovlev, who transferred the tsar from Tobolsk to Ekaterinburg. TsGAOR SSSR Collection.

Tikhmenev. *Vospominaniia o poslednikh dniakh prebyvaniia Nikolaia 2 v stavke.* Nice, 1925.

Trotsky, L. D. *Dnevniki i pis'ma.* Tenafly, N.J., 1986.

"U Grigoriia Rasputina." *Novoe vremia* 12/90 (1912).

Vil'ton, R. *Poslednie dni Romanovykh.* Berlin, 1923.

Voeikov, V. N. *S tsarem i bez tsaria.* Helsingfors, 1936.

Volkov, A. A. *Okolo tsarskoi sem'i.* N.d.

Vorob'ev, V. "Konets Romanovykh." *Prozhektor,* no. 9 (July 15, 1928).

"Vospominaniia P. M. Matveeva o tobol'skom zakliuchenii tsarskoi sem'i." *Ural'skii rabochii* (September 16, 1990).

Vyrubova, A. A. *Stranitsy iz moei zhizni.* Berlin, 1923.

Witte, S. Iu. *Vospominaniia*. Vols. 1–2. Moscow, 1960.

"Zapiski (Vospominaniia) P. M. Matveeva o tobol'skom zakliuchenii tsarskoi sem'i." Sverdlovsk Oblast Party Archive, f. 41, op. 1, d. 149, ss. 88–149. Excerpt published in *Ural'skii rabochii* (September 16, 1990).

Zhil'iar [Gilliard], P. *Tragicheskaia sud'ba russkoi imperatorskoi familii*. Revel, 1921.

PHOTO CREDITS

1. Central State Archive of the October Revolution, High Organs of State Government, and Organs of the State Administration of the U.S.S.R.
2. Central State Museum of the Revolution of the U.S.S.R., Archives.
3. Museum named for Feodor Ivanovich Tyutchev (1803–73), Muranovo, Russia.
4. Museum named for Feodor Ivanovich Tyutchev (1803–73), Muranovo, Russia.
5. Central State Archive of Film and Photographic Documents of the U.S.S.R.
6. Min. Imp. Dvora udelov. Koronatsionnyi sbornik. (Court Ministry of Crowned Lands. Coronation Collection.)
7. Central State Archive of Film and Photographic Documents of the U.S.S.R.
8. Central State Archive of Film and Photographic Documents of the U.S.S.R.
9. Central State Archive of Film and Photographic Documents of the U.S.S.R.
10. *Album du Bal Costumé au Palais D'Hiver, février 1903.* Volume 1, I. (St. Petersburg, Expédition pour la confection des papiers d'état, 1904).
11. *Album du Bal Costumé au Palais D'Hiver, février 1903.* Volume 1, II. (St. Petersburg, Expédition pour la confection des papiers d'état, 1904).
12. Central State Archive of Film and Photographic Documents of the U.S.S.R.
13. Central State Archive of Film and Photographic Documents of the U.S.S.R.
14. Central State Archive of Film and Photographic Documents of the U.S.S.R.
15. The Luton Hoo Foundation, Wernher Collection.
16. Central State Archive of Film and Photographic Documents of the U.S.S.R.
17. Central State Archive of Film and Photographic Documents of the U.S.S.R.
18. Central State Archive of Film and Photographic Documents of the U.S.S.R.
19. Central State Archive of Film and Photographic Documents of the U.S.S.R.
20. Central State Archive of Film and Photographic Documents of the U.S.S.R.
21. Central State Archive of Film and Photographic Documents of the U.S.S.R.
22. The Luton Hoo Foundation, Wernher Collection.
23. Central State Museum of the Revolution of the U.S.S.R., Archives.

24. Central State Archive of Film and Photographic Documents of the U.S.S.R.
25. Central State Archive of Film and Photographic Documents of the U.S.S.R.
26. Central State Museum of the Revolution of the U.S.S.R., Archives.
27. Central State Museum of the Revolution of the U.S.S.R., Archives.
28. Archives of the Novosti Russian Information Agency.
29. Archives of the Novosti Russian Information Agency.
30. Central State Archive of Film and Photographic Documents of the U.S.S.R.
31. Archives of the Novosti Russian Information Agency.
32. Archives of the Novosti Russian Information Agency.
33. Archives of the Novosti Russian Information Agency.
34. Archives of the Novosti Russian Information Agency.
35. State Archives of the October Revolution, Fund of Alexandra Feodorovna.
36. The Luton Hoo Foundation, Wernher Collection.
37. Archives of the Novosti Russian Information Agency.
38. Archives of the Novosti Russian Information Agency.
39. Central State Archive of Film and Photographic Documents of the U.S.S.R.
40. Central State Archive of Film and Photographic Documents of the U.S.S.R.
41. Archives of the Novosti Russian Information Agency.
42. Archives of the Novosti Russian Information Agency.
43. Central State Archive of Film and Photographic Documents of the U.S.S.R.
44. Central State Archive of the October Revolution, High Organs of State
    Government, and Organs of the State Administration of the U.S.S.R.
45. The Luton Hoo Foundation, Wernher Collection.
46. Central State Museum of the Revolution of the U.S.S.R., Archives.
47. The Luton Hoo Foundation, Wernher Collection.
48. Central State Museum of the Revolution of the U.S.S.R., Archives.
49. Central State Museum of the Revolution of the U.S.S.R., Archives.
50. The Luton Hoo Foundation, Wernher Collection.
51. The Luton Hoo Foundation, Wernher Collection.
52. The Luton Hoo Foundation, Wernher Collection.
53. The Luton Hoo Foundation, Wernher Collection.
54. Central State Museum of the Revolution of the U.S.S.R., Archives.
55. The Luton Hoo Foundation, Wernher Collection.
56. Central State Museum of the Revolution of the U.S.S.R., Archives.
57. Radzinsky Archives, Moscow.
58. Central State Museum of the Revolution of the U.S.S.R., Archives.
59. Radzinsky Archives, Moscow.
60. Radzinsky Archives, Moscow.
61. The Luton Hoo Foundation, Wernher Collection.
62. The Luton Hoo Foundation, Wernher Collection.
63. The Luton Hoo Foundation, Wernher Collection.
64. *Vechernii Ekaterinburg.*

INDEX

ABOUT THE AUTHORS

EDVARD RADZINSKY is Russia's most frequently staged playwright, after Chekhov, and his plays have won him international acclaim. A trained historian, Radzinsky has been working on the life of Tsar Nicholas II for the past twenty-five years.

MARIAN SCHWARTZ is a freelance Russian translator living in Texas. Her published translations include a biography of Constructivist Liubov Popova and the prose of many contemporary Russian women, outstanding among them being Nina Berberova (*The Tattered Cloak*).